The Racial Crisis in American Higher Education

Third Edition

SUNY series, Critical Race Studies in Education
—————
Derrick R. Brooms, editor

The Racial Crisis
in American Higher Education

Third Edition

Edited by

KOFI LOMOTEY and WILLIAM A. SMITH

**SUNY
PRESS**

Published by State University of New York Press, Albany

© 2023 State University of New York

All rights reserved

Printed in the United States of America

No part of this book may be used or reproduced in any manner whatsoever without written permission. No part of this book may be stored in a retrieval system or transmitted in any form or by any means including electronic, electrostatic, magnetic tape, mechanical, photocopying, recording, or otherwise without the prior permission in writing of the publisher.

For information, contact State University of New York Press, Albany, NY
www.sunypress.edu

Library of Congress Cataloging-in-Publication Data

Names: Lomotey, Kofi, editor. | Smith, William A., editor.
Title: The racial crisis in American higher education / edited by Kofi Lomotey, William A. Smith.
Description: Third edition. | Albany : State University of New York Press, 2023. | Series: SUNY series, critical race studies in education | Includes bibliographical references and index
Identifiers: LCCN 2022035141 | ISBN 9781438492728 (hardcover : alk. paper) | ISBN 9781438492742 (ebook) | ISBN 9781438492735 (pbk. : alk. paper)
Subjects: LCSH: Minorities—Education (Higher)—United States. | Racism in higher education—United States. | Discrimination in higher education—United States. | College integration—United States. | United States—Race relations.
Classification: LCC LC3731 .R255 2023 | DDC 378.1/982—dc23/eng/20220830
LC record available at https://lccn.loc.gov/2022035141

10 9 8 7 6 5 4 3 2 1

Contents

List of Illustrations ix

Foreword xi
    Donald B. Pope-Davis

Introduction 1
    William A. Smith and Kofi Lomotey

Part 1. Contextualizing the Crisis

1 Institutionalized White Racism: The Impact on US Higher Education 9
    Kofi Lomotey

2 Who Gets "Left Out": Pacific Islanders, Data Aggregation, and Native Erasure 23
    Kēhaulani Vaughn

3 Black Male Genocide: Systemic Racism and Implications for Black Male Presence and Success in Higher Education 37
    Shiver, Maria Ashkin, Jimmy Kendall, and Evelyn Ezikwelu

Part 2. Considering History

4 Presidential Responses to Campus Racism: A Historical Perspective 79
    Eddie R. Cole

5 Race-Conscious Affirmative Action in US Higher Education in an Era of Pronounced White Racial Backlash   97
   María C. Ledesma, Uma Mazyck Jayakumar, and Kenyon L. Whitman

Part 3. The Day-to-Day Realities

6 The Psychosocial Antecedents of Racial Battle Fatigue   125
   William A. Smith

7 Outsiders Within: Black Faculty in US Higher Education   167
   Channel C. McLewis, Chantal Jones, Gadise Regassa, and Walter R. Allen

8 African American Faculty and Administrators in Higher Education: From Recruitment to Retention   209
   Na Lor and Jerlando F. L. Jackson

9 Asian American Faculty Discrimination: Why Does It Matter?   239
   Robert T. Teranishi, Rose Ann Rico Eborda Gutierrez, and Annie Le

Part 4. Leadership Does Matter

10 HBCU Activism: The Evolving Role of HBCUs in Resolving Racial Tensions and Advancing Racial Conciliation in Higher Education   259
   Ivory A. Toldson, Bianca M. Mack, and Temple R. Price

11 Exploring the Latinx-Servingness of Faculty at Hispanic-Serving Institutions   279
   Cheryl Ching

12 Black Women Faculty Engendering Brave (Online) Spaces for Black/Students of Color and Themselves   297
   M. Billye Sankofa Waters, Mounira Morris, and Cherese Childers-McKee

13 Diversity Leadership at the University of Michigan:
   From Desegregation to Diversity, Equity, and Inclusion   319
   *Phillip J. Bowman, Jamillah B. Williams, Angela Ebreo,
   and Nia D. Holland*

Afterword: Equity, Justice, and *The Racial Crisis*   347
   Valerie Kinloch

Contributors   351

Index   357

Illustrations

Figures

6.1	Offensive racist mechanisms. Author created.	141
6.2	Causes and stress responses of racial battle fatigue. Author created.	144
6.3	Trauma-informed care applied to racial battle fatigue. Author created.	151
8.1	Percentage of non-Hispanic White population by state. *Note:* US Census 2020 data. From Wikimedia Commons 2021.	215
8.2	Percentage distribution of faculty by race, 2017. Author created.	217
8.3	Regional distribution of administrators by race, 2014. Author created.	219
13.1	Percentage of Blacks enrolled in white colleges and universities.	322

Tables

7.1	Largest Black Population by State: List of States, Institution Name, and Institution Type	179
7.2	Numbers and Percentages of Black Full-Time Instructional Staff by Gender, 2017	182
7.3	Numbers and Percentages of Black Full-Time Instructional Staff by Tenure Status and Gender, 2017	185

8.1 Percentage Distribution of Regions among Faculty by Race and Year, 1999 and 2017. 213

8.2 Percentage Distribution of Region among Administrators by Race and Year, 1999–2014. Author created. 216

8.3 Percentage Distribution of Institutional Control and Institutional Type among Faculty by Race and Year, 1999 and 2017. Author created. 221

8.4 Percentage Distribution of Carnegie Classification among Faculty by Race and Year, Fall 2017. Author created. 221

8.5 Percentage Distribution of Institution Sector among Administrators, 2014. Author created. 222

8.6 Percentage Distribution of Institution Type among Administrators. Author created. 222

8.7 Total African American Men and Women by Academic Rank, 2017. Author created. 224

8.8 Percentage Distribution of Academic Rank by Race and Gender, 2017. Author created. 225

8.9 Percentage Distribution of Gender by Race and Year, 1999 and 2017. Author created. 225

8.10 Percentage Distribution of Academic Rank by Race and Year, 1999 and 2017. Author created. 226

8.11 Percentage Distribution of Highest Educational Credential Attained among Administrators by Race and Year, 1999 and 2014. Author created. 226

8.12 Salaries of Student Affairs Administrators by Race, 2014. Author created. 227

8.13 Age of Students Affairs Administrators by Race, 2014. Author created. 227

8.14 Years in Student Affairs Administrative Position by Race, 2014. Author created. 227

Foreword

Donald B. Pope-Davis

Those who have struggled know that it is the journey that will define you. It is a journey that requires each of us to be stubbornly persistent in our endeavors, for we shall find resistance in every effort along the way that will forever define our character.

With this third edition of *The Racial Crisis*, we find ourselves once again on a journey that seems all too familiar. It is a time of passionate discourse, social and economic distress, and racial and cultural animus. This condition, in part, is derived from our historical legacy that has failed to "hold these truths to be self-evident, that [all of us] are created equal, that [we] are endowed by [our] Creator with certain unalienable rights, that among these are Life, Liberty and the pursuit of Happiness."

For many of us, this prophetic belief has deep ties to our educational institutions, where formation takes place, and where opportunities emerge that will affect those unalienable rights for generations of students.

Given the cultural realities of our communities, institutions of higher education are beginning to resemble the inherent diversity of our society. At the same time, however, institutions hold on to practices, beliefs, and behaviors that still privilege a few, even while espousing a transformative agenda for the greater good.

What is this greater good, and how should we go about achieving it, given our current racial and cultural climate? Some important answers are presented in this edition by scholars and practitioners who are on a journey, not for themselves, but to invoke substantive change and progress when addressing diversity, inclusion, and social justice issues within our academic communities. Their scholarship adds fresh and original perspectives to this critical and ongoing relevant conversation.

As a young faculty member, I was once told by a colleague that I would not get tenured if I engaged in cross-cultural scholarship. My goal, I was told, should be to replicate and extend current perspectives so that my work would be seen by others as relevant. Needless to say, I did not listen. I suspect that many of the contributors to this book have had similar experiences. Yet here we are, relevant and needed now more than ever in the current state of affairs.

The contributing scholars in this book have served notice that the journey must continue so that the changes we seek will continue to make our institutions accountable for their inclusive ambitions. As they demonstrate, seizing the moment is insufficient. It must be followed by actions that result in tangible changes in higher education. Upon reading this book, you will undoubtedly want to get into "a little trouble." As the late John Lewis pointed out, "Sometimes change calls for a little trouble."

Introduction

WILLIAM A. SMITH AND KOFI LOMOTEY

In 1991, Philip G. Altbach and Kofi Lomotey published the first volume of *The Racial Crisis in American Higher Education* (*Racial Crisis I*). That volume was motivated by the growth and experiences of students, faculty, and administrators of color in predominantly white postsecondary institutions. Between the late 1970s and the publication of *Racial Crisis I*, there was tremendous growth in racial/ethnic enrollment in predominantly white institutions by African American, American Indian/Alaska Native, Asian American, Pacific Islander, and Latinx undergraduate students (i.e., Students of Color). African American student enrollment more than doubled from 1976 (943,355) to 1991 (approximately 1.2 million). All other racial/ethnic groups saw similar increases, with American Indian/Alaska Native student enrollment rising from roughly 70,000 to 96,000, or an increase of 37% between 1976 and 1991. Asian American and Pacific Islander student enrollment grew from 169,291 to 501,000, or almost three times their representation in that period. Latinx student enrollment grew from 352,893 in 1976 to 724,561 in 1991, or over 100% (National Center for Education Statistics, Fall 2000).

The racial/ethnic growth that was realized on these historically white college and university campuses could be partially attributed to the tremendous efforts and wins by the civil rights movement of the 1960s. However, what truly sparked the need to publish the *Racial Crisis I* were the ineffective responses by white students, faculty, staff, and administrators to this unprecedented racial/ethnic growth. Students of Color and the small numbers of racially underrepresented faculty, staff, and administrators were experiencing, at best, *Plessy*-like conditions on post-*Brown* campuses. In *Racial Crisis I*, Altbach (1991) stated that "race is one of the most volatile, and divisive, issues in American higher education" (p. 3). Unfortunately, little changed between the publication of *Racial Crisis I* and the inking of *Racial Crisis II* (2002), 11 years later, edited by William A. Smith, Altbach, and Lomotey.

In the spring of 2002, a white male Harvard Law student used the term *nigs* on the law school website, referring to African Americans. His position was that he was simply outlining the facts of a property case that used racially restrictive covenants, and he paid little to no attention to the racistly charged word (Moore & Bell, 2017). This racist act led to a campus-wide silent protest led by the Black Law Students Association at Harvard Law School. However, the campus protest did not stop further racist agitation. Another white male student sent an email to a first-year African American woman law student that said, in part, "We at the Harvard Law School, [are] a free, private community, where any member wishing to use the word 'nigger' in any form should not be prevented from doing so" (Moore & Bell, 2017, p. 100). Racist incidents were not confined to Harvard University. In fact, race and racism remained a *volatile and divisive* issue in US higher education during the tumultuous 1990s (Smith, Altbach, & Lomotey, 2002).

John P. Downey and Frances K. Stage (1999) examined college and university campus hate crimes during the 1990s. They indicated that the increased campus hate crimes of the 1990s were the biggest threat to safety and to building an overall sense of community. These researchers identified three common perpetrators of campus hate crimes, typically white males: the *thrill seeker*, the *reactive*, and the organized hate group perpetrator. The thrill seeker is a person who is out for a racistly good time and for peer validation for their bigotry and hatred toward People of Color. A reactive person sees themselves as a victim of the breaking down of the racial order. This person, for instance, might be provoked to commit racist acts based upon interracial dating or on the belief that too many Students of Color have been admitted on campus. Downey and Stage thought that the perpetrator, the organized hate group, was the least likely offender on campus. The skinheads and Ku Klux Klan would be examples of this group.

Since the publication of *Racial Crisis II*, we have been underwhelmed by the responses of university and college administrators to our highlighting of the racial dilemmas. Both overt and covert white supremacist activities have become more commonplace on campuses. In the 2018 academic year, the Anti-Defamation League's Center on Extremism confirmed 320 incidents of white nationalist propaganda perpetrated on more than 200 college and university campuses. By 2019, campus hate crimes grew to 630 of the total of 2,713 crimes. There were an additional 2,083 hate crimes committed off-campus. This increase more than doubled the total number from the previous year (1,214). According to the Anti-Defamation League's report, the fall 2019 semester saw a 159% increase in hate crimes from the spring 2019 semester (ADL, 2020). Sadly, hate crimes represent only one aspect of the campus racial crisis. In this volume, Lomotey lays out how institutionalized white racism on campuses is interconnected with power, white supremacy, and white privilege, and how each of these is symbiotically related to the 2020 US and global protests for social and racial justice.

At the time of publication, we are dealing with at least two pandemics: COVID-19 and racism. Throughout the country the streets have been filled with protestors demanding an end to institutionalized white supremacy and police violence, especially against innocent and unarmed Black people. Many empty campuses were spared these demonstrations as a result of the COVID-19 shutdowns of regular daily operations. However, we are confident that without the pandemic students, and perhaps faculty and staff, would have been protesting on campuses across the country for precisely the issues raised in this third edition of the *Racial Crisis*.

Racism has been solidified as the most pivotal issue in higher education. In his chapter, Smith defines it as "an act of violence." These racist acts are not just the behavior of white supremacists or overt hate crimes. The racial crisis is embedded in how higher education operates. While the number of Students and Faculty of Color has increased, specific subgroups are silently disappearing without much attention being given to their loss. Overall, persistence to graduation for Students of Color is still an issue. The path toward tenure, promotion, and full professorship remains a dubious process for many Faculty of Color. Administrators of Color are scarce, and they continue to hold the most unprotected yet visible positions on campus. Each of these groups has inherited the racial crises covered in the first two editions of *The Racial Crisis* while taking on new twenty-first-century forms of crises not yet covered.

This volume offers an overview of some of the most pressing racial issues on campuses across the country. We believe that the current volume is a companion edition to the first two. The concerns in *Racial Crisis I* and *II* are still relevant to today's crises. Yet the present volume offers a deeper dive into current critical matters that need further thought and action. We need to make immediate sound decisions about postsecondary education becoming a racially inclusive environment that does not uphold institutionalized white supremacy. Otherwise, the writing of the *Racial Crisis IV* may be the racial nadir of higher education.

While the topics in this volume are similar to those in the two previous volumes, the organization is somewhat different. We begin by contextualizing the crisis, explaining aspects of the crisis. From there, we offer a historical perspective. Next, we look at what happens on campus, focusing on psychosocial issues, Black faculty, and Asian American faculty as illustrations. Finally, we offer insights on the significance of leadership, addressing issues of race and racism in higher education.

Kofi Lomotey sets the tone by opening part 1 with a sophisticated analysis of institutionalized white supremacy on campus and the social relationship to off-campus racial issues. Next, Kēhaulani Vaughn takes a critical look at the Campaign for College Opportunity publication *How Exclusion in California's Colleges and Universities Hurt Our Values, Our Students, and Our Economy* and critiques the publication's aggregation of Pacific Islanders with Asian Americans, highlighting the negative implications of such an analysis for the status of Pacific Islanders in the US higher education pipeline. Furthermore, through a three-city analysis, Shiver, Maria Ashkin, Jimmy Kendall, and Evelyn Ezikwelu explore the grim status of Black males in academia. Using a combination of three frameworks—social dominance theory, racial battle fatigue, and the analysis framework of the UN Office of the Special Advisor on the Prevention of Genocide—the authors offer a compelling analysis of the lifelong experiences of Black males, wherein they conclude that there is an externally imposed genocidal tendency toward Black males in US society.

In part 2, Eddie R. Cole sets the historical tone by investigating presidential responses to the racial crisis on postsecondary campuses. Then María C. Ledesma, Uma Mazyck Jayakumar, and Kenyon L. Whitman nicely extend this conversation by addressing the successes and failures of implementing affirmative action in postsecondary institutions.

William A. Smith's chapter nicely introduces part 3 with a conversation about the psychosocial antecedents of racial battle fatigue and how understanding the interlocking identities of racially minoritized groups better explains the racial pandemic impact. Channel C. McLewis, Chantal Jones, Gadise Regassa, and Walter R. Allen add to this utilizing critical race theory to explore the impact of anti-Blackness on the recruiting, hiring, promoting, and tenuring of Black faculty. They call for a serious rethinking of academia, including a reconsideration of the status of Black faculty. Na Lor and Jerlando F. L. Jackson examine the challenges associated with African American faculty and administrators' employment across the intersections of gender, institution type, sector, size, and degree credentials. Robert T. Teranishi, Rose Ann Rico Eborda Gutierrez, and Annie Le conclude this part by providing a provocative look at Asian American faculty. While this group is not numerically underrepresented, campuses have continued to fail to create an inclusive and productive environment for them. These authors discuss the unique needs, challenges, and contributions of Asian American faculty.

While many campuses have struggled to provide a sense of belonging for Black students, historically Black colleges and universities (HBCUs) have and continue to produce some of the country's greatest leaders. In the final part, Ivory A. Toldson, Bianca M. Mack, and Temple R. Price consider in granular detail how HBCUs play a deep-rooted role in forming Black people's intellectual, cultural, and spiritual development. Then Cheryl Ching explains how faculty at Hispanic-serving institutions perceive Latinx students, their role in advancing students' learning and development, and the support efforts they undertake. Next, in a powerful autoethnography M. Billye Sankofa Waters, Mounira Morris, and Cherese Childers-McKee each look at their academic and political lives, exploring issues of their work in the academy and the curriculum they develop and teach. Finally, Phillip J. Bowman, Jamillah B. Williams, Angela Ebreo, and Nia D. Holland provide an in-depth and instructive examination of diversity leadership development at the University of Michigan through the administrations of seven campus leaders from 1951 to the present. Through document analysis and personal experiences, the authors provide a chronological picture of the institution's advancement.

On one level, the conceiving—and compiling—of this volume has been inspiring; there are so many outstanding scholars included herein who describe race in US higher education from historical and contemporary perspectives. They also offer aspects of the solutions that can aid us in bringing about a more socially just environment in US higher education institutions.

However, as we indicated above, we are dealing with many of the same issues in 2021 that we dealt with in 1991—30 years ago: the status of Black, Latinx, Asian American, and Indigenous Peoples as students in US higher education, and as faculty in these institutions. In addition, the curriculum continues to be a challenge in terms of the limited discussion of the experiences of these groups.

In the spirit of the late Congressman John Robert Lewis, we posit that this book is dedicated to the millions of Students and Faculty of Color who have been, are, or will be in US institutions of higher education. We each have a responsibility to do our part to make the circumstances better for these groups. Social justice is a collective and collaborative responsibility.

References

ADL (2020). Year-over-Year: White supremacists double down on propaganda in 2019: A report from the center on extremism (Rep.). Anti-Defamation League.

Altbach, P. G. (1991). The racial dilemma in American higher education. In P. G. Altbach & K. Lomotey (Eds.), *The racial crisis in American higher education* (pp. 3–17). State University of New York Press.

Altbach, P. G., & Lomotey, K. (Eds.) (1991). *The racial crisis in American higher education*. State University of New York Press.

Downey, J. P., & Stage, F. K. (1999). Hate crimes and violence on college and university campuses. *Journal of College Student Development, 40,* 3–9.

Moore, W. L., & Bell, J. M. (2017). The right to be racist in college: Racist speech, white institutional space, and the First Amendment. *Law & Policy 39,* 99–120. doi:10.1111/lapo.12076

National Center for Education Statistics. (Fall 2000). *Integrated postsecondary education database system, fall enrollment and degree completion by race/ethnicity and gender*. US Department of Education.

Smith, W. A., Altbach, P. G., & Lomotey, K. (Eds.) (2002). *The racial crisis in American higher education: Continuing the challenges for the twenty-first century* (Rev. ed.). State University of New York Press.

PART 1
CONTEXTUALIZING THE CRISIS

Chapter 1

Institutionalized White Racism
The Impact on US Higher Education

Kofi Lomotey

Institutionalized White Racism Overview

In this chapter, I explore institutionalized White racism and its components—including power, White supremacy, and White privilege. I then look at society's contemporary responses to institutionalized White racism, including the widespread protests across the country and, indeed, the world. Next, I review, specifically, the reactions in higher education before exploring an opportunity for higher education to begin to address the impact of institutionalized White racism today—in the area of curriculum reform—broadly defined.

I begin with brief discussions of the origin, meaning, and components of institutionalized White racism. St. Clair Drake (1987) posits that institutionalized white racism replaced less severe forms of European color prejudice as well as the Mediterranean multicultural enslavement of the 15th and 16th centuries. One of the earliest and most brutal and inhumane acts of institutionalized White racism occurred beginning in the 16th century with the kidnapping of millions of Africans from the continent of Africa; their forced transportation to the Americas, with the murdering of some; and the enslavement upon their arrival here of those who were not killed in the process—for nearly 250 years. As we enter the third decade of the 21st century, one of the most—if not the most—significant factors negatively affecting the life chances of Black, Latinx, Asian American, and Indigenous peoples in the United States continues to be institutionalized White racism (Shockley & Lomotey, 2020).[1]

Institutionalized White racism, according to Alan Colon (2016), is systemic, and it facilitates divisiveness and the distinction between the privileged and those without privilege based largely upon race. As Colon (2016) points out, the disproportionate effect of institutionalized White racism on Black, Latinx, Asian American, and Indigenous peoples in the United States can be seen in disparities in physical and mental health, life spans, income and wealth, justice and public service experiences, employment, homeownership, the quality of education, and the legitimacy afforded to the histories and cultures of various groups. One illustration of this phenomenon of institutionalized White racism here in the United States is the systemic land loss experienced by the Indigenous peoples upon the arrival of Europeans. They were relegated to reservations after previously being free to roam the entire landmass. More recently, Blacks have experienced a massive loss of property (Love, 2017).

Colon (2016) discusses how higher education in the United States was initially designed to work in concert with religious institutions and with the government to maintain institutionalized White racism and the oppression of Black, Latinx, Asian American, and Indigenous peoples. The works of William Watkins (2001) and James Anderson (1988) support this view. Higher education was designed, Colon says, to prepare upper-class Whites to govern others, including poor White, Black, Latinx, Asian American, and Indigenous peoples. The curriculum within the schools supported these racist priorities. It reinforced those expected roles for particular groups in the United States. This systemic phenomenon was modeled after the English system wherein the White aristocracy similarly oppressed others within the society.

Power

Institutionalized White racism is the belief in the inferiority of Black, Latinx, Asian American, and Indigenous peoples *coupled with* the exercise of power and privilege by White people over these groups. It is a process through which White supremacy is executed. Wade Nobles (1978) defines power as the ability to explain reality and convince others that it is their reality. I provide three examples of this view. The first illustration relates to the continents on the planet Earth. In the United States (and presumably elsewhere), children are told beginning in elementary school that there are seven continents, and that a continent is a large body of land surrounded by water. So, when asked to name the continents, most students include Europe. (You cannot get to seven if you do not include Europe.) In fact, Europe is not a large body of land, nor is it surrounded by water; it is connected to Asia. The name of the continent is Eurasia. Claiming that Europe is a continent is reflective of a European worldview. Whenever Europe is referred to as a continent it upholds a White supremacy worldview. Many Black, Latinx, Asian American, and Indigenous peoples have been convinced that it is also their worldview.

The second illustration of power being used to define reality and to convince others that it is their reality is the world map. The Mercator projection map is the map of the world we are accustomed to viewing. This map was developed for sea merchants in the sixteenth century and has predominated since that time. While it is not possible to accurately display a sphere on a flat surface, this particular depiction of the world is excessively problematic for several reasons:

- It distorts and dramatically enlarges Eurasia and North American countries.
- It makes Alaska look nearly as large as the continental United States; Alaska can fit inside the continental United States about three times.
- It makes Greenland appear nearly the size of Africa; Greenland can fit into Africa almost 14 times.
- It makes Europe (excluding Russia) appear slightly larger than South America; the landmass of South America is nearly twice as large as that of Europe.
- It makes Antarctica appear to be the largest continent; Antarctica is the fifth-largest continent.
- It makes the landmass in the Northern Hemisphere look larger than the landmass in the Southern Hemisphere; the landmass of the Southern Hemisphere is 38.6 million square miles, while the landmass of the Northern Hemisphere is 18.9 million square miles.

Generally speaking, the inaccuracy (and cultural bias) portrayed by the Mercator projection of the world is that the landmass above the equator (mainly inhabited by White people) is significantly larger than the landmass below the equator (occupied predominantly by Black, Latinx, and Indigenous peoples). While the assertion is not true, it reflects power: the worldview of one group is imposed upon other groups and becomes their reality—while simultaneously embedding White supremacy as objective and normal.

The third illustration of the exercise of power by Whites in the United States refers to the "discovery" of the United States. Children are taught in US schools that Christopher Columbus discovered the modern-day North American continent in 1492. This fallacy is reinforced each October, when the United States celebrates Columbus Day. But there were Africans in the Americas before Columbus arrived (Van Sertima, 1976). And, of course, Indigenous peoples lived on this land centuries before Columbus arrived. How is it possible that Columbus discovered the United States? Obviously, he did not, but the perpetuation of that myth reflects power: White reality being imposed upon Black, Latinx, Asian American, and Indigenous peoples—for hundreds of years. In this case, the land was not recognized until it was seen and acknowledged by Whites.

Institutionalized White racism affects all of us: Whites, Blacks, Latinx, Asian Americans, and Indigenous peoples. But its most significant, persistent, and negative impact is on Black, Latinx, Asian American, and Indigenous peoples upon whom White power and reality are imposed. Joel Spring (1991) proposes that power is the capacity to control others, and adds that it is also the ability to avoid being controlled by others.

White Privilege

According to the Transnational Racial Justice Initiative (2001), because of White privilege, Whites amass more riches and other holdings and have greater entrée to societal benefits. They have an advantage in the legal system and every realm of US society. The large majority of Black, Latinx, Asian American, and Indigenous peoples, in contrast, face poverty and gross social injustices and inequities because of White privilege. This privilege is broad-based and functions within every sphere of US society. It affects local, state, and national protocols, processes, and patterns. Examples of this phenomenon include the redlining that occurs when Black people seek to purchase homes, and the internment of more than 125,000 Japanese Americans during World War II. A complete comprehension of this phenomenon—White privilege—the Transnational Racial Justice Initiative (2001) argues, necessitates understanding the impact on Black, Latinx, Asian American, and Indigenous peoples *and* on those with the privileges: the oppressors.

Institutionalized White racism begets White privilege. White privilege leads some to make statements wherein the summer 2020 protests are seen as the problem rather than White privilege (and institutionalized White racism). White racists deny that institutionalized White racism is a problem in the United States and instead blame Black, Latinx, Asian American, and Indigenous peoples—using victim blaming as a strategy to escape responsibility and the need to correct wrongs.

Indeed, institutionalized White racism has had a devastating and long-lasting impact on Black and other oppressed people in the United States. An opportunity for a more significant response to institutionalized White racism came in 2020, when the pronounced and collective response of the general public to acts of institutionalized White racism (e.g., police brutality toward Black people and the disproportionate impact of COVID-19 on Black, Latinx, and Indigenous peoples) reflected the initial stages of a much-needed cultural shift.

Institutionalized White Racism: Contemporary Responses

The United States is in a heretofore unseen position with regard to its response to issues of race, racism, and oppression. We are in the midst of what could become a significant cultural shift. With the visually documented plethora of state-sanctioned murders of Black men, women, and children, many Blacks—and others—have said "Enough is enough." From the slaughter of a multitude of enslaved Africans to the senseless and brutal murder of Emmett Till to the killings of Ahmaud Arbery, George Floyd, Breonna Taylor, and many others, many people in this country—of all colors—have stepped up to a degree and with a factual understanding previously unseen. But, of course, racist killings do not occur only within the Black community. We must not forget Sitting Bull,[2] Vincent Chin, Andrés Guardado, Carlos Ingram-Lopez, and many other Latinx, Asian American, and Indigenous peoples who have suffered a similar fate.

The massive interracial and intergenerational protests of 2020—in all 50 states and beyond—were unprecedented. Many are irate, frustrated, and tired. It is difficult to tell what's next, but the multiracial nature of these protests appeared to portend a significant outcome—a cultural shift.

Political leaders at the local, state, and congressional levels spoke up and made decisions seemingly designed to address some of the effects of institutionalized White racism. These included the removal of statues of confederate leaders, the reorganization of police forces, and the replacement of racially insensitive flags. For a while, the US Supreme Court appeared to become more liberal than previously anticipated (Liptak and Parlapiano, 2020). The rhetoric of corporations and their leaders suggested that their intentions were significantly more meaningful than in the past—even the recent past.

US Higher Education Today

> The racial situation in American higher education has been the focus of widespread coverage in the American media. . . . Reports of racial incidents are invariably followed by finger-pointing, inaccurate assessments and a general lack of understanding on the part of many. Some place the blame on underrepresented students, others blame university faculty and administrators, some blame white students and still others blame society at large. All too often these assessments are too simplistic and do not derive from an adequate consideration of the context in which these incidents occur.
>
> —Lomotey, 1991, p. 263

Although I made this statement over 30 years ago, it could just as well have been made yesterday. We are still burdened by numerous racist incidents on campuses (and elsewhere), and as a society, we still are unable or unwilling to address them adequately (see the case studies in this volume). If we explore the economic, political, health, military, housing, religious, and labor institutions in the United States, Black, Latinx, Asian American, and Indigenous peoples are still oppressed by institutionalized White racism. Indeed, the same is true of education, including higher education.

As for higher education, we have only to look at the racially biased admission process in which standardized tests are still used to measure college readiness. The faculty's expectations for the potential for success of Black, Latinx, and Indigenous students are still relatively low. The curriculum is still racially biased; the experiences of Black, Latinx, Asian American, and Indigenous peoples are still underrepresented and inaccurately documented. Black, Latinx, and Indigenous faculty are underrepresented in the academy, and in the classroom, Black students, for example, are 20 times more likely to see a professor of another race in front of them than they are to see one who looks like them. It is important to acknowledge this, because many students have difficulty envisioning themselves being successful when they have few successful role models who look like them.

Even though most campuses were largely deserted for some time due to COVID-19, the protests and their byproducts were not absent from higher education. Many higher education leaders have published statements condemning institutionalized White racism, White privilege, and police brutality toward Blacks. Unfortunately, many were not careful in their wording and had to backtrack and clarify their intentions (Ellis, 2020; McKenzie, 2020). In addition, an increasing number of schools removed standardized achievement examinations (e.g., SAT, ACT, and GRE) from their admission requirements. I suspect that this is at least in part a response to the well-known truism that these tests do not correlate well with academic potential and are even less predictive of the potential of Black and other oppressed students.

The multicultural protests affected collegiate athletics and other aspects of college life. The schools in the Southeastern Conference threatened not to hold any athletic competitions in the state of Mississippi if that state did not change its state flag, which had a confederate logo in the upper right-hand corner; the state quickly responded by abandoning the flag. Schools such as Princeton removed statues of individuals associated with the US confederacy or with forms of overt racism that were commonplace in the early United States. After the president of North Central University in Minneapolis announced the creation of a George Floyd Scholarship, several other colleges and universities followed his lead. Some institutions of higher education disassociated their campuses from local police departments.

Schooling versus Education: A Dilemma

Institutions, by definition, are subjective; they are often designed to seamlessly produce people and systems that further the status quo. Maintaining the status quo ensures that the existing power relations continue. Institutionalized White racism is a social justice issue. It is about providing freedom, justice, and equality for oppressed people. In discussing social justice leadership in the K–12 context, Martin Scanlan and George Theoharis (2015) suggest that there are four key components to social justice leadership: "(a) raising student achievement, (b) improving school structures, (c) re-centering and enhancing staff capacity, and (d) strengthening school culture and community" (p. 3). These components have relevance for higher education also, though they might be defined differently. For tertiary education, I would add curriculum reform as a fifth and critically important component of social justice leadership. We have an important opportunity in higher education to address institutionalized White racism head-on by revamping the curriculum to better address the needs of oppressed students. This opportunity is embedded in a distinction between schooling and education made by Mwalimu J. Shujaa. Shujaa (1995) profoundly differentiates between schooling and education: "Schooling is a process intended to perpetuate and maintain society's existing power relations and the institutional structures that support those arrangements. . . . Education in contrast to schooling is our means of providing for intergenerational transmission of cultural identity through knowledge of the values, beliefs, traditions, customs, rituals, and sensibilities that have sustained a people" (p. 15). Shujaa argues that schooling extends prevailing power relationships and perpetuates the existing politically controlling cultural orientation. Schooling occurs when one group has power over another. Through schooling, the culture of a dominant group is imposed upon another group. The group that is imposed upon adjusts and adapts in response to contact with the dominant (privileged) group.

Education, Shujaa (1993) argues, involves learning and internalizing one's cultural norms. It occurs in informal and formal settings. It provides the wherewithal for members of a group to effectively function within their family, community, and race and to retain the integrity of their own culture in social contexts where unequal power relations exist among cultures.

According to Shujaa (1993), we are all being schooled as a result of institutionalized White racism, White privilege, and the power that White people hold over other groups in society. In addition, I suspect that Shujaa would argue that Black, Latinx, and Indigenous peoples in the United States (and elsewhere) receive much less education because of the power exerted by Whites. Because of power relations in the United States, Black, Latinx, and Indigenous peoples receive significantly more schooling than education. The idea that there are seven continents could be thought of as reflective of the schooling that Black, Latinx, and Indigenous people receive in the United States. It is a reality created by Whites and foisted upon Black, Latinx, and Indigenous peoples. Conversely, the notion that there are only six continents reflects the education of these groups.

Presently, the curriculum in US higher education, even in historically Black colleges and universities, Hispanic-serving institutions, Pacific Islander colleges, and Indigenous colleges, does not provide Black, Latinx, Asian American, and Indigenous students with the opportunity to learn to think critically, to learn and know about self, to learn the cultures and stories of one's people, to learn to appreciate different worldviews, or to learn to work toward self-actualization. More particularly, Jake Carruthers (1995) describes a worldview as "the way a people conceive of the fundamental questions of existence and organization of the universe" (p. 53). Lomotey and Sessi Aboh (2009) expand this discussion of a worldview, specifically as it relates to Black people: "It is, in a sense, the lens through which one views the world. Too often, students of African descent in the United States receive an educational experience from a European worldview perspective that does not instill in them any desire to develop the communities populated by people of African descent" (315). When we consider the impact of institutionalized White racism, White privilege, and the exertion of power, a greater effort at providing education for Black, Latinx, Asian American, and Indigenous peoples seems to be in order and consistent with the cultural shift in which we find ourselves.

Curriculum Reform, Broadly Defined: An Opportunity

One way that our current circumstances might be addressed in higher education is through the provision of a curriculum wherein these groups no longer see their experiences, cultures, and lifestyles as appendages, or as tangential, to the curriculum but instead as intricately embedded in the curriculum. This more appropriate curriculum is one way in which colleges and universities can affect the racial crisis in US higher education today.

I am calling for a culturally relevant curriculum in higher education. All students deserve an effective teaching/learning experience facilitated by faculty who draw upon the culture of the student/learner, enabling them to "see themselves" in the curriculum (Gay, 2000; Lomotey, 1989). Perhaps the most cited definition of culturally relevant teaching is that of Gloria Ladson-Billings (1994) wherein she states, "Culturally relevant teaching is pedagogy that empowers students intellectually, socially, emotionally, and politically by using cultural referents to impart knowledge, skills, and attitudes" (p. 18). What might this look like in higher education?

The study of various European groups has been part of the US higher education curriculum since the beginning. Such areas of study include Greek mythology and the Latin, French, Italian, and German languages, and the curriculum is pregnant with European literature, music, and more. The systematic introduction of the experiences of Black, Latinx, Asian American, and Indigenous peoples came about with the advent of ethnic studies in the late 1960s and early 1970s. The battle to include these programs has been tumultuous and persists. By way of illustration, the struggle to gain additional support for the African and African American Studies program at Stanford University (*The Stanford Daily*, 2020) has been going on for more than 50 years. The argument in opposition to departmentalizing Black studies at Stanford is that the field is "too narrow." The same argument could be made for the European studies courses discussed above.

Like European cultural studies, these so-called ethnic studies do not just serve the groups for whom they are named; they benefit all students. Thus, while it is critically important to know about one's own people, it is also important to know about others.

Even within ethnic studies programs, in many instances, the experiences of various groups (e.g., Blacks, Latinx, Asian Americans, Indigenous peoples, LBGTQQ[3] people, and women) have recently been placed under one umbrella, limiting the emphasis and understanding of each individual group. *There is a need for more Black studies, Latinx studies, Asian American studies, and Indigenous studies programs (certificate programs, minors, and majors) in US institutions of higher education.*

As suggested in the earlier illustrations of an oppressor's worldview being imposed on others, too often the exposure to experiences of groups in the United States is extremely limited and does not reflect a worldview beyond the US shores. *There is a need for more international programs and services linking all students to other parts of the world.* It is most important to link Black students to Africa, Latinx students to the Latinx countries, Asian American students to Asia, and indigenous students to other parts of the Americas. Again, these international programs and services advantage all students; they enable all students to expand their worldview.

Where can one go to study Black people? Latinx people? Asian American people? Indigenous peoples? The pickins are slim. *There is a need for more databases on the experiences of Black, Latinx, Asian American, and Indigenous people.*

There is a need to develop more opportunities for university faculty to better understand the history, culture, and experiences of Black, Latinx, Asian American, and Indigenous peoples. *There is a need for more opportunities for university faculty to become more culturally literate or culturally competent.*

The implementation of these four suggestions will positively affect the experiences that students have in their classes and their degree programs.

Additionally, there is a need to reengineer the course and degree programs to explicitly incorporate the histories, cultures, and experiences of Black, Latinx, Asian American, and Indigenous peoples, enabling the stories of their lives to be more than appendages, or tangential, to the *main* curriculum.

Summary

Institutionalized White racism, White supremacy, and White privilege have a long, excruciating history in the United States and beyond and remain painfully impactful today. Most notably, for our purposes, they continue to negatively affect the experiences of Black, Latinx, Asian American, and Indigenous students in US higher education. Christiane Warren (2020) speaks of the current responsibility of higher education institutions, given the state of race relations in this country: "Higher education professionals want to take the lead now and engage more deliberately and jointly in revising our programs so that they are intellectually inclusive, skills focused, and fully transferable, thereby moving significantly forward to achieving true equity not only in access but also in outcome for all students. America remains an utterly unique experiment that continues to justify its claim of exceptionality. We need to see addressing injustice against one of us as an affirmation of freedom for all of us" (4). We have a responsibility to serve as social justice warriors struggling against all forms of social injustice and inequity—most notably, institutionalized White racism, White supremacy, and White privilege. One opportunity that we have today to take a significant step in addressing institutionalized White racism is to reengineer the curriculum, enabling Black, Latinx, Asian American, and Indigenous students to see themselves in the heart of the curriculum—to receive education and not just schooling. We can begin this task in five areas:

- establishing more ethnic studies programs
- creating additional international programs and services
- developing more databases about the experiences, culture, and history of Black, Latinx, Asian American, and Indigenous peoples
- creating more professional development opportunities for higher education faculty, enabling them to increase their cultural

competence—their knowledge of other cultural groups in the United States

- enabling Black, Latinx, Asian American, and Indigenous students to see themselves in the explicit curriculum for courses and degree programs.

As I said in the first volume of this text (Lomotey, 1991), "In the final analysis, we must all do everything that we can to eliminate [institutionalized white] racism and the accompanying racial conflict in American higher education—and in America" (pp. 268).

Notes

1. I am taking the liberty of spelling out the names of racial groups herein. I prefer not to use the more common catchall terms for the conglomeration of groups that are not White (e.g., "minorities," "minoritized groups," "people of color," et cetera). In a few instances I have excluded Asian Americans from the list. Their history, culture, and experiences in the United States are in many ways significantly different from those of the other oppressed groups. For example, in US schools there generally is an expectation that Asian American students will do well academically; this is not the case for these other groups. Also, Asian Americans are not as underrepresented on the faculties of US higher education institutions.

2. Indigenous peoples numbered as many as 15 million in North America at the close of the 16th century. By the end of the 19th century, after more that 1,500 attacks, wars, and raids, there were less than 240,000 Indigenous peoples in North America.

3. Lesbian, bisexual, gay, transgender, queer, and questioning.

References

Anderson, J. D. (1988). *The education of Blacks in the South, 1860–1935*. The University of North Carolina Press.

Carruthers, J. H. (1995). Black intellectuals and the crisis in Black education. In M. J. Shujaa (Ed.), *Too much schooling, too little education: A paradox of Black life in White societies* (pp. 35–55). Africa World Press.

Colon, A. (2016). Racism in colleges and universities. In K. Lomotey (Ed.), *People of color in the United States: Contemporary issues in education, work, communities, health, and immigration. Education: K–12 and higher education* (Vol. 1, pp. 267–275). Greenwood.

Drake, S. C. (1987). *Black folks here and there: An essay in history and anthropology.* Vol. 1. Center for Afro-American Studies, University of California at Los Angeles.

Du Bois, W. E. B. (1903). *The souls of Black folk.* Dover Publications.

Ellis, L. (2020, June 12). For colleges, protests over racism may put everything on the line. *The Chronicle of Higher Education.*

Gay, G. (2000). *Culturally responsive teaching: Theory, research, and practice.* Teachers College Press.

Ladson-Billings, G. (1994). *The dreamkeepers: Successful teachers for African-American children.* Jossey-Bass.

Liptak, A., & Parlapiano, A. (2020, June 30). The major supreme court cases this term and what the public thinks. *The New York Times.*

Lomotey, K. (1989). Cultural diversity in the urban school: Implications for principals. *NASSP Bulletin, 73*(521), 81–85.

Lomotey, K. (1991). Conclusion. In P. G. Altbach and K. Lomotey (Eds.), *The racial crisis in American higher education* (pp. 263–268). State University of New York Press.

Lomotey, K., & Aboh, S. F. (2009). Historically Black colleges and universities: Catalysts to liberation? In L. C. Tillman (Ed.), *The sage handbook of African American education.* Sage Publications.

Love, D. (2017, June 30). From 15 million acres to 1 million: How Black people lost their land. *Atlanta Black Star.*

McKenzie, L. (2020, June 8). Words matter for college presidents, but so will actions. *Inside Higher Education.*

Nobles, W. (1978). African consciousness and liberation struggles: Implications for the development and construction of scientific paradigms. (Unpublished monograph).

Scanlan, M., & Theoharis, G. (2015). Introduction: Intersectionality in educational leadership. In G. Theoharis and M. Scanlan (Eds.), *Leadership for increasingly diverse schools* (pp. 1–11). Routledge.

Shockley, K. G., & Lomotey, K. (2020). Introduction. In K. G. Shockley & K. Lomotey (Eds.), *African-centered Education: Theory and Practice* (pp. xvii–xxxiii). Myers Education Press.

Shujaa, M. J. (1993). Education and schooling: You can have one without the other. *Urban Education, 27*(4), 328–351.

Shujaa, M. J. (1995). *Too much schooling, too little education: A paradox of Black life in White societies.* Africa World Press.

Spring, J. (1991). Knowledge and power in research into the politics of urban education. In J. G. Cibulka, R. J. Reed, and K. K. Wong (Eds.), *The Politics of Urban Education in the United States* (pp. 45–56). Taylor and Francis.

Stanford Daily. (2020, July 6). Letter to the president and provost: The inadequacy of "The Impacts of Race in America."

Transnational Racial Justice Initiative. (2001). *The persistence of white privilege and institutionalized racism in US policy: A report on US Government compliance* with the International Convention on the elimination of all forms of racial discrimination. Applied Research Center.

Van Sertima, I. (1976). *They came before Columbus: The African presence in ancient America.* Random House.

Warren, C. (2020, June 9). Colleges must take a new approach to systemic racism. *Inside Higher Education,* 1–4.

Watkins, W. H. (2001). *The White architects of Black education: Ideology and power in America, 1865–1954 (The Teaching of Social Justice Series).* Teachers College Press.

Chapter 2

Who Gets "Left Out"

Pacific Islanders, Data Aggregation, and Native Erasure

KĒHAULANI VAUGHN

In March 2018, the Campaign for College Opportunity published "Left Out: How Exclusion in California's Colleges and Universities Hurt Our Values, Our Students, and Our Economy." Unequivocally emphasizing the distinction between diversity and inclusion, the report demonstrates that while the vast majority of students enrolled at California's public colleges and universities are from underrepresented groups, the faculty and leadership at these institutions remain largely male and white. Although *Left Out* emphasizes the importance of inclusion and provides recommendations to improve diversity at the faculty and leadership levels, through its practice of data aggregation, the report continues the exclusion of some of California's most vulnerable populations, including Native Americans and Pacific Islanders. With specific attention to Pacific Islanders, this chapter focuses on the problematic nature of aggregating Pacific Islanders with Asian Americans as a form of systemic erasure. This erasure continues to have consequences for a higher educational pipeline for Pacific Islanders that would include a greater number of students, faculty, and administrators.

Despite *Left Out*'s recommendations of disaggregating data, it continued the practice of aggregating Pacific Islanders into the Asian American rubric. Although calls for disaggregated data are not new, *Left Out* and similar reports maintain exclusion by grouping Pacific Islanders with Asian Americans, erasing Pacific Islanders and their distinct needs as Indigenous people, and imposing a racial category for the sake of inclusion. By utilizing *Left Out*, this chapter argues for the distinct separation of Pacific Islanders in data collection as a foundation in the discussions and the corresponding practices needed for a more inclusive higher education system for Pacific Islanders. This chapter provides a background on Pacific Islanders, a history of the Asian Pacific Islander category, Pacific Islanders as Indigenous people, the need for race in *Left Out*, the startling statistics, and disaggregated data. It emphasizes the importance of disaggregating Pacific Islander data within higher education by employing the same logic and arguments used by *Left Out*. It also reminds scholars and practitioners engaged in educational equity discussions of the pervasiveness of Indigenous erasure, which takes many forms, including data aggregation. These practices continue to have consequences for Pacific Islander students, faculty, and administrators, and the potential for a greater pipeline within higher education.

Who Are Pacific Islanders?

Before colonial powers landed in the Pacific, Pacific Islanders traversed seas spanning the islands and oceans of the Micronesian, Melanesian, and Polynesian archipelagos. However, colonialism, settler colonialism, and neo-colonialism have caused growing displacement in the Pacific. In response to military incursions, tourism, and environmental stressors, Pacific Islanders are taking up residence in new places, including the continental United States. Pacific Islanders possess varied citizenship and immigration statuses due to their unique histories and relationships with colonial powers, including the United States. These statuses include US citizen, US national, Compact of Free Association immigrant, and undocumented immigrant. In the United States, categorized by the federal government as Native Hawaiian and Pacific Islander (NHPI), Pacific Islanders encompass a group of more than twenty ethnically and linguistically diverse Indigenous communities (Empowering Pacific Islander Communities and Asian Americans Advancing Justice [EPIC & AAAJ], 2014). Currently, Native Hawaiians and Pacific Islanders represent over 1.2 million people and account for less than 1% (0.40%) of the US population (Hixon, Hepler, & Kim, 2012). According to the 2010 Census, Pacific Islanders are one of the fastest-growing populations in the United States; they are the second-fastest-growing group behind Asian Americans

(Asian Americans Advancing Justice [AAAJ], 2016). However, the NHPI population is expected to grow to over 2 million by 2030 (EPIC & AAAJ, 2014).

While Native Hawaiians and Pacific Islanders reside in all 50 states, California is home to the largest population of Pacific Islanders in the contiguous United States (EPIC & AAAJ, 2014). Reports such as *Left Out*, which give valuable information about California's public higher education institutions, need to accurately reflect the state's populations. Continuing the aggregation of Asian Americans and Pacific Islanders produces inaccurate data on Pacific Islanders, which has grave policy implications. For example, since Asian Americans are often not seen as an underrepresented minority in higher education, Pacific Islanders are also not considered an underrepresented minority in need of specific outreach and retention services. Furthermore, for the Pacific Islanders who exist in higher education, there often are no mechanisms to document their existence that could lead to a greater pipeline of Pacific Islander students, faculty, and administrators. Although the creators of the *Left Out* report emphasized the need for inclusion, Pacific Islanders and their educational needs continue to be erased and excluded when they are placed within an aggregated category. As Indigenous communities, including Pacific Islanders, continue to occupy a marginal space in the academy, Linda Smith (2012) reminds us of the importance of representation. She states, "Representation is an important concept because it gives the impression of truth" (p. 37). Therefore, the continued aggregation of Pacific Islanders not only gives a false representation but also does not allow Pacific Islanders to see themselves in higher education, which could lead to greater relevancy. This erasure continues to affect Pacific Islander students, faculty, and administrators and the possibility of a greater pipeline.

History of the Asian Pacific Islander Category

The US federal government established the racial category of Asian or Pacific Islander or Asian American and Pacific Islander (API or AAPI) in 1977 (Office of Management and Budget [OMB], 1995). After more than a decade of advocacy, the Office of Management and Budget passed Directive 15 in 1997, which required federal agencies to disaggregate NHPI from Asian Americans as two separate racial categories in all federal data collection (McGregor & Moy, 2003; OMB, 1997). Although Directive 15 was passed, the aggregation of Asian Americans and Pacific Islanders continues in data collection efforts. Combining two diverse pan-ethnic groups representing over 48 diverse ethnicities, the API/AAPI category often invisibilizes the NHPI community with serious policy implications (Kana'iaupuni, 2011). For example, according to the *Community of Contrasts Report*, about 18% of Native Hawaiians and Other Pacific Islanders (NHPI) hold a bachelor's degree, compared with an aggregate figure of 45% of Asian American and Pacific Islanders (EPIC & AAAJ, 2014). Asian Americans, by and large, are racialized and stereotyped as the model minority because of their professed educational success. However, OiYan A. Poon and associates assert that there is both a need to disaggregate among the Asian American category itself and a need to discuss Asian Americans in ways that encapsulate their unique racialized experiences in education (Poon et al., 2016). Although the Asian American racial category is problematic itself, as it also aggregates a large number of ethnic groups with diverse histories, the aggregation of the AAPI is even more problematic, as it further aggregates Asian American and Native Hawaiian Pacific Islander (The Campaign for College Opportunity, 2015). Because Asian Americans and Pacific Islanders have widely divergent statistical portraits in education and most data collection categories, the continued practice of aggregating Asian Americans and Pacific Islanders has critical policy and programming implications for Pacific Islanders. This practice of aggregation reproduces the exclusion of Pacific Islanders as a specific community with distinct needs through false data reporting (Kana'iaupuni, 2011; Kauanui, 2008). This custom affects a greater pipeline of Pacific Islander students, faculty, and administrators in higher education.

Pacific Islanders as Indigenous People / What Does Indigeneity Have to Do with It?

In order to implement an education system that is culturally relevant for Indigenous communities, Indigenous educators and students need to be identified, including those that are Pacific Islander. Without their identification, mainstream education continues to exclude their identities and forestall the creation of possible curriculums that could assist with the pathways to higher education moving forward. To address various issues affecting Indigenous communities, including the colonial education system, Native Hawaiian scholar Noelani Goodyear-Ka'ōpua (2013) reminds us of the importance of Indigenous scholars and says, "Indigenous scholars have shown that the power to define what counts as knowledge and to determine what our people should be able to know and do is a fundamental aspect of peoplehood, freedom, collective well-being, and autonomy" (p. 6). Therefore, being able to identify Indigenous scholars, including those who are Pacific Islander, is necessary to assist with creating education as a place where Indigenous communities can positively transform in order to flourish. Instead of imposing a racial category on Pacific Islanders that largely erases their identities as Indigenous people for the sake of inclusion, advocacy around data collection that is disaggregated and accurate needs to be a priority. Instead, higher education needs to document an Indigenous presence that could lead to a greater number of Indigenous students, faculty, and administrators in higher education, including Pacific Islanders.

Pacific Islanders are and continue to be Indigenous people. Aggregating Asian Americans and Pacific Islanders also erases Pacific Islanders as Indigenous people and solely applies an ethnic minoritized status. J. Kēhaulani Kauanui (2008) notes that the grouping of Pacific Islanders with Asian Americans erodes political claims based on Indigeneity (p. 2). Reducing Pacific Islanders as ethnic minorities elides claims to self-determination and sovereignty. For example, she states, "Pacific Islanders who have ties to islands that were forcibly incorporated into the United States (Hawai'i, Guam, American Samoa) have outstanding sovereignty and land claims, based on international principles of self-determination, which get erased by the categorization with Asians. Hence the frameworks for understanding the ills affecting Pacific peoples and their political claims are shaped by imperialism and settler colonialism, not simply civil rights" (p. 2). Continuously categorizing Pacific Islanders simply within a minoritized status effectively erases claims to self-determination and sovereignty and the associated rights to a culturally relevant education. A culturally relevant education could lead to a greater higher education pipeline for Pacific Islanders. Thus, identifying Pacific Islanders accurately is not simply about identity politics; it is also about recognizing Indigenous self-determination and Native sovereignty. This identification could be a first step in recognizing what is necessary for a culturally relevant education for Pacific Islanders and would increase the pipeline of students, faculty, and staff.

As Indigenous people, Pacific Islanders have inherent rights to a culturally relevant education. Whereas the United States is and continues to be a settler-colonial nation, the settler education system is built to maintain the settler nation-state. Within the settler education system, Western epistemologies and values define and shape what is considered knowledge and, more importantly, what is considered valuable knowledge (Smith, 2012). This erroneous belief means that other knowledge systems, including Indigenous ones, are not taught or valued within the mainstream public education system. In particular, the histories of Indigenous communities are largely taught from the perspective of the colonizer (Calderon, 2014; Goodyear-Kāʻopua, 2013). In education, colonialism is depicted as an ahistorical event where Native communities are mostly extinct. In addition, public education has mainly been an assimilatory project that teaches the social and cultural norms of the settler nation. For all of these reasons, the educational system is considered hostile for many Indigenous communities.

Many scholars have noted the adverse impacts that this type of education has had on Native/Indigenous communities, including Pacific Islanders (Kāʻopua, 2013). One indication of the impact is the lack of Pacific Islanders attending and completing higher education, which leads to fewer Pacific Islander peers, faculty, and college professional staff in higher education institutions. Overall, Indigenous students continue to occupy a marginal space within the academy, where their cultures and histories are absent from the higher education curriculum. Documenting Indigenous people, including Pacific Islanders, as living people works against the logics of Native erasure and the naturalized tendencies within education that solely portray Indigenous people as no longer existing, as not relevant, or as casualties for the greater good. Sometimes, the racial crisis in America means that society will overlook the needs of racially marginalized communities for capitalistic gains. Having a greater presence of Pacific Islanders could transform the curriculum and increase the relevancy of higher education for Pacific Islanders and other Indigenous groups, leading to a greater pipeline.

The Need for Race in *Left Out*

Education data that disaggregate by race and ethnicity are needed to understand the gaps within education. As the creators of the *Left Out* report recognized, having both diversity and inclusion at public higher education institutions is important because they will lead to a more culturally competent workforce that is fundamental to the health and growth of California's economy (Campaign for College Opportunity, 2018, p. 5). However, although *Left Out* identifies important data on underrepresented populations, the report simultaneously excludes Native/Indigenous populations, including Pacific Islanders, through practices of data aggregation. In particular, in the report,

Pacific Islanders fall under the label of Asian Americans, Native Hawaiians, and Pacific Islanders (AANHPI). Although AANHPI is a different label from the more recognized AAPI or API, it continues to categorize Pacific Islanders with Asian Americans, systematically erasing them as a discrete population with distinct experiences regarding retention, leadership, and racialization within higher education.

While data aggregation between Asian Americans and Pacific Islanders is not new, the mission and goals of the report were to identify populations that continue to be left out of California's public higher education systems. Systematically, Pacific Islanders are left out because there is no way to identify them. Therefore, data on Pacific Islander student enrollment, faculty, and leadership are unknown because the community has been erased by data aggregation with Asian Americans. This erasure signals to the community that their unique experiences and lived realities as Pacific Islanders are not important enough for a separate category through data disaggregation. Reported small sample sizes of Pacific Islanders are used for the basis to aggregate. However, calls for data disaggregation and techniques, including oversampling, targeted surveys, and working with community organizations, have been recommended by Indigenous scholars, including Pacific Islanders, as a necessity to provide more accurate data of the community (Kana'iaupuni, 2011). Without identifying the number of Pacific Islanders within California's public higher educational system, programs that address pipeline issues among underrepresented students will not identify Pacific Islanders within their recruitment and retention efforts. Additionally, this prohibits the growth of Pacific Islander studies and Indigenous studies that would benefit Pacific Islander and other Indigenous students. Leilani Sabzalian (2019) argues that Indigenous studies would benefit all students. Identifying Pacific Islanders as ethnic minorities also erases their ties with other Indigenous groups, leading to collaborative work that could retain Pacific Islander students, faculty, and staff in higher education.

The report emphasizes the importance of diverse leadership and how it contributes to students' sense of belonging on campus. Yet the report's practice of data aggregation implicitly negates the importance of having Pacific Islanders within California's higher education leadership. Examining the leadership of the UC, CSU, and CCC systems, the report states, "Above all, leaders set the tone and tenor of the institution, from the values they uphold to the culture they promote. All of this communicates to students and aspiring leaders that vital sense of belonging or devastating sense of exclusion" (Campaign for College Opportunity, 2018, p. 5). It continues, "Contributing to their sense of belonging are faculty and senior leaders who look like them, whose experiences are like theirs, and who help them flourish" (p. 5). Having the mechanisms to identify diverse leadership or the lack thereof is vital to creating cultures of inclusion within higher education, especially among traditionally underrepresented populations. However, the report fails to identify Pacific Islanders as a specific population and fails to recognize the need for more Pacific Islanders among students, faculty, and administration. How inclusive are campus cultures and a system of higher education that fail to do that? By their argument, Pacific Islander students, faculty, and aspiring leaders continue to feel a sense of exclusion that would lead them to feel "left out."

While the report discusses the importance of evaluating race and being critical of race with the hope of creating more educational equity by maintaining the AANHPI category, the architects of the report assume that these racial categories are fixed rather than understanding race as a social construct. The report states, "A focus on racial equity requires us to examine race with a critical eye, looking at historical patterns of bias and exclusion that have prevented AANHPI, African Americans, AI/AN, and Latinx students and professionals from achieving access and equitable outcomes in higher education. To ignore race—or use race-neutral language—is to ignore the inequities in academic achievement, education opportunity, workforce participation, and social integration that continue to plague our communities of color" (Campaign for College Opportunity, 2018, p. 27). Since educational experiences vary and can be affected by race and how people are racialized, it is important to look at race critically, even among data collection. Aggregating for the sake of "inclusion" can also be harmful because it excludes through erasure, creating inequality itself. Being critical of race is important, and data collection and disaggregation also need to be considered practices that can and do perpetuate exclusion among populations that continue not to be counted. This inclusion continues to affect a greater pipeline of Pacific Islanders in higher education. It is an argument not only about misrepresentation but also about the ways that Indigenous people, including Pacific Islanders, are racialized and grouped. These categories are usually imposed upon them and are outside of their determination or creation. Thus, this is also about the ability to self-identify, which is a part of self-determination. Pacific Islanders, like others, want their experiences to be validated, which would lead to greater chances of being retained and succeeding in higher education.

The Startling Statistics

Left Out brings attention to populations within California's higher education system that continue to be excluded. However, the aggregation of Pacific Islanders within the API rubric continues the completely inaccurate reporting of data. For example, the report states that "AANHPI have the third largest enrollment at California's public higher education (16%), with nearly 470,000 students. They are almost 40% of enrollments at the UC, 18% at the CSU and 14% at the community colleges" (Campaign for College Opportunity, 2018, p. 15). Contradicting these statistics, *The State of Higher Education in California: Asian American Native Hawaiian Pacific Islander Report*, published in 2015 by the Campaign for College Opportunity, reports that only 5% of NHPI undergraduates enrolled at the UC (p. 12). With a difference of 35%, the aggregation of Asian Americans and Pacific Islanders persists even among efforts purported to highlight diversity and inclusion. Additionally, *The State of Higher Education* highlights the differences between Asian American and NHPI first-time freshmen enrollment at the UC. The report notes that Asian Americans make up 40%, while NHPIs represent .03% of the entering cohort at the UC (p. 14). *The State of Higher Education* also notes that educational attainment rates vary by 60% among AAPIs (p. 11). With such extreme differences between aggregated and disaggregated data, it should be considered unethical to continue aggregating these two groups in data collection and reporting. Furthermore, this erasure affects the population of Pacific Islander students who continue to navigate higher education who are misrepresented and miscategorized.

To add insult to injury, *Left Out* describes the importance of faculty representation and provides statistics of AANHPI faculty compared to AANHPI student enrollment at California public higher education institutions. It states, "The percentage of tenured and non-tenured AANHPI faculty provide interesting insight into the question of representation. The good news is that, at the CSU campuses, tenured AANHPI faculty are reflective of the AANHPI body. At the community colleges, both tenured and non-tenured faculty are just under representational equity for AANHPIs. The bad news is that at the UC, where 39% of the student body are AANHPI, fewer than one-fifth of the tenured faculty members and one-fourth of the non-tenured faculty members are AANHPI" (Campaign for College Opportunity, 2018, p. 17). While the report highlights that faculty representation among certain higher education systems in California is reflective of AANHPI student enrollment, it is more accurate to say that the percentage of faculty is a representation of the Asian American community. Just as the data vary significantly among Asian American and Pacific Islander student enrollments, the aggregated data regarding AANHPI faculty would also perpetuate a highly inaccurate figure among Pacific Islander faculty. It is disingenuous to say that Pacific Islander faculty reflect a campus's student body, which is reported in *Left Out*. The reported reason for aggregating Pacific Islanders with Asian Americans is due to small sample sizes (Campaign for College Opportunity, 2018, p. 51). Therefore, it is not possible for Pacific Islander faculty to be reflective of the student body. Additionally, the report highlights the fact that at the UC, AANHPI represents only 11% of those serving on the academic senate, and 8% of senior leadership positions (p. 17). Although *Left Out* emphasizes a leadership issue that is shared among Asian Americans and Pacific Islanders, the data are disingenuous because the reports do not disaggregate. The number of Pacific Islander faculty and leadership positions at California public higher educational institutions is unknown, and the lack of inquiry represents an absence of care for the community. This lack of care undergirds a system of higher education that projects its nonrelevance to Indigenous communities, including Pacific Islanders.

Disaggregated Data

When data are disaggregated, we have a more accurate depiction of the NHPI community. This helps in understanding possible interventions and policies that can be implemented to assist with growing the pathways to higher education for NHPIs. It also matters for representation. For example, *The State of Higher Education* highlights the varying differences between college attainment for NHPIs and other groups: "NHPI adults (15 percent) are not only less likely than Asian Americans (49 percent) to have a college degree, but also they are much less likely than Whites (40 percent), the average California adult (31 percent), and Blacks (23 percent) to hold a college degree" (Campaign for College Opportunity, 2015, p. 11). Additionally, *The State of Higher Education* observes that NHPI undergraduates attend for-profit colleges at a rate of 20%, which is twice the rate of the state average (p. 12). In particular, NHPI students are just as likely to transfer to a four-year for-profit college as they are to a CSU—the highest proportion relative to other racial/ethnic groups (p. 15). Without disaggregating data, we would not have these unique findings among Pacific Islanders. Instead, the data in *Left Out* reflects an entirely different picture of students, faculty, and NHPI leadership.

The State of Higher Education makes some noteworthy points regarding disaggregating data among Asian Americans and Pacific Islanders, as well as the need for disaggregation, particularly in California. The report notes that while California's three segments of higher education collect disaggregated data on Asian Americans and NHPIs, they do not publicly report ethnic-specific data (Campaign for College Opportunity, 2015, p. 5). This flaw in reporting means that educators and policy makers need to advocate for such data in order to publish accurate portraits of communities. *The State of Higher Education* also recommends CSUs add NHPI and certain Asian American ethnic groups to their definition of underrepresented minority because their graduation rates are more similar to the African American than the Asian American community (p. 17). Whereas Asian Americans are included among those groups considered underrepresented in *Left Out* (which is not always the case due to the model minority myth), Pacific Islanders continue to be regarded as a subpopulation of Asian Americans. Therefore, when Asian Americans are not considered an underrepresented minority group, Pacific Islanders are automatically not considered underrepresented either, even though disaggregated data reveal that they are one of the most underrepresented and vulnerable populations. This misrepresentation affects the pipeline and curriculum potential of Pacific Islander students, faculty, and administrators.

Despite the Campaign for College Opportunity's acknowledgment of the importance of such data disaggregation practices in *The State of Higher Education* (2015), in which they disaggregated data on Asian American and Pacific Islanders, their publication two years later of *Left Out* (2017), in which they reaggregated the data, demonstrates the pervasiveness of aggregating figures due to so-called statistical reliability. Both reports offer an array of statistics and insights into segments of the higher education population in California, including insight into the leadership of California's public educational institutions and whether the leadership is reflective of the student body. However, *Left Out* failed even to acknowledge the need for disaggregated data; instead, the report stated that it elected to combine the data due to small sample sizes. By doing so, the report itself also did not understand the difference between diversity and inclusion—one of its purported key points. By including Pacific Islanders in the AANHPI category, the report and its architects continued practices that falsify data, minoritized Pacific Islanders instead of recognizing their Indigenous status, and erased

Pacific Islanders from the much-needed discussions about student enrollment and leadership at California's public higher educational institutions. While *Left Out* asks for race to be regarded critically within discussions of diversity and inclusion, it failed to recognize the complexities of race and how those complexities affect educational outcomes among Pacific Islanders. Interrogating race critically would also require an understanding of how certain groups are racialized. By including Pacific Islanders in AANHPI, the architects of *Left Out* performed inclusion while Pacific Islanders are not seen as a population with unique needs and educational experiences. Pacific Islander students, faculty, and administrators continue to be *left out*.

Conclusion

The *Left Out* report, instead of detailing the need for better data collection practices that would include Pacific Islanders as a separate category, simply did not include Pacific Islanders. It would have been better to admit this data limitation than to deny the distinct differences within the AANHPI populations completely. This act of exclusion would have been genuine in addressing the needs of creating a separate category that would have been critical of race and eventually would have led to more inclusion. Reports such as *Left Out* can discuss why there is a distinct need for disaggregated data among certain groups, including Pacific Islanders, because of their unique status and needs as Indigenous people. Partnerships with Pacific Islander community organizations can also assist with data collection efforts. For example, in partnership with Asian Americans Advancing Justice, Empowering Pacific Islander Communities, a community organization in Southern California created the *Community of Contrasts Reports* in 2014. The *Community of Contrasts Reports* contained disaggregated data on Pacific Islanders in national and California state reports. Both reports included disaggregated educational data on Pacific Islanders. Additionally, Hafoka et al. (in press) have offered an alternative to aggregating Pacific Islanders with Asian Americans when disaggregating Pacific Islanders in data is not possible. They suggest that a possible solution is to aggregate data among Pacific Islanders and Native Americans. Although the priority will always be to disaggregate, they suggest this as an alternative because both groups are Indigenous and possess similar higher educational statistics.

Programs and higher educational initiatives need to be created to support Pacific Islander faculty in order for them to be mentored into leadership roles. Pacific Islander faculty and leadership in higher education are necessary to understand the needs of the community. Programs also need to be created for students to increase the pathways to professoriate and leadership roles in higher education. More education about Pacific Islanders and other Indigenous groups could lead to a more inclusive higher education system in which a culturally relevant education can be supported and amplified. Disaggregated data and reporting Pacific Islanders separately is necessary to build pathways in which Pacific Islanders are seen and recognized as a distinct community that ultimately matters within higher education.

References

Asian Americans Advancing Justice. (2016). *Asian Americans and NHPI are the two fastest-growing racial groups, according to new census population estimates.* Authors. Retrieved from http://www.advancingjustice-la.org/sites/default/files/20160628%20Census%20Report%20PR.pdf

Calderon, D. (2014). Speaking back to manifest destinies: A land education-based approach to critical curriculum inquiry. *Environmental Education Research, 20*(1), 1–13.

The Campaign for College Opportunity. (2015). *The state of higher education in California: Asian American Native Hawaiian Pacific Islander report.* University of California, Los Angeles. Author. Retrieved from http://care.gseis.ucla.edu/wp-content/uploads/2015/08/2011_CARE_Report.pdf

The Campaign for College Opportunity. (2018). *Left out: How exclusion in California's colleges and universities hurts our values, our students, and our economy.* Author. Retrieved from https://collegecampaign.org/wp-content/uploads/2018/03/2018-Left-Out-Executive-Summary-Final.pdf

Empowering Pacific Islander Communities and Asian Americans Advancing Justice. (2014). *A community in contrast: Native Hawaiians and Pacific Islanders in the United States.* Authors. Retrieved from http://empoweredpi.org/wp-content/uploads/2014/06/A_Community_of_Contrasts_NHPI_US_2014-1.pdf

Goodyear-Ka'ōpua, N. (2013). *The seeds we planted: Portraits of a Native Hawaiian charter school.* University of Minnesota Press.

Hafoka, 'I., Vaughn, K., Aina, I., & Aleantar, C. M. (in press). The "invisible" minority: Finding a sense of belonging after imperialism, colonialism, and (im)migration for Native Hawaiian and Pacific Islanders in the United States. In R. T. Teranishi, B. M. D. Nguyen, C. M. Alcanter, & F. R. Curamineng (Eds.), *The racial heterogeneity project: Unmasking educational inequality in aggregation.* Teachers College Press.

Hixon, L., Hepler, B. B., & Kim, M. O. (2012). *The native Hawaiian and other Pacific Islander population: 2010.* US Census. Retrieved from http://www.census.gov/prod/cen2010/briefs/c2010br-12.pdf

Kanaʻiaupuni, S. M. (2011). Lot of aloha, little data: Data and research on Native Hawaiian and Pacific Islanders. *AAPI Nexus, 9*(1–2), 207–211.

Kauanui, J. K. (2008, September 8). Where are all the Native Hawaiians and Pacific Islanders in higher education? *Diverse Issues in Higher Education: The Academy Speaks.* Retrieved from https://diverseeducation.wordpress.com/author/kauanui/

McGregor, D., & Moy, E. (2003). Native Hawaiians and Pacific Islander Americans. *Asian-Nation: Asian American History, Demographics, & Issues.* Retrieved from http://www.asian-nation.org/hawaiian-pacific.shtml

Office of Management and Budget. (1995, August 28). *Standards for the classification of federal data on race and ethnicity.* White House Office of Management and Budget. Retrieved from https://www.whitehouse.gov/omb/fedreg_race-ethnicity

Office of Management and Budget (1997, October 30). *Revisions to the standards for the classification of federal data on race and ethnicity.* White House Office of Management and Budget. Retrieved from https://www.whitehouse.gov/omb/fedreg_1997standards

Poon, O., Squire, D., Kodama, C., Byrd, A., Chan, J., Manzano, L., Furr, S., & Bishundat, D. (2016). A critical review of the model minority myth in selected literature on Asian Americans and Pacific Islanders in higher education. *Review of Educational Research, 86*(2), 469–502.

Sabzalian, L. (2019). The tensions between Indigenous sovereignty and multicultural citizenship education: Toward an anticolonial approach to civic education. *Theory & Research in Social Education, 47*(3), 311–346.

Smith, L. T. (2012). *Decolonizing methodologies: Research and Indigenous Peoples.* Zed.

Chapter 3

Black Male Genocide

Systemic Racism and Implications for Black Male Presence and Success in Higher Education

SHIVER, MARIA ASHKIN, JIMMY KENDALL,
AND EVELYN EZIKWELU

Not since the landmark report *We Charge Genocide* was presented at the United Nations in Paris in 1951 has critical academic scholarship sought to examine linkages between social equity issues in higher education and the implications of the genocide occurring within Black communities across the United States.

Many critical scholars and individuals are vested in ameliorating adverse economic, social, and developmental outcomes for Black folk and continue to advance scholarship examining varying tenets of systemic racism, deficit frameworks, social equity issues, and institutionalized discrimination. However, few of these scholars have acknowledged the degrees to which their examinations dually make a case for charging genocide and how these examinations' reframing can advance scholarship specific to social equity, systemic racism, and Black males in higher education.

Due to the way in which Black males are situated at the nexus of gendered racism, as will be explained more shortly, the phenomenon of Black genocide affects Black males in a particular way, which has not been fully explored in academic literature. This focus is not to say that other groups are not also facing genocide (in fact, Native and Indigenous peoples are undeniably still facing genocide, and Black women, especially Black trans women, are certainly also targets for Black genocide, although the data and the literature for these groups differ from those for Black males; see chapter 6 in this volume). Nor is it to say that these groups do not warrant further attention (they do). In fact, the need for a close look at each subject position prompts our narrow focus here. As Black males are subject to heightened degrees of racial discrimination, psychological trauma, adverse mental and physical health outcomes, and labor market marginalization when compared to almost every other demographic, it is paramount to examine how Black males specifically are targeted for genocide or how Black male genocide is occurring in the United States, and what this means for Black male success within and outside of higher education.

As will be observed through data across Black males' lifespans, both nationally and locally within the specific cities for this case study (Oakland, California; Durham, North Carolina; Atlanta, Georgia), Black males are targeted through varying machinations of social institutions and systemic racism. These machinations operate through specific forms of genocide, which we detail below, illustrating the intentionality of social institutions to debilitate Black males from birth to death, resulting in both the occurrence of Black male genocide and the implicit exclusion of Black males from higher education. We consider data at both the national, or macro, level and the state and city, or micro, level to expose how this genocide, defined as "acts committed with intent to destroy, in whole or in part, a national, ethnical, racial or religious group" (United Nations, n.d.), permeates the nation's structure and is not an artifact of conglomerated data, nor is it accidental. We contend that Black male genocide is occurring at every level and in every city, affecting Black male involvement and attainment in higher education at each of these levels as well. The disparity between Black male and Black female involvement and achievement in higher education foregrounds our specific attentiveness to this phenomenon, as recent data found that undergraduate enrollment for Black men at community colleges fell 19.2% compared to 9% for Black women, alongside data that found that 36.1% of Black women have a college degree versus 26.5 % of Black men (Anthony, Nichols, & Pilar, 2021). In short, compounding factors of systemic racism and white supremacy adversely affect acceleration into higher education and degree obtainment for Black males more than for most other groups.

Our examination of Black male genocide and implications for Black males in higher education uses three theoretical frameworks: social dominance theory (SDT), racial battle fatigue (RBF), and the United Nations' Office of the Special Advisor on the Prevention of Genocide (OSAPG) analysis framework. Alongside these theoretical frameworks, specific attention will be paid to the subordinate male target hypothesis (SMTH), as the evidence supporting this hypothesis necessitates our particular focus on Black males.

Social dominance theory is a complex theoretical framework that addresses group-based hierarchies, wherein individuals are situated in a hierarchical social model based on their membership in certain social groups. The theory posits that these groups are stratified according to three identity features: age, gender, and "arbitrary set," including race and ethnicity (Sidanius & Pratto, 1999). Due to the interaction between gender and arbitrary-set features, in which males are more engaged in intergroup aggression than females, the Subordinate Male Target Hypothesis claims that subordinate males take the brunt of arbitrary-set discrimination, and this discrimination takes a different form than the discrimination that subordinate females face (Sidanius & Pratto, 1999). Moreover, subordinate males are particularly targeted, as they are seen as the foundation of the arbitrary-set group by dominant males and are therefore particularly threatening to dominant males' status. The SMTH is an important feature of SDT to note throughout this case study, as Black males are included in SMTH and are the population that most often gets forced into the lowest social stratum.

Although this case study focuses specifically on Black males, we acknowledge more than two sexes and two polarized genders. As SDT addresses only male and female sex identification categories under the label of "gender," and the data tends to reflect this categorization, this case study also limits the discussion to the male and female groups. The authors also acknowledge that while the current literature is limited in its labeling, the data likely include folks of varying sex and gender identities under these limited, inaccurate labels. Future work should expand this look at "gendered" racism to include trans and nonbinary folks explicitly.

Racial battle fatigue provides a crucial accompanying theory to SDT, as the relegation of Black males to a subordinate class necessitates examining both the social and the psychological stressors associated with varying forms of systemic racism and social hierarchies, as well as how under the guidelines of the OSAPG analytical framework, such stressors are indicative of an ongoing legacy of Black male genocide in the United States (Sidanius &; Pratto, 1999; Smith, 2004). Racial battle fatigue is similar to the post-traumatic stress disorder experienced by military personnel but represents the racial stressors that people of color experience due to the buildup of pervasive and mundane racism throughout their lives (Smith, 2004, 2010). According to Smith (2004), RBF includes several psycho-physiological symptoms, including tension headaches and backaches, trembling and jumpiness, chronic pain in healed injuries, a pounding heartbeat, rapid breathing in anticipation of conflict, an upset stomach, frequent diarrhea or urination, extreme fatigue, constant anxiety and worrying, increased swearing and complaining, inability to sleep, sleep broken by haunting conflict-specific dreams, loss of confidence in oneself and one's colleagues/department/college/university/community, difficulty in thinking coherently or being able to speak articulately under stressful conditions, rapid mood swings, elevated blood pressure, and emotional/social withdrawal (p. 181).

People of color experience these effects even when not under direct racial attack (Smith, 2004). Moreover, stress-related diseases result from the overfunctioning of the originally adaptive strategy of staying prepared for acute situations by constantly staying in this hypervigilant state to deal with ongoing micro and macro aggressions (Smith, 2004).

An integral theoretical framework necessary for examining how our data make a case for Black male genocide is provided by the Office of the UN Special Advisor on the Prevention of Genocide. The OSAPG outlines eight categories of factors that build to the charge of genocide:

- Intergroup relations, including the record of discrimination and/or other human rights violations committed against a group.
- Circumstances that affect the capacity to prevent genocide.
- Presence of illegal arms and armed elements.
- Motivation of leading actors in the state/region; acts that serve to encourage divisions between national, racial, ethnic, and religious groups.
- Circumstances that facilitate the perpetration of genocide (dynamic factors).
- Genocidal acts.
- Evidence of intent "to destroy in whole or in part."
- Triggering factors (n.d.).

This framework clarifies the cumulative effect that is important in charging genocide—not whether there is evidence of all factors, necessarily, but whether the available evidence amounts to an *intentional eradication* of a specific population.

While many of these factors seem to be obvious accounts of ongoing structural racism, intentionality is notoriously tricky to prove. According to OSAPG, eight issues can be analyzed to show intent to "destroy in whole or in part," in which genocidal intent can develop over time and "can be inferred from a set of existing facts which would suggest that what is unfolding or ongoing may be genocide (OSAPG, n.d., p. 4)." This case study addresses four out of these eight issues, namely:

- In a nonconflict situation, widespread and/or systematic discriminatory and targeted practices culminating in gross violations of human rights of protected groups, such as extrajudicial killings, torture, and displacement;

- The specific means used to achieve "ethnic cleansing," which may underscore that the perpetration of the acts is designed to reach the foundations of the group or what is considered as such by the perpetrator group;

- Targeted elimination of community leaders and/or men and/or women of a particular age group (the "future generation" or a military-age group);

- Other practices designed to complete the exclusion of the targeted group from social/political life. (OSAPG, n.d., p. 3)

Additionally, it should be noted that another of these issues listed by OSAPG could also be addressed within a paper concerned with the racial crisis in higher education, namely "statements amounting to hate speech by those involved in a genocidal campaign" (OSAPG, n.d., p. 3). While much scholarship discusses the prevalence of hate speech against black males in higher education institutions, this case study does not address this issue.

As this case study will make clear, data pertaining to infant mortality, the school-to-prison pipeline (STPP), income disparity, economic and institutional exclusion (including the exclusion from higher education), and overall health outcomes and life expectancy, alongside a discussion of how these data evidence intent to destroy according to OSAPG, the case for

Black male genocide is both empirically and theoretically justified, and the phenomenon of Black male genocide proves an instrumental and necessary theoretical addition to the ongoing project of advancing Black male success inside and outside higher education.

Infancy

Black males' disparate life chances start in utero. This section will show how Black male physiological development is affected by the conditions in which the pregnant parent lives, and will provide evidence for how these early life health disparities influence Black male presence in higher education and facilitate genocide against Black males. There is ample evidence that Black females face greater health risks, overall and in both pregnancy and birth, specifically, than females in other groups. Although these data do not reflect the infant mortality rates of Black males specifically, they do indicate that Black males are facing greater risk and lower life chances than are males in other groups in utero, at birth, and in infancy. These data provide support for the major claims of SDT, showing that Black males start facing structural disparities immediately, even before birth, and set the tone for SMTH, showing one way that Black males' position in the social strata is ensured—through a reduction in population numbers and the resulting reduction in numbers of Black males in higher education. Moreover, these data begin to show how these structural disparities are dually evidence of the "intent to destroy in whole or in part" required by the OSAPG definition of genocide by targeting Black males as the foundation of the overall Black population and by systematically eradicating them at every turn.

Infant Mortality

Black females are 22 times more likely than White females to have poor cardiovascular health, which immediately puts Black infants at greater risk for low birth weight and higher infant mortality (Kalinowski, Taylor & Spruill, 2019). The leading causes of infant mortality include low birth weight, congenital malformations, maternal complications, and sudden infant death syndrome (US Department of Health and Human Services, 2017). Blacks have higher rates than Whites of each of these causes, with the highest rate being low birth weight, at 3.2 times greater than Whites (US Department of Health and Human Services, 2017). Prematurity is also a leading cause of infant mortality in Oakland and Georgia (Broda, 2019; Chapple-McGruder et al., 2012). Pregnant Black people also are 2.2 to 2.3 times more likely to receive late or no prenatal care (US Department of Health and Human Services, 2017), which compounds the chances of negative health outcomes for Black infants.

According to the US Department of Health and Human Services (2017), in 2014, the national infant mortality rate for Whites was 4.9 per 1,000 births. For Blacks, however, the rate of infant mortality was 10.9 per 1,000 births, or 2.2 times the rate of infant mortality for Whites. The rates of infant mortality for Blacks in both Georgia and North Carolina are even higher than the national average, at 12.2 and 12.9 per 1,000 births, respectively, compared to 5.4 per 1,000 births for Whites in both states (Georgia Department of Public Health, 2017; Kaiser Family Foundation, n.d.). In Durham in 2014, 12.5% of Black infants were born at a low birth weight, compared to 5.9% of White infants, and in 2018 over 50% of infant deaths in North Carolina were Black infant deaths (Bowden, n.d.). While this disparity is lower for California at the state level (3.8 for Whites and 8.2 for Blacks; Kaiser Family Foundation, n.d.), it is much higher in Oakland County, at 13.5 per 1,000 for Blacks compared to 3.8 per 1,000 for Whites (Broda, 2019). These disparities in infant mortality across groups naturally result in disparities in living Black children, and later in Black adults, influencing the number of Black males in higher education. In other words, the population size of Blacks overall, including Black males, is reduced immediately due to health disparities faced in utero and at birth, eliminating much of the future generation of Black males in total; by design, there are simply fewer surviving Black males to go to college than there are males in other groups. Subsequent sections will explicate factors that influence the disparities in higher education attendance and achievement within the Black population that result in an ingroup disparity between males and females, as well, such that Black males have the lowest level of engagement with higher education overall.

RACIAL BATTLE FATIGUE

These data also begin to show the impact of RBF on the Black population overall and on Black males specifically. Black females facing RBF have poorer health overall than females in other groups due to their increased stress levels, which lead to a variety of poorer health outcomes. These poorer health conditions for pregnant Black females affect the health and survival rates of Black infants, including Black male infants, reducing their life chances immediately and unequivocally. Through both an immediate reduction in population numbers and longer-term health outcomes, these reduced life chances contribute to Black males' low representation in higher education and to their genocide. Racial battle fatigue affects Black males both directly, through their own stress experience throughout their lives, and indirectly, in utero, through the levels of stress that pregnant Black females experience. Racial battle fatigue, then, for Black males, begins before birth.

The effects of SDT, SMTH, and RBF do not end at birth, however. Those Black males who survive infancy face ongoing obstacles and threats as they grow up and move through or are pushed out of the education system (and as they move from the education system to engage with the incarceration or employment systems). Regardless of the specific path that Black males take, their life expectancy and life chances are lower than is the case for most other groups.

The School-to-Prison Pipeline

Black males are systematically deprived of educational opportunities readily available to their White peers. Even when Black males obtain the same educational achievements as their White peers, it does not provide them the same power as it does Whites. This section observes how systemic racism intentionally extracts and blockades Black males from educational environments, both nationally and at the state or city level in Atlanta, Durham, and Oakland, ultimately leading to their exclusion from higher education. These data provide evidence for how the school-to-prison pipeline contributes to Black male genocide by excluding Black males from social and political life by removing them from everyday life via death or incarceration such that they cannot become community leaders. Thus, we can simultaneously analyze the intentionality of genocide as addressed by the OSAPG.

Zero Tolerance and Suspensions

In 2015, Black male representation in national K–12 public school enrollment reflected their numbers in the overall population, at 13% (Snyder, de Brey & Dillow, 2019). As Marcia Caton (2012) notes, however, zero-tolerance policies result in an overrepresentation of Black males being suspended and expelled, and the parity for Black male representation in education does not last long. Due to zero-tolerance policies and other discriminatory disciplinary practices, Black males face obstacles and blockades in their educational experience as soon as they arrive at school. For example, while Black preschoolers comprise only 18% of preschool enrollment, they comprise 48% of suspended students. In contrast, White preschoolers comprise 43% of enrollment, but only 23% of suspensions, with males representing a much higher suspension rate than females (US Department of Education Office for Civil Rights, 2014). Overall, Black males are suspended four times more than White students nationally, while in some areas near Durham, the rate of Black male suspension is as high as 14 times that of White students (Johnson, 2018). In California, 12.8% of Black males are suspended; this rate is 3.6 times greater than the overall statewide suspension rate, which is only 3.6% (Wood, Harris, & Howard, 2018). Black males overall have a 70% chance of being suspended between preschool and 12th grade (US Department of Education Office for Civil Rights, 2014).

One of the implications of the disparity in suspension rates across racial groups is that Black males miss more class time than students in other groups. From 2015 to 2016, Black students missed five times as many school days at the national level as White students due to suspensions (Washburn, 2018). According to Discriminology Beta (n.d.), in Georgia, Black males are three times as likely to get out-of-school suspension (OSS) than White males, and 18% of Black males receive OSS. In Georgia, Black male K–12 students lose 180 hours of instruction to OSS, compared to 51 hours for White students (Discriminology Beta, n.d.). The amount of instruction missed due to suspension contributes to the push-out rate. Push-out happens when students experience such high rates of adversity and disconnection in schooling environments that they feel discouraged from continuing their education and are forced out of educational settings. Push-out affects Black students at high rates, as they are targeted as troublemakers, and spend so much time out of the classroom due to suspensions that they fall too far behind to catch up (Stearns & Glennie, 2006). Feeling behind in classes, continued educational disruption, dislike of teachers and school in general, and feeling intellectually inferior contribute to an early exit from school systems (Stearns & Glennie, 2006). With Black males primarily targeted for suspensions, they are at the greatest risk for push-out, reducing the numbers of Black males in K–12 schools and later in higher education.

Push-out through suspensions comes atop lacking resources in K–12 that are vital to college success. For example, only 57% of Black students had access to math and science courses pivotal to "college readiness," compared to 71% for White students and 81% for Asian students nationally (United Negro College Fund, 2019). This disparate access to the courses, knowledge, and skills necessary to succeed in college also directly contributes to low numbers of Black males in higher education. Even when they successfully navigate a system designed to push them out through suspensions, Black males stay in school. Black males are not provided the same education as their White peers, resulting in disparate college readiness.

Arrests

Suspension is not the only form of punishment in which Black males are overrepresented. According to the ACLU, 36 out of 10,000 Black male students are referred for arrest, compared to 24 out of 10,000 Black female students (Whitaker et al., n.d.). In Georgia, 80 per 10,000 students are referred for arrest overall (Whitaker et al., n.d.), meaning that Black male students make up roughly half of those referred for arrest despite being a significantly smaller percentage of the student population. These arrest referrals affect Black males' criminal record, their opportunities for both education and civic engagement, and their motivation to engage with an education system that sends them to prison while they are at school. The disproportionate representation of Black males in various disciplinary settings predisposes Black male youth for RBF (Committee on Racial Equity, 2019), as they see themselves being targeted for disciplinary action, disciplined at higher rates and to greater extents than other students, and facing serious repercussions for this disparate treatment, including push-out, incarceration, and pull-out (defined below), all of which limit their access to higher education. Police also patrol low-income Black neighborhoods and school districts more than they do White suburban neighborhoods, further increasing the rate of Black male youth arrests (Lacoe, 2015; Lipsitz, 2011).

Incarceration

According to the Sentencing Project (2021), "Black males have a 32% chance of serving time in prison at some point in their lives; Hispanic males have a 17% chance; White males have a 6 percent chance." With Black males making up roughly half of the referrals for arrest for K–12 students, as seen above, this disparity in incarceration rates across groups should not be surprising; Black male incarceration is a direct implication of the system of referrals for arrest while in school. Additionally, "For all young males, high school dropouts were 47 times more likely to be incarcerated than their similar aged peers who held a four-year college degree" (US Department of Education Office for Civil Rights, 2014, p. 11). Moreover, 68% of incarcerated males "did not graduate from high school, with 35% of prisoners reporting behavior, academic problems, and academic disengagement as the main reasons for not obtaining their high school diploma" (Darensbourg, Perez, & Blake, 2010, p. 197). That Black males are more likely to be pushed out or arrested than are most other groups, including Black females, is an indicator that Black males are being funneled from the education system into the incarceration system, contributing to the overall disparity in life chances between Black males and other groups, and disenfranchising Black males in everyday life (Maciag, 2021). The mass incarceration of Black males serves as one form of ethnic cleansing, contributing to their overall genocide and low representation in higher education simultaneously. This well-known phenomenon, known as the school-to-prison pipeline is not the only way Black males are disproportionately affected by being barred from engaging with the education system.

Pull-Out

Poverty is the number one determinant of high school dropout, push-out, and pull-out (Sum et al., 2009). Pull-out occurs when other responsibilities lure students away from completing their education (i.e., earning a living, financial pressures, family, mother/fatherhood, illness; Doll, Eslami & Walters, 2013; Stearns & Glennie, 2006). Schools situated in high-poverty districts, historically redlined districts serving a predominantly Black student body, tend to have the highest dropout rates (Lipsitz, 2011; Rumberger, 2013). Students from these districts have few options available to them; given their financial constraints, and once they leave school, the possibility of economic mobility is largely cut off. High school dropouts are most likely to struggle financially and are therefore systemically forced to seek income in riskier occupational areas, resulting in increased contact with the criminal justice system (Burrus & Roberts, 2012). The impact of these economic constraints is compounding, as having a criminal record also limits employment opportunities due to the practice of requiring background checks even for low-paying jobs (Rich & Grey, 2005).

Additionally, Ashley Archibald (2019) found that employers in Oakland, California, were less likely to hire Black men for low-skill service industry jobs if more low-level and high-level violent crime than usual had been recently committed in the area. The suggestion here is that the pathological criminalization of Black males as individuals prone to violence can serve as a deterrent to economic and social advancement, further limiting the economic and life chances of those Black males pushed or pulled out of school. School closures also disproportionately displace and pull out urban Black students and set them back academically, as these closures make finding, enrolling, and commuting to a new school arduous, and often this effort seems pointless. Data indicate that more displaced Black students are sent to lower-income and lower-performing schools that will likely be closed than are White students (Stanford's Center for Research on Education Outcomes, 2017).

Violent Deaths and Murders

The higher concentrations of police and Black males on urban streets that result from the relationship between overpolicing and push-out and pull-out of Black males from the K–12 education system leads to the increased likelihood of arrests, police brutality, and the use of lethal force (Lopez, 2016). While police brutality and the ongoing murder of Black males by police have received heightened media attention and increased scholarships (too much to be covered in this paper) has been devoted to these issues since the founding of the Black Lives Matter movement in 2013 and the murder of George Floyd in the summer of 2020, these issues warrant some discussion here as well, as they are salient to the charge of the genocide of Black males and serve as particularly strong evidence of the intention behind this genocide.

Black males are often killed by police or other violence in their neighborhoods. These deaths start early, sometimes as early as elementary school. In fact, the leading cause of death for Black males between the ages 15 and 34 nationally is homicide (A Call for Gun Violence Prevention, 2018), and violent injury is a significant cause of disability among young Black males (Rich & Grey, 2005). Data about violence against Black males are further complicated by the recurrent nature of the violent injury and the lack of trust that young Black males have in the police (Rich & Grey, 2005), as they feel they cannot call police to protect them from violent injury due to racial profiling, police brutality, and extrajudicial killings by police. While Blacks make up only 13% of the overall population, they constitute 26% of victims killed by police and are 2.8 times more likely to be killed by police than Whites (Males, 2014). For example, between 2000 and 2016 in Oakland, 67 out of the 90 individuals shot and killed by police were Black and overwhelmingly male (Barreira & Swedback, 2019). Specifically, college-aged Black males between 20 and 24 are most likely to be killed by police (Males, 2014). About 25% of Blacks who were killed were unarmed, a full 8% higher than Whites. Gun violence kills more Black and Native or Indigenous males than is the case for any other groups (Firearms Deaths North Carolina, 2015).

Police homicides are examples of largely state-sanctioned extrajudicial killings and serve as clear evidence of one of the OSAPG's issues to be analyzed for intentionality, which looks for "a non-conflict situation, widespread and/or systematic discriminatory and targeted practices culminating in gross violations of human rights of protected groups, such as extrajudicial killings, torture and displacement" (OSAPG, n.d., p. 3). By August 2020, police had killed 164 Black people, most of whom were male (Cohen, 2020). The age ranges of Black males who are mainly targeted through homicide are important, to both the case for the intentionality of Black male genocide and this phenomenon for higher education. College-aged Black males are targeted for homicide in general and in homicides committed by police more than most other groups. This age group (whether broadly construed at 15–34 or more narrowly construed at 20–24) is precisely the one that would otherwise be attending higher education. This age group of Black males, already reduced through high infant mortality, is the Black community's future generation of community leaders, seen as the foundation of the community, according to SMTH, and therefore is targeted explicitly for homicide, and often extrajudicially murdered by police, thereby eliminating them from sociopolitical engagement and community leadership, and making their genocide directly connected to the racial crisis in higher education.

These data show that Black males' attempts to navigate the education system encounter continuous and often unavoidable roadblocks. Through disproportionate suspension and referrals for arrests starting in elementary school and the implications of those continued practices through high school; through push-out and pull-out due to low academic achievement, school closures, and financial need; and through limited economic options and police murder, Black males are being actively and continuously removed from the K–12 education system, which, as we address in the next section, also affects their access to and involvement in higher education and overall life chances. In fact, Black males are removed from K–12 education at such a rate that in North Carolina, only 60.9% of Black males graduate high school; in California, that rate is 61.6%; and in Georgia, it is only 55.3%

(Schott Foundation for Public Education, 2013). The same practices that reduce the number of Black male students also contribute to their experience of RBF and, worse, their rate of death. In line with the central tenets of SDT and in support of our claim of Black male genocide, the clearly discriminatory practice of denying access to or removing Black males from educational institutions reduces their access to power and relegates them to the lowest social strata; those Black males who are removed from educational environments, including higher education, face poverty and death at higher rates than almost any other group.

Higher Education

The rates of Black males graduating from high school and continuing into higher education are alarmingly low. Scholarship on the admission, retention, and persistence of Black males in higher education have long attributed low enrollments to systemic and institutional racism factors. In addition, literature has also extensively examined how racialized essentialisms and phobias of Black males exacerbate latent cultures of both implicit and explicit racial bias in higher education. While such contributions have provided invaluable insights into anti-Black misandry and ongoing legacies of white supremacy prevalent in higher education, we feel that the OSAPG framework adds valuable contributions to these literatures, specifically regarding the intentionality of systemic racism and exclusion of Black males from higher learning as an intention to destroy, and not an accidental consequence of a racist US social order.

The OSAPG framework's relevance to understanding Black male genocide and higher education can lead to more comprehensive understandings of how the STPP, incarceration, and violent death statistics for Black males are part of a pervasive pattern of systemic racism that coalesces to stifle Black male college enrollment overall. By the time Black males reach college age, many are already removed from the educational system and are moving into the incarceration system at high rates. According to the Prison Policy Initiative, the numbers of Black males in higher education and those in prison were roughly equal (Prison Policy Initiative, n.d. b). This parity is partly due to the high rates at which Black males are referred for arrest in school before they can even apply to or attend higher education institutions. Adultification of Black youth and the stigma of the Black male as "violent" have long operated as the hegemonic rationale for the forced removal of

Black males from educational spaces, wherein racialized pathologies of Black males as "deviant" have been observed to follow them from preschool to college (Ferguson, 2000). As we discuss in this section, the continuation of these discriminatory practices against Black males once they enter college further reduces the already low enrollment and achievement numbers, ultimately resulting in low college and postsecondary graduation rates and reduced earning and sociopolitical power overall. Again, these data dually evidence both the charge of genocide and specifically the intentionality behind observed factors of systemic racism and institutional racism, all of which operate to exclude Black males from sociopolitical life and community leadership strategically.

ENROLLMENT

Black males enter higher education at lower rates than most other groups. For example, the incoming first-year class at the University of North Carolina in 2013 had nearly 4,000 first-year students but included only 98 Black males; Black males comprised only 2.5% of the incoming class, compared to 26.7% for White males (Craven, 2013). These low numbers for Black male enrollment exist in nearly every institution and persist throughout overall college enrollment. For instance, Black males accounted for less than 3.4% of the total undergraduate enrollment numbers (3,414 out of 101,613) in the University of California (2019) school system enrollment in fall 2018. In Georgia, while Blacks make up 35% of the general population, they account for only 28% of the University System of Georgia's (USG) undergraduate enrollment (Lee, 2019), with numbers of Black male students and their percentage of the overall undergraduate student population staying consistent since at least fall 2014 (University System of Georgia, 2019e). While national data gathered from the National Center for Educational Statistics (NCES) has observed increased enrollment of Black males in higher education (33% in 2018 measured against 25% in 2000), retention and persistence of Black males in higher education remains markedly lower than their White counterparts (PRiME, 2021).

The low representation of Black males in college enrollment is even starker compared to other groups. For example, in fall 2018, 31,002 Black males were enrolled in the USG's institutions, compared to 55,246 Black females and 74,003 White males (University System of Georgia, 2019d, 2019e, 2019f). This comparative trend is long-established, with the ratio of Black females to Black males enrolled anywhere in the USG in 2001 at 2:1, with over 28,000 Black females enrolled, compared to over 14,000 Black males enrolled (Perry-Johnson et al., 2003). While the USG includes several predominantly White institutions (PWIs), this comparative trend is also seen in enrollment in historically Black colleges and universities (HBCUs). According to Ernie Suggs (2012), "Women outnumber men 3-to-2 at Black colleges, according to the Department of Education's National Center for Education Statistics. At the 100 accredited HBCUs, 61.5 percent of the students are women." These data show that Black males are not enrolling in higher education institutions at rates equal to their percentage of the population at the national or state level. In other words, very few Black males are accessing higher education, contributing to the overall racial crisis in higher education.

The OSAPG framework illustrates how disparities in access to higher education result from intentionally manufactured racial crises derived from and produced by systemic racism. While endemic issues of racialized pathologies undoubtedly contribute to overall Black male removal and attrition from secondary education (adultification, RBF, overt and implicit bias, racist policy formation, etc.) that bar access to higher education, the material implications of removal and eradication (mass murder, economic exploitation, mass incarceration) must be dually considered as factors contributing to the racial crisis in higher education overall. In short, disregarding the larger context and problematics of systemic racism as intentional acts of genocide should amplify the need to examine issues of access, retention, and persistence of Black males as indicative of issues primarily external to student performance and/or institutional policy altogether.

Black Male Attrition and Disparities in Degree Attainment in Higher Education

Those Black males who do go to college continue to face obstacles and have lower retention and graduation rates than students in other groups. Past data and publications observing disparities in attrition between Black males and other groups typified the Black male college graduate as "an endangered species" (Washington, 2013), noting specific disparities in degree attainment within California State universities being markedly lower for Black males in comparison to overall degree attainment rates (on average 10–25% lower, however at Chico State, Black male degree attainment was 18.2% compared to 61.8% for the general student population; Washington, 2013). Since Michael Washington's publication, degree attainment across all groups has accelerated, but disparities still exist in educational attainment for Black males compared to most other groups. The most recent national data examining degree attainment from 2017–2018 observed that 8.9% of bachelor's degrees were awarded to Black males compared to 11.4% for Black females (National Center for Education Statistics, n.d.). Conversely, degree attainment remains markedly higher for White males (65.2%) and higher for Hispanic males (13.2%; National Center for Education Statistics, n.d.). Data also found that Black females comprise higher overall college enrollment (41%) compared to Black males (33%), yet the percentage of Black males versus Black females with some college and no degree remains almost even (26.3% for Black females vs. 24.3% for Black males; Anthony, Nichols, & Pilar, 2021). In summary, Black males are accepted into higher education institutions at lower rates than other groups and conversely face higher attrition rates than other groups.

The prevalence of Black male attrition in higher education and compounding factors of systemic racism that all but guarantee unequal school experiences for Black males in US society must be considered here. As the OSAPG framework illustrates, ample evidence of disparate K–12 schooling experiences for Black males versus their White counterparts illustrates how state actors, namely educational professionals, encourage racial divisions. As observed by Lawrence Scott and Laurie Sharp (2019), Black males in K–12 and higher education were observed to have incurred higher rates of prejudice, stereotypes, unequal treatment, and degraded self-belief from teachers, professors, and guidance counselors. Numerous reports have long observed how Black boys in K–12 schooling are suspended and disciplined at rates far higher than other groups, with one study finding that Black boys in kindergarten through third grade in California State school systems comprised 6.2% of suspensions compared to 1.1% of suspensions statewide (Wood, Harris, & Howard, 2018). As Scott and Sharp (2019) note, "Black males who experience disparate K–12 school experiences may not recognize academic shortfalls until later in life" (p. 46); disparate schooling experiences must be understood as playing a contributing factor to both the shortage and attrition of Black males in higher education overall. Such disparities can help inform retention and persistence policy and programming in higher education related to the success of Black male students.

While multiple scholars contend how systemic racism on college campuses impedes the success and educational attainment of Black males in higher education (Owens et al., 2019; Scott & Sharp, 2019; Smith, 2016), it must be acknowledged how such campus cultures reflect the larger hegemonic and racist rationales of US society. As observed by Ann Ferguson in her seminal text *Bad Boys: Public Schools in the Making of Black Masculinity*, "Educational institutions are organized and reflect the interests of dominant groups in the society" (2000, p. 50). As referenced earlier, the OSAPG framework helps illustrate that the nature of disparate economic realities between Black students and White students are not the result of unintended consequences but a crisis manufactured by White supremacist formations of economic exploitation, economic violence, and sociopolitical control over material resources and social dominance. The OSAPG framework clarifies how such disparities operate to intentionally exclude and push out Black males from higher education through limited access to economic means and mobility, which translates to limited access to overall economic and sociopolitical power.

Arrest and Death of College-Aged Black Males

Black males are also less likely to remain unincarcerated or otherwise survive their college years than students from other groups; absence from higher education, then, is not just an issue of unequal school experiences and access. Additionally, Black male absence from higher education sits at the intersection of systemic racism and state-sponsored surveillance, both of which collude to criminalize and incarcerate college-aged Black males at much higher rates than any other group (Nellis, 2021). According to Robert Brame et al. (2014), "Non-Hispanic, Black males have the highest risk of arrest by age 18 (29.6%), followed by Hispanic males (26.2%) and non-Hispanic, non-Black (White) males (21.5%)." By the age of 23, that rate has risen to 48.9% for Black males, compared to 43.8% for Hispanic males and 37.9% for White males, and males overall are twice as likely to be arrested as females (Brame et al., 2014). Moreover, Black males are more likely to have been arrested by the age of 23 (48.9%) than they are to have graduated from college (roughly 40% overall). Furthermore, recall that college-aged Black males (ages 20–24) are the group most likely to be killed by police (Males, 2014). These data show that during the ages most typical for college attendance, Black males are being incarcerated or murdered at disproportional rates compared to other groups, pulling them out of higher education and society at these higher comparative rates and rates higher than their rates of engagement with and achievement in higher education, thus eliminating them from everyday life and civic engagement. These data show that the low rate of Black males in higher education is connected to removing them from society; the racial crisis in higher education is directly informed by the genocide being enacted against Black males.

Achievement

Due to these widely varied factors, Black males complete college and post-secondary degrees at extremely low rates. According to Jennifer Lee (2019), Blacks are underrepresented compared to the overall graduation rate at almost every type of institution (research institutions 77%, Blacks 62%; comprehensive universities 56%, Blacks 53%; state universities 52%, Blacks 39%; state colleges 31%, Blacks 19%; technical colleges 34%, Blacks 30%). Nationally, only 4 in 10 Black students graduate within 6 years (compared to a 62% graduation rate for White students; Quinn, 2017). Regarding degree attainment by Black males specifically, US Department of Education aggregate data from 2015 found that approximately 17.6% received a bachelor's degree compared to 24.6% for Black females and 39.5% for White males nationally. Stark disparities in master's degree attainment between Black males and other groups are prevalent, with Black males earning 2.5% of master's degrees compared to 7.2% for Black females and 8.2% for White males (Scott & Sharp, 2019). In addition, only 37.4% of Black males in the fall 2012 cohort graduated from all institutions within the USG with a bachelor's degree within six years (University System of Georgia, 2019g). This percentage is compared to 51.3% of Black females (University System of Georgia, 2019h) and 59.9% White males (University System of Georgia, 2019i). Moreover, in all of USG, 4,663 Black males achieved graduate degrees of any kind (University System of Georgia, 2019b), compared to 10,257 Black females (University System of Georgia, 2019a) and 15,706 White males (University System of Georgia, 2019c).

While these numbers for Black male degree attainment and academic achievement are low, there are institutions with higher Black male achievement rates. In Georgia, several institutions graduate Black students at higher rates (Quinn, 2017) and are doing better than the national average, including Emory University, University of Georgia, Georgia Technical Institute, Georgia College and State University, and Georgia State University (Quinn, 2017). Georgia State University (GSU) has the largest percentage of Black students, including 29.5% Black first-year students, and graduates them at a higher rate than the national average and a higher rate than White students, with a 55.5% Black student graduation rate (Quinn, 2017). This success is partially due to GSU providing "retention grants" for students who cannot continue to pay tuition, and partially due to greater representation of African American faculty (10% versus the national average of about 4%, excluding HBCUs; Chiles, 2016). The increased success of Black males at these institutions supports our claim that the low representation of Black males in higher education overall is due to systemic factors that are designed to result in this exclusion of Black males from social, political, and community engagement and leadership. When these systemic factors (such as the financial accessibility of higher education) are reduced or removed, Black males can persist and achieve in higher education. In other words, Black males would see far greater higher education persistence and achievement if it were not for the multiple forms of genocide perpetrated against them.

Postgraduation Employment and Income

Even when Black males graduate from college, their employment and income do not match those of graduates from other groups. Nationally, Black students with bachelor's degrees earn approximately $20,000 less per year than their White counterparts (National Center for Education Statistics, 2016). Regarding Black male earnings versus other groups, the most recent report from the Bureau of Labor Statistics found that Black men's weekly earnings were $813 compared to $1,134 for White men (US Department of Labor, 2022). Other data specifically found that Black men earned $0.98 for every dollar a White man with the same qualifications made. While a benign gap, the disparity in such earnings increases exponentially when accounting for salaries (Gruver, 2019). Such data remain important given overall data that confirms that Black boys raised in wealthy American households earn markedly less than White boys with similar backgrounds (Badger et al., 2018). Approximately 39% of White males born rich remained rich compared to 17% for Black males, while it was found that Black boys fare worse than White boys in 99% of America (Badger et al., 2018). While data examining gendered disparities of generational wealth and net worth remains scant, overall data concludes that the net worth of White families remains ten times greater than that of Black families ($171,000 vs. $17,150; McIntosh et al., 2020). Such data should make clear how the OSAPG framework and prevalent factors of systemic racism (be it affectations posed to Black male and community prosperity through redlining, criminalization, mass incarceration, and/or racist campus cultures that exacerbate Black male attrition and degree attainment) frame such economic realities as relevant to the argument of Black male genocide, as far as such economic disparities operate with the intent to destroy in whole, or in part.

Black college graduates also face disparate unemployment rates compared to all other groups. As of 2021, Black men have the highest unemployment rate of any racialized or gendered group (Holzer, 2021). Of further issue are how Black male absence from labor data sets results from factors of mass incarceration, meaning that the hypercriminalization of Black males overall accounts for significant gaps in findings that attempt to account for Black male labor participation, economic earnings, and so on (Holzer, 2021). Such circumstances of Black male absence due to mass incarceration support the argument for Black male genocide, insofar as the criminalization of Black men operates to exclude Black males from social and political life (OSAPG, n.d.). Hence, college-aged Black males, even those with degrees, still experience heightened obstacles and less earning potential overall compared to other groups.

Similar disparities exist even amid prosperous economic climates that signify job expansions. Black workers today are twice as likely to be unemployed as White workers overall (6.4% vs. 3.1%). Furthermore, they experience higher rates of unemployment with a college degree than do White workers with a college degree (3.5% vs. 2.2%; Williams & Wilson, 2019). These disparities in postgraduation employment and income show that even when Black males attain college degrees, their life chances are unequal to those of their peers in dominant social groups. Despite post-racial rhetoric that contends otherwise, the reality remains that educational attainment does not mitigate discrimination against Black males or result in their obtaining equal social or economic power. In short, factors of systemic racism continue to dramatically reduce the tangible benefits higher education should bestow on Black males, which directly contributes to the ongoing record of discrimination and violence against Black males overall.

Economic Exclusion

Economic disparity as a result of limited educational attainment, changing economic conditions, labor discrimination, and systemic racism between Black and White communities, including the lasting impacts of redlining, is a long-observed phenomenon (Cawthorne Gaines, 2009; Curry, 2017; Dau-Schmidt & Sherman, 2013; Feagin, 2010; Gould, 2018; Kendi, 2016;

Lipsitz, 2011; Staples, 1987). Educational attainment does not lead to equal employment and income opportunities or to economic parity for Black males compared to other groups. The historic context of the economic exclusion of Black males and redlining, combined with the data about the STPP, make clear how systemic racism and economic policies adversely affect Black males over other groups, further illustrating how underenrollment in higher education and exclusion from key professions function to remove Black males from society. This section addresses how Black males are excluded from economic stability and wealth attainment despite their educational achievement and provides evidence for one way that genocide is enacted against Black males—systemically limited economic mobility and exclusion from social and political life.

Professional Occupations and Higher Education

Disproportionate adverse economic impacts for Black males compared to other groups can be found in gross disparities in overall earnings and exclusion from professional occupations and higher education. When looking at employment data regarding several high-end occupations, Adia Harvey Wingfield (2014) found that Black males comprised only 2.6% of physicians/surgeons, 2% of lawyers, 3% of engineers, and 2.5% of bankers nationally, despite constituting approximately 6.5% of the overall population. Data regarding rates at which Black males are suspended, incarcerated, and/or experience varying levels of educational disruption (pull-out, push-out, etc.) before entering higher education are also data about the factors leading to the low representation of Black males in these professional occupations. In short, Black males remain absent from key professions, positions of leadership, and higher education not solely as a result of limited access and resources but also as a result of the ways in which their lives remain threatened by cultures of systemic racism within the very institutions purported to uplift them.

Such data make clear how factors of systemic racism work to exclude Black males from higher education and the labor force, contributing to their subordinate position in the social strata and building to the charge of genocide. Lower overall earnings, low rates of four-year degree obtainment, the inability to escape poverty, and, as we discuss below, the physiological threat of systemic racism in the form of RBF place Black males in an almost impossible socioeconomic and biological predicament—their placement in the lowest social strata is reinforced and maintained, ensuring that Black males most often cannot economically afford safety, education, or positive healthcare outcomes. Paired with the rising costs of higher education overall, low enrollment and graduation rates for Black males in higher education is not tantamount to just a problem of socioeconomic opportunities, nor is it simply a reflection of the already well-documented systemic and structural racism that Black males face. Instead, these combined features of higher education contribute to the racial crisis in higher education, specifically as it pertains to Black males both as evidence of and as the continuation of Black male genocide. While numerous scholars ascertain that Black males face difficulties succeeding within majority historically white institutions (HWIs), there is a greater need to investigate these linkages between the ways externalizing forces of systemic racism place Black male students at a disadvantage beyond that of deficit framings.

Health and Life Expectancy

Regardless of professional and economic achievement, Black males are overrepresented in various adverse health outcomes that often lead to death. The prevalence of these poor health outcomes for Black males further reduces their ability to participate in society, specifically in higher education, and reduces the population, contributing to their genocide. Although the following data is not comprehensive, it is illustrative of how Black males suffer from health disparities compared to members of other groups.

Negative Health Outcomes

Black males are overrepresented in HIV/AIDS rates (Fullilove, 2006; *Atlanta*, 2020); cardiovascular disease (Bayakly, 2015; Durham County Community Health Assessment, 2017), including high blood pressure (Bayakly, 2015; Centers for Disease Control and Prevention, 2010;); diabetes (Walker, Williams, & Egede, 2016); obesity (Bayakly, 2015); kidney disease (Duru et al., 2008); and prostate cancer (Durham County Community Health Assessment, 2014). In fact, at just around 75 years, Blacks have the lowest life expectancy out of all groups, compared to around 79 years for Whites, and 81 years for Hispanics (Cook, 2016). Additionally, according to the Prison Policy Initiative, every year lived in incarceration reduces an individual's life expectancy by an average of two years (Widra, 2017). Given the disproportionately high rates at which Black males are incarcerated, this reduction in life expectancy results in further disparities between Black males and all other groups. Overall, the combination of high rates of infant mortality, the STPP, police murders, incarceration, and the many health disparities that Black males face reduces the time that Black males are expected and able to live and participate in society, including all levels of education.

Racialized Stress

Racialized stress and RBF compound each of these health issues, increasing the rate at which Black males suffer from them and reducing Black males' ability to mediate them. According to Derek Griffith, Katrina Ellis, and Julie Ober Allen (2013), "Stress is a key factor that helps explain racial and gender differences in health" (p. 19S), contributing directly to the negative health outcomes detailed above. Stress has a significant impact on, for example, the cardiovascular system and blood pressure; the body's response to stress is to raise your blood pressure and blood sugars. According to Gordon (2014), "Constant stress results in allostatic load, which is when the body's protective mechanisms become destructive from over usage." Chronic stress leads to chronic high blood pressure and high blood sugar, increasing the risk of diabetes. The CDC defines social determinants of health that include "the circumstances in which people are born, live, work, and age, as well as the healthcare system" that make up "four categories of interacting factors: 1) socioeconomic circumstances, 2) psychosocial factors, 3) neighborhood environment, and 4) political, economic and cultural drivers" (Walker, Williams, & Egede, 2016). All of these categories interact with, for example, diabetes, so that they exacerbate the impact of the disease on the Black population and can produce negative health outcomes where there may not have been any before. While socioeconomic status (SES) affects health disparities for all racial groups, David R. Williams (2006) found that even within particular levels of SES, racism added to the health disparities seen for Blacks: "Racism is an added burden for nondominant populations." Racism is a common stressor for Black males in college, along with financial and employment stress, stress about their college readiness (which results at least in part from the STPP detailed above), and stress from interpersonal relationships, with stress from the school environment and various expressions of racism being greater at HWIs (Goodwill et al., 2018). In addition to stress from direct, overt racism, Black males in college also experience the particular stress of navigating the world as Black males, trying to achieve against the strain of systemic racism (Watkins et al., 2007). This stress of trying to make something of themselves continues throughout their lives (Griffiths,

Ellis, & Allen, 2013), acting as an ongoing, compounding stressor for Black males. Additionally, young Black males are subject to the traumatic stress associated with violent injury, which is often recurring due to intentional violence (Rich & Grey, 2005). This trauma increases adverse health outcomes and increases young Black males' likelihood of substance abuse as a coping mechanism for this trauma (Rich & Grey, 2005).

Black male college students also adopt various other coping strategies for dealing with their stress, including isolating themselves from others and disengaging from their emotions (Goodwill et al., 2018), which are informed by raced and gendered behavioral norms and expectations (Griffiths, Ellis, & Allen, 2013) and have a disparate impact on Black males' mental and physical health in both the short and long term. According to Sean Joe (2008), "Black men are caught in the gender straightjacket of hyper-masculinity, which discourages help-seeking and undervalues emotional concerns, while exaggerating the importance of work and material indicators of success in a context in which economic success may be almost unattainable" (p. 235). The specific combination of concerns that Black males face at the nexus of gender, race, and class has resulted in Black males' experiencing disparate amounts of stress, and lower overall health outcomes, including mental health outcomes (Watkins, Walker & Griffith, 2010). Recent increases in Black male suicide, for example, are such that suicide is the third most common cause of death for young Black males aged 15–24, with even greater numbers of young Black males attempting but not completing suicide (Joe, 2008). Young Black males under the age of 32 are significantly more likely to attempt suicide than are older Black males or Black females of any age (Joe, 2008). The phenomenon of racialized stress is particularly important to a discussion of the racial crisis in higher education, as racialized stress in its various forms and outcomes further reduces the already low numbers of Black males attending institutions of higher education whether via suicide or via choosing not to attend or not to continue attending college after stressful life events (Watkins et al., 2007), and affects the emotions, stress, and overall well-being of those who do attend.

On average, stress from racism in the form of both abject and abstract racialized microaggressions was shown to increase Black males' chances of developing hypertension and heart disease by 44–45%, as well as to increase their chances of developing clinical depression and post-traumatic stress disorder (Owens et al., 2019). In line with RBF, racial profiling results in higher levels of stress for Blacks, even when they merely anticipate an experience with racism (Silverstein, 2013). Furthermore, this stress is not reduced as Black males attain education, economic stability, and positions of power. Instead, it increases, leading Black males of all SES levels to face higher rates of stress and negative health outcomes due to their arbitrary set membership or being Black males.

The abundance of data concerning Black males' health and life expectancy and the layered ways in which these data come to play out in Black males' lives show a complicated relationship between education and Black males' health, lives, and deaths. Although educational attainment leads to greater economic resources and stability and greater access to healthcare and health information, this does not, in turn, lead to greater overall health outcomes for Black males as it does for White males. Instead, greater levels of stress and racialized stress lead to poorer health outcomes for Black males throughout their lives regardless of educational attainment (Griffith, Ellis, & Allen 2013; Miller et al., 2015). These greater levels of stress will undoubtedly affect their ability to achieve academically and their ability to lead fulfilling lives. This complex, cyclical, compounding relationship between education and Black male health, then, perfectly illustrates the structure and functioning of SDT and SMTH and supports the charge of genocide against Black males in the United States. Black males face a catch-22 in terms of health outcomes—they die early without education, through infant mortality, police murders and other civilian violence, incarceration, and poor health outcomes due to lack of education and access. They also die prematurely, despite attaining higher education, through higher levels of race-related stress and the incumbent impact on their health overall. Contrary to popular rhetoric, educational attainment changes how Black males experience discrimination and poor outcomes but does not eliminate them. Instead, we can infer from the preponderance of evidence that Black males are systematically targeted and removed from social and political life through various and persistent methods, amounting to Black male genocide.

Conclusion

In short, genocide is responsible for the racial crisis in higher education pertaining to Black males. In line with SMTH, the data discussed in this paper relegate Black males to the status of subordinate males. The ways that Black males are subordinated are dually the ways that the United States is committing genocide against them and why they are largely missing from higher education. The OSAPG outlines eight categories of factors that build to the charge of genocide, requiring that the cumulative effect of evidence show an intentional eradication of a specific population, along with eight issues to be analyzed to show "intent to destroy in whole or in part." The data provided in this case study detail how four of those sets of categories are satisfied regarding Black males, providing ample evidence that supports the charge of Black male genocide and that shows how this phenomenon helps explain both the underenrollment and underrepresentation of Black males inside and outside higher education overall:

- Intergroup relations, including record of discrimination and/or other human rights violations committed against a group
- Circumstances that affect the capacity to prevent genocide
- Circumstances that facilitate perpetration of genocide (dynamic factors)
- Evidence of intent "to destroy in whole or in part"

Evidence of intent "to destroy in whole or in part" includes the following issues to be analyzed:

- In a nonconflict situation, widespread and/or systematic discriminatory and targeted practices culminating in gross violations of human rights of protected groups, such as extrajudicial killings, torture and displacement;
- The specific means used to achieve "ethnic cleansing," which may underscore that the perpetration of the acts is designed to reach the foundations of the group or what is considered as such by the perpetrator group;
- The targeted elimination of community leaders and/or men and/or women of a particular age group (the "future generation" or a military-age group);
- Other practices designed to complete the exclusion of targeted group from social/political life. (OSAPG, n.d., p. 3)

The STPP that runs from K–12 into higher education, disparate arrest, extrajudicial murder rates, limited employment opportunities, and disparate income provides a clear record of discrimination against Black males throughout their life span. Moreover, this discrimination record further perpetuates their genocide through widely disparate, negative health outcomes for Black males, including racialized stress and RBF, a condition specifically resulting from this discrimination. From in utero to end of life, Black males are killed and otherwise die at higher rates and earlier than other groups; have limited access to education, employment, and economic power; and see limited positive outcomes from pursuing higher education, all of which serve to both facilitate their deaths and genocide and affect their ability to prevent that genocide by placing them in a subordinate position with little to no social power. Through creating and maintaining social hierarchy, the United States ensures that Black males are stuck in the lowest social strata; they are removed from social and political life through incarceration, killed, or indirectly ensured to die early from other negative health outcomes. Their means of survival are prevented or removed, thereby significantly reducing their chances. Furthermore, there is a damaging catch-22 in higher education: Black males are simultaneously expected to pursue education, yet they are prevented from doing so at every step, making education so difficult for them to access and giving them such limited benefits that it is largely unobtainable and fails to be a worthwhile pursuit. The systemic, compounding ways in which these threats to Black males affect their lives, engagement with higher education, and ability to succeed amounts to an unquestionable intent to destroy.

The charge of genocide is crucial if we position critical educational scholarship to examine threats of systemic racism and institutionalized discrimination beyond posing as just an existential deterrent to success. Indeed, we must question our current line of logic and scholarship if we acknowledge that the very institution(s) that we claim benefit all people simultaneously contributes to the genocide of Black males and is inaccessible to them due to this genocide.

Our case study's foci could be extended to other subordinate populations beyond that of Black males. In acknowledging this, we feel that further research is needed in two specific areas. First, we need continued scholarship that specifically looks at whether other gender and racial groups are experiencing a genocide, as well as how stress factors related to systemic racism prevalent within HWIs and RBF affects success within and beyond higher education overall. And second, we need further research about the ways in which Black males specifically are affected academically by acknowledging the existence of both genocide and RBF. Research of this kind will prove paramount to positioning calls to action for higher education to either come to terms with the fact that a genocide has been occurring and thus admit its complicity and monetary gain from such atrocities, and/or take robust and radical critical, academic, social, and institutional action to end it. We hope for and demand the latter.

References

A Call for Gun Violence Prevention. (2018, March 23). *North Carolina Health News*. Retrieved from https://www.northcarolinahealthnews.org/2018/03/23/a-call-for-gun-violence prevention/

Anthony Jr, M., Nichols, A. H., & Pilar, W. D. (2021). A look at degree attainment among Hispanic women and men and how COVID-19 could deepen racial and gender divides. *The Education Trust*.

Archibald, A. (2019, August 7). Study: Proximity to violent crime affects hiring practices. *Real Change*. Retrieved from https://www.realchangenews.org/news/2019/08/07/study-proximity-violent-crime-affects-hiring-practices

Atlanta. (2020, December 11). AIDSVu. https://aidsvu.org/local-data/united-states/south/georgia/atlanta/

Badger, E., Miller, C. C., Pearce, A., & Quealy, K. (2018). Extensive data shows punishing reach of racism for black boys. *The New York Times*. Retrieved from https://www.nytimes.com/interactive/2018/03/19/upshot/race-class-white-and-black-men.html

Barreira, A., & Swedback, A. (2019, April 14). Law enforcement killed 90 oakland residents since 2000, and 74 percent were black. *East Bay Express*. Retrieved from https://www.eastbayexpress.com/oakland/law-enforcement-killed-90-oakland-residents-since-2000-and-74-percent-were-black/Content?oid=4940357

Bayakly, R. (2015). Burden of cardiovascular disease in Georgia. [PowerPoint slides]. Georgia Department of Public Health. Retrieved from https://dph.georgia.gov/sites/dph.georgia.gov/files/Cardiovascular%20Burden_CDU_10.22.15_RBayakly.pdf.

Board of Regents University System of Georgia. (2018, October 30). Semester enrollment report fall 2018. Retrieved from https://www.usg.edu/assets/research/documents/enrollment_reports/SER_Fall_18_Final_11072018.pdf.

Bowden, A. (n.d.). *Black infant deaths are soaring in North Carolina*. Center for Health Journalism. https://centerforhealthjournalism.org/2022/10/10/black-infant-deaths-are-soaring-north-carolina

Brame, R., Bushway, S. D., Paternoster, R., & Turner, M. G. (2014). Demographic patterns of cumulative arrest prevalence by ages 18 and 23. *Crime & Delinquency, 60*(3), 471–486. https://doi.org/10.1177/0011128713514801

Broda, Natalie. (2019, June). What infant mortality means in Oakland County. *The Oakland Press*. Retrieved from https://www.theoaklandpress.com/news/tiny-casualties-what-infant-mortality-means-in-oaklandcounty/article_4d836312-9395-11e9-aa0d-b329b0b00926.html

Burrus, J., & Roberts, R. D. (2012). Dropping out of high school: Prevalence, risk factors, and remediation strategies. *R & D Connections, 18*(2), 1–9.

Caton, M. T. (2012). Black male perspectives on their educational experiences in high school. *Urban Education, 47*(6), 1055–1085.

Cawthorne Gaines, A. (2009). Weathering the storm: Black men in the recession. *Center for American Progress*. Retrieved from https://www.americanprogress.org/article/weathering-the-storm-black-men-in-the-recession/

Centers for Disease Control and Prevention. (2010). *A closer look at African American men and high blood pressure control: A review of psychosocial factors and systems-level interventions.* US Department of Health and Human Services.

Centers for Disease Control. (2014). 500 cities project: Local data for better health: Oakland, CA. Retrieved from ftp://ftp.cdc.gov/pub/MAPBOOKS/CA_Oakland_MB_508tag.pdf

Chapple-McGruder, T., Zhou, Y., Freymann, G., & Castrucci, B. (March 2012). *From preconception to infant protection*. Georgia Department of Public Health, Maternal and Child Health Program, Office of Epidemiology.

Chiles, N. (2016, November 25). At Georgia State, more black students graduate each year than at any US college. *The Hechinger Report*. Retrieved from https://hechingerreport.org/at-georgiastate-black-students-find-comfort-and-academic-success/.

Cohen, Li. (2020, September 10). Police in the US killed 164 Black people in the first 8 months of 2020: These are their names. (Part I, January–April). *CBS News*. Retrieved from https://www.cbsnews.com/pictures/black-people-killed-by-police-in-the-u-s-in-2020/

Committee on Racial Equity. (2019). Action plan and recommendations. *Public School Forum*. Retrieved from https://www.ncforum.org/committee-on-racial-equity/

Cook, L. (2016, April 20). Life expectancy drops for Whites, rises for Blacks and Hispanics. *US News & World Report*. Retrieved from https://www.usnews.com/news/blogs/data-mine/articles/2016-04-20/life-expectancy-drops-for-whites-rises-for-blacks-and-hispanics.

Craven, J. (2013, October 10). Only 98 of nearly 4,000 new first-years are black males. *The Daily Tar Heel*. Retrieved from https://www.dailytarheel.com/article/2013/10/only-98-of-nearly-4000-newfirst-years-are-black-males

Criminal Justice Facts. (n.d.). The Sentencing Project. Retrieved from https://www.sentencingproject.org/criminal-justice-facts

Curry, Tommy. (2017). The Political economy of Niggerdum: Racist misandry, class warfare, and the disciplinary propagation of the super-predator mythology. In Tommy J. Curry, *The man-not: Race, class, genre, and the dilemma of black manhood* (PP. 104–136). Temple University Press.

Darensbourg, A., Perez, E., & Blake, J. J. (2010). Overrepresentation of African American males in exclusionary discipline: The role of school-based mental health professionals in dismantling the school to prison pipeline. *Journal of African American Males in Education (JAAME), 1*(3), 196–211.
Dau-Schmidt, Kenneth G., and Sherman, Ryland. (2013). The employment and economic advancement of African-Americans in the twentieth century Articles by Maurer Faculty. Paper 1292.
Department of Education. (2011). Merit aid for undergraduate students statistics. United States Department of Education. Retrieved from https://nces.ed.gov/pubs2012/2012160.pdf
Discriminology Beta. (n.d). Georgia: State level out-of-school suspension report. Retrieved from https://www.discriminology.org/state-level/ga.
Doll, J. J., Eslami, Z., & Walters, L. (2013). Understanding why students drop out of high school, according to their own reports: Are they pushed or pulled, or do they fall out? A comparative analysis of seven nationally representative studies. *Sage Open, 3*(4), 2158244013503834.
Durham County Community Health Assessment. (2014). Durham County Public Health. https://www.dcopublichealth.org/home/showpublisheddocument/24474/636537006906770000
Durham County Community Health Assessment. (2017). Durham County Public Health. https://www.dcopublichealth.org/home/showpublisheddocument/29424/637079609137330000
Duru, O. K., Li, S., Jurkovitz, C., Bakris, G., Brown, W., Chen, S. C., Collins, A., Klag, M., McCullough, P. A., McGill, J., Narva, A., Pergola, P., Singh, A., & Norris, K. (2008). Race and sex differences in hypertension control in CKD: Results from the Kidney Early Evaluation Program (KEEP). *American Journal of Kidney Diseases: The Official Journal of the National Kidney Foundation, 51*(2), 192–198. https://doi.org/10.1053/j.ajkd.2007.09.023
Feagin, J. R. (2010). *The White racial frame: Centuries of racial framing and counter-framing.* Routledge.
Ferguson, A. (2000). *Bad boys: Public schools in the making of black masculinity.* University of Michigan Press.
Firearms Deaths North Carolina. (2015). North Carolina injury and prevention. NCDHHS. Retrieved from https://www.injuryfreenc.ncdhhs.gov/
Fullilove, R. (2006, November). African Americans, health disparities, and HIV/AIDS: Recommendations for confronting the epidemic in Black America. National Minority AIDS Council. Retrieved from https://static.prisonpolicy.org/scans/aids.pdf
Goodwill, J. R., Watkins, D. C., Johnson, N. C., & Allen, J. O. (2018). An exploratory study of stress and coping among Black college men. *American Journal of Orthopsychiatry, 88*(5), 538–549.
Gordon, B. (2014, January 20). The silent genocide in Black America: Race-based stress and negative health outcomes in US Blacks. *Psychology Today.*

https://www.psychologytoday.com/us/blog/obesely-speaking/201401/the-silent-genocide-in-black-america

Gould, E. (2018). Manufacturing decline has hurt Black Americans more. *VOX EU*. Retrieved from https://voxeu.org/article/manufacturing-decline-has-hurt-black-americans-more

Griffith, D. M., Ellis, K. R., & Allen, J. O. (2013). An intersectional approach to social determinants of stress for African American men: Men's and women's perspectives. *American Journal of Men's Health, 7*(4, Suppl.), 19S–30S.

Gruver, J. (2022, June 23). Racial wage gap for men | Payscale. Payscale—Salary Comparison, Salary Survey, Search Wages. https://www.payscale.com/research-and-insights/racial-wage-gap-for-men/

Harvey Wingfield, A. (2014). Crossing the color line: Black professional men's development of interracial social networks. *Societies, 4*(2), 240–255.

Henry K. Kaiser Family Foundation. (2013, March 13). Health coverage by race and ethnicity: The potential impact of the Affordable Care Act. Retrieved from https://www.kff.org/disparities-policy/issue-brief/health-coverage-by-race-and-ethnicity-the-potential-impact-of-the-affordable-care-act

Holland, K. (2016, May 5). College debt is much worse for black students. CNBC. Retrieved from https://www.cnbc.com/2016/05/05/college-debt-is-much-worse-for-black-students.html

Holzer, H. J. (2022, March 9). *Why are employment rates so low among Black men?* Brookings. https://www.brookings.edu/research/why-are-employment-rates-so-low-among-black-men/

Incarcerated Women and Girls. (2018, May 10). The Sentencing Project. Retrieved from https://www.sentencingproject.org/publications/incarcerated-women-and-girls/

Joe, S. (2008). Suicide patterns among Black males. In E. Anderson (Ed.), *Against the wall: Poor, young, Black, and male* (pp. 218–241). University of Pennsylvania Press.

Johnson, D. (2018, August 21). 20-to-1: Black male suspensions in Durham public schools. *Carolina Political Review*. https://www.carolinapoliticalreview.org/editorial-content/2018/8/20/20-to-1

Kaiser Family Foundation. (n.d.). *Infant mortality rate*. https://www.kff.org/other/state-indicator/infant-death-rate/?currentTimeframe=0&sortModel=%7B%22colId%22:%22Infant%20Deaths%22,%22sort%22:%22desc%22%7D#notes

Kalinowski, J., Taylor, J. Y., & Spruill, T. M. (2019). Why are young black women at high risk for cardiovascular disease? *Circulation, 139*(8), 1003–1004. https://doi.org/10.1161/CIRCULATIONAHA.118.037689

Kendi, I. (2016). *Stamped from the beginning: The definitive history of racist ideas in America*. Nation Books.

Lacoe, J. R. (2015). Unequally safe: The race gap in school safety. *Youth Violence and Juvenile Justice, 13*(2), 143–168. Retrieved from https://doi.org/10.1177/1541204014532659

Lee, J. (2019, September 12). 2019 Georgia higher education data book. Retrieved from https://gbpi.org/2019/georgia-higher-education-data-book-2019/.

Lipsitz, G. (2011). *How racism takes place*. Temple University Press.

Lopez, G. (2016, August 13). There are huge racial disparities in how US police use force. *VOX*. Retrieved July 11, 2019, from https://www.vox.com/identities/2016/8/13/17938186/police-shootingskillings-racism-racial-disparities

Maciag, M. (2021, April 21). *Where have all the Black men gone?* Governing. https://www.governing.com/archive/gov-black-men-gender-imbalance-population.html

Males, M. (2014, August 26). Who are police killing? Center on Juvenile and Criminal Justice. Retrieved from http://www.cjcj.org/news/8113

Marshall, M., Nichols, A., & Pilar, W. (2021). Raising undergraduate degree attainment among black women and men takes on new urgency amid the pandemic. The Education Trust. Retrieved from https://edtrust.org/resource/national-and-state-degree-attainment-for-black-women-andmen/

McIntosh, K., Moss, E., Nunn, R., & Shambaug, J. (2020, February 27). *Examining the Black-White wealth gap*. Brookings. https://www.brookings.edu/blog/up-front/2020/02/27/examining-the-black-white-wealth-gap/

Miller, Gregory, Yu, Tianyi, Edith, Chen, et al. (2015). Self-control forecasts better psychosocial outcomes but faster epigenetic again in low-SES youth. *National Academy of Sciences, 112*(33), 10325–10330.

NAACP. (2005). *Interrupting the school-to-prison pipe-line*.

National Center for Education Statistics. (2016). Post-bachelor's employment outcomes by sex and race/ethnicity. Retrieved from https://nces.ed.gov/programs/coe/pdf/coe_tbb.pdf

National Center for Education Statistics. (n.d.). Bachelor's degrees conferred to females by postsecondary institutions, by race/ethnicity and field of study: 2017–18 and 2018–19. https://nces.ed.gov/programs/digest/d20/tables/dt20_322.50.asp

Nellis, A. (2021). The color of justice: Racial and ethnic disparity in state prisons. The Sentencing Project. Retrieved from https://www.sentencingproject.org/publications/color-of-justice-racialand-ethnic-disparity-in-state-prisons/

Office of Civil Rights (n.d.). *2013–14 State and National Estimations*. Civil Rights Data Collection. https://ocrdata.ed.gov/estimations/2013-2014

Office of the Special Adviser on the Prevention of Genocide. (n.d). Analysis Framework. Retrieved from https://www.un.org/ar/preventgenocide/adviser/pdf/osapg_analysis_framework.pdf

Owens, D., Lockhart, S., Matthews, D. Y., & Middleton, T. J. (2019). Racial battle fatigue and mental health in Black men. In J. Butcher, J. O'Connor Jr., & F. Titus (EdS.), *Overcoming challenges and creating opportunity for African*

American male students (pp. 99–107). IGI Global. https://doi.org/10.4018/978-1-5225-5990-0.ch005

Perry-Johnson, A., Papp, D., Butler, F., Levine, S., Nickel, S., & Wolfe, J. (2003, May 21). Summary and final recommendations of the University System of Georgia's African-American Male Initiative. Retrieved from https://www.usg.edu/assets/aami/files/Summary_and_Final_Recommendations.pdf

PRiME. (2021, April 15). *The condition of education 2020*. PRiME Center | St. Louis University. https://www.sluprime.org/prime-blog/2020conditionofeducation

Prison Policy Initiative. (n.d. a). Georgia profile. Retrieved from https://www.prisonpolicy.org/profiles/GA.html.

Prison Policy Initiative. (n.d. b). African American male populations, 2000. Retrieved from https://www.prisonpolicy.org/graphs/blackmalepop.html.

Quinn, C. (2017, March 8). These Georgia colleges graduate the highest percentage of Black students. *The Atlanta Journal Constitution*. Retrieved from https://www.ajc.com/news/local-education/these-georgia-colleges-graduate-the-highestpercentage-black-students/jTeYr6tU7j3p4LXYV0zppN/

Rich, J. A., & Grey, C. M. (2005). Pathways to recurrent trauma among young Black men: Traumatic stress, substance use, and the "code of the street." *American Journal of Public Health, 95*(5), 816–824.

Ross, J. (2014, May 27). African-Americans with college degrees are twice as likely to be unemployed as other graduates. *The Atlantic*. Retrieved from https://www.theatlantic.com/politics/archive/2014/05/african-americans-with-college-degreesare-twice-as-likely-to-be-unemployed-as-other-graduates/430971/

Rumberger, R. (2013). *Poverty and high school dropouts*. American Psychological Association. Retrieved from https://www.apa.org/pi/ses/resources/indicator/2013/05/poverty-dropouts

Schott Foundation for Public Education. (2013). Interactive map dashboard: Black male grad rates. *Black Boys Report*. Retrieved from http://blackboysreport.org/interactive-map-dashboard/

Scott, L., & Sharp, L. A. (2019). Black males who hold advanced degrees: Critical factors that preclude and promote success. *The Journal of Negro Education, 88*(1), 44–61.

Sidanius, J., & Pratto, F. (1999). *Social Dominance*. Cambridge University Press.

Silverstein, J. (2013, March 12). How racism is bad for our bodies. *The Atlantic*. Retrieved from https://www.theatlantic.com/health/archive/2013/03/how-racism-is-bad-for-our-bodies/273911/

Sirota, A. (2018, January 15). Unemployment levels for Black workers two times that for Whites in NC. North Carolina Justice Center. Retrieved from https://www.ncjustice.org/publications/unemployment-levels-for-black-workers-two-times-thatfor-whites-in-nc/

Smith, W. A. (2004). Black faculty coping with racial battle fatigue: The campus racial climate in a post-civil rights era. In Darrell Cleveland (Ed.), *A long way to go: Conversations about race by African American faculty and graduate students at predominately White institutions* (pp. 171–190). Peter Lang Publishers.

Smith, W. A. (2010). Toward an understanding of misandric microaggressions and racial battle fatigue among African Americans in historically White institutions. In E. M. Zamani-Gallaher & V. C. Polite (Eds.), *The state of the African American male* (pp. 265–277). Michigan State University Press.

Smith, W. A. (2016, June 26). Understanding the corollaries of offensive racial mechanisms, gendered racism, and racial battle fatigue. Center for Critical Race Studies at UCLA. https://issuu.com/almaiflores/docs/was_research_brief?e=25160478/39889684

Smith, W., Hung, M., & Franklin, J. (2011). Racial battle fatigue and the miseducation of black men: Racial microaggressions, societal problems, and environmental stress. *The Journal of Negro Education, 80*(1), 63–82.

Smith W. A., Bishop J., Jones C., Curry T. J., & Allen, W. R. (2016). "You make me wanna holler and throw up both my hands!": Campus culture, Black misandric microaggressions, and racial battle fatigue. *International Journal of Qualitative Studies in Education, 29*(9), 1189–1209.

Snyder, T.D., de Brey, C., & Dillow, S.A. (2019). *Digest of education statistics 2017* (NCES 2018–070). National Center for Education Statistics, Institute of Education Sciences, US Department of Education. Washington, DC.

Spencer, M. R., Warner, M., Bastian, B. A., Trinidad, J. P., & Hedegaard, H. (2019, March 21). Drug overdose deaths involving fentanyl, 2011–2016. *National Vital Statistics Reports 68*(3), 1–14.

Stanford's Center for Research on Education Outcomes. (2017). Lights off: Practice and impact of closing low-performing schools. Retrieved from https://credo.stanford.edu/closure-virtualcontrol-records.

Staples, R. (1987). Black male genocide: A final solution to the race problem in America. *The Black Scholar, 18*(3), 2–11.

Stearns, E., & Glennie, E. J. (2006). When and why dropouts leave high school. *Youth & Society, 38*(1), 29–57. https://doi.org/10.1177/0044118X05282764

Suggs, E. (2012, February 1). Males a distinct minority at HBCUs. *The Atlanta Journal-Constitution*. https://www.ajc.com/news/local/males-distinct-minority-hbcus/RXb5FLlpCc2H2ViJ39ZYNM/

Suggs, E., & Peebles, J. (2019, July 25). Atlanta is known as a black mecca: Jobs data tell a different story. *The Atlanta Journal-Constitution*. Retrieved from https://www.ajc.com/business/employment/atlanta-known-blackmecca-jobs-data-tell-different-story/yyQlvuMGBzbFIwLnhPeiiJ/

Sum, A., Khatiwada, I., McLaughlin, J., & Palma, S. (2009). The consequences of dropping out of high school. *Center for Labor Market Studies Publications, 23*, https://www.prisonpolicy.org/scans/The_Consequences_of_Dropping_Out_of_High_School.pdf

The Sentencing Project. (2021, February 21). *Parents in prison.* https://www.sentencingproject.org/app/uploads/2022/09/Parents-in-Prison.pdf

Torres, Nicole. (2018). Research: Having a black doctor led black men to receive more-effective care. *Harvard Business Review.* Retrieved from https://hbr.org/2018/08/research-having-a-black-doctor-led-black-men-toreceive-more-effective-care

United Nations. (n.d.). United Nations Office on Genocide Prevention and the Responsibility to Protect. Retrieved September 13, 2022, from https://www.un.org/en/genocideprevention/genocide.shtml

United Negro College Fund. (2019). *K–12 disparity facts and statistics.* Retrieved from https://www.uncf.org/pages/k-12-disparity-facts-and-stats

United States Department of Health and Human Services. (2017). *Infant mortality and african americans.* Office of Minority Health Resource Center. https://www.minorityhealth.hhs.gov/omh/browse.aspx?lvl=4&lvlid=23

United States Department of Labor. (2022, October 18). *Usual weekly earnings of wage and salary workers third quarter 2022.* Bureau of Labor Statistics. https://www.bls.gov/news.release/pdf/wkyeng.pdf

United States Census Bureau. (2018). QuickFacts US. Retrieved from https://www.census.gov/quickfacts/nc

University of California. (2019). UC enrollment data. Retrieved from https://www.universityofcalifornia.edu/infocenter/fall-enrollment-glance

University System of Georgia. (2019a). University System of Georgia degrees and awards conferred fiscal year 2018 female Black or African American. Retrieved from https://analytics.usg.edu/cognos/cgibin/cognos.cgi?b_action=cognos Viewer&ui.action=run&ui.o bject=%2fcontent%2ffolder%5b%40name%3d %27Public%27%5d%2ffolder%5b%40name%3d %27Reports%27%5d% 2ffolder%5b%40name%3d%27Academic%27%5d%2freport%5b%40na me%3d%27Degrees%20Conferred%27%5d&ui.name=Degrees%20 Conferred&run.outputForma t=PDF&run.prompt=true&CAMUsername= cognosguest&CAMPassword=R3adOnlyUs3r&CAMNamespace=BOROUD

University System of Georgia. (2019b). University System of Georgia degrees and awards conferred fiscal year 2018 male black or African American. Retrieved from https://analytics.usg.edu/cognos/cgibin/cognos.cgi?b_action= cognosViewer&ui.action=run&ui.o bject=%2fcontent%2ffolder%5b %40name%3d%27Public%27%5d%2ffolder%5b%40name%3d %27R eports%27%5d%2ffolder%5b%40name%3d%27Academic%27%5d%2 freport%5b%40na me%3d%27Degrees%20Conferred%27%5d&ui.name= Degrees%20Conferred&run.outputForma t=PDF&run.prompt=true& CAMUsername=cognosguest&CAMPassword=R3adOnlyUs3r&CAMName space=BOROUD

University System of Georgia. (2019c). University System of Georgia degrees and awards conferred fiscal year 2018 male White. Retrieved fromhttps://analytics.usg.edu/

cognos/cgibin/cognos.cgi?b_action=cognosViewer&ui.action=run&ui.o bject=%2fcontent%2ffolder%5b%40name%3d%27Public%27%5d%2ffolder%5b%40name%3d %27Reports%27%5d%2ffolder%5b%40name%3d%27Academic%27%5d%2freport%5b%40na me%3d%27Degrees%20Conferred%27%5d&ui.name=Degrees%20Conferred&run.outputForma t=PDF&run.prompt=true&CAMUsername=cognosguest&CAMPassword=R3adOnlyUs3r&CAMNamespace=BOROUD

University System of Georgia. (2019d). University System of Georgia fall headcount enrollment fall 2014–fall 2018 Black or African American female. Retrieved from https://analytics.usg.edu/cognos/cgibin/cognos.cgi?b_action=cognosViewer&ui.action=run&ui.o bject=%2fcontent%2ffolder%5b%40name%3d%27Public%27%5d%2ffolder%5b%40name%3d %27Reports%27%5d%2ffolder%5b%40name%3d%27Academic%27%5d%2freport%5b%40na me%3d%27Enrollment%27%5d&ui.name=Enrollment&run.outputFormat=PDF&run.prompt=tr ue&CAMUsername=cognosguest&CAMPassword=R3adOnlyUs3r&CAMNamespace=BOROUD

University System of Georgia. (2019e). University System of Georgia fall headcount enrollment fall 2014–fall 2018 Black or African American male. Retrieved from https://analytics.usg.edu/cognos/cgibin/cognos.cgi?b_action=cognosViewer&ui.action=run&ui.o bject=%2fcontent%2ffolder%5b%40name%3d%27Public%27%5d%2ffolder%5b%40name%3d %27Reports%27%5d%2ffolder%5b%40name%3d%27Academic%27%5d%2freport%5b%40na me%3d%27Enrollment%27%5d&ui.name=Enrollment&run.outputFormat=PDF&run.prompt=tr ue&CAMUsername=cognosguest&CAMPassword=R3adOnlyUs3r&CAMNamespace=BOROUD

University System of Georgia. (2019f). University System of Georgia fall headcount enrollment fall 2014–fall 2018 White male. Retrieved from https://analytics.usg.edu/cognos/cgibin/cognos.cgi?b_action=cognosViewer&ui.action=run&ui.object=%2fcontent%2ffolder%5b%4 0name%3d%27Public%27%5d%2ffolder%5b%40name%3d%27Reports%27%5d%2ffolder%5b%40name%3d%27Academic%27%5d%2freport%5b%40name%3d%27Enrollment%27%5d&ui. name=Enrollment&run.outputFormat=PDF&run.prompt=true&CAMUsername=cognosguest&CAMPassword=R3adOnlyUs3r&CAMNamespace=BOROUD

University System of Georgia. (2019g). University System of Georgia graduation rate report bachelor degree six-year rates first-time freshmen black or African American male fall 2012 cohort. Retrieved from https://analytics.usg.edu/cognos/cgibin/cognos.cgi?b_action=cognosViewer&ui.action=run&ui.o bject=%2fcontent%2ffolder%5b%40name%3d%27Public%27%5d%2ffolder%5b%40name%3d %27Reports%27%5d%2ffolder%5b%40name%3d%27Academic%27%5d%2freport%5b%40na me%3d%27Graduation

%27%5d&ui.name=Graduation&run.outputFormat=PDF&run.prompt=tr ue&CAMUsername=cognosguest&CAMPassword=R3adOnlyUs3r&CAM Namespace=BOROUD

University System of Georgia. (2019h). University System of Georgia graduation rate report bachelor degree six-year rates first-time freshmen Black or African American female fall 2012 cohort. Retrieved from https://analytics.usg.edu/ cognos/cgibin/cognos.cgi?b_action=cognosViewer&ui.action=run&ui.o bject= %2fcontent%2ffolder%5b%40name%3d%27Public%27%5d%2ffolder %5b%40name%3d %27Reports%27%5d%2ffolder%5b%40name%3d%27 Academic%27%5d%2freport%5b%40na me%3d%27Graduation%27%5d&ui. name=Graduation&run.outputFormat=PDF&run.prompt=tr ue&CAMUser name=cognosguest&CAMPassword=R3adOnlyUs3r&CAMNamespace= BOROUD

University System of Georgia. (2019i). University System of Georgia graduation rate report bachelor degree six-year rates first-time freshmen White male fall 2012 cohort. Retrieved from: https://analytics.usg.edu/cognos/cgibin/cognos. cgi?b_action=cognosViewer&ui.action=run&ui.o bject=%2fcontent%2ffolder %5b%40name%3d%27Public%27%5d%2ffolder%5b%40name%3d %27 Reports%27%5d%2ffolder%5b%40name%3d%27Academic%27%5d%2 freport%5b%40na me%3d%27Graduation%27%5d&ui.name=Graduation &run.outputFormat=PDF&run.prompt=tr ue&CAMUsername=cognosguest& CAMPassword=R3adOnlyUs3r&CAMNamespace=BOROUD

US Rights. (2014). Civil rights data collection data snapshot: School discipline. Issue brief no. 1.

Valenzuela, A. (1999). Subtractive schooling: US-Mexican youth and the politics of caring. State University of New York Press.

Walker, R. J., Williams, J. S., & Egede, L. E. (April 2016). Impact of race/ethnicity and social determinants of health on diabetes outcomes. *American Journal of the Medical Sciences, 351*(), 366–373. Retrieved from https://www.amjmedsci. org/article/S0002-9629(15)37995-7/fulltext

Washburn, D. (2018, August 31). The price of punishment: New report shows students nationwide lost 11 million school days due to suspensions. EdSource. Retrieved from https://edsource.org/2018/the-price-of-punishment-new-report-shows-students-nationwide-lost-11-million-school-days-due-to-suspensions/601889

Washington, M. (2013). Is the Black male college graduate becoming an endangered species? A multi-case analysis of the attrition of Black males in higher education. *LUX: A Journal of Transdisciplinary Writing and Research from Claremont Graduate University, 3*(1), 20.

Watkins, D. C., Walker, R. L., & Griffith, D. M. (2010). A meta-study of Black male mental health and well-being. *Journal of Black Psychology, 36*(3), 303–330.

Watkins, D. C., Walker, R. L., Griffith, D., Watkins, D. C., Green, B. L., Goodson, P., Guidry, J. J., & Stanley, C. A. (2007). Using focus groups to explore the stressful life events of Black college men. *Journal of College Student Development, 48*(1), 105–118.

Whitaker, A., Torres-Guillen, S., Morton, M., Jordan, H., Coyle, S., Mann, A., & Sun, W. (n.d). Cops and no counselors: How the lack of school mental health staff is harming students. American Civil Liberties Union. Retrieved from https://www.aclu.org/report/cops-and-nocounselors

Widra, E. (2017, June 26). Incarceration shortens life expectancy. Prison Policy Initiative. Retrieved from https://www.prisonpolicy.org/blog/2017/06/26/life_expectancy/.

Williams, D. R. (2006, February 6). Race, socioeconomic status, and health: The added effects of racism and discrimination. *Annals of the New York Academy of Sciences*. Retrieved from https://nyaspubs.onlinelibrary.wiley.com/doi/abs/10.1111/j.1749-6632.1999.tb08114.x

Williams, J., & Wilson, V. (2019, August 27). Black workers endure persistent racial disparities in employment outcomes. Economic Policy Institute. Retrieved from https://www.epi.org/publication/labor-day-2019-racial-disparities-in-employment/

Williams, J. P. (2018, May 31). Why are black children killing themselves? *US News & World Report*. Retrieved from https://www.usnews.com/news/healthiest-communities/articles/2018-05-31/whats-behind-the-higher-suicide-rate-among-black-children?fbclid=IwAR38hqCMRoomlRTQd1cl_N9qA_hp4D-ZqnPogOhOnDOx5ynLbTAcXfzP8Es

Wood, J. L., Harris III, F., & Howard, T. C. (2018). Get out! Black male suspensions in California public schools. Community College Equity Assessment Lab and the UCLA Black Male Institute.

Young Invincibles. (2017). Race and ethnicity as a blueprint to opportunity: A blueprint for higher education equity. Retrieved from https://younginvincibles.org/wpcontent/uploads/2017/05/Higher-Education-Equity.pdf

PART 2
CONSIDERING HISTORY

Chapter 4

Presidential Responses to Campus Racism
A Historical Perspective

Eddie R. Cole

College presidents are critical to addressing campus racism. Consequently, these academic leaders' responses, or the lack thereof, to racial incidents are frequently the focus of media coverage, as seen with recent events at the University of Missouri and the University of Virginia. In 2015, Missouri's university system president, Tim Wolfe, and the flagship campus chancellor, R. Bowen Loftin, resigned after weeks of muffled responses to a series of racial incidents on campus (Svrluga, 2015). In 2017, a violent clash between white nationalists and counterprotesters turned deadly, and Virginia President Teresa Sullivan's handling of the "Unite the Right" rally on campus garnered widespread criticism (Jarvis, 2019; Stripling, 2017). In both instances, the critiques demonstrate the direct link between college presidents and the processing of campus racism by the public. However, the incidents at Missouri and Virginia and those elsewhere are only a reminder of the persistence and prominence of racism on college campuses.

Racism has been embedded within American higher education since its beginning. In 1622, the initial plan for the first college in the colonies was abandoned following a massacre in the Virginia colony more than a decade before Harvard was founded (Fausz, 1977; Kramer, 2016; Torrence, 1915; William & Mary, 1855). The massacre was the Powhatan's defense of their land, but white historians later described it as "an insurrection of savages" (Adams, 1887, p. 11). In turn, the white supremacists who led the colonial colleges enrolled indigenous youth and subscribed to the "propagation of the gospel among the natives" (p. 14). Following the American Revolution, subsequent generations of white academic leaders extended those same racist ideas toward Chicano and Asian American students throughout the 1800s (Anderson, 2002; Horsman 1981; MacDonald, 2013; McClain, 1994). All the while, for nearly two centuries, the earliest colleges and universities profited from the enslavement of Africans (Wilder, 2013).

History has shaped the current racial crisis in American higher education; however, contemporary presidents consistently fail to acknowledge history when responding to racial incidents (Cole & Harper, 2017). This lack of history is vital because the racist-themed parties in which white students dress in stereotypical costumes mocking other racial groups, the videos of them using racial epithets, and other forms of harassment are not isolated incidents. This racist behavior may appear more pronounced since social media and other forms of digital media capture and disseminate it faster than ever before. Yet in actuality, the present-day racist's repertoire is merely an ode to the past, and this brief exploration of the last century demonstrates what we know and what remains to be understood about college presidents' responses to campus racism.

In October 1915, during World War I, Black physicians publicly criticized Johns Hopkins University officials for an uptick in racist practices. As customary during Jim Crow, Black patients were treated in segregated wards of the Johns Hopkins Hospital, where Black physicians were freely admitted to treat their patients. The facilities were indicative of the "separate but equal" ethos that guided much of American society, and Black medical professionals functioned within that environment with equal access to their patients no different than their white medical counterparts. However, there was "a change [in] attitude on the part of some folks connected with the hospital" ("Physicians Get Raw Deal," 1915). Johns Hopkins officials started requiring Black physicians to see the hospital superintendent for a permit or wait until visiting hours before seeing their patients. "This latter arrangement," the Black-owned *Baltimore Afro-American* reported, "the physicians consider a humiliation" ("Physicians Get Raw Deal," 1915).

The Black physicians' treatment became the focus of discussion at the Maryland Medical, Pharmaceutical, and Dental Association meeting that fall. Later, Black leaders called for Black Baltimoreans to support Provident Hospital, a local facility that served Black patients without segregationist practices, "rather than trying to get them in 'Jim Crow' wards in other institutions" ("Physicians Get Raw Deal," 1915). The actions of Johns Hopkins officials were reflective of the broader societal shifts that were tightening the social chains on Black people. For instance, some Black veterans returning from World War I were lynched for refusing to remove their military uniforms upon arriving in the United States (Davis, 2008). This behavior was a form of white rage in response to Black people having any outwardly dignified status, and Johns Hopkins academic leaders essentially stripped Black doctors of their white coats.

This type of behavior remained common at Johns Hopkins during this era. It was an accepted fact that academic leaders of the Baltimore university held the color line ("The Jew and the Negro," 1920), and the hospital was the epitome of this. By 1925, Black leaders juxtaposed the racism on campus with the university namesake's will, which stated his original intention for the institution. As an abolitionist, Johns Hopkins had intended for funds from his estate to be used to educate the children of Baltimore. Concerning the purpose of the hospital, the will read, "The hospital shall be for the indigent sick of this city and its environs without regard to age, sex, or color . . . and the poor of this city and state of all races . . . shall be received into this hospital without charge" (Winchester, 1925). Paul Winchester, a Maryland journalist, further explained that "trust funds . . . have been perverted to other uses and a very large portion of the work of that institution is devoted to other purposes than the donor intended" (Winchester, 1925).

As such, the critiques of Johns Hopkins were widespread. In 1926, W. E. B. Du Bois, a distinguished scholar and leading Black intellectual of the time, considered it one of the nation's more racially prejudiced colleges ("Johns Hopkins Leads," 1926). Two years later, the university was critiqued during the South Atlantic Championships hosted on campus because Black athletes were initially barred from competing. Following pressure from the Amateur Athletic Union and the South Atlantic Committee, Henry Iddins, assistant to the campus treasurer, publicly stated that Johns Hopkins would allow the Black athletes to compete ("Hopkins Official Denies," 1928).

Throughout this period, Johns Hopkins President Frank J. Goodnow, who led the University from 1914 to 1929, was largely silent about campus racism, although he was not a quiet leader. For example, in June 1926, he was quoted in *The New York Times* saying, "Stand for freedom of thought and expression. Fight intolerance." Goodnow added, "It is only as we can know the truth that this land can really be made 'the land of the free'"

("Fight Intolerance," 1926). The irony in Goodnow's statements delivered during the graduate school commencement was that all Americans were not free at Johns Hopkins. White academic leaders called for intellectual freedom. However, in the same breath, they also maintained strict racial segregation. This attitude highlighted Goodnow's nonresponse approach to campus racism as college presidents perpetuated campus racism regardless of institutional type.

At Hampton Institute in Virginia, white administrators enforced segregated practices at the private Black college (Anderson, 1988; Kendi, 2012). Because white missionary organizations and philanthropists founded numerous Black colleges, it was common for many private Black colleges to have a white president and several white faculty members in the first half of the 20th century. In the 1920s, however, tensions boiled at Hampton as Black students protested white professors' opposition to hiring qualified Black teachers and the operation of a segregated club on campus (Anderson, 1988). The Black resistance to campus racism was punctuated under James E. Gregg, who led Hampton from 1918 to 1929 ("Discrimination Rife," 1934).

In January 1931, following the less-than-one-year presidency of George P. Phenix, Arthur Howe was named Hampton president ("Dr. Arthur Howe Quits," 1940; "Hampton Principal Drowns," 1930). On the one hand, Howe did not maintain a strict color line within the Mansion House on campus. On the other, this shift made him different from his predecessors, who had not allowed Black guests to attend events or mingle across races, and Howe's actions angered some white campus stakeholders who protested events at the mansion with mixed company ("Discrimination Rife," 1934).

Howe upheld other racist traditions. For example, the B&B Club, a literary and drama organization, admitted only white members and often used campus facilities for its events (Howe was a member). Hampton also operated the Winona School, an on-campus school exclusively for the children of the white faculty and staff ("Discrimination Rife," 1934). Additionally, in 1934, Howe fired Wilhelmina B. Patterson, a Black music instructor at Hampton. It was speculated that her dismissal was in retaliation toward those who had charged white administrators and faculty with racial discrimination, but Howe was "mum" on the Patterson matter ("Ousted Music Teacher," 1934). His silence was shortly afterward supported by other whites when the Baptist Ministers Conference in southeastern Virginia declined to adopt a resolution that condemned the "alleged discrimination in the administration of Hampton Institute" ("Ministers Decline," 1934). Thus, societal norms allowed racism on campus to manifest itself unabated, even on Black college campuses ("Jim-Crowism at Hampton," 1934).

Of course, racism knows no regional boundaries, and Chicago was a leading example of this throughout the 20th century. Chicago was notorious for its racist housing practices (see Hirsch, 1983; Moore, 2016; Winling, 2017). These issues existed before World War II, but the presidents of Chicago's universities only amplified the racism. Postwar migration brought more Southerners to Chicago, and Black neighborhoods soon expanded beyond long-standing racial boundaries. Unfortunately, academic leaders at the University of Chicago (UChicago) and Northwestern University helped maintain those borders (Cole, 2020).

In 1945, Milton Mayer, assistant to UChicago Chancellor Robert M. Hutchins, charged the university as responsible for the upkeep of the local housing restrictions. He then urged local residents to "badger the university day and night, in season and out, until it does something to attack restrictive covenants" ("Chicago U. Aide Hits Own," 1945). Throughout the 1930s and the early 1940s, UChicago spent more than $100,000 on "community interests," the bulk of which was used to protect restrictive covenants (Hirsch, 1983). Hutchins was hired in 1929 and responded by adamantly explaining that UChicago did not tolerate campus racism. As an example, he said the institution admitted Black students on the same terms as white students, citing as evidence that the fall 1937 freshman class's youngest student was a 13-year-old Black student. "It is the constant effort of the faculty of the university to educate men and women to resist all sorts of prejudice and to guide their loves by the light of reason," he stated (Hutchins, 1937). Nevertheless, this was a deflection from the reality of housing, and Hutchins was partly to blame for the city's segregation as academic leaders financially supported local whites' efforts to keep neighborhoods segregated.

Considering this, some students took heed of Mayer's charge and demanded that UChicago officials adjust their housing practices. In 1947, a number of students threatened to strike if a conference with Hutchins did not result in an agreement to end racism within the UChicago medical facilities. This demand included the denial of medical treatment to nonwhites and, when treated, segregated rooms aimed at keeping whites from other racial groups. Multiple student groups—including the American Veterans Committee and the Committee on Racial Equality (later named the Congress of Racial Equality)—rallied to end Jim Crow at UChicago, and more than 400 students supported the demands made to Chancellor Hutchins (Jarrett, 1947).

In 1948, Hutchins was at the center of another racial conflict when Mary F. Hutchins, a Northwestern senior and his daughter, accused Northwestern administrators of forcing a women's counselor to resign. The younger Hutchins charged in the *Daily Northwestern* that the counselor, Ruth McCarn, was sympathetic to racial problems and that Franklyn B. Snyder, president of Northwestern, considered her "too liberal about Jews and Negroes" ("Student Paper Revives," 1948). In a written statement, the Northwestern president responded and denied "any truth to the [Mary F. Hutchins] statement" ("Fired for Race Interest," 1948; "Student Paper Revives," 1948). He then called the McCarn situation a nonissue, saying that when the "matter came up originally, it was thoroughly discussed by the proper committees of the board of trustees, which recommended that Mrs. McCarn's resignation be accepted" ("Student Paper Revives," 1948).

As Snyder responded to the controversy at Northwestern, there was a larger shift in the role and scope of the college presidency—a shift that would further influence how racism on campuses emerged. The international pressure that accompanied World War II and the Cold War, alongside increasing college attendance, resulted in a remarkable amount of power and influence being bestowed upon college presidents. As a result, many of them used their new realm of influence to mold institutional, state, and national racial policies and practices. This influence was clear with "urban renewal," the informal name for a federal program that revitalized land use by removing what many considered slum areas to acquire property near their universities. In 1948, the Supreme Court ruled in *Shelley v. Kraemer* that racially restrictive covenants were unconstitutional (see Gonda, 2015). Afterward, urban renewal programs enticed academic leaders who used institutional, state, and federal resources to halt urban encroachment while simultaneously taking over slum areas in an effort to expand their facilities (Cole, 2020). Nevertheless, the interests of these college presidents were often self-serving and, thus neglected one of the nation's most prevalent modes of campus racism.

In 1951, UChicago trustees hired Lawrence A. Kimpton as chancellor. However, during Hutchins's last years as chancellor, the encroachment of Black residents from west of the Hyde Park neighborhood had negatively affected the university. At the time, people living in "the South Side's Negro ghetto spilled into the area," and by the close of the 1940s, undergraduate enrollment at the university fell to 1,350. Overcrowding affected enrollment more than the Great Depression, did as enrollment fell to its lowest since the 1915–2016 academic year when 1,403 students were enrolled. "We must find ways to reverse the trend," Kimpton noted ("The Campus Fights Back," 1960). The dismal student numbers, coupled with the Housing Act of 1949 and its appropriation of federal funds for slum clearance programs, presented new opportunities for college presidents despite public critiques.

Chicago Urban League President Nathaniel Oglesby Calloway questioned the contradictory nature of the urban renewal plans. "It's not that we don't want slum clearance; decaying areas and outmoded streets must be rebuilt," said Calloway, who held a PhD from Iowa State University and an MD from the University of Illinois (Anderson, 1993; Chicago Urban League, 1958). "But can we, in justice, tear down people's homes when we continue to restrict their free movement into new homes? In other words, can slum clearance and the perpetuation of residential segregation live together?" (Chicago Urban League, 1958).

By 1956, two-thirds of the city's 86,000 residents displaced by urban renewal projects were Black (Chicago Urban League, 1958). When pressed about the displacement of Black residents, particularly on the South Side near campus, Kimpton prioritized the university's existence over the local housing segregation that UChicago administrators had long perpetuated. "A great university must be part of a great urban environment," he said, "but how does a university remain great as it participates in the deterioration of our American cities?" ("Urban Decay Feared," 1957). He then explained how UChicago had "destroyed" 48 acres of South Side "blight" and spent $5.3 million to buy dilapidated buildings for razing ("Urban Decay Feared," 1957).

Kimpton led the South East Chicago Commission, a white citizens group that was the driving arm behind South Side displacement. UChicago officials and their affiliates repeatedly lobbied federal and state officials to amend housing policies to allow the nation's academic leaders to proceed with urban renewal projects (Cole, 2020). When pressed on the racial implications, Kimpton's response was simply, "The very life of the university is at stake" (Wehrwein, 1958).

In 1960, Black college students in the South introduced a new element to the urban renewal crisis unfolding near college campuses, and many white students in the Northeast, Midwest, and West sympathized with their Southern counterparts. This element heightened the criticism of the presidents of urban universities who supported these programs. During the 1961–1962 academic year, UChicago students held a sit-in in the office of the new chancellor, George W. Beadle, to demand the University end its involvement in housing discrimination. The first sit-in demonstration was staged by the Congress of Racial Equality (CORE) north of the Mason–

Dixon line ("Winds of Change," 1962). Beadle's response was straightforward: changing housing policy needed to be slow to prevent white flight and the destruction of the University ("UC Segregation Criticized," 1962). However, when it came to urban renewal, college presidents elsewhere did not adopt the institutional-minded responses at UChicago.

The following year, 1963, was especially violent and pivotal to the fight for racial equality, as historians, civil rights leaders, and journalists have repeatedly documented (J. Baldwin, 1963; Chow, 2013, Goduti, 2013). In May 1963, some 250 residents of Syracuse, New York, participated in a sympathy rally against recent events in Alabama, where Birmingham police officers used high-powered water hoses and police dogs on civil rights demonstrators, primarily children (Hailey, 1963). Ten days after the Syracuse rally for Birmingham, *The Post-Standard* reported that most local Black families being relocated by urban renewal plans did not want to move ("Human Rights," 1963; Moss, 1963). By the fall, some Syracuse University faculty and students made a direct connection between racial violence in the South and the urban renewal program in their city.

In September 1963, only days after the March on Washington for Jobs and Freedom, the first Syracuse protest occurred at an urban renewal site. Shortly afterward, 14 CORE demonstrators were arrested for trespassing on a site where a building was being demolished. Within the first three days of demonstrations, there were 38 arrests, 25 of which were Syracuse students (Case, 1963; "Nab 14," 1963). On September 17, more than 200 people—faculty, students, and administrators—assembled in Hendricks Chapel on campus to hear CORE leaders and members of the Syracuse University Committee on Equality discuss the recent protests. This gathering was two days after four young girls were murdered in the bombing of the 16th Street Baptist Church in Birmingham. As a result, Syracuse activists had no worry of arrest when Blacks in the South were losing their lives. "We don't argue that laws against trespassing are unjust," one demonstrator told the audience. "We may violate literal laws, but spiritual laws are more important" ("Demonstrations, Arrests Continue," 1963).

Immediately following the gathering, at 10:30 p.m., Chancellor William Pearson Tolley issued a statement printed on the front page of *The Daily Orange*. He stated that citizens have the right to object to what they felt was an unjust law, but that those who intentionally violated the law would face consequences. The chancellor said, "For those whose conscience dictates a deliberate violation of law and order, the university may have compassion, but it cannot stand between them and the civil authorities or offer them institutional aid. Civil disobedience is a grave act fraught with serious consequences for the individual and for society." Tolley continued, "Those who feel or reason their way to this position must be willing to accept the penalties and consequences for themselves. Such penalties and consequences may entail extended imprisonment by civil authorities. For those associated with the university, the trustees and administrative officers must reserve the right to impose such penalty as individual actions warrant" (Tolley, 1963). When this response is combined with his others, it is clear that Tolley envisioned racism as a Southern issue but events in Syracuse as a matter of civil disobedience—thus ignoring the racism in New York. The Southern violence also stirred new questions about race and free speech for college presidents. In late 1963, a cohort of Ivy League presidents responded differently to the racist rhetoric of white supremacists invited to their campuses in the Northeast. In October 1963, segregationist and Mississippi Governor Ross Barnett spoke at Princeton University following an invitation from the student debate society. The invitation ignited a debate over whether Barnett's presence would represent an implied endorsement of his racist views while Princeton was also beginning to recruit more Black students (Cole, 2020).

Prior to Barnett's visit, Princeton President Robert F. Goheen had condemned the Mississippi governor. "The invitation to Governor Barnett to speak here the night of October 1st runs hard against this basic tenet of the university, and personally, I judge the invitation to be untimely and ill considered," he said. Yet he also agreed that Barnett deserved to be heard: "At the same time, we have no less a commitment to the principle of free inquiry and debate" (Goheen, 1963). After Barnett's visit, Goheen responded by launching a series of initiatives to enroll and hire more Black people at Princeton.

Invitations to white supremacists were handled differently by other college presidents. For example, segregationist and Alabama Governor George C. Wallace was invited to the University of Pennsylvania and was scheduled to speak in November 1963. There, President Gaylord P. Harnwell initially denied that Wallace had been invited by the university, saying no invitation had been offered; however, Donald Angell, vice president of Penn, later admitted that a group of law students had invited Wallace in July 1963 before the bombings in Birmingham (Peters, 1963). Wallace's invitation to Yale that fall was rescinded, but he did speak at Harvard shortly after Barnett spoke at Princeton in October 1963 (Chauncey, 2017; "The Wallace Speech," 1963).

Related to free speech was the push for predominately white institutions to truly embrace the free exchange of ideas by becoming more racially and ethnically diverse across student bodies and faculty. Up to that point, Black, Latinx, Asian, Chicano, and indigenous students experienced segregation on campus, if they were not denied outright enrollment, at mainstream institutions. The same applied to faculty jobs as well (Anderson, 1993). As a result, racism took new forms on college campuses, with more underrepresented students and faculty being hired during the late 1960s. Scholars have carefully outlined the challenges and pitfalls associated with white academic leaders' recruitment and enrollment of the first significant wave of nonwhite students and the trauma many of those students experienced at white colleges and universities (Biondi, 2012; Bradley, 2018; Karabel, 2005; Kendi, 2012; Williamson, 1999, Williamson, 2003). However, college presidents were also tasked with responding to the campus racism experienced by faculty with those same backgrounds.

In August 1969, on the campus of the University of California, Los Angeles, Black, Mexican American, Asian American, and indigenous faculty and students formed a coalition to demand housing for students from those groups. In that instance, UCLA Chancellor Charles E. Young advocated for the housing solution in response to the isolation those students felt on campus ("UCLA Capitulates," 1969); however, Young could not respond as affirmatively when it came to the controversy surrounding the 25-year-old Angela Davis, who had just joined the UCLA faculty. Davis was a member of the Black Panther Party and a self-admitted Communist. In September 1969, she was fired from her position as a philosophy professor by the university system's board of regents. In a rebuttal, Davis characterized the firing as an attack "on an individual. It affects the entire black community and the university and obviously is an attack on the autonomy of the university" ("Fired UCLA Professor," 1969).

Her final point about the autonomy of UCLA was significant. Throughout the 1960s, UCLA chancellors had reoccurring conflicts with UC central administration located in Berkeley. This conflict was most pronounced between former UCLA Chancellor Franklin D. Murphy and former UC President Clark Kerr (Cole, 2018). Nevertheless, the UC academic council unanimously opposed the termination and defended Davis's right to be a member of the Communist Party ("Academic Council Defends," 1969). Shortly afterward, in late October, a California superior court judge ruled the firing illegal, and Davis remained on the UCLA faculty. It was determined that "mere membership" in the Communist Party was not grounds for firing ("Angela Safe," 1969). However, as historian Ibram X. Kendi

(2016) explained, "[Conservative Governor Ronald] Reagan began searching for another way to fire her" (p. 411).

In May 1970, despite Davis's victory the previous fall, the regents fired her again. Instead of citing her Communist affiliations, this time Reagan and the regents justified their action as simply being a case of not renewing her contract as a visiting assistant professor. The regents' decision overrode her academic department and Chancellor Young's recommendation that Davis continue to serve on the UCLA faculty ("Miss Davis Fired," 1970). The attempt to rehire Davis was further complicated when, in August 1970, a shootout in a Marin County, California, courtroom ended with a judge and three Black men being killed (Kendi, 2016). The Federal Bureau of Investigation charged Davis with murder, among other charges, because she had purchased a firearm involved in the shooting. After a two-month search, the FBI arrested Davis in New York in October. Two years later, however, jurors found Davis not guilty (Kendi, 2016).

Many citizens, former colleagues, and others had long believed that racism was at the heart of the public critique and elected officials' actions against Davis. Therefore, following her being found not guilty after the three-year ordeal, rumors soon swirled that Davis could be rehired at UCLA. Regent John E. Canaday said that rehiring Davis "would be outrageous and inconceivable" (Trombley, 1972). Yet in response Chancellor Young said, "There is a possibility that she might want to teach in California again." However, when asked if UCLA officials had been in contact with Davis, he said, "That would not be proper for other than confidential discussion at this time" ("Chancellor Mum," 1972). Years later, as Young neared retirement, the *Los Angeles Times* assessed, "If anything made his reputation, it was his defense of acting professor Angela Davis, a Communist whose politics drew the ire of UC regents. In a test of wills, Young refused to fire her" (Wallace, 1996).

"A test of wills" is a fair description of the delicate situation in which college presidents find themselves when addressing racism. Although they are looked upon as leaders, various campus stakeholders have affected how, or even if, college presidents respond to campus racism. Moreover, over the past century, these issues still have not been reconciled. As a result, historical perspectives—across Black or white campuses, private or public, and multiple regions—demonstrate how college presidents' responses mirror many of those that academic leaders employ today. Thus, the central questions now are, what is the role of the college president in advancing equity on college campuses, and what lessons for practice can contemporary presidents heed from the past?

One historical takeaway is that college presidents' silence has been one of the most dangerous responses to campus racism. It has been a passively violent approach that perpetuates the racist practices, ideas, and policies that have reverberated throughout American higher education since its founding. This tactic was evident when citizens publicly challenged campus discrimination and college presidents did not acknowledge the issue. Although legalized segregation does not function as it did a century ago, college presidents today are still hesitant to directly condemn racism (see Cole & Harper, 2017; Jarvis, 2019).

Another lesson is that institutional-minded responses also run counter to racial justice. By the mid-20th century, societal pressure over the image of American democracy and the reality of racial exclusion altered how several college presidents, particularly those at non-Southern institutions, responded to campus racism. Those presidents often touted themselves as being more enlightened than their Southern counterparts. Yet their responses to campus racism prioritized public relations over acknowledging their racist behaviors. This strategy was employed by urban university presidents who used urban renewal programs to displace thousands of families—especially Black, Puerto Rican, or Asian American households—during the 1950s and 1960s. Those college presidents championed their willingness to admit students of all races (compared to segregated Southern institutions). The irony is that the focus on public relations, not racism, persists as a guiding philosophy for several contemporary presidents (Schmidt, 2015).

Finally, the presidential responses of the 1960s and 1970s provide distinct lessons for free speech policies, academic freedom, and campus racism. White supremacists being invited to speak on college campuses is not new, considering that racist ideas guided the development of American higher education. Historically, these figures' invitations were rescinded or honored. Nevertheless, in one instance, at Princeton, a dramatic shift in racial policy was advanced following the visit from a white supremacist Southern governor. That presidential response demonstrates how academic leaders can condemn racist speech and also use the moment to implement campus policies that validate how the campus condemns racism. Yet the handling of these polarizing figures remains controversial and varies, with little certainty of how to protect free speech and maintain racial inclusivity (Nossel, 2018).

These lessons and others are critical. College presidents are pertinent to setting campus diversity agendas (Kezar, 2007; Kezar & Eckel, 2008), and their responses to racism are the foundation for any actions aimed at achieving equity. Despite how societal contexts and social movements have evolved over the decades, this is important, because the broader trends in racist incidents on college campuses are consistent. College campuses continue to "swallow cities" and displace communities of color (D. L. Baldwin, 2017). Like the "Tequila Sunrise" party at UCLA in 1985, when the Beta Theta Pi fraternity used racist tropes that denigrated Latinx culture (see Haraguchi, 1985; Howell, 1985; Ramos, 1985), themed parties and blackface still regularly occur on campuses (Murphy, 2019). Likewise, since the election of US President Donald J. Trump, the engagement with federal officials has stirred controversy regarding how the presidents of historically Black colleges and universities (HBCU) respond to racism (Hartocollis & Weiland, 2017). Considering that these racial issues have been constant, college presidents' historical responses to racism are ripe for contemporary presidents and those interested in understanding how academic leaders can embrace the influence of their position and commit to racial justice—a commitment that is the hallmark of any institution *truly* dedicated to liberation.

References

Academic council defends Angela Davis. (1969, October 2). *Los Angeles Sentinel*, p. A11.

Adams, H. B. (1887). *The College of William & Mary: Contribution to the history of higher education*. Government Printing Office.

Anderson, J. D. (1988). *The education of Blacks in the South, 1860–1935*. University of North Carolina Press.

Anderson, J. D. (1993). Race, meritocracy, and the American academy during the immediate post–World War II era. *History of Education Quarterly 33*(2), 151–175.

Anderson, J. D. (2002). Race in American higher education. In W. A. Smith, P. G. Altbach, & K. Lomotey (Eds.), *The racial crisis in American higher education: Continuing challenges for the twenty-first century* (2nd ed., pp. 3–21). SUNY Press.

Angela safe—for a while. (1969, October 23). *Los Angeles Sentinel*, p. A1.

Baldwin, D. L. (2017, July 30). When universities swallow cities. *The Chronicle of Higher Education*. Retrieved from https://www.chronicle.com/article/When-Universities-Swallow/240739

Baldwin, J. (1963). *The fire next time*. Dial Press.
Biondi, M. (2012). *The Black revolution on campus*. University of California Press.
Bradley, S. M. (2018). *Upending the ivory tower: Civil rights, Black Power, and the Ivy League*. New York University Press.
The campus fights back. (1960, January 4). *Newsweek*.
Case, R. G. (1963, September 15). Pickets plan return: Mayor orders job continued. *Syracuse Herald-Journal*.
Chancellor mum on Angela's UCLA chances. (1972, September 21). *Los Angeles Sentinel*, p. C7.
Chauncey Jr., S. (2017, November 29). On hard decisions. (Letter to the editor). *The Yale Daily News*. Retrieved from https://yaledailynews.com/blog/2017/11/29/letter-11-28/
Chicago U. aide hits own school for racism. (1945, August 25). *Chicago Defender*, p. 11.
Chicago Urban League. (1958, June). *Urban renewal and the Negro in Chicago: Chicago Urban League Report*. University of Chicago, Hyde Park Historical Society Collection (Box 78, Folder 15), Special Collections Research Center (archival location abbreviated as "SCRC" hereafter).
Chow, K. (2013, December 31). As 2013 winds to an end, so do the tweets of 1963. National Public Radio. Retrieved from https://www.npr.org/sections/codeswitch/2013/12/31/258664831/as-2013-winds-to-an-end-so-do-the-tweets-of-1963.
Cole, E. R. (2018). College presidents and Black student protests: A historical perspective on the image of racial inclusion and the reality of exclusion. *Peabody Journal of Education, 93*(1), 78–89.
Cole, E. R. (2020). *The campus color line: College presidents and the struggle for Black freedom*. Princeton University Press.
Cole, E. R., & Harper, S. R. (2017). Race and rhetoric: An analysis of college presidents' statements on campus racial incidents. *Journal of Diversity in Higher Education 10*(4), 318–333.
Davis, D. A. (2008). Not only war is hell: World War I and African American lynching narratives. *African American Review 42*(3/4), 477–491.
Demonstrations, arrests continue: Rally speakers explain "why." (1963, September 18). *The Daily Orange*.
Discrimination rife on campus of Hampt'n Inst. (1934, February 17). *Norfolk Journal and Guide*, p. 1.
Dr. Arthur Howe quits Hampton Institute post. (1940, March 12). *The Herald Tribune*.
Fausz, J. F. (1977). *The Powhatan uprising of 1622: A historical study of ethnocentrism and cultural conflict*. (Unpublished PhD diss.). The College of William & Mary, Williamsburg, Virginia.
Fight intolerance, Dr. Goodnow urges. (1926, June 9). *The New York Times*, p. 9.

Fired for race interest, says ex-aid at N.U.: Asserts liberal views roused Dr. Snyder. (1948, November 18). *Chicago Daily Tribune*, p. 11.

Fired UCLA professor charges racial bias. (1969, September 25). *Los Angeles Sentinel*, p. A1.

Goduti, Jr., P. A. (2013). *Robert F. Kennedy and the shaping of civil rights, 1960–1964*. McFarland & Company.

Goheen, R. F. (1963, September 24). Robert F. Goheen statement on Barnett. Goheen President Records (Box 425, Folder 2), Princeton University Archives.

Gonda, J. D. (2015). *Unjust deeds: The restrictive covenant cases and the making of the civil rights movement*. University of North Carolina Press.

Hailey, F. (1963, May 4). Dogs and hoses repulse Negroes at Birmingham: 3 students bitten in second day of demonstrations against segregation. *The New York Times*, p. 1.

Hampton principal drowns at Buckroe: Dr. Phenix, 66, headed institute for less than a year. (1930, October 11). *The Baltimore Afro-American*, p. 10.

Haraguchi, S. (1985, April 15). UPC continues theme party debate. *The Daily Bruin*, p. 1.

Hartocollis, A., & Weiland, N. (2017, March 4). Campus backlash after leaders of Black colleges meet with Trump. *The New York Times*. Retrieved from https://www.nytimes.com/2017/03/04/us/backlash-black-colleges-trump.html

Hirsch, A. R. (1983). *Making the second ghetto: Race and housing in Chicago, 1940–1960*. University of Chicago Press.

Hopkins official denies color bar: Race athletes welcome at Homewood if o.k. with A.A.U., Iddins says. (1928, May 26). *The Baltimore Afro-American*, p. 10.

Horsman, R. (1981). *Race and manifest destiny: The origins of American racial Anglo-Saxonism*. Harvard University Press.

Howell, C. (1985, April 15). Beta party sparks anti-racism protest. *Daily Bruin*, p. 1.

Human rights luncheon: Negro families opposing move to public housing (1963, May 23). *The Post-Standard*.

Hutchins, R. M. (1937, November 6). Hutchins statement on restrictive covenants, University of Chicago, George W. Beadle Records (Box 265, Folder 1), SCRC.

Jarrett, V. (1947, December 6). U. of C. medical bias under fire. *Chicago Defender*, p. 9.

Jarvis, W. (2019, June 27). Dozens of presidents condemned hatred in Charlottesville. What were they really saying? *The Chronicle of Higher Education*. Retrieved from https://www.chronicle.com/article/Dozens-of-Presidents-Condemned/246581

The Jew and the Negro. (1920, November 12). *The Baltimore Afro-American*, p. 9.

Jim-Crowism at Hampton Inst. causes stir: Visiting white college students' presence is responsible. (1934, May 5). *Norfolk Journal and Guide*, p. 10.

Johns Hopkins leads in race prejudice. (1926, March 20). *The Baltimore Afro-American*, p. 14.

Karabel, J. (2005). *The chosen: The hidden history of admissions and exclusion at Harvard, Yale, and Princeton*. Houghton Mifflin Company.

Kendi, I. X. (formerly Ibram H. Rogers) (2012). *The Black campus movement: Black students and the racial reconstruction of higher education, 1965–1972*. Palgrave Macmillan.

Kendi, I. X. (2016). *Stamped from the beginning: The definitive history of racist ideas in America*. Basic Books.

Kezar, A. J. (2007). Learning from and with students: College presidents creating organizational learning to advance diversity agendas. *NASPA Journal, 44*(3), 578–610.

Kezar, A. J., & Eckel, P. (2008). Advancing diversity agendas on campus: Examining transactional and transformational presidential leadership styles. *International Journal of Leadership in Education, 11*(4), 379–405.

Kramer, M. J. (2016). *The 1622 Powhatan uprising and its impact on Anglo-Indian relations*. (Unpublished master's thesis). Illinois State University, Bloomington.

MacDonald, V. M. (2013). Demanding their rights: The Latino struggle for educational access and equity. In *American Latinos and the Making of the United States: A Theme Study*, pp. 306–329. National Park Service. US Department of Interior.

McClain, C. J. (1994). *In search of equality: The Chinese struggle against discrimination in nineteenth-century America*. University of California Press.

Minsters decline to voice disapproval of reported discrimination at Hampton. (1934, March 17). *Norfolk Journal and Guide*, p. 1.

Miss Davis fired: Will file suit. (1970, June 25). *Los Angeles Sentinel*, p. A1.

Moore, N. Y. (2016). *The south side: A portrait of Chicago and American segregation*. St. Martin's Pres).

Moss, S. (1963, May 13). Orderly contrast: 250 march protesting treatment of Negroes. *The Post-Standard*.

Murphy, B. (2019, February 21). Blackface, KKK hoods and mock lynchings: Review of 900 yearbooks finds blatant racism. *USA Today*. Retrieved from https://www.usatoday.com/in-depth/news/investigations/2019/02/20/blackface-racist-photos-yearbooks-colleges-kkk-lynching-mockery-fraternities-black-70-s-80-s/2858921002/

Nab 14 CORE demonstrators. (1963, September 17). *Syracuse Herald-Journal*.

Nossel, S. (2018, May 25). You can only protect campus speech if you acknowledge racism. *The Washington Post*. https://www.washingtonpost.com/outlook/you-can-only-protect-campus-speech-if-you-acknowledge-racism/2018/05/25/5c26bbcc-59ed-11e8-b656-a5f8c2a9295d_story.html

Ousted music teacher forced to quit Hampton Inst. campus: Presidn't Howe demands she leave Jan. 29. (1934, February 3). *Norfolk Journal and Guide*, p. 1.

Peters, A. (1963, September 28). Official admits Wallace invited to speak at U. of P.: Earlier story quoting Harnwell conflicts with new admission. *The Philadelphia Tribune*, p. 3.

Physicians get raw deal: Policy of discrimination against colored physicians practiced at Johns Hopkins Hospital. (1915, October 9). *The Baltimore Afro-American*, p. 1.

Ramos, G. (1985, April 19). "Tequila sunrise" party sparks protests of racism at UCLA, p. SD24.

Schmidt, P. (2015, April 21). Colleges respond to racist incidents as if their chief worry is bad PR, studies find. *The Chronicle of Higher Education*. Retrieved from https://www.chronicle.com/article/Colleges-Respond-to-Racist/229517

Stripling, J. (2017, November 20). Inside the U. of Virginia's response to a chaotic white-supremacist rally. *The Chronicle of Higher Education*. Retrieved from https://www.chronicle.com/article/Inside-the-U-of-Virginia-s/241832

Student paper revives "race" charge at N.U. (1948, November 17). *Chicago Daily Tribune*, p. 21.

Svrluga, S. (2015, November 9). U. Missouri president, chancellor resigns over handling of racial incidents. *The Washington Post*. Retrieved from https://www.washingtonpost.com/news/grade-point/wp/2015/11/09/missouris-student-government-calls-for-university-presidents-removal/

Tolley, W. P. (1963, September 18). Bulletin: Chancellor Tolley statement. *The Daily Orange*.

Torrence, W. C. (1915). Henrico County, Virginia: Beginnings of its families: Part I. *The William & Mary Quarterly 24*(2), 116–142.

Trombley, W. (1972, September 15). Reemployment of Angela Davis under consideration at UCLA. *Los Angeles Times*, p. A1.

UC segregation criticized. (1962, January 17). *Chicago Maroon*, p. 1.

UCLA capitulates to demands of minorities. (1969, August 28). *Los Angeles Sentinel*, p. A8.

Urban decay feared: Chicago U. chancellor cities threat to school. (1957, November 6). *The New York Times*, p. 72.

Wallace, A. (1996, February 15). UCLA Chancellor Young to retire. *Los Angeles Times*. Retrieved from http://articles.latimes.com/1996-02-15/news/mn-36332_1_chancellor-young/2

The Wallace speech. (1963, October 24). *The Harvard Crimson*. Retrieved from https://www.thecrimson.com/article/1963/10/24/the-wallace-speech-pone-can-hardly/

Wehrwein, A. C. (1958, September 28). Urban renewal project dividing Chicago: Racial issue marks clash over big rebuilding plan for university region. *The New York Times*, p. 54.

Wilder, C. S. (2013). *Ebony and ivy: Race, slavery, and the troubled history of America's universities*. Bloomsbury Press.

William & Mary. (1855). Catalogue of William and Mary College. The W&M Digital Archive. Retrieved from https://digitalarchive.wm.edu/bitstream/handle/10288/13564/catalogueofwilli1855coll.pdf;jsessionid=4B73D3DC50B5299892A35A1755412CFE?sequence=2

Williamson, J. A. (1999). In defense of themselves: The Black student struggle and recognition at predominantly white colleges and universities. *The Journal of Negro Education 68*(1), 92–105.
Williamson, J. A. (2003). *Black power on campus: The University of Illinois, 1965–75.* University of Illinois Press.
Winchester, P. (1925, June 13). Late Johns Hopkins' will disregarded by trustees: Johns Hopkins Univ. perverted its funds. *The Baltimore Afro-American*, p. A10.
Winds of change over the Chicago campus. (1962, February 6). *The London Times.*
Winling, L. C. (2017). *Building the ivory tower: Universities and metropolitan development in the twentieth century.* University of Pennsylvania Press.

Chapter 5

Race-Conscious Affirmative Action in US Higher Education in an Era of Pronounced White Racial Backlash

María C. Ledesma, Uma Mazyck Jayakumar, and Kenyon L. Whitman

Critical race legal scholar Kimberlé Crenshaw (2007) has written, "What most people think they know about affirmative action isn't right, and what is right about affirmative action most people don't know" (p. 131). Indeed, since its inception, affirmative action has remained among the most maligned and misunderstood social policies in both public and legal debates surrounding educational opportunity, especially concerning postsecondary access (Chemerinsky, 1996). Too often, these debates are dehistoricized (Crenshaw, 2007; Ledesma, 2012; Torres, 2015), resulting in (at best) simplistic and (at worst) disingenuous (mis)characterizations. Moreover, the policy is described very differently by supporters and detractors (Ledesma, 2012). Those who seek to uphold affirmative action within college admissions suggest it is an indispensable tool in the quest for educational equity and social justice. Opponents see it as nothing more than a blatant—even illegal—attempt to privilege race above all else in granting admission to the nation's most sought-after postsecondary institutions (e.g., Thernstrom & Thernstrom, 1997).

Confusion about affirmative action begins with misunderstandings about what the policy is and is not (Holloway, 1989). The policy can be traced back to Executive Order 11246, signed into law by President Lyndon Johnson in 1965 in an effort to promote civil liberties and civil rights for those historically shut out of employment and educational opportunities. Citing the American Psychological Association, John Richardson and Karen Lancendorfer (2004) defined affirmative action as "a catchall phrase referring to laws, customs, and social policies intended to alleviate the types of discrimination that limit opportunities for a variety of demographic groups in various social institutions" (p. 76). In theory, affirmative action has sought to "mitigate the current blindnesses of institutions and decisionmakers" (Young, 1990, p. 198) and "to [extend] a hand to eminently qualified people previously held back by bias" (Cose, 1997, as cited in Tierney & Chung, 2002, p. 271). In the practice of college and university admissions, affirmative action allows for race to be one factor among many in the holistic review of applicants for college entrance (Wright & Garces, 2018). Ironically, race-conscious affirmative action wields less power than other more deeply institutionalized but less scrutinized forms of affirmative action, such as legacy admissions (Jayakumar & Page, 2021; Oppenheimer, Onwuachi-Willig, & Leong, 2019).

The term *affirmative action* itself triggers visceral and polarizing reactions, as it has been strategically weighted down with a history of misinformation and stereotypes (Crenshaw, 2007; Ledesma, 2012). Opponents of the policy have exploited this to call for an end to all race-conscious practices (Garces & Poon, 2018). Thus, we use *race-conscious admissions practices* to refer to affirmative action in postsecondary settings. This terminology zeroes in on the center of the controversy—that is, the limited use of race as one factor in holistic admissions decisions. Likewise, it separates it from other, less familiar forms of affirmative action, including aggressive outreach and recruitment efforts, reliance on goals and timetables, financial support (Chemerinsky, 1996), and priority based on class, geography, family legacy, and athletic ability (Anderson & Svrluga, 2019; Cashin, 2014; Jayakumar & Page, 2021; Kahlenberg, 2014; Oppenheimer, Onwuachi-Willig, & Leong, 2019). Most of these are overlooked in mainstream affirmative action debates (Lamb, 1992; Massey & Mooney, 2007).

This chapter describes the current state of race-conscious admissions practices in higher education by contextualizing the contemporary affirmative action debate. We cannot do so without first understanding the legacy of *Regents of the University of California v. Bakke* (1978) and, more specifically, Justice Lewis Powell's "diversity rationale." In *Bakke's* fractured decisions,

Powell framed his reasoning in support of race-conscious admissions practices not in terms of restorative justice but rather in terms of how racial diversity enhances the experiences of predominantly White students. Lost in this exchange were three of the university's defenses of race-conscious practices: (1) reducing the deficit of historically underrepresented minorities in medical schools and the medical profession; (2) countering the effects of societal discrimination; and (3) increasing the number of physicians practicing in underserved communities.

Powell was persuaded only by the institution's *fourth* rationale—that an ethnically diverse student body has educational benefits. Notably, he also listed a fifth (often overlooked) rationale: "fair appraisal of each individual's academic promise in the light of some cultural bias in grading or testing procedures" (Powell opinion in *Regents of the University of California v. Bakke*, p. 306). He added, "To the extent that race and ethnic background were considered only to the extent of curing established inaccuracies in predicting academic performance, it might be argued that there is no 'preference' at all" (p. 306). Per Powell, had race-conscious admissions been used purely as a corrective measure to account for existing racial/ethnic/cultural biases in predicting academic success, then race-conscious practices would *not* function as a preference or advantage of any kind. Curiously, proponents of race-conscious practices have never seized on Powell's fifth rationale. After all, countless studies have confirmed Powell's suspicion that standardized testing is culturally biased against historically underrepresented students (e.g., Santelices & Wilson, 2010; Valencia & Suzuki, 2000).

When it comes to defenses of race-conscious admissions practices, courts have been primarily disinclined to support all but the diversity rationale. As such, these defenses embody Derrick Bell's (1980, 2004) *interest convergence dilemma*, which posits that the interests of Blacks and other historically minoritized racial groups will be accommodated only when they converge with the interests of Whites. The predominance of the diversity rationale exemplifies Bell's thesis: in short, race-conscious practices are tolerated because the educational benefits that flow from a racially and ethnically diverse student body are valued by majoritarian institutions, and are most beneficial to White students who tend to come from segregated neighborhoods and to have the least precollege exposure to people from different racial backgrounds (Jayakumar et al., 2018). Notably, Bell cautioned that when practices based on interest convergence are no longer perceived as valuable to dominant interests, they will be retracted. Indeed, over the past three decades, affirmative action has been consistently restricted and depleted with each new legal challenge, with many of these challenges coming since the turn of the 21st century.

Race-Conscious Admissions Practices in the New Millennium

Although race-conscious admissions practices have been a political lightning rod since their inception, recently, we have seen a reinvigorated and unrelenting level of legal scrutiny. Since 2000, the US Supreme Court has deliberated at least seven cases that directly or indirectly concern the future of race-conscious admissions practices: *Grutter v. Bollinger* (2003), *Gratz v. Bollinger* (2003), *Parents Involved in Community Schools v. Seattle School District No. 1* (2007), *Ricci v. DeStefano* (2009), *Fisher v. University of Texas* (2013), *Schuette v. Coalition to Defend Affirmative Action* (2014), and *Fisher v. University of Texas* (2016).

Grutter v. Bollinger (2003) and *Gratz v. Bollinger* (2003) are notable for many reasons, not the least of which is that they brought the topic of race-conscious admissions before the Supreme Court for the first time since *Bakke* in 1978. Both cases deliberately cast White women as victims of race-conscious practices, even though they remain among the greatest beneficiaries of affirmative action (Cho, 2002). Each plaintiff posited that she had been unfairly disadvantaged because of race in seeking admission to the University of Michigan. In *Gratz*, the justices struck down the university's undergraduate admissions policy, suggesting the approach was too mechanistic—reflecting a quota for race—and thus did not satisfy the legal standard of review. In *Grutter*, the court was persuaded, albeit by the slimmest of margins, that the law school's holistic race-conscious admissions review was more narrowly tailored. In the final 5–4 decision, the court upheld and rearticulated *Bakke's* core diversity rationale, again endorsing the theory that educational benefits flow from an ethnically diverse student body.

Parents Involved in Community Schools v. Seattle School District No. 1 (2007) and *Ricci v. DeStefano* (2009) were not explicitly focused on higher education but are nevertheless crucial in understanding the evolution of anti-race-conscious arguments. The questions at the center of *Parents Involved* was whether (1) decisions in *Grutter* and *Gratz* apply to public high school students; (2) racial diversity is a compelling interest that can justify the use of race in public high school admissions; and (3) a school district that generally permits a student to attend a high school of choice violates the Equal Protection Clause of the Fourteenth Amendment if the student is denied admission to a preferred school in order to achieve a desired racial balance. The justices responded "no, no, and yes" (Oyez, n.d., para. 7).

Reversing a Ninth Circuit ruling, the court declared that the 2003 Grutter case did not control the school district. They further reasoned that "Racial balancing is not transformed from 'patently unconstitutional' to a compelling state interest simply by relabeling it 'racial diversity'" (*Parents Involved* majority opinion, 2007, p. 24). The court's conservative plurality rested its opinion on the fact that, unlike in *Grutter*, the school district lacked both an individualized and narrow approach to its use of race. In this case, Chief Justice Roberts (in)famously declared, "The way to stop discrimination on the basis of race is to stop discriminating on the basis of race" (*Parents Involved* majority opinion, 2007, pp. 40–41).

The question at the heart of *Ricci v. DeStefano* (2009) was whether the city of New Haven, Connecticut, could reject a service exam when its outcomes proved to be racially skewed, thereby preventing the promotion of minority candidates. The case centered on petitioner Frank Ricci and 17 other New Haven firefighters—16 were White, and one was Latino—who contended that their civil rights had been violated when city officials failed to promote any of them into the available captain and lieutenant positions. Ricci maintained that the city engaged in racial discrimination by refusing to honor the "merit"-based exam outcomes. The court's conservative majority ruled in favor of Ricci, arguing that city officials had violated Title VII and the petitioners' civil rights. Ironically, the very real and long history of racial discrimination against historically underrepresented groups was utterly overlooked in the case (Harris & West-Faulcon, 2010).

In *Fisher v. University of Texas* (2013, 2016) and *Schuette v. Coalition to Defend Affirmative Action* (2014), deliberations focused explicitly on race-conscious postsecondary admissions. In *Fisher I* (2013), Abigail Fisher—a White woman—challenged the race-conscious admissions practices at the University of Texas (UT), claiming she had been a victim of racial discrimination. She contended that she had been harmed by the university's use of race in admissions. She added that it was unnecessary and discriminatory for UT to employ race-conscious practices because they admitted a majority of each incoming class (75%–80%) through the state's Top Ten Percent Plan (TTPP), which guaranteed admission to graduating seniors in the top 10% of their class (Flores & Horn, 2015). Fisher's legal team made no attempt to override *Grutter* or, by extension, the diversity rationale.

The justices took nine months to deliberate *Fisher I*, and the highly anticipated decision proved to be anticlimactic. They remanded the case to the appellate court, where UT's race-conscious practices prevailed, laying the foundation for an appeal to the Supreme Court. In that appeal, *Fisher II* (2016) contended that UT's use of race in admissions was unnecessary and violated the Equal Protection Clause. In fact, Fisher's academic record was less than stellar and was likely the major reason for her denial of admission. Moreover, while the court once again upheld UT's limited use of race, it also introduced new arguments. The issue of classroom diversity was debated before the justices in *Fisher II*. The reasoning is that while programs like TTPP are useful in diversifying the overall student body, race-conscious measures are still necessary to avoid segregation across academic disciplines and majors. The key arguments in UT's defense were also avoiding the harms of racial isolation and the relevance of critical mass. While the *Fisher II* decision upheld race-conscious practices, it also introduced a more "demanding evidentiary burden" (Robinson, 2016, p. 188), requiring post-secondary institutions to prove they had exhausted *all* race-neutral means before employing race-conscious practices.

Sandwiched between *Fisher I* and *Fisher II*, *Schuette v. Coalition to Defend Affirmative Action* (2014) affirmed states' rights to use ballot initiatives to curtail the use of sex- and race-based preferences in public education, public employment, and public contracting. Led by then Michigan Attorney General William Schuette, petitioners contended that voters had the right to choose whether to prohibit the use of race "preferences" in governmental bodies, including public colleges and universities. Building upon the lessons of California's Proposition 209—also known as the California Civil Rights Initiative—which in 1996 became the first statewide prohibition of the use of race-based preferences in public education, public employment, and public contracting, *Schuette* successfully withstood legal challenge. In a 6–2 decision, the court granted states permission to curtail and/or terminate the use of race-conscious policy via ballot initiative or constitutional amendment. To date, race-conscious admissions are banned in seven states, including California, Washington, Colorado, Michigan, Arizona, Oklahoma, and Florida. However, in November 2020, efforts to reinstate affirmative action in California fell short. By a 56%–44% margin, California voters rejected Proposition 16, which would have overturned Proposition 209 and once again allowed the considerations of race, ethnicity, and gender in public education, employment, and contracting.

The question at the center of each of the related cases was what role, if any, race-conscious practices should play in policymaking, including university admissions, K–12 school assignments, and employment promotions. Five of these cases—*Grutter, Gratz, Schuette, Fisher I,* and *Fisher II*—specifically addressed postsecondary admissions. Moreover, while *Bakke* remains law, these petitioners all sought to curb the limited use of race in university admissions. More recently, two additional lawsuits filed in 2014—*Students for Fair Admissions v. Harvard* (2019) and *Students for Fair Admissions v. University North Carolina at Chapel Hill*—have advanced with the sole intent of upending *all* forms of race-conscious policies. While the UNC case remains undecided at the time of this writing, on September 30, 2019, US District Court Judge Allison Burroughs upheld Harvard's race-conscious admissions practices. In her 130-page ruling, Judge Burroughs provided a thorough and detailed analysis of the claims against Harvard, including the allegation that the university discriminated against Asian American applicants. Since Judge Burroughs's ruling, *SFFA v. Harvard* has arrived before the Supreme Court. Unfortunately, the outcomes do not bode well for proponents of race-conscious admissions policies. Indeed, in the wake of Justice Anthony Kennedy's retirement in 2018 and the death of Justice Ruth Bader Ginsburg in 2020, the case will be argued before a much more conservative court. With three Trump-appointed conservative justices, the Supreme Court is expected to once again deliberate and rule on the future of affirmative action in higher education during the 2021–2022 term.

With each legal challenge to the use of race in university admissions, court mandates have become increasingly limited, resulting in "increased evidentiary burdens" for postsecondary institutions per Kimberly Robinson (2016). This limitation, coupled with the court's hesitancy to embrace any reasoning to uphold race-conscious practices other than Justice Powell's diversity rationale (articulated in *Bakke*), has further weakened distributive justice arguments supporting affirmative action. In short, race-conscious practices have become synonymous with upholding diversity (Moses & Chang, 2006).

White Backlash: Universities under Threat

"White backlash" is a phenomenon that Matthew Hughey (2014) described as one "sewn together by the narrative that non-white success is purposefully engineered at the expense of white sacrifice" (p. 721). In this country, majoritarian contempt against perceived "special benefits" dates as far back as the 1865 founding of the Freedmen's Bureau, established to assist newly freed enslaved Blacks reintegrate into society. Even then, such efforts were derided and framed as unjust "preferences" against Whites, who felt aggrieved that they did not accrue such benefits (Oakes, 1979). More recently, these sentiments peaked following the 2008 election of the first African American US president, Barack Obama. The election of his successor was arguably a direct rebuke of Obama and all he represented (Bobo, 2017). Likewise, President Donald Trump's 2016 campaign slogan, "Make America Great Again," embodied the fears of a White electorate, which will cede its demographic dominance as early as 2045, when White Americans are expected to become a minority (Danbold & Huo, 2014; Outten et al., 2012).

The plight for educational access and opportunity for historically marginalized and minoritized students of color is likewise full of similar instances of White backlash. Since the first Black students integrated American colleges and universities, White majoritarian groups have resisted, often resulting in riots and violence that required military intervention to restore peace. For example, in 1963, in a public display of defiance, Alabama Governor George C. Wallace protested the integration of the University of Alabama by literally blocking its entryway (Durr, 2003). Across the country, White people "lash[ed] back" (Carter, 1995). The White middle class thought they had to fight Blacks over a supposed "dearth" of resources (Hughey, 2014). As a result, for many Whites, desegregation policies were seen as an unjustified handout to "inferior" beneficiaries who lacked the values, merit, and resources to take advantage of such opportunities (Hughey, 2014). The issue of White victimhood and White innocence is a consistent trope in the debate over race-conscious admissions practices (Gotanda, 2004). Universities, in particular, are at the epicenter of the nation's cultural wars, hosting a new wave of far-right nationalist movements (Bobo, 2017; Scobey, 2019) and sparking renewed White backlash (Hughey, 2014).

The epitome of such White backlash occurred on January 6, 2021, when hundreds of aggrieved white nationalists stormed the US Capitol to halt the inauguration of the 46th president of the United States, Joseph Biden. The onslaught, the first upon the US Capitol since the Civil War, left officers defending the Capitol both slain and maimed. However, in some corners, the mob's violent assault was consistently downplayed. Relying on narratives of victimhood and a nostalgia for a White America that never was, conservative media outlets as well as Republican officials alike attempted to rationalize the domestic terrorist attack as the misguided response of innocent voters who felt victimized by a "rigged" election that ousted their preferred candidate—Trump—from office (Jalonick, 2021; Smith, 2021). Months on, the gaslighting continued, with only a fraction of the hundreds of white nationalist extremists being tracked down after the fact to finally face legal consequences. These actions highlight the vast contrast to the hypermilitarized response and harsh treatment of largely peaceful Black Lives Matter protesters in the summer of 2020, who took to the streets to call for an end to white supremacy after the brutal murders of George Floyd, Breonna Taylor, and countless Black, Indigenous, and People of Color at the hands of the police-state.

Student Activism and Race-Conscious Admissions

The struggle for access to quality educational opportunities for historically minoritized groups has been long and arduous, and these fights have often been spearheaded by a history of agitation (Cho, 2005; Ferguson, 2017). Student activism has been and continues to be a critical instrument in the quest for educational equity and social justice. Per Richard Peterson (1966), the "surge of student unrest and active protest must certainly be among the most significant developments in American higher education, perhaps in American society" (p. 1).

Fifty years ago, one of the longest student strikes in US history took place at San Francisco State College—now called San Francisco State University. Students protested institutional recalcitrance by putting pressure on the college to create a Black studies department and increase the admission of Black students. The Black Student Union pressed the college to admit more Black students and organized the community so that more Black parents could send their children to the college. After months of protesting, the administration made available hundreds of admissions slots (Meraji, 2019). As other student groups, including Asian and Latina/o/x student groups, sought similar arrangements, they were advised to request slots from their Black counterparts. A joint effort across all student groups would eventually become the Third World Liberation Front, which empowered students to work as a collective against campus administration. Established in 1968, the organization pioneered contemporary student protest movements, paving the way for the nation's first college of ethnic studies and spearheading efforts to increase admission and enrollment of historically underrepresented students of color (Meraji, 2019).

Although central in the push for equity and social justice, these social movements have not been without political complications. For instance, student protests in higher education have been met with increased corporatization and administrative expansion. While some might cast these developments as a direct response to meeting the needs of postsecondary constituents, Ferguson (2017) maintained that "the ascendency of the administrator was not occasioned by the visibility of minority communities and the need for transformation" (p. 62). Rather, the increased number and visibility of administrators "was principally motivated by an interest in widening the university's powers against the kinds of social transformations that minority visibility demanded" (p. 62). While promising in theory (Ahmed, 2012), these positions are too often symbolic, relegated to putting out fires rather than implementing meaningful long-term change (Ferguson, 2017).

Racial matters debated on college campuses echo the larger societal issues. For example, in the fall of 2015, the University of Missouri became ground zero of the #BlackLivesMatter (BLM) movement. The killing of unarmed black teenager Michael Brown by a Ferguson police officer launched one of the most significant student movements of recent time (Joseph, 2017). While the BLM movement shined the light on the epidemic of police brutality, it also provided a platform for students of color to push back against campus administrators seen as dragging their feet on institutional issues of diversity and inclusion.

BLM was a sober backdrop to the Supreme Court pronouncement upholding the limited use of race admissions in *Fisher II* (2016). As Elise Boddie (2016) recounted, "It is hard to ignore that the Court decided *Fisher II* against the backdrop of deep racial unrest, spurred by long-simmering frustrations over police brutality and the multiple failures of our institutions to address pervasive inequality, including concentrated, racialized poverty" (p. 47). Conceivably, the court's plurality was persuaded to delay the cessation of race-conscious admissions practices when confronted with nationwide student- and civilian-led protests calling attention to systemic racism and entrenched White supremacy (Boddie, 2016; Lempert, 2016).

The court's decision to uphold the limited use of race in *Fisher II* also underscores the power of activism. After all, the emergence of social movements protesting state-sanctioned shootings of unarmed Black men and youth, coupled with the campus-based rise of the BLM movement between *Fisher I* and *Fisher II*, ensured that the issues of racism and White supremacy could not be easily dismissed or ignored during final deliberations in *Fisher II*. Richard Lempert (2016) acknowledged as much: "By themselves these shootings might have moved Justice Kennedy to look with greater sympathy on efforts to boost the life chances of black people by placing a small thumb on the scale of college admissions" (p. 114). Lempert's treatment of BLM is more provocative, contending that the "riotous" behavior that sometimes accompanied these protests might have given Kennedy pause to support the expansion of race-conscious efforts. Regardless, student activists giving voice to the historically marginalized and scholars producing reams of empirical evidence on the value of race-conscious practices have arguably helped to stave off the end of affirmative action.

Implications of Current Court Cases and Judicial Updates

Today's assaults on race-conscious admissions practices stretch back to earlier efforts orchestrated by conservative activists, foundations, and organizations that have long sought to dismantle all progressive race-conscious social policy (Cokorinos, 2003; Stefancic & Delgado, 1996). Many of these same entities, including the Center for Individual Rights, the Cato Institute, and businessman Edward Blum, to name a few, are responsible for coordinating and financing the current legal barrage. As founder and director of Project on Fair Representation and Students for Fair Admissions, Blum, a wealthy White businessman, has spearheaded, organized, and funded multiple high-profile legal challenges whose sole purpose has been to upend all race-conscious social policy. Blum was the chief architect behind *Fisher I* (2013) and *Fisher II* (2016), and *Schuette v. Coalition to Defend Affirmative Action* (2014), as well as the 2013 voting rights case *Shelby County v. Holder* (2013). Blum is also the lead strategist behind the two most recent high-profile anti–affirmative action cases, *SFFA v. Harvard* and *SFFA v. University of Carolina, Chapel Hill* (Hinger, 2018).

In the UNC case, Blum claims that the school runs afoul of legal standards set in *Fisher II*, which say postsecondary institutions can employ race-conscious practices only when all race-neutral means to increase racial diversity are exhausted. Instead, he posits that the University of North Carolina uses race in a "mechanical and formulaic way" (Hoover, 2019). Blum's framing in the Harvard case is more insidious, playing on the fears of Asian Americans and seeking to pit them against other minoritized groups for the ultimate benefit of white students. He posits that Harvard engages in "invidious discrimination" by limiting the number of Asian American admits. Notably, Blum casts a collective of Asian American students (not White females) as the victims: "The rampant discrimination against Asian-Americans at Harvard, and [Harvard and UNC-Chapel Hill's] failure to comply with recent Supreme Court directives with regard to race preferences, are emblematic of the unfair, counterproductive, and illegal behavior of the vast majority of competitive colleges throughout the country" (Schmidt, 2014, para. 4). While affirmative action has thus far withstood a salvo of attacks, the latest round comes at a time of a reconstituted Supreme Court with a firmly established conservative majority. In his limited tenure, President Trump has shifted the court, with the addition of Justices Neil Gorsuch, Brett Kavanaugh, and, most recently, Amy Coney Barrett. Notably, Trump has also appointed a record number of federal judges who will (re)shape the legal system for decades to come (Bannan, 2016).

Color-Blind Policy Framework Challenges and Myths

Legislation from *Bakke* onward treats all acts, including those designed to address past and current racial exclusion, effectively the same as those rooted in racial animus and resulting in racial exclusion (Bell, 1980; Garces, 2014; Harris, 2003). Similarly, the *Bakke* rationale invokes the notion of "White innocence," characterizing Whites as faultless victims of affirmative action (for more on white innocence within the affirmative action debate, see Jayakumar, Garces, & Park, 2018). Rooted in this logic, Justice Powell cautioned that "broadening affirmative action would be racially divisive because it would cost whites, as a group, access and power" (Boddie, 2016, p. 49). This argument led to the "protective measure" of strict scrutiny in affirmative action litigation, centered on maintaining White interests and White innocence (Boddie, 2016; Jayakumar, Garces, & Park, 2018).

In *Schuette* (2014), Justice Sonia Sotomayor reasoned that her fellow justices would prefer to bypass a candid examination of the racial impact of legislation. She observed that the "refusal to accept the stark reality that race matters is regrettable" (*Schuette*, Sotomayor dissenting, p. 46). She further emphasized, "As members of the judiciary tasked with intervening to carry out the guarantee of equal protection, *we ought not sit back and wish away, rather than confront, the racial inequality that exists in our society*. It is this view that works harm, by perpetuating the facile notion that what makes race matter is acknowledging the simple truth that race *does* matter" (p. 46; emphasis added). As Sotomayor pointed out, moving toward color-blind legal approaches that deny ongoing sociohistoric realities of racial discrimination keeps racial inequality intact. Thus, it is essential that we interrogate false narratives, within both legal discourse and the broader public conversation, which fan the flames that threaten to burn down race-conscious practices once and for all.

RACE-NEUTRAL ALTERNATIVES

Among these dangerous false narratives is the myth that race-neutral alternatives—particularly percentage plans and income-based affirmative action—are a viable alternative to race-conscious admissions practices. Yet a multitude of studies have demonstrated that these approaches, such as those implemented by the University of Texas and the University of California, do not restore underrepresented student enrollment to rates experienced prior to the dissolution of affirmative action (Ledesma, 2019). Indeed, studies based on national data sets or subgroups of top-tier institutions, as well as those examining "natural experiment" states—where affirmative action is banned—all demonstrate a reduction in underrepresented student enrollment numbers at the most selective colleges and universities (Epple, Romano, & Sieg, 2008; Horn & Flores, 2003; Howell, 2010; Kurlaender, Friedmann, & Chang, 2015).

There is agreement across all studies that elimination of affirmative action leads to significant declines in Black and Latina/o/x student percentages at selective postsecondary institutions, and race-neutral alternatives alone do not recover these losses (Kurlaender, Friedmann & Chang, 2015; Reardon, Baker, & Klasik, 2012). For example, Bowen and Bok's (1998) famous study of elite colleges predicted a 29% drop (from 42% to 13%) among Black students; another simulation based on three highly selective private research universities predicted a 5.7% decline in matriculants (from 9.0% to 3.3%) and a 4.1% decline (from 7.9% to 3.8%) in Latina/o/x matriculants enrolling as traditional first-year students.

In natural experiment states, where race-neutral alternatives are the only option, percentages of underrepresented students have not fully recovered. For example, even in California, where institutions have had over two decades to adjust, UC Berkeley and UCLA have not recovered percentages of underrepresented students of color, despite their population growth at the state level (Ledesma, 2019). In Texas, where the TTPP recovers some numbers (versus no plan at all), a closer look reveals that underrepresented students enrolling in the most selective institutions would likely have been admitted without the plan (Horn & Flores, 2003). Moreover, the university loses *diversity within diversity*—that is, differences in characteristics, such as income, within particular racial groups (Brief of 823 American Social Science Researchers, 2016).

The Mismatch Hypothesis

Another popular narrative is the mismatch hypothesis, suggesting that affirmative action harms Black, Latina/o/x, and Native American students by placing them in institutions where they are less likely to graduate and succeed. This myth, propagated by Richard Sander and Stuart Taylor (2012), continues to receive disproportionate attention in the legal debate—even in the face of studies (some using the same data set) showing different results and serious flaws in their analyses and thesis (Kidder & Lempert, 2015; Park, 2018). In *Fisher II*, a brief filed by over 800 social scientists who study college access, race, and related issues rejected the mismatch hypothesis, given the overwhelming evidence against it (Brief of 823 American Social Science Researchers, 2016).

The reality, based purely on the (mostly White) racial composition of applicants to elite and selective schools, suggests that an Asian American with high scores who is rejected would be edged out by a White applicant with slightly lower scores (Kidder, 2006). Critics of race-conscious admissions promote the false notion that affirmative action is to blame for this. In fact, the evidence suggests that race-conscious admissions do not significantly harm Asian American applicants (Hughes, Thompson, & Carrillo, 2016; West-Faulcon, 2017). Thus, ending such policies would not address discrimination, as actual ceilings placed on Asian American admits (West-Faulcon, 2017).

Myth of Meritocracy

Perhaps the most harmful and long-standing myth embedded in the very structures of postsecondary institutions is that of meritocracy. After all, as Lani Guinier and Gerald Torres (2003) and others (Oakes et al., 2002) have argued, we need affirmative action because of problematic notions of merit within admissions processes that are purported to be race-neutral. Historically and currently, there are changing standards of merit and a willingness of institutions and the public to shift supposedly objective notions of merit when it fits institutional and elite White interests (Karabel, 1984). For example, in the 1920s, when Jewish students were showing higher results than

White Protestant upper-class students on entrance exams, the trend-setting elites—Harvard, Yale, and Princeton—shifted their admissions practices to include character, personality, academic promise, and scholarly attainments, as well as interviews and photographs. This move was a strategic institutional effort to eradicate "the Jewish problem" by redefining merit and transforming admissions practices to continue to favor White elite interests (Karabel, 2005). More recently, Frank Samson (2013) showed that the factors that define merit are subject to White Americans' perceptions of group threat. Specifically, Whites are more likely to decrease the emphasis on grades in response to Asian American threat, but increase it when thinking about Latina/o/x and Black competition. This fluidity in the notion of meritocracy privileges White applicants.

Research underscores this pattern. High school grades, access to honors and advanced placement courses, and standardized test scores correlate with socioeconomic status (Atkinson & Geiser, 2009). Moreover, standardized test scores have limited predictive power in forecasting student success, with more than 80% of variance attributable to more holistic factors (Darling-Hammond & Dintersmith, 2014). Nonetheless, limiting definitions of merit—often based on measures such as these—are legitimized and used to justify the exclusion of marginalized students and to privilege White applicants. Thus, admissions criteria that disproportionately advantage those with privilege—especially affluent White students—further challenge racial justice in college access. In reality, race-conscious practices play a very small role in shaping the racial demographics of the student body, despite popular rhetoric about its overinflated impact.

Post-Racial Myths

Related to the myth of meritocracy is the notion that we are beyond race, or *post-racial*. Within this myth, advances in student body diversity based on overall racial composition are seen as sufficient or complete. It has become common practice on college campuses to dilute conversations about diversity with other forms of difference without attention to intersections around race or power relations in society (Warikoo, 2016). Furthermore, post-racial myths obscure persistent underrepresentation, particularly when it comes to more selective institutions.

For example, based on 1982–2004 enrollment data, Sean Reardon, Rachel Baker, and Daniel Klasik (2012) found that, despite an exponential increase in nonindigenous students of color entering postsecondary education, there was a decline in Black students at selective institutions, and the growth in the number of Latina/o/x students was not commensurate with population changes. In 1982, 15% of students were nonindigenous students of color (5.6% Black, 6% Latina/o/x, 3.5% Asian American), whereas in 2004 the percentage was 22% (3.4% Black, 6.9% Latina/o/x, and 12.1% Asian American). Asian Americans collectively show enrollment growth, but particular subgroups are persistently underrepresented (Jaschik, 2013), and indigenous students remain severely underrepresented (Center for Native American Youth at the Aspen Institute, n.d.). The myth that we are beyond the need to address racial diversity on college campuses ignores persistent racism, color-blind frames, and a lack of critical mass for various severely underrepresented groups (Jayakumar, 2015), all of which remain pervasive problems.

Countering these narratives in multiple spheres of influence—including the legal audience, scholars and practitioners, public opinion, and within the context of building a movement and supporting agitation—is essential to a strategic counterattack aimed at addressing the reality that race continues to affect college access and educational outcomes (Jayakumar & Adamian, 2015).

Conclusion

Race-conscious practices did not materialize out of nowhere. Rather, they resulted from sustained advocacy and long-fought social movements. Moreover, they were developed in part to respond to student activism and a desire for equal access to educational environments and resources (Cho, 2005; Rogers, 2012; Zamani-Gallaher et al., 2009). However, just as student agitation and researcher advocacy have helped safeguard the limited use of race in university admissions, sustained protest from anti–affirmative action pundits has helped ensure the policy remains under scrutiny.

In order to appreciate the complexity of race-conscious practices, policy makers, practitioners, and researchers need a critical understanding of affirmative action anchored in its historical roots—one that first and foremost acknowledges that it is, by definition, a *race-conscious* approach, but was never, by design, *racism-conscious*. Although borne of the civil rights context, its approach to meritocracy and equality has reflected a mainstream consciousness that has helped maintain majoritarian systems of advantage. From an interest convergence perspective, affirmative action was never a revolutionary policy that could bring about racial justice in higher education;

rather, it carried the promise of incremental progress and momentary racial relief that could be depleted as soon as it posed a threat to the privileged status of (mostly middle- and upper-class) Whites.

This perspective was made clear during *Bakke* when the plurality of Supreme Court justices dismissed all distributive justice arguments that spoke to reparations for past discrimination and instead established the diversity rationale as the sole legally permissible justification for race-conscious admissions practices. Supreme Court cases over the last four decades have provided context for continued consideration of race in postsecondary admissions and for interventions that improve campus racial dynamics without threatening White interests, but efforts designed to more radically and holistically address racial equity have consistently been thwarted (Ahmed, 2012; Warikoo, 2016).

Affirmative action has always faced harsh legal challenges, but its current challenges are unique. Prior cases have benefited from a Supreme Court that, although ideologically divided, still carried the hope of a swing vote; today's court is hyperpartisan, with a heavy conservative leaning. Prior attempts to dismantle affirmative action were rooted in individual allegations of unfair treatment; today's legal challenges point to group harms filed by collective plaintiffs. Moreover, the problematic myths and false narratives outlined in this chapter are deep-seated, even among the highest arbiters of justice. In his passionate dissenting opinion in *Fisher II*, Justice Samuel Alito, joined by Justices Clarence Thomas and John Roberts, proclaimed that UT's justification for race-conscious practices in addition to the TTPP was "affirmative action gone wild" (*Fisher* 2016, Alito dissenting at 2216). This comment, at its core, suggests that affirmative action has succeeded beyond measure. In truth, 40 years post-*Bakke*, historically minoritized students, faculty, and administrators continue to be severely underrepresented in the most selective US postsecondary institutions.

All of these factors are complicated (and compounded) by pronounced White backlash, as evidenced by the election of Donald Trump, the steep rise of overt White nationalist organizations and movements, and the blatant disregard of historical facts. Arguably, this signals the heightened perceived threat among a politically emboldened group of Whites who fear they are losing their grip on power (Bannan, 2016). This perceived threat is apparent on college campuses where white student groups are starting to emerge as a direct backlash to consciousness raising by the #BLM movement and student protests across nearly 100 college campuses demanding that institutions address racial bias, stereotypes, underrepresentation, and structural racism on their campuses.[1] One example of the growing white student backlash is the Union of White Cornell Students, who submitted their own set of demands to administration and expressed their purpose in a social media post as "a community of white students who wish to preserve and advance their race." Their open letter grievance regarding the black student demands on their campus also suggests white fragility, even hostility, and fractured racial dynamics.

Affirmative action has been a helpful, albeit imperfect, mechanism for countering problematic admissions practices, but relying on it as the only avenue for increasing racial equity in higher education may not be the best strategy. In an increasingly color-blind legal context with severe restrictions on the terms of affirmative action policy (Orfield, 2015), we must more seriously engage with the critiques that critical race scholars have offered (Jayakumar, Garces, & Park, 2018; Warikoo, 2016). We need greater institutional accountability and advocacy to change the very standards and normalized practices that have helped recreate racial inequities in college access. We must go beyond traditional notions of merit to find new avenues to identify students with potential for success.

As evidenced by the two newest legal challenges, those seeking to end affirmative action want more than to shut down race-conscious admissions practices—which, when all is said and done, have a minimal impact on who gets into college. Indeed, by design, today's assault on affirmative action is intended to produce collateral damage. *All* race-conscious educational programing—from ethnic studies programs to outreach and retention efforts—are in the line of fire. Moreover, race-conscious efforts to diversify graduate and professional schools are at risk, but so are faculty recruitment and retention and administrative leadership programs. In the shadow of a resurgent white nationalist movement, all analytical tools that center race and racism, such as critical race theory (CRT), are under assault (Kilgore, 2021). Indeed, the virulent attack on CRT, which was ushered in with the Trump administration's anti-CRT memo, which became Executive Order 13950 on September 22, 2020, labeled CRT as "divisive, anti-American propaganda" (Fortin, 2021; Gabriel & Goldstein, 2021), has deliberately misconstrued CRT and framed it as an anti-American boogieman. Many of the same forces that defended and justified the insurrection of January 6 have sought to whitewash history by prohibiting any attempts at acknowledge, let alone discussion, of America's racist past.

The complexities of the shifting legal context and restrictions on race-conscious practices call for complex and multifaceted responses from scholars, institutional agents, and grassroots organizations, including more done on multiple levels and from multiple parties. While the future of race-conscious admissions policies remains perilous, postsecondary institutions that value and support racial diversity should be proactive in preparing a defense of race-conscious policies because more legal challenges are inevitability on the horizon.

Note

1. For more on the demands put forth by Black student organizations and allied groups in recent years, see http://www.thedemands.org, as well as Chessman and Wayt (2016).

References

Ahmed, S. (2012). *On being included: Racism and diversity in institutional life*. Duke University Press.

American Council on Education. (2018). *Education department reverses Obama-era guidance on diversity in admissions*. Retrieved from https://www.acenet.edu/news-room/Pages/Education-Department-Reverses-Obama-era-Guidance-on-Diversity-in-Admissions.aspx

Anderson, N., & Svrluga, S. (2019, June 12). Varsity athletes admissions and enrollment at top colleges. *Washington Post*.

Atkinson, R. C., & Geiser, S. (2009). Reflections on a century of college admission tests. *Educational Researcher, 38*(9), 665–676.

Bannan, N. L. O. (2016). Building on 80 years of radical lawyering in the age of Trump. *National Lawyers Guild Review, 73*, 189–192.

Bell, D. (1980). *Brown v. Board of Education* and the interest convergence dilemma. *Harvard Law Review, 93*, 518–533.

Bell, D. (2004). *Silent covenants:* Brown v. Board of Education *and the unfulfilled hopes for racial reform*. Oxford University Press.

Berrey, E. (2015). *The enigma of diversity: The language of race and the limits of racial justice*. University of Chicago Press.

Bobo, L. D. (2017). Racism in Trump's America: Reflections on culture, sociology, and the 2016 US presidential election. *British Journal of Sociology, 68*(1), S85–S104.

Boddie, E. C. (2016). The future of affirmative action. *Harvard Law Review Forum, 130*, 38–50.

Bowen, W. G., & Bok, D. (1998). *The shape of the river: Long-term consequences of considering race in college and university admissions*. Princeton University Press.

Brief of 823 American Social Science Researchers as amici curiae in support of respondents, Fisher v. University of Texas II, 136 S. Ct. 2198 (2016).

Carter, D. T. (1995). *The politics of rage: George Wallace, the origins of the new conservatism, and the transformation of American politics*. Simon & Schuster.

Cashin, S. (2014). *Place not race: A new vision of opportunity*. Boston, MA: Beacon Press.

Center for Native American Youth at the Aspen Institute. (n.d.). Fast Facts on Native American Youth and Indian Country (pp. 1–3).

Chemerinsky, E. (1996). Making sense of the affirmative action debate. *Ohio Northern University Law Review, 22*, 1159–1176.

Chessman, H., & Wayt, L. (2016). What are students demanding? Higher Education Today. Retrieved from https://www.higheredtoday.org/2016/01/13/what-are-studentsdemanding/

Cho, S. (2002). Understanding white women's ambivalence towards affirmative action: Theorizing political accountability in coalitions. *UMKC Law Review, 71*(2), 399–418.

Cho, S. (2005). From massive resistance, to passive resistance, to righteous resistance: Understanding the culture wars from *Brown* to *Grutter*. *Journal of Constitutional Law, 7*(3), 809–835.

Cokorinos, L. (2003). *The assault on diversity: An organized challenge to racial and gender justice*. Rowman & Littlefield Publishers.

Crenshaw, K. W. (2007). Framing affirmative action. *Michigan Law Review First Impressions, 105*, 123–133.

Danbold, F., & Huo, Y. J. (2014). No longer "All-American"? Whites' defensive reactions to their numerical decline. *Social Psychological and Personality Science, 6*, 210–218.

Darling-Hammond, L., & Dintersmith, T. (2014, July 17). A basic flaw in the argument against affirmative action. (Blog post). Retrieved from http://www.washingtonpost.com/blogs/answer-sheet/wp/2014/07/17/a-basic-flaw-in-the-argument-against-affirmative-action/

Durr, K. D. (2003). *Behind the backlash: White working-class politics in Baltimore, 1940–1980*. University of North Carolina Press.

Epple, D., R. Romano, & Sieg, H. (2008). Diversity and affirmative action in higher education. *Journal of Public Economic Theory, 10* (4), 475–501.

Ferguson, R. (2017). *We demand: The university and student protests*. University of California Press.

Fisher v. University of Texas I, 133 S. Ct. 2411 (2013).

Fisher v. University of Texas II, 136 S. Ct. 2198 (2016).

Flores, S. M., & Horn, C. L. (2015). *Texas top ten percent plan: How it works, what are its limits, and recommendations to consider*. Educational Testing Service.

Fortin, J. (2021). Critical race theory: A brief history. *New York Times*. https://www.nytimes.com/article/what-is-critical-race-theory.html?fbclid=IwAR1JFP04PTdwR8HdiNaKAtRrn_OnfsBNoTgzT88nGqyBp75TC98LVt7Ocbk

Gabriel, T., & Goldstein, D. (2021). Disputing racism's reach, Republicans rattle American schools. *New York Times.* https://www.nytimes.com/2021/06/01/us/politics/critical-race-theory.html

Garces, L. M. (2014). Aligning diversity, quality, and equity: The implications of legal and public policy developments for promoting racial diversity in graduate studies. *American Journal of Education, 120,* 457–480.

Garces, L. M., & Poon, O. (2018). *Asian Americans and race-conscious admissions: Understanding the conservative opposition's strategy of misinformation, intimidation, and racial division.* Los Angeles, CA: The Civil Rights Project. Retrieved June 26, 2019 from https://escholarship.org/uc/item/3560g5qq

Gotanda, N. (2004). Reflections on *Korematsu, Brown,* and White innocence. *Temple Political and Civil Rights Law Review, 13,* 663–674.

Gratz v. Bollinger, 539 US 244 (2003).

Grutter v. Bollinger, 539 US 306 (2003).

Guinier, L., & Torres, G. (2003). *The miner's canary: Enlisting race, resisting power, transforming democracy.* Harvard University Press.

Harris, C. I. (2003). What the Supreme Court did not hear in Grutter and Gratz. *Drake Law Review, 51,* 697–713.

Harris, C. I., & West-Faulcon, K. (2010). Reading *Ricci*: Whitening discrimination, racing test fairness. *UCLA Law Review, 58,* 73–165.

Hinger, S. (2018, October 18). Meet Edward Blum, the man who wants to kill affirmative action in higher education. ACLU. Retrieved June 26, 2019 from https://www.aclu.org/blog/racial-justice/affirmative-action/meet-edward-blum-man-who-wants-kill-affirmative-action-higher

Holloway, F. A. (1989). What is affirmative action? In F. A. Blanchard & F. J. Crosby (Eds.), *Affirmative action in perspective* (pp. 9–19). Springer.

Hoover, E. (2019, January 18). That other affirmative-action case: The battle over UNC's admissions policies heats up. *The Chronicle of Higher Education.* Retrieved from https://www.chronicle.com/article/That-Other-Affirmative-Action/245519

Horn, C. L., & Flores, S. M. (2003). *Percent plans in college admissions: A comparative analysis of three states' experiences.* Cambridge, MA: Civil Rights Project, Harvard University.

Hughes, S. A., Thompson Dorsey, D., & Carrillo, J. F. (2016). Causation Fallacy 2.0: Revisiting the myth and math of affirmative action. *Educational Policy, 30*(1), 63–93.

Hughey, M. W. (2014). "White Backlash in the 'Post-Racial' United States," *Ethnic and Racial Studies 37*(5): 721–730.

Jalonick, M. C. (2021) What insurrection? Growing number of GOP downplay January 6. The Associated Press. https://www.theguardian.com/us-news/2021/jul/06/republicans-effort-to-deny-the-capitol-attack-is-working-and-its-dangerous

Jaschik, S. (2013) *The Deceptive Data on Asians.* Retrieved on June 30, 2019, from https://www.insidehighered.com/news/2013/06/07/report-calls-end-grouping-asian-american-students-one-category

Jayakumar, U. M. (2015). *Why are all the black students still sitting together in the proverbial college cafeteria? A look at research informing the figurative question being taken by the Supreme Court in Fisher*. Higher Education Research Institute.

Jayakumar, U. M., & Adamian, A. A. (2015). Toward a critical race praxis for educational research: Lessons from affirmative action and social science advocacy. *Journal Committed to Social Change on Race and Ethnicity, 1*(1), 22–58.

Jayakumar, U. M., Garces, L. M., & Park, J. (Spring 2018). Reclaiming diversity: Advancing the next generation of diversity research toward racial equity. In M. B. Paulsen (Ed.), *Higher education: Handbook of theory and research* (pp. 11–79). Springer.

Jayakumar, U. M., & Page, S. E. (2021). Cultural capital and opportunities for exceptionalism: Bias in university admissions. *The Journal of Higher Education*. DOI: 10.1080/00221546.2021.1912554

Joseph, P. E. (2017, April 6). Why Black Lives Matter still matters. *The New Republic*. Retrieved from https://newrepublic.com/article/141700/black-lives-matter-still-matters-new-form-civil-rights-activism

Kahlenberg, R. (Ed.). (2014). *The future of affirmative action: New paths to higher education after* Fisher v. University of Texas. Century Foundation Press.

Karabel, J. (1984). Status-group struggle, organizational interests, and the limits of institutional autonomy: The transformation of Harvard, Yale, and Princeton, 1918–1940. *Theory & Society, 13*, 1–40.

Karabel, J. (2005). *The chosen: The hidden history of exclusion at Harvard, Yale, and Princeton*. Houghton Mifflin.

Kidder, W. C. (2006). Negative action versus affirmative action: Asian Pacific Americans are still caught in the crossfire. *Michigan Journal of Race and Law, 11*, 605–624.

Kidder, W. C. & Lempert, R. O. (2015). The mismatch myth in US higher education: A synthesis of empirical evidence at the law schools and undergraduate levels. In U. M. Jayakumar & L. M. Garces (Eds.), *Affirmative Action and Racial Equity: Considering the Evidence in Fisher to Forge the Path Ahead* (pp. 105–129). Routledge Press.

Kilgore, E. (2021). Why Republicans want voters to panic about critical race theory. *Intelligencer*. https://nymag.com/intelligencer/article/republicans-voters-panic-critical-race-theory.html

Kurlaender, M., Friedmann, E., & Chang, T. (2015). Access and diversity at the University of California in the post-affirmative action era. In U. M. Jayakumar & L. M. Garces, with F. Fernandez (Eds.), *Affirmative action and racial equity: Considering the Fisher case to forge the path ahead* (pp. 80–101). Routledge, Taylor & Francis.

Lamb, J. D. (1992). The real affirmative action babies: Legacy preferences at Harvard and Yale. *Columbia Journal of Law and Social Problems, 26*, 491–522.

Ledesma, M. C. (2012). Revisiting *Grutter* and *Gratz* in the wake of *Fisher*: Looking back to move forward. *Equity & Excellence in Education, 46*, 220–235.

Ledesma, M. C. (2019). California sunset: O'Connor's post-affirmative action ideal comes of age in California. *The Review of Higher Education, 42*, 227–254.

Lempert, R. (2016). Justice Kennedy and the *Fisher* revisit: Will the irrelevant prove decisive? *Texas Law Review, 94*, 108–120.

Massey, D. S., & Mooney, M. (2007). The effects of America's three affirmative action programs on academic performance. *Social Problems, 54*(1), 99–117.

Meraji, S. M. (2019, March 21). *50 years ago students shut down this college to demand ethnic studies courses.* (Radio program). NPR. Retrieved from https://www.npr.org/2019/03/21/705594577/50-years-ago-students-shut-down-this-college-to-demand-ethnic-studies-courses

Moses, M. M., & Chang, M. J. (2006). Toward a deeper understanding of the diversity rationale. *Educational Researcher, 35*, 6–11.

Oakes, J. (1979). A failure of vision: The collapse of the Freedman's Bureau courts. *Civil War History, 25*, 66–76.

Oakes, J., Rogers, J., Lipton, M., & Morrell, E. (2002). The social construction of college access: Confronting the technical, cultural, and political barriers of low-income students of Color. In W. G. Tierney & L. S. Hagedorn (Eds.), *Increasing access to college: Extending possibilities for all students* (pp. 105–121). SUNY Press.

Oppenheimer, D., Onwuachi-Willig, A., & Leong, N. (2019) Affirmative action. *Berkeley Journal of African-American Law & Policy, 20*(2), 1–17.

Orfield, G. (2015). Foreword. In U. M. Jayakumar & L. M. Garces (Eds.), *Affirmative action and racial equity: Considering the Fisher case to forge the path ahead* (pp. i–xxi). Routledge.

Outten, H. R., Schmitt, M. T., Miller, D. A., & Garcia, A. L. (2012). Feeling threatened about the future: Whites' emotional reactions to anticipated ethnic demographic changes. *Personality and Social Psychology Bulletin, 38*, 14–25.

Oyez. (n.d.). *Parents Involved in* Community Schools v. Seattle School District No. 1. Retrieved from https://www.oyez.org/cases/2006/05-908

Parents Involved in *Community Schools v. Seattle School District No. 1*, 551 US 701. (2007).

Park, J. (2018). *Race on campus: Debunking myths with data.* Harvard Education Press.

Peterson, R. (1968). *The scope of organized student protest in 1967–1968.* Oxford University Press.

Reardon, S. F., Baker, R., & Klasik, D. (2012). *Race, income, and enrollment patterns in highly selective colleges, 1982–2004.* Center for Education Policy Analysis, Stanford University.

Regents of the University of California v. Bakke, 438 US 265 (1978).

Ricci v. DiStefano, 557 US 557 (2009).

Richardson, J. D., & Lancendorfer, K. M. (2004). Framing affirmative action: The influence of race on newspaper editorial responses to the University of Michigan cases. *International Journal of Press/Politics, 9,* 74–94.

Robinson, K. J. (2016). *Fisher's* cautionary tale and the urgent need for equal access to an excellent education. *Harvard Law Review, 130,* 185–240.

Rogers, I. H. (2012). The black campus movement: Black students and the racial reconstruction of higher education, 1965–1972. Palgrave Macmillan.

Samson, F. L. (2013). Multiple group threat and malleable White attitudes towards academic merit. *Du Bois Review: Social Science Research on Race, 10,* 233–260.

Sander, R., & Taylor Jr., S. (2012). *Mismatch: How affirmative action hurts students it's intended to help, and why universities won't admit it.* Basic Books.

Santelices, M. V., & Wilson, M. (2010). Unfair treatment? The case of Freedle, the SAT and the standardization approach to differential item functioning. *Harvard Educational Review, 80*(1), 106–134.

Schmidt, P. (2014, November 18). Lawsuits against Harvard and UNC-Chapel Hill urge an end to race conscious admissions. *Chronicle of Higher Education.* Retrieved from http://www.chronicle.com/article/Lawsuits-Against-Harvard-and/150113

Schuette v. Coalition to Defend Affirmative Action, 572 US (2014).

Scobey, D. (2019, February 18). The path across America's divide starts at its colleges. *Chronicle of Higher Education.* Retrieved from https://www.chronicle.com/interactives/Trend19-Intrusion-Opinion

Shelby County v. Holder, 570 US (2013).

Smith, D. (2021). Republicans' effort to deny Capitol attack is working—and it's dangerous. *The Guardian.* https://www.theguardian.com/us-news/2021/jul/06/republicans-effort-to-deny-the-capitol-attack-is-working-and-its-dangerous

Stefancic, J., & Delgado, R. (1996). *No mercy: How conservative think tanks and foundations changed America's social agenda.* Temple University Press.

Thernstrom, S., & Thernstrom, A. M. (1997). *America in black and white: One nation indivisible.* Touchstone.

Tierney, W. G., & Chung, J. K. (2002). Affirmative action in a post-*Hopwood* era. In W. A. Smith, P. G. Altbach, & K. Lomotey (Eds.), *The racial crisis in American higher education* (rev. ed., pp. 271–283). SUNY Press.

Torres, G. (2015). Neoliberalism and affirmative action. *Cultural Dynamics, 27*(1), 43–62.

Valencia, R. R., & Suzuki, L. A. (2000). *Intelligence testing and minority students: Foundations, performance factors, and assessment issues.* Sage.

Warikoo, N. K. (2016). The diversity bargain and other dilemmas of race, admissions, and meritocracy at elite universities. University of Chicago Press.

West-Faulcon, K. (2017). Obscuring Asian penalty with illusions of Black bonus. *UCLA Law Review Discourse, 64,* 592–646.

Wright, D. K., & Garces, L. M. (2018). Understanding the controversy around race-based affirmative action in American higher education. In J. Blanchard (Ed.), *Controversies on campus: Debating the issues confronting American universities in the 21st century* (pp. 3–21). Praeger.

Young, I. M. (1990). *Justice and the politics of difference*. Princeton University Press.

Zamani-Gallaher, E. M., Green, D. O., Brown, M. C. II, & Stovall, D. O. (2009). *The case for affirmative action on campus: Concepts of equity, considerations for practice*. Stylus.

PART 3
THE DAY-TO-DAY REALITIES

Chapter 6

The Psychosocial Antecedents of Racial Battle Fatigue

WILLIAM A. SMITH

Tuesday, November 8, 2016, marked the 58th quadrennial presidential election and the positioning of Donald J. Trump as the 45th president-elect of the United States of America. Numerous people counted Trump out early on during his campaign. Doubters believed that Hilary Rodham Clinton would be the most likely person to follow President Barack H. Obama in the highest position in the country. Pundits said that Trump would come up short because his campaign was anchored in racist, sexist, and xenophobic rhetoric. Consequently, many were surprised that this did not happen.

Some analysts tried to blame the win on non-college-educated Whites. This theory did not stand up to the postelection analyses using the American Trends Panel (ATP) created by the Pew Research Center (PRC). The ATP is a nationally representative online survey panel of over 10,000 verified voters. The findings from the PRC's ATP report produced interesting results. For instance, President Trump received 62% and 47%, respectively, of White men's and women's vote, 38% of the college-educated White vote, and 64% of the non-college-graduate White vote (For most Trump voters, "very warm" feelings for him endured, 2018). The Pew Research Center reported another critical finding. About one-third (35%) of those who voted for Trump initially felt "cold" toward him in April 2016. These voters increasingly became "warmer" toward Trump by September 2016

(57%). They progressively warmed up to him by November 2016 (71%) and maintained their enthusiasm through to March 2018 (67%). About two-thirds (65%) of those Trump voters who started with "warm" feelings sustained their passion in September 2016 (81%), November 2016 (86%), and into March 2018 (83%).

Concomitantly, while Trump-positive feelings were growing, we watched a dramatic rise in and recognition of racial hatred and white supremacy in society and on postsecondary campuses. In fact, counties where Trump won by larger margins, or those that simply hosted a Trump campaign rally in 2016, witnessed more than twice as many hate crimes as did areas that did not host a rally (Edwards & Rushin, 2018; Williams & Gelfand, 2020). Under the Trump presidency, many believed that higher education was under attack by the president's right-wing populists (Giroux, 2019). Some critics have suggested that Trump has shaped the cultural landscape in higher education as a "poisonous public pedagogy of sensationalism, easy consumption, bigotry, fear, and distraction" (Giroux, 2019, p. 9). On the one hand, Trump labeled undocumented Mexicans as a problem people who are rapists and drug dealers illegally coming across the border along with a few good people mixed in. On the other hand, Trump also claimed that there were "very fine people on both sides" of the deadly violence during the 2017 march on the University of Virginia campus in Charlottesville, Virginia, by white nationalists, neo-Nazis, Ku Klux Klan members, and other tiki torch–carrying white supremacists. These racist protesters were met by anti-racist demonstrators and counterprotesters. Trump's intentional straddling of the fence between racist hate-filled ideologues and the counterprotestors was more than just tacit support—some would argue it was a full-throated endorsement—of white supremacists and a nationalists' dogma (Giroux, 2019). The backing of a racist ideology and climate and the attack on the democratic mission is new neither to the United States nor to its institutions of higher education. Given the current racial crisis in American higher education and society, we must have a more precise understanding of and vocabulary for the psychosocial antecedents of racial battle fatigue for targets of white supremacy.

This chapter provides an overview of the psychosocial antecedents of racial battle fatigue. At the very foundation of US society, including postsecondary education, are racism, institutionalized white supremacy, and colonialism (see chapter 1 in this volume). Also foundational to US society is sexism—and, later, what would be named as *homophobia* and *transphobia*. Long-standing patterns of institutional and systemic racism have been maintained in *Plessy*-like conditions on today's post-*Brown* campuses. Racialized targets of white supremacy (ToWS; i.e., American Indians, African Americans/Blacks, Asian Americans, Latinas/os/x, Pacific Islanders, and bi- and multiracial people) have—as students, faculty, staff, and administrators—been forced to resist daily against racistly hostile conditions while being required to be competitive, productive, and successful, without consideration to the racist ecology.

"Racism" is a commonly used term, yet its definition does not always provide a proper view of the varied experiences scholars have for diverse interpretations of race-related stress. By specifying a more explicit description of anti-Black racism, I offer an effective supplementary way of linking anti-Black racism to understanding racial battle fatigue as an outcome and a theoretical framework. However, while I use anti-Black racism as an example to create this understanding, it is notwithstanding that anti-American Indian, anti-Asian American, anti-Latina/o/x, anti-Pacific Islander, anti-multiracial, and anti–racially ambiguous racism follow this same logic. I also address the psychosocial adaptation experiences that ToWS encounter on historically white campuses. In this way, I describe a more elucidated framework, a manifesto, for connecting racial microlevel aggressions (i.e., where racial microaggressions occur) to racial battle fatigue. I conclude with a discussion on trauma-informed care, role strain, and racial socialization as tools for individuals and helping professionals to reduce racial battle fatigue, disrupt racism, and promote social justice.

Defining Racism and Subordinate-Racialized Groups

The Anti-Defamation League's (ADL) Center on Extremism tracked the increasing number of white supremacist propaganda activities in 2019, including racist fliers, stickers, banners, and posters (ADL, 2020). The most alarming finding was that US white supremacist propaganda incidents rose by 120% in 2019. In addition, the ADL report provided data showing increased events both on and off campus, more than doubling the activity in 2018. There were a total of 2,713 cases reported in 2019, with 630 on campus, compared to 1,214 in 2018, with 320 on campus (ADL, 2020). The 2019 incidents of racist propaganda were on 433 separate campuses in 42 states and the District of Columbia. Clearly, historically white colleges and universities are a racist microcosm of society at large. However, before understanding the dynamics of these institutions, the weight of racism must be clarified.

Racism is a complex and oppressive system supported by white history, laws, policies, culture, political economies, traditions, organizations, schooling, and institutions (Feagin, 2013). Sociologist Joe R. Feagin (2014) defines systemic racism as "a diverse assortment of racist practices: the unjustly gained economic and political power of Whites; the continuing resource inequalities; the rationalizing White-racist frame; and the major institutions created to preserve White advantage and power" (p. 9). Critical race theorist Tommy J. Curry (2017) defines racism as "a complex nexus, a cognitive architecture used to invent, reimagine, and evolve the presumed political, social, economic, sexual, and psychological superiority of the White races in society while materializing the imagined inferiority and hastening the death of inferior races. Said differently, racism is the manifestation of the social processes and concurrent logics that facilitate the death and dying of racially subjugated peoples" (p. 4). Taken together, I believe these two definitions provide the backdrop for understanding systemic white advantage and power along with the coexisting reasons that foster premature death and dying that result from the biopsychosocial violence that is the system of anti-Black racism.

Racism is a violent act that the body codes as an attack at the organism level. As a result, racism can be experienced as macro-level (e.g., at the societal level or communities/states/government/institutions), meso-level (e.g., groups, workplace, and decisionmakers practices), and micro-level (e.g., at the individual, daily, or smaller group levels) stressors/aggressions that negatively affects the psychological, emotional, and physiological health of racialized targets of white supremacy (Anderson, 1989; Brondolo et al., 2011; Carter & Forsyth, 2010; Pierce, 1970, 1974, 1975a, 1975b, 1988, 1995; Ramos, Jaccard, & Guilamo-Ramos, 2003; Smith, 2004, 2008a, 2008b; Williams, 2021). In addition, Dr. Eduardo Bonilla-Silva (2015) reminds us that it is *racism* that constructs and buttresses *race*, and *racism* is at the foundation of this violence experienced by targets. Subsequently, I use *anti-Black racism* as an example of linking a racism-related definition to this systemic process.

Anti-Black racism is a dangerous and specific stressor that poses a violent threat to the biological, physical, cultural, mental, and social health and the associated interlocking identities of the Black person (e.g., anti-Black misogyny, anti-Black misandry, anti-Black homophobia, anti-Black transphobia, colorism, anti-Black ableism oppression [or anti-Black ableism], etc.). One of the most significant challenges is the quest for biopsychosocial equilibrium versus disequilibrium in a racist society that marginalizes ToWS into substandard, subordinated racial groups. This challenge is one in which the marginalized person must constantly try to maintain a state of homeostasis and psychological clarity during external threats that can negatively affect their biology, thoughts, attitude, emotions, and behavior.

The charge to more fully understand racial disequilibrium raises a corollary charge to comprehend better how racial misogyny, racial misandry, and racism against racially minoritized queer people affect their lives, achievements, ambitions, wealth, safety, and health.[1] The goal of optimal health is in identifying and counteracting the biopsychosocial and behavioral consequences of actual or perceived racism and the social determinants of racism. This articulation of anti-Black racism (or anti-American Indian racism, anti-Asian American racism, anti-Latina/o/x racism, anti-Pacific Islander racism, anti-racially ambiguous racism, anti-biracial, anti-multiracial people racism, etc.) eliminates the need for arguing about the intentions of the perpetrator(s) or the institutions of racism instead of looking more critically at their effects.

The threat to optimal health and safety in a racist society is the inability to respond with effective measures. For instance, most racialized individuals have a psychosocial orientation obviously (but not solely) based on their racial group's culture, customs, traditions, and socialization processes (I talk more about this in the section on trauma-informed care). Racism disrupts this cultural psychosocial orientation process through a disturbed person-environmental racist relationship (Ahmed, 2006). Consequently, racism attacks this group-centered position and may throw the unsuspecting target into psychosocial disorientation. Depending on the target's previous commitment to an adaptive racial socialization process, they may stay in this confusing, inferior, and harmful position for a longer or shorter time. The successful target emerges from this attack with a new psychosocial orientation, having learned or employed a defensive resilience strategy to avoid racism's utter grip (Smith, 2016).

We Charge Genocide:
Identifying (Racist) Racial Misandry and Racial Misogyny

> Out of the inhuman black ghettos of American cities, out of the cotton plantations of the South, comes this record of mass slayings on the basis of race, of lives deliberately warped and distorted by the willful creation of conditions making for premature death, poverty and disease. It is a record that calls aloud for condemnation, for an end to these

> terrible injustices that constitute a daily and every-increasing violation of the United Nations Convention on the Prevention and Punishment of the Crime of Genocide.
>
> —William L. Patterson, "We Charge Genocide" (1952)

This quote is from "We Charge Genocide: The Historic Petition to the United Nations for Relief from a Crime of the United States Government against the Negro People," a petition was delivered at the United Nations' Paris meeting of 1951 by petition editor William L. Patterson, the executive director of the Civil Rights Congress, with many significant copetitioners, such as W. E. B. Du Bois and Paul Robeson. The petition argued that an inaccurate understanding of genocide is to believe that it means the total annihilation of a group of people (i.e., Black people). In fact, the Genocide Convention's definition, adopted by the General Assembly of the United Nations on December 9, 1948, stated that "any intent to destroy, in whole or in part, a national, racial, ethnic or religious group is genocide" (Patterson, 1951, p. xi). However, more importantly, the definition went on to declare that "causing serious *bodily or mental harm* to members of the group" (p. xi; emphasis added) is an act of genocide.

Bodily or mental harm to a racial group is the key to understanding oppression, discrimination, subordination, white supremacy, and the effects on racialized targets (Yosso et al., 2022). Ample research has shown that ToWS, who are subordinated by race and any one of these other factors regarding their gender, sexuality, physical ability, social class, and neurodiversity, are besieged, punished, and imprisoned by the US criminal justice system more than Whites who are subordinated by the same factors (Quigley, 2011). They also suffer from racism in health care, which is associated with their higher morbidity and mortality (McKenzie, 2003). They have fewer opportunities for the benefits of homeownership (Perry, 2019), face barriers to their advancement in employment (Dovidio & Gaertner, 2004) and earnings (Darity, 2003), and endure unjust impoverishment (Feagin, 2014). Additionally, Black members of the LGBTQ+ community report higher levels of stigma in queer spaces (McConnell et al., 2018). Phenotype also plays a role in the subordination of groups. Using data from the 1980 National Survey of Black Americans, Verna Keith and Cedric Herring (1991) found that being Black with a darker skin tone was positively correlated with lower education, less prestigious occupations, lower personal income, and less family income than was being Black with a lighter complexion.

Adolfo Cuevas and his research team (Cuevas, Dawson, & Williams, 2016) analyzed more than 1,000 studies on race and skin color in Latinx health. Their findings reported that skin color is a critical factor for predicting life chances and health. Afro-Latinx and darker-skinned Latinx faced significantly poorer racial and social determinants of health than White Latinx, especially when living in the United States's 48 contiguous states. These are acts of bodily and mental harm coded as violence (Smith, 2004). Racism, as a result, is a violent act, and the body remembers!

In a study on Asian, Black, and Latina/o/x adults, Elizabeth Brondolo et al. (2011) found that the impact of racism and self-report health was significant and did not differ across racialized groups. Subsequently, the lives of racialized targets of white supremacy are consistently placed in danger. Therefore, we must continue to properly define racism as an act of violence, and racial micro-level aggressions as weapons of mass destruction of human lives. Every racist microaction has corresponding racial microaggressions. To be sure, there is a systemic and institutional aversion to ToWS. I define these racist institutional and systemic antipathies as racial (racist) misandry, racial (racist) misogyny, and racial (racist) queer-and-trans* phobia.[2]

Thus, anti-Black misandry, anti-Black misogyny, and anti-Black queer-and-trans*-phobic mechanisms are systemic and ideological justifications toward the aversion, oppression, subordination, violence, silencing, controlling, hyperpolicing, and justified killing of Black boys and men (anti-Black misandry; e.g., George Floyd), Black girls and women (anti-Black misogyny; e.g., Sandra Bland), and queer, trans*, nonbinary, gender-nonconforming Black people (e.g., Monika Diamond, a Black transgender woman who was killed in Charlotte, North Carolina in 2020). Anti-Black misandry, anti-Black misogyny, and anti-Black queer-and-trans*-phobic mechanisms exist to support and perpetuate a permanent underclass of Black people and threaten their mental and physical life. We have witnessed these oppressive mechanisms propagated through racist scholarly ontologies (through pro-White understandings of how things exist), axiologies (through pro-White values, ethics, aesthetics, religious practices, and even spiritual interpretations), epistemologies (through pro-White racial ways of knowing), and cosmologies (e.g., pro-White origin stories and beliefs) (Smith, 2010; Smith, Yosso, & Solórzano, 2007). As a result, white supremacy and oppression form America's quintessential racial contract, a sociopolitical and racist system that primarily operates in the background to rule over racialized targets of white supremacy (Mills, 1997).

Using lenses for racial (or racist) misandry, misogyny, and anti-queer-and-trans* mechanisms are crucial because it allows us to challenge frameworks, theories, biases, and inadequate interpretations of the lives of subordinated, casted, and racialized people. These lenses require us to disaggregate the often used categorical or group-based explanations. For example, instead of examining data about US Latinx–grouped people, we learn much more when we disaggregate by ethnic gender groups (e.g., Mexican American men [Chicano] and Mexican American women [Chicana], Puerto Rican men and Puerto Rican women, Cuban American men and Cuban American women, Salvadoran American men and Salvadoran American women, and Dominican American men and Dominican American women) and nonbinary identities, such as a Salvadoran American queer nonbinary person. These considerations and their ethnic or racialized identities, while representing the many different genders and queer identities, offer a more accurate insight into a person's lived ethnoracial experiences. The aim is to prevent the *flattening* of race, gender, sexuality, class, ability, and other critical factors of a person's interlocking identities.

It is essential to disaggregate data/experiences by more unique group identities to understand the effects of racism more thoroughly. For instance, examining only one reference group (e.g., Korean American gender-fluid people) provides more relevant and detailed information than suppressing or silencing their minoritized experiences within the overall racial groups' experience. Kathryn Stockton (2021) describes in her book *Gender(s)* the historical problems of the gender concept as we know. She states, "Gender is made of things that are not gender: race and money. Gender is fundamentally raced and classed in these United States." Stockton further explains, "The history of the concept 'gender' bears this out, in ways that may amaze you. When we know this history, the notion of 'opposite sexes' falls apart. In fact, the notion of there being 'two sexes' forcefully crumbles" (p. 11–12). Stockton provides an essential point of clarification that is historically and contemporarily grounded. She goes on to say, "Since the thirteen colonies, we have made legal and often biological distinctions between at least six categories (are they six sexes?): white man, white woman, Black man, Black woman, Native man, Native woman . . . joined by other sexes in other territories. There can be no opposites with six or more sexes. Due to the US system of race, the 'opposite sex' is a phantom concept. Nobody lives it. Yet what stunning power it wields. It's had consequences (what an understatement) for this country's dealings with race" (p. 11–12). Tommy J. Curry's book *The Man-Not* (2017) adds to this history on how Black men have explicitly been treated. He writes, "The Black male is negated not from an origin of (human) being, but from nihility. Frantz Fanon's reflection on objecthood and nonbeing are not simply descriptions of negation; they are not terms of proxemics but terms to register. Nonbeing expresses the condition of Black male being—the nihility from it is birthed" (p. 6–7). Our research, assessments, and interpretations must consider these valuable perspectives. However, unfortunately, most of today's social science perspectives and analyses of racial or gender matters are suppressed and controlled through who gets accepted in graduate admissions or who receives scholarships, fellowships, employment, tenure, publications, and professional presentations based upon conforming to elite decision makers' and academic power brokers' biases (Feagin, 2020).

Subsequently, unique racial subcategories (*race+*, which can be viewed as micro-races) better inform appropriate responses to racism (*racism+*, which is an aspect of micro group-level racism). Thus, we should avoid population bias reporting when we do not have a representative sample in our qualitative and quantitative studies. Too often, a study on African American postsecondary students will report 70–86% Black women participants and claim that the findings honestly tell us something about Black people while marginalizing the *race+* experiences of Black men, Black queers, and Black people with disabilities. Stockton explains, "[Here] is the danger of binary thought. Dangers to many good things—our health, income distribution, fairness in labor, modes of well-being, relation to the land—result from masculine/feminine mandates that con us into thinking that devotion to these norms will deliver the good life that, in reality, corporate power and white supremacy reserve for themselves. We can scout these dangers via racial histories. Each strikes a blow to 'opposites attract.' Each shows the harm of this fateful concept" (Stockton, 2021, p. 149). Instead, it would be better and more honest to focus exclusively on self-identified African American cis-gender straight able-body middle-class women rather than making a generalized claim for all Blacks. Unfortunately, this is the weaknesses in most studies, and it reflects our bias-centered views of the world.

For instance, Patricia Coogan and colleagues (2020) were interested in determining how racism affected African American women's subjective cognitive functioning (SCF) based on psychological stress and memory decline. In a prospective cohort study of 59,000 Black women aged 21 through 69 years, they used health questionnaires to elicit demographic and lifestyle factor information such as reproductive history and medical conditions. Analyses were run on women 55 years old and older (a total of 17,323 who met a specific criterion and had complete data). The findings showed that women who experienced both daily and institutional racism had decreased SCF. Black women in the highest quartile of the everyday racism score had almost three times (2.75) the risk of poor SCF as women in the lowest quartile.

Furthermore, Black women who indicated that they were experiencing institutional racism in five to six domains also had almost three times (2.66) the risk of poor SCF as those who reported not undergoing any such experiences. Thus, this study is essential for understanding how institutional racism, in its chronic forms, can explain why rates of dementia and Alzheimer's disease are higher in African American women than among other women, but how the impact of racism was not considered a factor in the differential. Unfortunately, sexuality was not identified, as is the case in most studies, which would have given us critical *race+* or micro-racial components to consider.

Jim Sidanius and Felicia Pratto (1999) studied African American boys and men as a racially subordinated group. In *Social Dominance Theory of Social Hierarchy and Oppression*, Sidanius and Pratto explain that one of the main components of social dominance is the *arbitrary-set system*: "The arbitrary-set system is filled with socially constructed and highly salient groups based on characteristics such as clan, ethnicity, . . . caste, social class, religious sect, . . . or any other socially relevant group distinction that the human imagination is capable of constructing" (p. 33). They assert that recognizing the existence of the arbitrary-set system provides us with a more nuanced understanding of control by the dominant group. "The arbitrary-set system is also, by far, associated with the greatest degree of violence, brutality, and oppression" (p. 34). According to the authors, part of the arbitrary-set system is the subordinate-male target hypothesis (SMTH). For instance, the SMTH might have offered a valuable way to explain additional findings in my studies on encounters with the policing of Black men's bodies (Smith, Allen, & Danley, 2007; Smith et al., 2016). These collegiate Black men reported experiencing hypervisibility while also being racialized targets of hypersurveillance on historically white campuses. They described being continually threatened and controlled by law enforcement and community reign, all components of SMTH. The arbitrary-set system's SMTH is valuable, in this regard, for explaining subordinated racialized men's experiences. SMTH is an example of moving closer to what I call an *Afrisandric-centered analysis* (i.e., maintaining a positive orientation toward Black boys and men's race, class, sexuality, gender, and (dis)ability identities and forms of oppression at the center of your viewpoint and research construction while keeping their strength-based and societal/institutional coping responses at the forefront of analysis).

The SMTH does not suggest the nonexistence of discrimination, domination, or violence against women. Instead, it offers an intersecting psychology of genders and arbitrary-set conflict. In fact, James Sidanius and colleagues (2018) have better articulated the ability of social dominance theory (SDT) to explain the intersectional intricacies of racism and sexism by introducing a theory of gender prejudice (TGP), a derivative of SDT. In a similar manner of offering a complex examination, Lourdes D. Follins, J. J. Walker, and Michelel K. Lewis (2014) state that "Black lesbian, gay, bisexual, and transgender (LGBT) individuals in the United States are more likely to experience violence across the lifespan than are LGBT individuals of other ethnoracial backgrounds or heterosexuals of any ethnoracial group" (pp. 190–191). Understanding this propensity to experience violence, the authors were interested in sharing the forms of resilience Black LGBT people use. For instance, African consciousness (a strong connection and group attachment to Black individuals and ancestors) was a very prominent and vital finding in creating a strong sense of self-acceptance among some Black lesbians. These African conscious Black lesbians defined themselves and resisted accepting sexual orientation and gender identity labels given to them by others.

Possessing a clearer understanding of racially minoritized LGBTQ+ people's racial experiences and resilient responses on and off campus is critical. Before COVID-19, suicide was the 10th leading cause of death in the United States. This paints one gruesome picture of suicidality (e.g., attempts and ideations) among all US citizens. Unfortunately, a more precise and horrific picture develops when we examine the effects of sexual and gender identities. People who are LGBTQ+ are approximately twice as likely to have suicidal ideation and greater rates of attempting suicide than their straight and cisgender counterparts (Sutter and Perrin, 2016). In a study on LGBTQ People of Color (POC), Megan Sutter and Paul B. Perrin (2016) found that racism directly affected their mental health but was not associated with suicidal ideation. LGBTQ-based discrimination had a more direct effect on mental health than suicidal ideation. I recognize that aggregating the unique diversities of individual LGBTQ people and then adding a + (plus sign) is as problematic as putting all Asian American or Latina/o/x from various ethnic groups (*race*+) into one group. This is a limitation in our current data collection and articulation. We must do better!

Fortunately, Kimberly Balsam and colleagues (2011) have come very close in this regard with the development of their LGBT People of Color Microaggressions Scale. The scale offers valuable insight into LGBTQ POC microaggressive experiences. For instance, certain stereotypical beliefs about race/ethnicity and sexual prowess and endowment might lead to feelings of rejection and sexual objectification of LGBTQ POC by White LGBTQ members (Balsam et al., 2011). Furthermore, their findings suggested that racism displayed by romantic partners and close friends had a negative impact on their mental health. Additionally, they found an association between depression and perceived stress in the LGBT Relationship Racism subscale. Along this same line, the researchers reported a significant finding: "Asian American men were considered among the least sexually desirable by gay men from other races/ethnicities and were also perceived to be less desirable by other Asian American gay men. Finally, the fact that income and education level were not predictive of LGBT-POC microaggressions is notable; such experiences appear to be prominent for LGBT-POC regardless of social class or other types of privilege" (p. 171). This dynamic has powerful historical roots in the gendering of Asian Americans due to citizenship status (Stockton, 2021).

Research is sparser on Black self-identified gay, bisexual, and non-gay-identified men who have sex with men. Previous attention was paid more to their sexual risk behaviors and roles in transmitting HIV among other gay/bisexual men and Black straight cis-gendered women. However, Follins, Walker, and Lewis's (2014) literature review indicated that these men used similar coping strategies for dealing with racism (e.g., heightened levels of spirituality, extended family caring, self-love, and acceptance) as did African conscious Black lesbians. D.-L. Stewart (2021) warns us that mere diversity research can operate as a system of containment: "This containment drives focus and research to certain diversity issues deemed most important and creates research undesirables who are marginalized further by research/ers" (p. 9). Adopting "trickle up high impact practices" in our research and praxis can help ensure that trans* and queer people are visible, central, and in partnership with our desire to create a more liberatory space (Stewart & Nicolazzo, 2018). Researchers are calling for better scholarship, policy development, and programs that address the complexities that lie within the multiple identities among queer and trans* People of Color (QTPOC) (Akerlund & Cheung, 2000; Bey, 2017; Garvey et al., 2019; Misawa, 2010; Nicolazzo, 2016; Rankin, Weber, & Garvey; 2015). In summary, we should provide closer, more precise attention to disaggregating racially subordinated people by their gender and sexuality (*race+*). Racial misandry, racial misogyny, racial queer-and-trans*-phobic discrimination, microaggressions, SDT, SMTH, and TGP are appropriately sophisticated to capture many of the entanglements of violence, oppression, subordination, discrimination, and brutality within systems of white supremacy and sex/gender subjugation.

Equally as important as the aforementioned interlocking identities is anti-Black ableism. Kathleen R. Bogart and Dana S. Dunn (2019) define ableism as "stereotyping, prejudice, discrimination, and social oppression toward people with disabilities" (p. 651). I define racialized ableism (e.g., anti-Black ableism) in a similar way, as the *stereotyping, prejudice, discrimination, and social oppression toward racialized disabled targets of white supremacy*. As a result, this group should be centered in examinations of their unique experiences. For instance, the voices of the ToWS within the disability community are largely unheard and rendered invisible. Activists from this community, composed primarily of racialized targets of white supremacy, have stepped up to address this specific form of racism (Harriet Tubman Collective, 2018). The Harriet Tubman Collective has taken issue with the "disability/deaf rights community's white supremacy problem" (Harriet Tubman Collective, 2018). These activists claim that there has been a long history of "erasure, extraction, and exploitation of Disabled Black, Indigenous, PoC community builders and advocates by white researchers, journalists and the entities that fund them" (Harriet Tubman Collective, 2018). They charge White scholars with ignoring the centuries-long violence by the police against racialized disabled ToWS. They also accuse them of making elementary errors using a "white gaze" in their research and then claiming that their scholarship is "innovative and new."

Furthermore, as in other areas of society, White scholars co-opt and repackage contributions made by racialized disabled targets of white supremacy as "new and praiseworthy" scholarship when White people present it. The Harriet Tubman Collective points to the problem of white supremacy in reporting and recognizing the experiences of racialized disabled ToWS in larger data collections and article production. The development of DisCrit offers a promising insight into how patterns of oppression distinctively interlock to target individuals at the margins of whiteness and ability (Annamma, Connor, & Ferri, 2013; Annamma, Ferri, & Connor, 2018a,b).

Subini Ancy Annamma and colleagues (Annamma, Connor, & Ferri, 2013; Annamma, Ferri, & Connor, 2018a, 2018b) offer a hybridization of critical race theory and disability studies with the intention to demolish the system of inequality established upon racism and ableism while offering a theoretical framework called dis/ability critical race studies, or DisCrit. These scholars maintain that "DisCrit also accounts for the complex histories in which racially "othered" bodies are marked as physically, psychologically, or morally deficient, a status further codified through scientific racism. Intersectionality thus serves both as the impetus for DisCrit as well as a necessary corrective to what Chris Bell (2006) rightly names "White dis-ability studies" (p. 230). DisCrit proposes a legacy of historical beliefs and abuses about race and disability that has its roots in white supremacy. It also reports that African American students face the brunt of this form of racism and ableism. According to their research, and compared to White students, Black students are three times as likely to be labeled mentally retarded. They are twice as likely to be labeled as emotionally disturbed. Black students are also one and half times more likely to be considered learning disabled. While Black students are at risk of being in an alarming overrepresentation in these categories, American Indian, Latinx, and Native Alaskan students are also disproportionately represented (Annamma, Connor, & Ferri, 2013).

In summary, socioeconomic status (class), race, gender, sexuality, physical abilities, and neurodiversity are all nonnegotiables when it comes to understanding the full domination and subordination efforts that face targets of white supremacy.

Racial Battle Fatigue in Society and Schools

In 1970, Dr. Chester M. Pierce argued that racism in the United States was a public and mental health illness. Pierce (1970) claimed that white supremacy used offensive mechanisms in the form of racial microaggressions, and that the sum of these actions was racism, "a lethal disease" (p. 267). He went on to articulate, "The offensive mechanism which assures that the person in the inferior status is ignored, tyrannized, terrorized, and minimized constitute[s] the fabric from which is cut the cloth of statistics that describes the plight of the ghetto citizen. It is a summation of collective micro-offenses by the majority that ignores the fact that a massive commitment is needed to make the ghetto school fail" (pp. 267–268). In short, as I call them today, offensive *racist* mechanisms are intentionally used as psychosocial pollutants, which include physical threats of violence and examples of death to keep racialized people in their place (Curry, 2017; Pierce, 1970). These offensive racist mechanisms put additional frustration, confusion, and role strain on the racialized target, family, friends, and work life (Bowman, 2006). Pierce (1970) stated, "It is difficult, if not impossible, for a Black to understand how a White, particularly a privileged White, can exhibit offensive microaggressions without considering [himself/herself] a murderer" (268). These offensive racist micro-level aggressions also operate within systems of injustice, such as the hyperpolicing of racialized neighborhoods and in schools as local city uniformed police serving in the capacity of school "resource officers."

Critical race theory scholars have helped to popularize and extend our understanding about the impact of racial micro-level aggressions in education and society (Annamma, Connor, & Ferri, 2013; Annamma, Ferri, Connor, 2018a, 2018b; D. A. Bell, 1992, 1995; Brayboy, 2005; Brooms, 2016; Curry, 2017; DeCuir & Dixson, 2004; DeCuir-Gunby & Gunby, 2016; Delgado & Stefancic, 2017; Gómez, 2015; Gomez et al., 2011; Harper, 2012; Hughes & Giles, 2010; Jones, 2021; Kenny Nienhusser, Vega, & Carquin, 2016; Ladson-Billings, 2014; Ladson-Billings & Tate, 1995; Leonardo, 2009; McGee & Stovall, 2015; Parker, 2015; Parker & Lynn, 2002; Patton, 2016; Patton et al., 2007; Pérez Huber, & Solórzano, 2015; Stovall, 2006; Sue et al., 2007; Villalpando, 2003; Yosso, 2005; Yosso et al., 2009). In 1969, Pierce suggested that "probably the most grievous of offensive mechanisms spewed at victims of racism and sexism are microaggressions. These are subtle, innocuous, preconscious, or unconscious degradations, and putdowns, often kinetic but capable of being verbal and/or kinetic. In and of itself a microaggression may seem harmless, but the cumulative burden of a lifetime of microaggressions can theoretically contribute to diminished mortality, augmented morbidity, and flattened confidence" (Pierce, 1995, p. 281). Since these seminal contributions by Dr. Chester Pierce, scholars such as Daniel G. Solórzano, Walter R. Allen, and Grace Carroll (2002) have made significant advances in racial microaggressions research in higher education by explaining how they attack "one's race, gender, class, sexuality, language, immigration status, phenotype, accent or surname" (p. 17). Tara J. Yosso, William A. Smith, Miguel Ceja, and Daniel G. Solórzano (2009) adapted Dr. Pierce's definition to show how racial microaggressions affected Latina/o/x students at historically White campuses. This study found three types of racial microaggressive experiences that were replete on these campuses: first were frequent putdowns and racist jokes about Latina/o/x people, next was an overall system supporting interpersonal discrimination, and finally, institutional aggression toward Latina/o/x students reinforced a lowered sense of belonging. Derald Wing Sue et al. (2007) went further and classified racial microaggressions into three groups: microassaults, microinsults, and microinvalidations. These classifications suggest that racial microaggressions are multifaceted and take on many forms.

I extend Sue and colleagues' (2007) classification of racial microaggressions to capture the recent evidence of how they operate from a racial battle fatigue framing. I agree with Sue and his collaborators' findings that micro-insults frequently occur, and that they are "characterized by communications that convey rudeness and insensitivity and demean a person's racial heritage or identity. Microinsults represent subtle snubs, frequently unknown to the perpetrator, but that clearly convey a hidden insulting message to the recipient of color" (p. 274). However, microinsults can and do occur at the micro level, meso level, and macro level under certain contexts. Additionally, their definition of micro-invalidations is empirically evident as being "characterized by communications that exclude, negate, or nullify the psychological thoughts, feelings, or experiential reality of a person of color" (p. 274). J. Luke Wood and Frank Harris III (2021a, 2021b, 2021c) address an additional concern they identify as "racelighting." The intentions of racelighting ToWS are to make them question their thoughts, actions, and lived experiences based upon a racialized message. If racelighting is effective, ToWS will question their interpretation of reality or whether they are hypersensitive. One of the primary goals of whiteness and white supremacy, using offensive racist mechanisms such as racelighting and other racial microaggressions, mesoaggressions, and macroaggressions, is to force the nondominant racial group into ideological and cultural compliance. For instance, in African Americans, I identify this as *Afropenia*. Afropenia results from constant micro-level to macro-level anti-Black psychological attacks that produce deficiencies in a Black person's/group's Africanity, African Americanness, or Blackness and that can lead to alien-self disorders, anti-self disorders, self-destructive disorders, and organic disorders (Akbar, 1991). To be sure, all nondominant racial groups continuously fight to maintain a healthy racial/cultural identity under whiteness. These are prevalent occurrences in the lives of racialized targets of white supremacy. As a result, I offer a taxonomy to understand better how offensive racist mechanisms lead to racial battle fatigue at various forms and levels of aggression (see figure 6.1).

As shown in this chapter, racist micro-insults and micro-invalidations are common in the lives of ToWS. As a result, as shown in figure 6.1, I place them as part of the foundation of offensive racist mechanisms. Micro-insults and micro-invalidations can be viewed as subtle, innocuous, preconscious, or unconscious degradations and putdowns. However, increasingly, ToWS

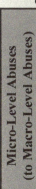

Figure 6.1. Offensive racist mechanisms. Author created.

Micro-Level Abuses (to Macro-Level Abuses)

Racial micro-level abuses (to macro-level abuses) are repetitive systemic and collective actions of purposeful assaults, aggressions, insults, and invalidations with the intentions to oppress, manipulate, hurt, weaken, marginalize, frighten, or torture a racialized person/group mentally, emotionally, physically, politically, economically, and socially that results in individual or group racial battle fatigue.

Micro-Level Aggressions

Racial micro-level aggressions are the racist insults and invalidations, or the summation of collective racist micro-offenses, perpetrated by a dominant racial group that tyrannizes, terrorizes, and marginalizes a racial target or group. In turn, the sum of these actions is the "lethal disease" of racism, which can turn into racial battle fatigue.

Micro-Level Invalidations

A racial micro-level invalidation is characterized by communications that are intended to exclude, negate, or nullify the psychological thoughts, feelings, or experiences of a racial target, group, or organization

Micro-Level Assaults

A racial micro-level assault is an overt racist physical, verbal, or nonverbal attack intended to cause harm to the racial target. This assault could be through defamation, ostracization, or other prejudicial actions, including psychological, physical, or emotional violence that results in racial battle fatigue.

Micro-Level Insults

A racial micro-level insult can be an intentional or fortuitous action by a perpetrator that the racial target, group, or organization codes as offensive, uncivil, or impertinent. These insults can be interpreted as the denigration of the racial target's culture, identity, background, perspective, or lived reality or organizational mission. Oftentimes, the perpetrator believes they are complimenting the target, but the target perceives it as a "backhanded compliment" (e.g., "Black people are so athletic and great dancers!")

are reporting the blatancy of offensive racist mechanisms. Consequently, micro-insults and micro-invalidations develop into micro-level aggressions to macro-level aggressions. I use micro-*level* to signal that these are mundane, smaller system threats to racialized individuals, families, groups, and race/ethnic-based organizations. This is where targets believe that something more aggressive and systemic is happening, irrespective of how they try to accommodate racism or make demands for the aggression to stop. Pierce (1995) writes that "it is a summation of collective micro-offenses by the Whites that applies economic terrors to poor Blacks who have the temerity to demand what the law provides" (p. 268). Thus, these offenses are a cumulation of subtle to blatant aggressions.

Sue and his research partners (2007) help explain the next part of the taxonomy I offer as micro-level assaults: "A microassault is an explicit racial derogation characterized by a verbal or nonverbal attack meant to hurt the intended victim through name-calling, avoidant behavior, or purposeful discriminatory actions" (p. 274). Thus, racist micro-level assaults are intended threats, many of which rise to the level of unaddressed or unreported hate crimes. Still, in effect, they contribute to the diminished mortality, augmented morbidity, and flattened confidence of ToWS. Sue's research team does not directly address the top of my taxonomy, racist micro-level and macro-level abuses. Abuse is commonly defined as "any action that intentionally harms or injures another person" (Tracy, 2012).

Consequently, racist micro-level and macro-level abuses are these collective actions and the overall harm and injuries they cause the racialized target, group, community, organization, or institution. Pierce (1995) explains, "The vehicle for these characteristics is the cumulative effect of offensive [racist] mechanisms, individually exhibited but collectively approved and promoted by the White sector of this society" (p. 268). This oppression is the systemic and institutionalized nature of racism and white supremacy that Kwame Ture (formerly known as Stokely Carmichael) and Charles Hamilton (1967) and Joe R. Feagin (2020) so eloquently describe in their research.

Operationalizing Racial Battle Fatigue as a Theoretical Framework

Offensive racist mechanisms are operated as routine exogenic racist micro-level aggressions in the daily lives of targeted groups. These offensive racist mechanisms cause race-related stress that leads to mental, emotional, and physical strain stored in the body, which is racial battle fatigue (Smith, 2004). Racial battle fatigue (RBF) is the unrelenting exhaustion of using coping and resilience strategies in racistly unsupportive and hostile environments (Pierce, 1970; Smith, 2008a, 2008b; Smith, Allen & Danley 2007; Smith, Yosso & Solórzano (2007). Racial battle fatigue results from a constant physiological, psychological, cultural, and emotional energy depletion after constantly fighting racist micro-level aggressions, micro-level/macro-level assaults, and micro-level/macro-level abuses in racistly hostile or unsupportive environments. Therefore, in operationalizing racial battle fatigue, we must view this as a public and mental health crisis, indeed, a pandemic. Thus, racial battle fatigue is caused by the exogenic biopsycho pollutants of racism. It is a systemic race-related (racism-related) repetitive stress injury resulting from the bioaccumulation of racist experiences.

Figure 6.2 outlines a few examples of the biopsychosocial responses of racial battle fatigue. Psychological stress responses may be one or more expressions of frustration, defensiveness, hypervigilance, apathy, shock, constant worrying, anger, anxiety, disappointment, resentment, and hopelessness after encountering racistly microaggressive conditions (Smith, 2004). Targets who report physiological stress responses from experiencing constant offensive racist mechanisms may indicate having prolonged headaches, backaches, teeth grinding, high blood pressure, and insomnia (Smith, 2004). Additionally, ToWS may suffer from memory suppression (forgetting or self-blame) because the brain will oftentimes repress highly stressful, traumatic, or fear-related events. This understanding is helpful as a short-term protective coping method following a traumatic event. However, long-term memory suppression can be a pathway to poor biopsychosocial health and racial battle fatigue.

There is a multiplicity of behavioral responses to exogenous offensive racist mechanisms. Some of the more commonly reported are stereotype threat, John and Jane Henryism (or prolonged, high-effort coping beyond what might be seen as reasonable odds), academic disidentification, social withdrawal, self-doubt, increased or decreased spiritual commitment, substance use or abuse, lower or higher job performance, self-silencing for fear of being ostracized, reduced or amplified sexual energy, and dramatic diet changes. Lesser studied are behaviors resulting from intra-racial battle fatigue and intragroup (nondominant group) shaming and silencing tactics. Intra-racial battle fatigue has at least three primary responses.

First, there are the endogenous biopsychosocial effects from internalized in-group racial antipathy. These effects are influenced by people having an affinity and need for acceptance from the dominant racial group that they

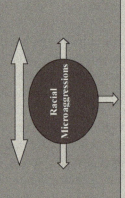

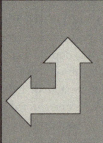

Figure 6.2. Causes and stress responses of racial battle fatigue. Author created.

cannot fully achieve. Second, are endogenous microaggressions dominant intragroup people inflict upon the racial group to which they are socially ascribed but from which they are ideologically and philosophically distant. Some critics go as far as classifying this as a form of Stockholm syndrome. However, these behaviors can be traced back as early as "The Meritorious Manumission Act of 1710," in which an enslaved person would gain material benefits from the enslaver for working against the liberation of other enslaved Africans. Drawing on the work of Frantz Fanon (2008), these conditions are responses to the effects of white supremacy on the target, who is tempted by "hallucinatory lactification" and conceptual whiteness. Yet this hallucinatory negotiation is flawed from the start because the fundamental dilemma that remains is the threat of accepting the "whiteness or perish" doctrine when acquiring whiteness is not a valid option. The third action is the endogenous silencing and shaming of a nondominant racial intragroup member(s) by the dominant racial intragroup to make that person (or subgroup) acquiesce to an accepted group story, opinion, secret, or identity.

This third action leads to a feeling of "pluralistic ignorance" and a "spiral of silence." Pluralistic ignorance is the consequence of being pressured by force or fear to be a submissive intragroup member and not speak out against an accepted flawed group norm, position, or opinion. A *spiral of ignorance* is the threat that an intragroup member's opinion will be classified as unpopular. Thus, the intragroup member is discouraged from publicly expressing what they believe is true out of risk of being socially ostracized. This endogenous threat of social isolation is strong enough that the individual must maintain the popular group opinion, story, or lie and appear to go along to maintain safety and allegiance within the group. Paraphrasing the thoughts of W. E. B. Du Bois, the muzzling of intragroup members' criticism as honest challengers is a hazardous position to hold. Social ostracization will only lead to some of the best observations, assessments, and contributions from intragroup critics to be placed in a position of doomed silence and intellectual paralysis. In contrast, other intragroup members will parrot out loud the accepted dominant position with passion and self-indulgence while losing the subgroup of critical thinkers who truly see, as in the Danish folktale, that the "emperor" is not wearing clothes.

Additionally, a person's attitude or behaviors coded as meanness or toxic can be behavioral responses to systemic micro-abuses and repetitive gendered racism. Racial trauma and antipathy are rarely seen as an explanatory factor for far too many vulnerable people, especially Indigenous and Black and Brown boys and men. The enumerations in figure 6.2 and the above paragraphs are not exhaustive; a target might simultaneously experience one or more of these symptoms or be oblivious and not practice proactive or protective self-defense. In the end, the cumulative impact of exogenous racism on racialized targets of white supremacy makes it a public and mental health disease characterized by adverse health sequelae on racially marginalized and oppressed people, blunted hope and dreams, perceptual distortion, overconsumption of time, and energy loss, racial battle fatigue contagion, and fatality (Pierce, 1970, 1974, 1995; Profit, Mino, & Pierce, 2000; Smith, 2004, 2010, 2016).

Racial battle fatigue makes essential claims, much like CRT's tenets, called the Ten Pillars, which are briefly identified as follows:

1. White supremacy, patriarchal domination, racism, heteronormativity, gender-binarism, ableism, classism, and settler/internal colonialism are endemic to society.

2. Race and racism are primary systemic categories for interpreting the realities of the targets of white supremacy.

3. Racialized people are subordinated by their identities of gender, sexuality, queerness, and mental/physical (dis)abilities, which are influenced by other socially constructed and highly salient group-based characteristics (e.g., social class), which is *race+* (or micro-race) social structure.

4. Racial misandry, racial misogyny, racial queer-and-transphobia, and racial ableism are interdependent, systemic, and ideological justifications for the aversion, oppression, dismissal, silencing, rejection, hypervisibility or hyperinvisibility, premature death, and subordination of racialized boys and men (racial misandry), racialized girls and women (racial misogyny), racialized people with disabilities, and racialized queer/trans/nonbinary/and gender non-conforming people.

5. The body codes racism as a violent act, which produces durable effects on the biological constitution and can be transmitted to a target's offspring and racial group members through racial battle fatigue contagion.

6. Offensive racist mechanisms destroy the biopsychosocial determinants of health, wealth, happiness, motivation, confidence, sense of belonging, and social ecologies.

7. Racism is experienced as both a macro-level and micro-level stressor that negatively impacts the psychological, emotional, and physiological health of racialized targets of white supremacy.

8. Offensive racist mechanisms cause severe bodily and mental harm to members of the targeted group.

9. Racist mechanisms are an act of genocide, causing the targeted group mental and physical destruction in whole and part as defined by the United Nations.[3]

10. RBF research is a social justice and liberatory practice that prioritizes racially marginalized people's voices in exposing and eliminating white supremacy and systems of subjugation by sex, sexuality, genders, ability, class, and other forms of offensive mechanisms for oppression.

I have described the Ten Pillars of racial battle fatigue in this section. This framework is rooted in a long-standing history of domination, colonialism, genocide, and slavery (Feagin, 2020). Since higher education is a microcosm of society at large, there is no surprise that we find similar patterns on historically white campuses across the country. Subsequently, racism touches every sector of our society, and ToWS are always in the process of trying to mitigate racial battle fatigue. The racial battle fatigue framework is robust enough for clinical health practitioners such as psychoanalysts, psychiatrists, psychotherapists, and psychologists to focus on individual-level interventions with people suffering from childhood trauma and other post-traumatic symptoms while experiencing systemic racism. They are not mutually exclusive. We know that the body and mind influence each other.

Therefore, if the body and mind are experiencing trauma, the individual will find adaptive or maladaptive methods to blunt the pain. We all have unique psychological, historical, and cultural filters through which we perceive stressors within our environment. As a result, the individual will become more attuned to painful events that others might not recognize or may feel are easier to manage. Threat perceptions, as a result, will make changes in the brain and keep that person on guard while others are relaxing and feeling peaceful in the same environment. Subsequently, public health professionals, social workers, community-based educators, and sociologists must be better informed of the risk factors and protective factors at the community level when they understand racial battle fatigue as a systemic race-related repetitive stress injury side by side with post-traumatic stress events. Epigeneticists and epidemiologists can work better together through a racial battle fatigue lens to determine the causes of diseases in populations and mechanisms of gene regulation. They must acknowledge that the traumatized person cannot fully heal in the same environment and under the same conditions that made them "sick." Lastly, critical legal scholars, lawyers, and all other race/ethnic "crits" can be more precise on the systemic level of biopsychosocial threats and offensive racist mechanisms in the communities they represent.

Offensive racist mechanisms run the whole gamut on historically white colleges and university campuses and contribute to the racial crisis in American higher education (Williams et al., 2020). For instance, Jeremy D. Franklin (2019) examined African American and Mexican American college students dealing with racial battle fatigue and their ability to use effective coping to alleviate racial stress. Elizabeth F. Desnoyers-Colas (2019) challenged the inauthenticity of campus-wide social justice workshops as causing heightened racial battle fatigue for racialized students. Rafael J. Hernández and Miguel T. Villodas (2019) found that consistent with the racial battle framework, Chicana/o/x and Latina/o/x college students were at risk for diminished well-being because of experiencing racial microaggressions. Noelle Witherspoon Arnold, Emily R. Crawford, and Muhammad Khalifa (2016) used the racial battle fatigue framework to explicate the fault lines in the tenure and promotion process and how racial microaggressions are consistent for Black faculty. Finally, Miracle Husband's (2016) research focused on the Black student affairs professional in the era of #BlackLivesMatter, who yet must struggle with racism, blocked opportunities, and environmental stress.

Using counterstorytelling from interview data, Nicola A. Corbin, William A. Smith, and J. Roberto Garcia (2018) expose the psychological tensions and silencing Black college women face while navigating social constructions of who they are under a white gaze. Tamara N. Stevenson (2012) examined the magnitude to which full-time African American faculty at public community colleges experienced racial battle fatigue associated with their faculty role. Lastly, Paul C. Gorski (2019) reported the burnout that racial justice activists of color face from dealing with conditions they experience at historically white colleges and universities, elevating the threat of racial battle fatigue.

Finally, in three edited books, Kenneth Fasching-Varner and colleagues (2015); Jennifer L. Martin (2015); and Nicholas D. Hartlep and Daisy

Ball (2019) chronicle the ongoing crisis in US higher education through a racial battle fatigue lens from the experiences of students, faculty, staff, and administrators. The prior two editions of *The Racial Crisis in American Higher Education* (1991, 2002), and the need for this third edition, along with the research cited in this section, indicate that we are not living in a post-racial (or, better stated, a post-racist) society. After an exhaustive literature search, I am unaware of any studies linking disability/ableism or non-gender-binary racism with racial battle fatigue. This exclusion is a void that must be filled. Until there is an end to white supremacy, racism, and other forms of oppression, we must continue to find strategies, as racism inhibitors, for mitigation.

Applying Trauma-Informed Care to Racial Battle Fatigue

In a study on racial battle fatigue among Black student affairs educators, Wilson K. Okello and colleagues (2020) discuss how they respond to anti-Blackness and everyday racism. These professionals felt like they had to wear the proverbial mask while on campus to cope with the constant onslaught of subtle and overt racism. These researchers highlighted the participants' efforts at self-care, self-definition, self-love, and agency as necessary components for resilience. Stephen Quaye and colleagues (2019) focused on 35 Black student affairs educators' engagement in resistance and resilience practices as self-care for racial battle fatigue. These educators reported that they attempt to unplug from work and the people and places that cause them racial harm.

Additionally, they turned to community building with other Black educators; they took time out to care for their bodies, create safe spaces for recovery, and commit to the use of counseling services. Thus, racialized targets of white supremacy spend additional time and energy to recover from the stress of enduring daily offensive racist mechanisms. Fortunately, many of these strategies have been passed down or otherwise communicated as successful tactics to other racial group members. However, to increase the chances of successful resilience strategies, the racialized target must realize the seriousness of their enduring conditions, as traumatic events.

A literature search on trauma-informed care reveals a plethora of research on this topic (e.g., mental health settings, child welfare, juvenile justice, domestic violence, and homeless services). These efforts are essential for providing the service, protection, and safety needed for people whose lives were at risk from traumatic events. Racism is endemic, so it is a daily traumatic event in the lives of ToWS. Targets are constantly being surveilled by coworkers, public safety, white students, or ordinary citizens. This hyper-surveillance causes additional anxiety and stressful conditions because the racialized target's space, time, energy, and movement are threatened. The pandemic sickness from racial battle fatigue, racial battle fatigue contagion, and intraracial battle fatigue will remain a constant concern until white supremacy and other forms of oppression are eliminated or controlled, or until effective counteroffensive mechanisms are developed. Therefore, we must understand the necessary toolkits for trauma-informed care to address racial battle fatigue.

As indicated in figure 6.3, four critical components must be considered for effective self-care and group care. First, there must be racial realism (D. A. Bell, 1992) in that one cannot deny that racism exists and is endemic. We must teach our children and reeducate our adults on the systemic, covert nature of racism. A firm understanding of the nature of racism and its effects will help produce more substantial commitments to resilient, adaptive coping strategies. Second, targets must be educated on the signs and symptoms of racial battle fatigue. Too often, psychosocial responses such as anger, hopelessness, projection (as a defense mechanism), and fear are misdiagnosed as sequelae of non-racism-related traumatic, stressful events. In addition, more educational leaders, medical doctors, public health professionals, social workers, probation officers, judges/justices, and counseling center therapists must understand the sociopsychological and sociophysiological effects of racism. A clear understanding will allow them to treat people with appropriate care and concern. To be sure, targets must seek out effective strength-based/asset-based coping strategies. Here, the work by Phillip J. Bowman (2006) and his role strain and adaptation model is very promising for helping to mitigate racial battle fatigue. One of the most exciting features of this model is that it offers a clear explanation of risk and protective factors at the individual, family, and community levels. Furthermore, this model "emphasizes the importance of cultural-ecological empowerment strategies that consider ethnic-specific, multilevel, and lifespan challenges facing at-risk populations" (p. 129).

Howard Stevenson (1998) offers a complementary strength-based/asset-based coping strategy that might work well with the "Bowman role strain and adaptation model." Stevenson provides three forms of racial socialization efforts often used by Black families. The first is the *protective racial socialization* in which "socialization beliefs view the world as racially

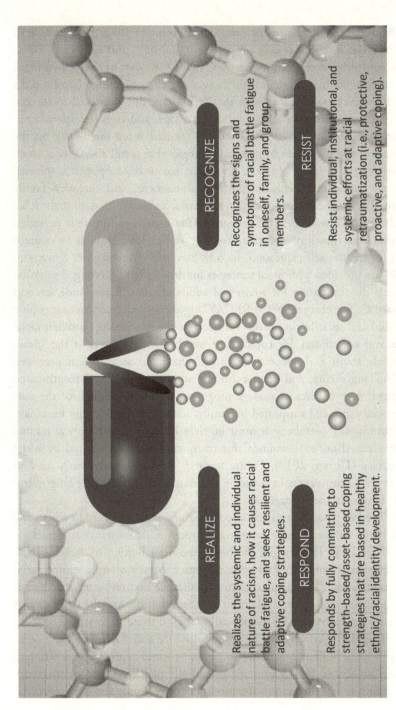

Figure 6.3. Trauma-informed care applied to racial battle fatigue. Author created.

hostile and worthy of distrust, encourage youth to discern supportive or hostile racial intentions, take on a tone of caution, and encourage youth to succeed despite external oppression" (p. 40). As part of this belief, Black parents provide their children with "racism awareness teaching." Second is the *proactive racial socialization beliefs* that "encourage the individual to succeed as a function of internal talent, cultural heritage, and pays less attention to external oppression. Proactive beliefs are focused more intensively on the respondent's endorsement of parental strategies that instill a sense of cultural empowerment in youth" (p. 41). This belief has three components: spiritual and religious coping, cultural pride reinforcement, and extended family caring. The final strategy is *adaptive racial socialization* that promotes "an orientation to the world that recognizes the racial hostility that pervades, identifies that hostility and then keeps it at bay long enough to create a space for creative self-expression" (p. 53). Stevenson (Anderson & Stevenson, 2019) has provided additional strategies for dealing with prolonged exposure to racial discrimination for youth and adults of color. Riana Anderson and Howard C. Stevenson's (2019) RECASTing theory (racial encounter coping appraisal and socialization theory) moderates the relationship between racial stress and self-efficacy for coping and well-being. The assets of the "Bowman role strain and adaptation model," the racial socialization practices, RECASTing theory, and other culturally and ethnic-specific strength-based practices, such as rites of passage programs, must be retooled for the current racial crisis and supported by family, schools, health care professionals, and community members. It must be clear in mind that historical trauma is experienced as "soul wounds" for many communities targeted by white supremacy (Duran, 2019). Future research should consider each method and test its effectiveness in reducing the trauma of racial battle fatigue and racial battle fatigue contagion.

The last component necessary for trauma-informed care in addressing racial battle fatigue is *resistance*. Racial/ethnic-specific resistance strategies are pivotal resources in reducing the biopsychosocial burden of racism. These strategies are learned from effective responses to racism and avoiding racial retraumatization. The main concern in resistance and resilience strategies is that the nature and operationalization of racism changes, and the target group's defensive position must be quickly adjustable to those variations. The main goal of resistance strategies is to acquire distance and the opportunity to be on the offense. Offensive counterstrategies to white supremacy, racism, and oppression should be the primary goal of the racially subordinated group. The ability to develop group interdependence or unity, self-determination, collective work and responsibility, and cooperative economics should be fundamental in resistance and resilience strategies (Karenga, 1998). Concurrently, racially minoritized groups should be able to use their time more effectively and joyfully in culturally responsive "places" that used to be culturally apathetic "spaces" (Tichavakunda, 2020). The outstanding higher education scholar Dr. Antar Tichavakunda (2021) stresses that postsecondary "institutions can either stand in the way of and inhibit Black celebration and recreation or institutions can create conditions and structures that facilitate Black joy" (pg. 316). Institutions and society must become a racially liberatory space of joy for the so-called racially marginalized people to no longer live between fear and risk from responding to racism. Yesteryear was the accepted and expected time for a change. Tomorrow is too late for developing another convenient excuse to have more meetings and discussions. Today is our last and best opportunity for turning the arc of the future toward truth, balance, order, reciprocity, harmony, righteousness, morality, and justice in US society and higher education. In order to accomplish this, we must continue to ask ourselves a fundamental question: Are we part of the trauma or treatment in the lives of targets of racism?

Conclusion

As I conclude, I begin where I started, with the 45th president of the United States. While penning this chapter, we have been devastated by the tragic killings of Ahmaud Arbery, Breonna Taylor, Antonio Valenzuela, Loreal Tsingine, Balbir Singh Sodhi, and George Floyd; the murders of the eight people at three Atlanta-area massage parlors (six of whom were women of Asian descent); and the violent insurrection on the US Capitol on January 6, 2021. However, many more racially subordinated people have died or been racially abused that are unknown to us. The violence they faced and the justice that will not be rendered should move us to more urgently espouse the prioritization of racial group consciences and survival over passive action. For example, between 2017 and 2019, there were at least 80 homicides of trans* or gender-non-conforming people in the United States. According to a report by the group Everytown for Gun Safety,[4] almost 80% of known trans* homicide victims were Black.

Nevertheless, the 45th president of the United States denied that systemic racism exists within law enforcement. Responding to a reporter's question on this topic, he blamed incidents (e.g., the police officer shooting

Jacob Blake Jr. in the back seven times) on a few "bad apples" or good cops who "choke" under pressure (Trump denies systemic racism, pushes "law and order" in Kenosha, 2020). After this, he moved to overhaul federal agencies' racial sensitivity training, calling it "divisive" and "un-American." Additionally, the former president ordered the Office of Management and Budget to stop funding training on critical race theory and diversity sensitivity training for federal employees, calling it a "propaganda effort." In addition, he tweeted, "Critical race theory is the greatest threat to western civilization, and it's made its way into the US federal government, the military, and the justice system" and "Not anymore!" (Dawsey & Stein, 2020).

If the then President and his constituents were correct, there is no racial problem or crisis in the United States, except for those who make a problem out of nothing. The problem is that supporters of critical race theory are ahistorical and anti-American. So, the real question remains, *How does it feel to be a problem?* If there is no problem with the United States, except for a few bad actors, then Indigenous, Black, Brown, and Asian people must be blamed for the conditions in which they find themselves. However, for a moment, from the early spring to the late summer of 2020, it appeared that most of the country suspended that judgment with the discovery of a video of Ahmaud Arbery's murder, the "public lynching" of George Floyd, and the subsequent protests. I heard from White friends and allies during this time to see if I was "all right." These friends and those protestors knew something that the 45th president failed to understand or covertly endorses—that there is a racial crisis in America, and it is on our college and university campuses. This crisis dates from the founding of Harvard University in 1636 to the 2020 attacks on diversity and social justice by the Trump presidential administration. Concurrently, college and university presidents are still struggling with race relations and justice, equity, diversity, and inclusion (JEDI) principles on their campuses. I am not sure if the 45th president has set the country back, as some would argue, or if he has helped expose where we are in this historical moment. To be sure, the obstinate culture and conditions of white supremacy will continue to have an evolving hold on the ideologies, beliefs, interactions, policies, and sense of belonging for students from diverse racial-ethnic-gender-sexual-ability-neurodiversity identities. These conditions will continue to affect the racial climate and crisis in society and postsecondary education.

The summer of 2020 could be a turning point in people's unwillingness to tolerate white supremacy and oppression. There might be some hope to be gleaned from this racially/ethnically diverse group of demonstrators that enough is enough. However, it will take more than one summer of protests to make this change happen. Hopefully, with a better understanding of the conditions that cause racial battle fatigue, more people will become informed and less passive about participating in direct social action on campus and the community. I am optimistic that this chapter will provide the reader and activist with a strategy for researching racial battle fatigue. For example, we need to learn more specifically about anti-Black, anti-Chicana/o/x/e, anti–Chinese American, anti-Navajo, anti–Korean American, anti–Hmong American, anti–Tongan American, anti–Samoan American, and anti–Puerto Rican racial battle fatigue. Regarding anti-Queer racial battle fatigue, we should examine the ways that anti-Black gender-non-conforming RBF affects the lives of students, faculty, and staff. DisCrit racial battle fatigue would help shed a brighter light on Black and Brown boys within the school-to-prison pipeline. Gendered racial battle fatigue could be used to interpret data on Korean American cis-women as an underrepresented population in specific majors or fields. Class-based racial battle fatigue is promising for exposing how specific resources and opportunities are structurally absent in certain minoritized communities. Moreover, we should be open and prepared for the emerging identities to be included in this comprehensive and continually expanding framework. This increased awareness and action is a movement that I can support.

Nevertheless, I remain restless and agitated because I believe in racial realism, like Derrick Bell (1992), rather than merely supporting an ideology of racial equality. The fight for justice has already been a long one. We must remember that our humanity and health are at stake when we do not resist oppression. Whatever trauma is not transformed is transferred (i.e., racial battle fatigue contagion). When the body feels protected, the mind feels safe and can be educated more effectively. The endemic racial crises on college and university campuses fail in its attempt to cover this safely. Thus, it is not about seeing the end of oppression during our lifetime. It is about fighting for the end of oppression so that it might occur within a lifetime.

Acknowledgments

My most profound appreciation goes to the anonymous external reviewers, along with Drs. Kofi Lomotey, Paula Smith, Kathryn Stockton, Claudia Geist, Tommy J. Curry, and Phillip J. Bowman for their thoughtful and thorough suggestions on improving this chapter. Thank you for pushing me to develop my points more effectively. During the final revisions of this chapter, I learned of the passing of Dr. Charles W. Mills. Dr. Mills and I were colleagues at the University of Illinois at Chicago, where he was a professor, and I was a postdoctoral research scholar. His book, *The Racial Contract*, and the generous conversations and advice he shared with me during that time helped shape my thinking. Lastly, I must acknowledge the impact that Dr. Chester M. Pierce's friendship and mentorship had on me. He continuously encouraged me to develop racial battle fatigue and never stop strengthening this "powerful concept." I hope this chapter would have made you proud. Rest in Power (RIP), my friend.

Notes

1. I use "queer" comprehensively to represent the full range of diversity within the LGBTQIA+ community in general discussion terms only. At the same time, I am arguing that it is important for researchers to consider the unique identities and experiences within this diverse group.

2. "Trans*" is used in this chapter to mean anyone who does not feel right in their "sex assigned" at birth.

3. The United Nations' Office of Genocide Prevention and the Responsibility to Protect (United Nations (n.d.), United Nations Office on Genocide Prevention and the Responsibility to Protect. Retrieved September 13, 2022, from https://www.un.org/en/genocideprevention/genocide.shtml.

The website offers a clear definition of genocide. Article 2 states that "genocide means any of the following acts committed with intent to destroy, in whole or in part, a national, ethnical, racial or religious group." Article 2 goes on to clarify its narrow definition of the crime of genocide in its two main "Elements of the crime":

A mental element: the "intent to destroy, in whole or in part, a national, ethnical, racial or religious group, as such"; and

A physical element, which includes the following five acts, enumerated exhaustively:

- Killing members of the group
- Causing serious bodily or mental harm to members of the group
- Deliberately inflicting on the group conditions of life calculated to bring about its physical destruction in whole or in part
- Imposing measures intended to prevent births within the group
- Forcibly transferring children of the group to another group.

4. "How does gun violence impact the communities you care about?," EveryStat.org, https://maps.everytownresearch.org/everystat.

References

Ahmed, S. (2006). Conclusion: Disorientation and queer objects. In *Queer phenomenology: Orientations, objects, others* (pp. 157–180). Duke University Press. https://doi.org/10.2307/j.ctv125jk6w.8

Akbar, N. (1991). Mental disorder among African Americans. In R. L. Jones (Ed.), *Black psychology* (pp. 339–352). Cobb & Henry Publishers.

Akerlund, M., & Cheung, M. (2000). Teaching beyond the deficit model: Gay and lesbian issues among African Americans, Latinos, and Asian Americans. *Journal of Social Work Education, 36*(2), 279–292.

Anderson, N. B. (1989). Racial differences in stress-induced cardiovascular reactivity and hypertension. Current Status and Substantive Issues. *American Psychological Association, 105*(1), 89–105. https://doi.org/10.1037/0033-2909.105.1.89

Anderson, R. E., & Stevenson, H. C. (2019). RECASTing racial stress and trauma: Theorizing the healing potential of racial socialization in families. *American Psychologist, 74*(1), 63–75.

Annamma, S. A., Connor, D. J., and Ferri, B. A. (2013). Disability critical race studies (DisCrit): Theorizing at the intersections of disability and race. *Journal of Race, Ethnicity, and Education, 16*(1), 1–31.

Annamma, S., Ferri, B. A., & Connor, D. J. (2018a). Cultivating and expanding disability critical race theory (DisCrit). In Katie Ellis, Rosemarie Garland-Thomson, Mike Kent, and Rachel Robertson (Eds.), *Manifestos for the future of critical disability studies* (pp. 230–238). Routledge.

Annamma, S. A., Ferri, B. A., Connor, D. J. (2018b). Disability critical race theory: Exploring the intersectional lineage, emergence, and potential futures of DisCrit in education. *Review of Research in Education, 42*(1): 46–71. doi:10.3102/0091732X18759041

Anti-Defamation League. (2020, February 11). White supremacist propaganda spikes in 2020. Retrieved September 7, 2022, from https://www.adl.org/white-supremacist-propaganda-spikes-2020

Arnold, N. W., Crawford, E. R., & Khalifa, M. (2016). Psychological heuristics and faculty of color: Racial battle fatigue and tenure/promotion. *The Journal of Higher Education, 87*(6), 890–919.

Balsam, K. F., Molina, Y., Beadnell, B., Simoni, J., & Walters, K. (2011). Measuring multiple minority stress: The LGBT People of Color Microaggressions Scale. *Cultural Diversity and Ethnic Minority Psychology, 17*(2), 163–174.

Bell, C. (2006). Introducing White disability studies: A modest proposal. In L. J. Davis (Ed.), *The Disability Studies Reader* (2nd ed., pp. 275–282). Routledge.

Bell, D. A. (1992). Racial realism. *Connecticut Law Review, 24,* 363–379.

Bell, D. A. (1995). Who's afraid of critical race theory. *U. Ill. L. Rev.,* 893.

Bey, M. (2017). The trans*-ness of blackness, the blackness of trans*-ness. *Transgender Studies Quarterly, 4*(2), 275–295.

Bogart, K. R., & Dunn, D. S. (2019). Ableism special issue introduction. *Journal of Social Issues, 75*(3), 650–664.

Bonilla-Silva, E. (2015). The structure of racism in color-blind, "post-racial" America. *American Behavioral Scientist, 59*(11), 1358–1376.

Bowman, P. J. (2006). Role strain and adaptation issues in the strength-based model: Diversity, multilevel, and life-span considerations. *The Counseling Psychologist, 34*(1), 118–133.

Boxall, K. (2018). Revisiting the foundations of (critical) disability studies: Manifesto for an inclusive social model. In Katie Ellis, Rosemarie Garland-Thomson, Mike Kent, and Rachel Robertson (Eds.), *Manifestos for the future of critical disability studies* (pp. 199–208). Routledge.

Brayboy, B. M. J. (2005). Toward a tribal critical race theory in education. *The Urban Review, 37*(5), 425–446.

Brondolo, E., Hausmann, L. R., Jhalani, J., Pencille, M., Atencio-Bacayon, J., Kumar, A., . . . & Crupi, R. (2011). Dimensions of perceived racism and self-reported health: Examination of racial/ethnic differences and potential mediators. *Annals of Behavioral Medicine, 42*(1), 14–28.

Brooms, D. R. (2016). *Being Black, being male on campus: Understanding and confronting Black male collegiate experiences.* SUNY Press.

Carmichael, S., & Hamilton, C. V. (1967). *Black Power: The politics of liberation in America.* Vintage Books.

Carter, R. T., & Forsyth, J. (2010). Reactions to racial discrimination: Emotional stress and help-seeking behaviors. *Psychological Trauma: Theory, Research, Practice, and Policy, 2*(3), 183–191.

Coogan, P., Schon, K., Li, S., Cozier, Y., Bethea, T., & Rosenberg, L. (2020). Experiences of racism and subjective cognitive function in African American women. *Alzheimer's & Dementia: Diagnosis, Assessment & Disease Monitoring, 12*(1), e12067.

Corbin, N. A., Smith, W. A., & Garcia, J. R. (2018). Trapped between justified anger and being the strong Black woman: Black college women coping with racial battle fatigue at historically and predominantly White institutions. *International Journal of Qualitative Studies in Education, 31*(7), 626–643.

Cuevas, A. G., Dawson, B. A., & Williams, D. R. (2016). Race and skin color in Latino health: An analytic review. *American journal of public health, 106*(12), 2131–2136.

Curry, T. J. (2017). *The man-not: Race, class, genre, and the dilemmas of black manhood.* Temple University Press.

Darity Jr, W. A. (2003). Employment discrimination, segregation, and health. *American Journal of Public Health, 93*(2), 226–231.

Dawsey, J., & Stein, J. (2020, September 5). White House cancels race-related training sessions it calls "un-American propaganda." *The Washington Post.* Retrieved from https://www.washingtonpost.com/politics/2020/09/04/white-house-racial-sensitivity-training/

DeCuir, J. T., & Dixson, A. D. (2004). "So when it comes out, they aren't that surprised that it is there": Using critical race theory as a tool of analysis of race and racism in education. *Educational researcher, 33*(5), 26–31.

DeCuir-Gunby, J. T., & Gunby, N. W., Jr. (2016). Racial microaggressions in the workplace: A critical race analysis of the experiences of African American educators. *Urban Education, 51*(4), 390–414. doi:10.1177/0042085916628610

Delgado, R., & Stefancic, J. (2017). *Critical race theory.* New York University Press.

Desnoyers-Colas, E. F. (2019). Talking loud and saying nothing: Kicking faux allyness to the curb by battling racial battle fatigue using White accomplice-ment. *Departures in Critical Qualitative Research, 8*(4), 100–105.

Dovidio, J. F., & Gaertner, S. L. (2004). Aversive racism. In M. P. Zanna (Ed.), *Advances in experimental social psychology* (Vol. 36, p. 1–52). Elsevier Academic Press. https://doi.org/10.1016/S0065-2601(04)36001-6

Duran, E. (2019). *Healing the soul wound: Trauma-informed counseling for Indigenous communities.* Teachers College Press.

Edwards, G. S., and Rushin, S. (2018, January 14). The effect of President Trump's election on hate crimes. Available at SSRN: https://ssrn.com/abstract=3102652 or http://dx.doi.org/10.2139/ssrn.3102652

Essed, P. (1991). *Understanding everyday racism: An interdisciplinary theory.* Sage.

Essed, P. (2002). Everyday racism: A new approach to the study of racism. In P. Essed & D. Goldberg (eds.), *Race critical theories* (pp. 176–194). Blackwell.

Fanon, F. (2008). *Black skin, white masks.* Grove Press.

Fasching-Varner, K. J., Albert, K. A., Mitchell, R. W., & Allen, C. (2015). *Racial battle fatigue in higher education: Exposing the myth of post-racial America.* Rowman & Littlefield.

Feagin, Joe R. (2013). *Systemic racism: A theory of oppression.* Taylor and Francis.

Feagin, J. R. (2014). *Racist America: Roots, current realities, and future reparations.* Routledge.

Feagin, J. R. (2020). *The White racial frame: Centuries of racial framing and counter-framing.* Routledge.

Follins, L. D., Walker, J. N. J., & Lewis, M. K. (2014). Resilience in Black lesbian, gay, bisexual, and transgender individuals: A critical review of the literature. *Journal of Gay & Lesbian Mental Health, 18*(2), 190–212.

For most Trump voters, "very warm" feelings for him endured. (2018, August 9). *Pew Research Center: US Politics & Policy.* Retrieved from https://www.pew

research.org/politics/2018/08/09/for-most-trump-voters-very-warm-feelings-for-him-endured/

Franklin, J. D. (2019) Coping with racial battle fatigue: Differences and similarities for African American and Mexican American college students. *Race Ethnicity and Education, 22*(5), 589–609. DOI: 10.1080/13613324.2019.1579178

Garvey, J. C., Mobley Jr., S. D., Summerville, K. S., & Moore, G. T. (2019). Queer and trans* students of color: Navigating identity disclosure and college contexts. *The Journal of Higher Education, 90*(1), 150–178.

Giroux, H. (2019). Authoritarianism and the challenge of higher education in the age of Trump. *Action, Criticism, and Theory for Music Education, 18*(1), 6–25.

Gómez, J. M. (2015). Microaggressions and the enduring mental health disparity: Black Americans at risk for institutional betrayal. *Journal of Black Psychology, 41*(2), 121–143. doi:10.1177/0095798413514608

Gomez, M. L., Khurshid, A., Freitag, M. B., & Lachuk, A. J. (2011). Microaggressions in graduate students' lives: How they are encountered and their consequences. *Teaching and Teacher Education, 27*(8), 1189–1199. doi:10.1016/j.tate.2011.06.003

Gorski, P. C. (2019). Racial battle fatigue and activist burnout in racial justice activists of color at predominately White colleges and universities. *Race Ethnicity and Education, 22*(1), 1–20.

Harper, S. R. (2012). Race without racism: How higher education researchers minimize racist institutional norms. *Review of Higher Education, 36*(1 Suppl.), 9–29. doi:10.1353/rhe.2012.0047

Harriet Tubman Collective (2018). Accountable reporting on disability, race and police violence: A community response to the "Ruderman Foundation paper on the Media Coverage of Use of Force and Disability." Retrieved from https://docs.google.com/document/d/117eoVeJVP594L6-1bgL8zpZrzgojfsveJwcWuHpkNcs/edit

Hartlep, N. D., & Ball, D. (Eds.). (2019). *Racial battle fatigue in faculty: Perspectives and lessons from higher education.* Routledge.

Hernández, R. J., & Villodas, M. T. (2019). Overcoming racial battle fatigue: The associations between racial microaggressions, coping, and mental health among Chicana/o and Latina/o college students. *Cultural Diversity and Ethnic Minority Psychology, 26*(3), 399–411.

Hughes, R., & Giles, M. (2010). CRiT walking in higher education: Activating critical race theory in the academy. *Race Ethnicity and Education, 13*(1), 41–57.

Husband, Miracle (2016). Racial battle fatigue and the Black student affairs professional in the era of #BlackLivesMatter. *The Vermont Connection, 37*, Article 10. Retrieved from http://scholarworks.uvm.edu/tvc/vol37/iss1/10

Jones, A. M. (2021). Conflicted: How Black women negotiate their responses to racial microaggressions at a historically White institution. *Race Ethnicity and Education*, 1–16.

Karenga, M. (1998). *Kwanzaa: A celebration of family, community, and culture.* University of Sankore Press.

Keith, V. M., & Herring, C. (1991). Skin tone and stratification in the Black community. *American Journal of Sociology, 97*(3), 760–778.

Kenny Nienhusser, H., Vega, B. E., & Carquin, M. C. S. (2016). Undocumented students' experiences with microaggressions during their college choice process. *Teachers College Record, 118*(2), 1–33. Retrieved from https://www.scopus.com/inward/record.uri?eid=2-s2.0-84957552518&partnerID=40&md5=acccd9335280c4dece3c27c1f2ecc23e

Ladson-Billings, G. (2014). Culturally sustaining pedagogy 2.0: A.k.a. the Remix. *Harvard Educational Review, 84*(1), 74–84. Retrieved from https://www.scopus.com/inward/record.uri?eid=2-s2.0-84897055930&partnerID=40&md5=8a0e44347af1a703b6e322454d8bfea7

Ladson-Billings, G., and Tate, W. F. (1995). Toward a critical race theory of education. *Teachers College Record, 97,* 47–68.

Leonardo, Z. (2009). *Race, whiteness, and education.* Routledge.

Martin, J. L. (Ed.). (2015). *Racial battle fatigue: Insights from the front lines of social justice advocacy.* ABC-CLIO.

McConnell, E. A., Janulis, P., Phillips, G. II, Truong, R., & Birkett, M. (2018). Multiple minority stress and LGBT community resilience among sexual minority men. *Psychology of Sexual Orientation and Gender Diversity, 5*(1), 1–12. https://doi.org/10.1037/sgd0000265

McGee, E. O., & Stovall, D. (2015). Reimagining critical race theory in education: Mental health, healing, and the pathway to liberatory praxis. *Educational Theory, 65*(5), 491–511.

McKenzie, K. (2003). Racism and health: Antiracism is an important health issue. *British Medical Journal, 326,* 65–66.

Meyer, D. (2008). Interpreting and experiencing anti-queer violence: Race, class, and gender differences among LGBT hate crime victims. *Race, Gender & Class, 15*(3/4), 262–282.

Mills, C. W. (1997). *The racial contract.* Ithaca, NY: Cornell University Press.

Misawa, M. (2010). Queer race pedagogy for educators in higher education: Dealing with power dynamics and positionality of LGBTQ students of color. *The International Journal of Critical Pedagogy, 3*(1), 26.

Nicolazzo, Z. (2016). "It's a hard line to walk": black non-binary trans* collegians' perspectives on passing, realness, and trans*-normativity. *International Journal of Qualitative Studies in Education, 29*(9), 1173–1188.

Okello, W. K., Quaye, S. J., Allen, C., Carter, K. D., & Karikari, S. N. (2020). "We wear the mask": Self-Definition as an approach to healing from racial battle fatigue. *Journal of College Student Development, 61*(4), 422–438.

Olkin, R., Hayward, H. S., Abbene, M. S., & VanHeel, G. (2019). The experiences of microaggressions against women with visible and invisible disabilities. *Journal of Social Issues, 75*(3), 757–785.

Parker, L. (2015). Critical race theory in education and qualitative inquiry: What each has to offer each other now? *Qualitative Inquiry, 21*(3), 199–205. doi:10.1177/1077800414557828

Parker, L., & Lynn, M. (2002). What's race got to do with it? Critical race theory's conflicts with and connections to qualitative research methodology and epistemology. *Qualitative inquiry, 8*(1), 7–22.

Patterson, W. L. (Ed.). (1951). We charge genocide: The historic petition to the United Nations for relief from a crime of the United States government against the Negro people. Civil Rights Congress.

Patton, L. D. (2016). Disrupting postsecondary prose: Toward a critical race theory of higher education. *Urban Education, 51*(3), 315–342.

Patton, L. D., McEwen, M., Rendón, L. and Howard-Hamilton, M. F. (2007). Critical race perspectives on theory in student affairs. *New Directions for Student Services, 2007*(120), 39–53. https://doi.org/10.1002/ss.256

Pérez Huber, L., & Solorzano, D. G. (2015). Racial microaggressions as a tool for critical race research. *Race, Ethnicity and Education, 18*(3), 297–320. doi:10.1080/13613324.2014.994173

Perry, V. G. (2019). A loan at last? Race and racism in mortgage lending. In G. D. Johnson, K. D. Thomas, A. K. Harrison, & S. G. Grier (Eds.), *Race in the marketplace: Crossing critical boundaries* (pp. 173–192). Palgrave Macmillan.

Pierce, C. M. (1970). Offensive mechanisms. In F. Barbour (Ed.), *The Black seventies* (pp. 265–282). Porter Sargent.

Pierce, C. M. (1974). Psychiatric problems of the Black minority. *American Handbook of Psychiatry, 2,* 512–523.

Pierce, C. M. (1975a). Poverty and racism as they affect children. In I. Berlin (Ed.), *Advocacy for child mental health* (pp. 92–109). Brunner/Mazel.

Pierce, C. M. (1975b). The mundane extreme environment and its effect on learning. In S. G. Brainard (Ed.), *Learning disabilities: Issues and recommendations for research* (p. 109–119). National Institute of Education, Department of Health, Education, and Welfare.

Pierce, C. M. (1988). Stress in the workplace. In A. F. Coner-Edwards & J. Spurlock (Eds.), *Black families in crisis: The middle class* (pp. 27–34). Brunner/Mazel.

Pierce, C. M. (1995). Stress analogs of racism and sexism: Terrorism, torture, and disaster. In C. V. Willie, P. P. Rieker, B. M. Kramer, & B. S. Brown (Eds.), *Mental health, racism, and sexism* (pp. 277–293). University of Pittsburgh Press.

Pratto, F., Sidanius, J., & Levin, S. (2006). Social dominance theory and the dynamics of intergroup relations: Taking stock and looking forward. *European Review of Social Psychology, 17*(1), 271–320.

Profit, W. E., Mino, I., & Pierce, C. M. (2000). Stress in Blacks. In G. Fink (Ed.), *Encyclopedia of stress* (pp. 324–330). Academic Press.

Quaye, S. J., Karikari, S. N., Rashad Allen, C., Kwamogi Okello, W., & Demere Carter, K. (2019). Strategies for practicing self-care from racial battle fatigue. *Journal Committed to Social Change on Race and Ethnicity, 5*(2), 95–131.

Quigley, W. (2011). Racism: The crime in criminal justice. *Loy. J. Pub. Int. L.*, *13*, 417.

Ramos, B., Jaccard, J., & Guilamo-Ramos, V. (2003). Dual ethnicity and depressive symptoms: Implications of being Black and Latino in the United States. *Hispanic Journal of Behavioral Sciences*, *25*(2), 147–173.

Rankin, S., Weber, G., & Garvey, J. (2015). LGBTQIAA: From invisibility to visibility: Queer-spectrum and trans-spectrum college students. In P. A. Sasso & J. L. DeVitis (Eds.), *Today's college students: A reader* (pp. 165–182). Peter Lang.

Sidanius, J., Hudson, S. K. T., Davis, G., & Bergh, R. (2018). The theory of gendered prejudice: A social dominance and intersectionalist perspective. *The Oxford handbook of behavioral political science*, *1*, 1–35.

Sidanius, J., & Pratto, F. (1999). *Social dominance: An intergroup theory of social hierarchy and oppression*. Cambridge University Press.

Smith, W. A. (2004). Black faculty coping with racial battle fatigue: The campus racial climate in a post-civil rights era. In Darrell Cleveland (Ed.), *A long way to go: Conversations about race by African American faculty and graduate students at predominantly white institutions* (pp. 171–190). Peter Lang Publishers.

Smith, W. A. (2008a). Campuswide climate: Implications for African American students. In L. Tillman (Ed.), *A Handbook of African American Education* (pp. 297–309). Sage Publications.

Smith, W. A. (2008b). Higher Education: Racial Battle Fatigue. In R. T. Schaefer (Ed.), *Encyclopedia of Race, Ethnicity, and Society* (pp. 615–618). Sage Publications.

Smith, W. A. (2010). Toward an understanding of misandric microaggressions and racial battle fatigue among African Americans in historically White institutions. In E. M. Zamani-Gallaher & V. C. Polite (Eds.), *The state of the African American male* (pp. 265–277). Michigan State University Press.

Smith, W. A. (2016). Understanding the corollaries of offensive racial mechanisms, gendered racism, and racial battle fatigue. *Center for Critical Race Studies at UCLA Research Brief*, *1*, 1–4.

Smith, W. A., Allen, W. R., & Danley, L. L. (2007, December). "Assume the position . . . You fit the description": Campus racial climate and the psychoeducational experiences and racial battle fatigue among African American male college students. *American Behavioral Scientist*, *51*(4), 551–578.

Smith, W. A., Mustaffa, J. B., Jones, C., Curry, T. J., & Allen, W. R. (2016, September). "You make me wanna holler and throw up both my hands!": Campus culture, Black misandric microaggressions, and racial battle fatigue. *International Journal of Qualitative Studies in Education*, *29*(9), 1189–1209.

Smith, W. A., Yosso, T. J., & Solórzano, D. G. (2007). Racial primes and Black misandry on historically White campuses: Toward critical race accountability in educational administration. *Educational Administration Quarterly*, *43*(5), 559–585.

Solórzano, D. G., Allen, W., & Carroll, G. (2002). Keeping race in place: Racial microaggressions and campus racial climate at the University of California, Berkeley. *Chicano-Latino Law Review*, *23*, 15–112.

Stevenson, H. C. (1998). Managing anger: Protective, proactive, or adaptive racial socialization identity profiles and African-American manhood development. *Journal of Prevention & Intervention in the Community, 16*(1–2), 35–61.

Stevenson, T. N. (2012). Racial Battle Fatigue, role strain, and African-American faculty at public community colleges (Order No. 3540464). Available from ProQuest Dissertations & Theses Global (1098782348). https://login.ezproxy.lib.utah.edu/login?url=https://www.proquest.com/dissertations-theses/racial-battle-fatigue-role-strain-african/docview/1098782348/se-2

Stewart, D-L. (2021). Performing goodness in qualitative research methods. *International Journal of Qualitative Studies in Education, 35*(1), 1–13.

Stewart, D-L., & Nicolazzo, Z. (2018). High impact of [whiteness] on trans* students in postsecondary education. *Equity & Excellence in Education, 51*(2), 132–145.

Stockton, K. B. (2021). *Gender(s)*. MIT Press.

Stovall, D. (2006). Forging community in race and class: Critical race theory and the quest for social justice in education. *Race ethnicity and Education, 9*(3), 243–259.

Sue, D. W., Capodilupo, C. M., Torino, G. C., Bucceri, J. M., Holder, A., Nadal, K. L., & Esquilin, M. (2007). Racial microaggressions in everyday life: Implications for clinical practice. *American psychologist, 62*(4), 271.

Sutter, M., & Perrin, P. B. (2016). Discrimination, mental health, and suicidal ideation among LGBTQ People of Color. *Journal of Counseling Psychology, 63*(1), 98.

Tichavakunda, A. A. (2020). Studying Black student life on campus: Toward a theory of Black placemaking in higher education. *Urban Education*, https://doi.org/10.1177/0042085920971354

Tichavakunda, A. A. (2021). Black joy on White campuses: Exploring Black students' recreation and celebration at a historically white institution. *The Review of Higher Education 44*(3), 297–324. doi:10.1353/rhe.2021.0003

Tracy, N. (2012, July 29). What is abuse? Abuse definition, HealthyPlace. Retrieved on September 6, 2020, from https://www.healthyplace.com/abuse/abuse-information/what-is-abuse-abuse-definition

Trump denies systemic racism, pushes "law and order" in Kenosha. (2020, September 1). *Al Jazeera & News Agencies*. Retrieved from https://www.aljazeera.com/news/2020/09/trump-denies-systemic-racism-pushes-law-order-kenosha-200901203137937.html

Villalpando, O. (2003). Self-segregation or self-preservation? A critical race theory and Latina/o critical theory analysis of findings from a longitudinal study of Chicana/o college students. *International Journal of Qualitative Studies in Education, 16*(5): 619–646.

Williams, M. T. (2021). Microaggressions are a form of aggression. *Behavior Therapy, 52*(3): 709–719. Doi:10.1016/j.beth.2020.09.001

Williams, M. T., Skinta, M. D., Kanter, J. W., Martin-Willett, R., Mier-Chairez, J., Debreaux, M., & Rosen, D. C. (2020). A qualitative study of microaggressions against African Americans on predominantly White campuses. *BMC Psychology, 8*(1). Doi:10.1186/s40359-020-00472-8

Williams, V., & Gelfand, I. (2019). *Trump and racism: What do the data say?* Brookings. Retrieved on August 11, 2020, from www.brookings.edu/blog/fixgov/2019/08/14/trump-and-racism-what-do-the-data-say/

Wingfield, A. H. (2007). The modern Mammy and the angry Black man: African American professionals' experiences with gendered racism in the workplace. *Race, Gender & Class, 14*(1/2), 196–212.

Wood, J. L., & Harris III, F. (2021a, February 12). Racelighting: A prevalent version of gaslighting facing People of Color. *Diverse Issues in Higher Education, 37*(26), 10–11. Retrieved from https://www.diverseeducation.com/opinion/article/15108651/racelighting-a-prevalent-version-of-gaslighting-facing-people-of-color

Wood, J. L., & Harris III, F. (2021b). *Racelighting in the normal realities of Black, Indigenous, and People of Color: A scholarly brief.* Community College Equity Assessment Lab (CCLEAL). Retrieved from http://bmmcoalition.com/racelighting/

Wood, J. L., & Harris III, F. (2021c, March 30). Racelighting: Three common strategies racelighters use. *Diverse Issues in Higher Education.* Retrieved from https://www.diverseeducation.com/opinion/article/15108908/racelighting-three-common-strategies-racelighters-use

Yosso, T. J. (2005). Whose culture has capital? A critical race theory discussion of community cultural wealth. *Race ethnicity and education, 8*(1), 69–91.

Yosso, T. J., Smith, W. A., Ceja, M., & Solórzano, D. G. (2009). Critical race theory, racial microaggressions, and campus racial climate for Latina/o undergraduates. *Harvard Educational Review, 79*(4), 659–690.

Yosso, T. J., Smith, W. A., Solórzano, D. G., & Hung, M. (2022). A critical race theory test of W. E. B. Du Bois's hypothesis: Do Black students need separate schools? *Race Ethnicity and Education* (CREE), *25*(3), 370–388. doi:10.1080/13613324.2021.1984099

Chapter 7

Outsiders Within

Black Faculty in US Higher Education

CHANNEL C. MCLEWIS, CHANTAL JONES, GADISE REGASSA, AND WALTER R. ALLEN

Diversifying the academy is an unfulfilled endeavor. Black student activists across college campuses insistently call for institutional change that includes hiring more Black faculty (Griffin, 2019; Kelly, Gayles, & Williams, 2017; Ndemanu, 2017), echoing the same demands made during the Black campus movement in the 1960s and 1970s (Rogers, 2012). Despite such efforts, the repression of Black people in the professoriate is relentless. In 1992, 27,000 Black faculty members comprised 5.11% of full-time faculty and instructional staff (Snyder, de Brey, & Dillow, 2019). Today, Black folks still constitute 5.53%, with 45,427 Black faculty members (NCES, 2018b). This dismal proportion of Black faculty is alarming, given that the Black population in the United States is 13.4% (US Census, 2020). The underrepresentation of Black faculty on college campuses is persistent.

The lack of Black college faculty poses a challenge to the growing number of Black and other Students of Color entering higher education. In 2016, Black students represented 15.2% of undergraduate students and 13.5% of graduate students, while full-time Black faculty are less than half of this proportion (Espinosa et al., 2019). Faculty of Color, specifically Black faculty, are critical mentors and role models who aid in retaining

Black students (Commodore et al., 2018; Griffin & Reddick, 2011; Wilder, Osborne-Lampkin, & Jackson, 2015). Yet Shaun Harper and Isaiah Simmons (2019) found the ratio of full-time Black undergraduates to full-time Black faculty to be as extreme as 369 to 1. The incongruence between the racial composition of college faculty and the demographics of the student population exemplifies the prevalence of Black exclusion in higher education.

The present study centers on full-time Black faculty at public higher education institutions to examine their representation on college campuses and expound on existing scholarship analyzing the prevalence of education violence in higher education (Mustaffa, 2017). Providing a descriptive portrait of Black college faculty, we aim to examine racial disparities within the opportunity structure in accessing and thriving in the professoriate. Through our analysis of data on full-time instructional staff and synthesis of current literature, we assess the conditions that perpetuate the subjugation and exclusion of Black folks and render them outsiders within the academy (Collins, 1986). The status of Black people in academe lends to our critique of the hypocrisy in higher education that subscribes to multicultural and diversity paradigms (Berrey, 2015; Ladson-Billings & Tate, 1995), yet preserves anti-Black racism and misogynoir (Bailey, 2021; Dumas & ross, 2016).

Theoretical Framework

CRITICAL RACE THEORY

Critical race theory (CRT), a framework with theoretical roots in critical legal studies, a radical civil rights tradition, and radical feminism, serves as a lens to center race, racism, and power in analyzing the inclusion and exclusion of Black faculty in higher education. Critical race theorists contend that racism and its intersection with other forms of oppression are embedded in the fabric of US society (Delgado & Stefancic, 2017). For higher education research, CRT aids in "disrupting postsecondary prose" to challenge "the ordinary, predictable, and taken for granted ways in which the academy functions as a bastion of racism/White supremacy" (Patton, 2016, p. 317). We utilized a critical race framework to "understand how a regime of white supremacy and its subordination of people of color have been created and maintained in America, and, in particular, to examine the relationship between that social structure and professed ideals" (Crenshaw et al., 1995, p. xiii). Pertinent to the present study is how "diversity" is a professed ideal propagated in the mythos of higher education.

Higher education is susceptible to the pervasive nature of racism and white supremacy. While higher education embraces diversity, institutions and their campus cultures maintain a white patriarchal order. Diversity reduced to a form of "token incrementalism in terms of racial heterogeneity does not substantially threaten generations of institutionalized racial privilege" (Harris, Barone, & Patton, 2015, p. 25). Multiculturalism and diversity are aspects of what Michael Dumas and kihana ross (2016) refer to as the *neoliberal-multicultural imagination* to describe the wavering attempts to provide recourse for legacies of structural racism and its impediment to advance opportunities for Black people. Racial justice in higher education is often restricted to "diversity mission statements or climate assessment data that is minimally (or never) used, and tend to be token gestures that place the burden of this systemic work on a few" (Harris, Barone, & Patton, 2015, p. 27–28). The few, in many instances, are minoritized faculty. In the present chapter, we focused on Black faculty and looked to Black critical theorists in framing the particulars of Black marginalization, subjugation, and resistance.

Black Critical Theory and Anti-Blackness

While critical race theories in education are useful, *anti-Blackness* as a conceptual lens provides specificity of the Black experience. Dumas and ross (2016) contend "only critical theorization of blackness confronts the specificity of *anti-blackness*, as a social construction, as an embodied lived experience of social suffering and resistance, and perhaps most importantly, as an antagonism, in which the Black is a despised thing-in-itself" (p. 416). Anti-Blackness is central to capturing the distinct ways Black people are regulated, marginalized, and dispossessed within educational spaces (Dei, 2017; Dumas & ross, 2016). We apply this lens to examine how anti-Blackness cultivates adverse conditions to suppress the entry, retention, and success of Black faculty.

Review of Literature

The professoriate is racially stratified and discriminative. In 2016, Native Hawaiian or Pacific Islander faculty were 0.1% of college faculty; American

Indian or Alaska Native faculty, 0.4%; multiracial faculty, 0.9%; faculty of unknown race or ethnicity, 2.6%; and international faculty, 3.1%. Latinx faculty represented 4.7%; Black faculty, 5.7%; Asian faculty, 9.3%; and white faculty, an overwhelming 73.2% (Espinosa et al., 2019). Among this demographic, Black faculty made up 105,616 of all faculty, with 61,063 in part-time and 44,553 in full-time positions (Snyder, de Brey, & Dillow, 2019). This representation reflects the steady rise of part-time faculty members who typically receive lower pay, fewer benefits and services, and are without professional development and tenure opportunities (Kezar & Bernstein-Sierra, 2016). While the experience of part-time Black faculty warrants more research, the focus of the present chapter is Black, full-time instructional staff. It should also be noted a disproportionate share of Black faculty work at historically Black colleges and universities (HBCUs).

Black faculty comprise 5.7% of full-time instructional staff (Snyder, de Brey, & Dillow, 2019), with one-third concentrated at the level of instructor, lecturer, and faculty with no academic rank (Espinosa et al., 2019). In addition to faculty rank, differences in the proportion of Black faculty varies based on the institutional sector. For example, Black faculty represent 11.2% of full-time instructional staff at for-profit institutions and 7.4% at public two-year institutions, where the vast majority of Black faculty are employed as instructors, lecturers, and faculty with no academic rank (Espinosa et al., 2019). Comparatively, Black faculty represent just over 5% of full-time instructional staff at private and public four-year institutions (Espinosa et al., 2019). Our focus is on public, four-year institutions because they employ 35,513 Black college faculty, the majority across sectors (Snyder, de Brey, & Dillow, 2019).

Among the 5.1% of Black faculty at public, four-year institutions, 45.3% have tenure, 22.3% are on the tenure track, and 32.3% are not on the tenure track. More specifically, in examining faculty rank and tenure status, among tenured Black faculty, 19.4% are full professors, 23.1% are associate professors, 2.3% are assistant professors, and 0.5% are instructors, lecturers, and faculty with no academic rank. Across Black tenure-track faculty, 0.3% are full professors, 2.5% are associate professors, the majority at 19% are assistant professors, and 0.6% are instructors, lecturers, and faculty with no academic rank. Lastly, among Black non-tenure-track faculty, 1.2% are full professors, 3% are associate professors, 10.5% are assistant professors, and the vast majority, at 17.6%, are located among instructors, lecturers, and faculty with no academic rank (Espinosa et al., 2019).

Public four-year colleges and universities are expected to serve the public good (Harper & Simmons, 2019) as it pertains to research, access, and affordability. Black students represent 10.9% of students at public four-year institutions (Snyder, de Brey, & Dillow, 2019). However, histories of anti-Blackness within education systems have shortchanged Black students and communities (Allen et al., 2018; McLewis, 2021) in which "too many public colleges and universities fail to offer Black students equitable access to one of our nation's most valuable public goods" (Harper & Simmons, 2019, p. 6). Instead, "African American student enrollment, college degree attainment, and economic advancement continue to be undermined by anti-Black perspectives, institutional biases, racial discrimination, and white privilege" (Allen et al., 2018, p. 68). These same processes undermine Black faculty.

Obstacles Encountered by Black Faculty

The underrepresentation of Black college faculty is commonly attributed to the low number of Black graduate students (Griffin, 2019; Kayes, 2006; Myers & Turner, 2004). Reliance on the "too few" claim justifies departments asserting that racial diversity is unachievable. This rationale ignores the many graduates of Black-serving institutions (BSIs) and historically Black colleges and universities (Allen et al., 2018). The reality is many historically white institutions (HWIs) look to other institutions that replicate and mirror the social norms of their institutions (Light, 1994), especially in their evaluations of candidates (Posselt et al., 2020). Caroline Turner and Samuel Myers (2000) also challenged supply-side theory as they described the realities of tokenism, marginalization, and hostile campus climates for Faculty of Color and found that wages predict representation. They concluded, "Among those who already have advanced degrees market forces may play a more prominent role in affecting faculty representation than pipeline factors designed to increase the supply of minority faculty" (Myers & Tuner, 2004, p. 300). Endorsements of supply-side theory breed deficit rationales, leaving unchallenged how senior college administrators and search committees rely on traditional approaches to recruit a diverse applicant pool and use biased assessment processes like "fit" and "merit" to determine whether candidates are "qualified" (White-Lewis, 2020).

A challenge to diversifying the academy is posed by search committees, the decision makers and gatekeepers in racially restructuring academic departments. Search committees impose racism when the screening process often codes "qualified" and "fit" as white and/or whiteness and rules out candidates of color (Griffin, 2020; Liera, 2020, White-Lewis, 2020). Further, the status quo is reproduced when preferred candidates are similar or a cultural match to search committee members (Kayes, 2006; Rivera, 2017; Tuitt, Sagaria, & Turner, 2007). Though search committee members increasingly receive training or manuals on equal opportunity and affirmative action hiring practices, the content of the materials vary and is often reduced to a "bureaucratic activity" (Tuitt, Sagaria, & Turner, 2007); or implicitly rejected if it is not valued by members (Kayes, 2006; Turner, Gonzalez, & Wong [Lau], 2011). Efforts to diversify are troubled when plans to prioritize diversity are not implemented before searches begin, or backlash is feared (Kayes, 2006; White-Lewis, 2020). Attempts to diversify often fall on the tokenized members of search committees, rather than being integrated into faculty search processes and embraced by all (Wilder, Osborne-Lampkin, & Jackson, 2015).

Hiring Black faculty through diversity and opportunity hiring programs is one of the strategies institutions employ to increase representation (Kelly, Gayles, & Williams, 2017). However, tokenism and hostile campus cultures diminish opportunities to broaden and advance faculty diversity; facts evident in the anti-Black challenges to Black faculty's existence within academic spaces. For example, following *Gratz v. Bollinger* (2003) and *Grutter v. Bollinger* (2003), Women of Color faculty at predominantly white research institutions describe a "perception that once search committees have made attempts to diversify the applicant pool that no further efforts are required to hire and retain diverse faculty" (Turner, Gonzalez, & Wong [Lau], 2011, p. 208).Recruitment and hiring do not ensure that faculty will be retained (Kelly, Gayles, & Williams, 2017).

Retention and Campus Racial Climate and Cultures

Beyond the hiring process, scholars describe higher education institutions' lack of urgency and commitment to retaining Black faculty (Kelly, Gayles, & Williams, 2017). Across HWIs, the experiences of racial battle fatigue, surveillance, stereotyping, gendered racism, and isolation are pervasive (Carter Andrews, 2015; Corbin, Smith, & Garcia, 2018; Smith, 2004). Racist chants, threats, violence, policing, and assumptions that Black faculty "are out of place," "just visiting," and "temporary" all reveal the anti-Blackness within higher education. Hostile campus climates negatively affect job satisfaction for Black faculty (Jayakumar et al., 2009; Kelly & Winkle-Wagner, 2017). Retention efforts must engage the impact of hostile and racist campus climates on Black faculty.

Issues of retention stemming from hostile campus climates show little change in practice, despite the rhetoric of diversity supported in the courts. Equal employment opportunity is expected to be implemented by higher education institutions, yet the procedures and conditions to hire and retain Black faculty are insufficient. Retention requires clearly defined standards for advancement, enhanced communication about institutional resources and opportunities, and greater mentorship and professional development opportunities across all faculty ranks (Croom, 2017; Turner, Gonzalez, & Wong [Lau], 2011), which is especially critical for Black faculty across institutional types (Ethridge et al., 2018). However, the expectations of the professoriate—research, teaching, and service—are not neutral standards for all but are consistently upheld in disparate impact challenges (Ware, 2000). A stark example is *Scott v. University of Delaware* (1978).

Scott v. University of Delaware (1978) personifies how university interests are prioritized, while Black faculty are disposable and protections for Black faculty are obliterated. The contract of Dr. Nolvert Scott, a Black assistant professor, was not renewed due to his productivity and complaints about his teaching, which did not meet the new standards imposed by the department. The district court acknowledged the requirements and conditions "probably has a disparate impact upon blacks," but explained "that this disparate impact is justified by the legitimate interest of the University in hiring and advancing persons who are likely to be successful in adding to the fund of knowledge" (p. 1126). The supposedly neutral criteria and practices resulting in the exclusion of Black faculty are lawful so long as they fulfill a "business necessity" (Ware, 2000). The negative determinations about teaching in *Scott* mimic the biased and negative evaluations Black faculty regularly receive. These evaluations target Black faculty members' pedagogy and knowledge, especially those with intersecting oppressed identities, such as gender and sexual identity, and whose research and teaching disrupt the power of white supremacy (Haynes et al., 2020; Porter et al., 2020).

Promotion and Tenure

Far from neutral and routine examinations of teaching, research, and service, anti-Blackness and misogynoir pervert the promotion and tenure of Black faculty. The previous discussion of disparate impact shows how protections for Black faculty are severely limited amid institutional climates of hostility and anti-Black sentiments of disposability. Another example of disparate impact was *Carpenter v. Board of Regents of University of Wisconsin System* (1984), which illuminates "the deeply embedded nature of White supremacy is also evident in faculty promotion and tenure processes, which are presumed to be fair and impartial" (Patton, 2016, p. 323). A Black faculty member and former chairman of the Afro-American Studies Department, Dr. Joseph Carpenter, had a teaching and service record deemed acceptable. However, he was denied tenure based on a lack of publications. The case describes the anomalous and extensive administrative, counseling, advising, and mentorship demanded of Dr. Carpenter because of the hostile campus racial climates and efforts to develop the newly established Afro-American Studies Department, which were not typical requirements of junior faculty in other departments. Arguably, the conditions of the campus environment that necessitated Dr. Carpenter's involvement in service became the grounds for punitive measures (Ware, 2000). Like *Scott*, the Court of Appeals in *Carpenter* (1984) stated, "Even if we were to find that the evidence supported a finding of disparate impact, there is no question that UW-M has a legitimate business interest" (p. 914). These examples show how Black faculty are penalized by the extreme service demands of combatting hostile campus racial climates created by institutions. Nonetheless, the "legitimate business interests" of the university often reigns supreme and is used as a rationale to dismiss and dispose of Black faculty.

Tenure is among the highest, most coveted levels of achievement within academia. An indefinite appointment able to be terminated only under extraordinary circumstances, its purpose is to "safeguard academic freedom, which is necessary for all who teach and conduct research in higher education" (AAUP, n.d., para. 3). Paradoxically, despite professed ideals of academic freedom, research by Black faculty who center marginalized communities is deemed suspicious, invalid, and less rigorous (Griffin, Bennett, & Harris, 2013; Settles et al., 2021), possibly forcing Black faculty research interests and tenure requirements to take separate paths (Jayakumar et al., 2009). Kimberly Griffin, Jessica Bennett, and Jessica Harris (2013) advise departments and institutions that espouse values of intellectual diversity to keep "a vigilant eye to cases of tenure-denial for faculty who study race or any other topics that are often maligned as 'identity politics'" (p. 508). Derrick Bell (1993) also speaks to the preservation of the status quo power and the conflict between academic freedom and faculty diversity in the example of law schools: "Academic freedom has never translated into an unfettered individual right to teach and research. Rather, faculty peers are primarily responsible for determining both who should be admitted to the academy, and what sort of teaching and scholarship should be necessary to gain permanent status there" (p. 373). Epistemic exclusion prevails as a tool to subjugate the labor and knowledge production of Black intellectuals, particularly Black women (Collins, 1986; Settles et al., 2021). Epistemic exclusion is heavily politically implicated and can be a mechanism to restrict minoritized groups' access to the professoriate and success in the academy. For example, the University of North Carolina–Chapel Hill Board of Trustees failed to approve tenure for Nikole Hannah-Jones, a MacArthur Genius and Pulitzer Prize–winning journalist, and creator of the 1619 Project, despite prior approval from the University of North Carolina faculty, dean, provost, and chancellor (Hannah-Jones & NAACP LDF, 2021). In addition, the 1619 Project is the target of numerous equity gag orders alongside CRT (African American Policy Forum, 2021). In a joint announcement, Howard University revealed that Nikole Hannah-Jones and Ta-Nehisi Coates would join its faculty. This move underscores how HBCUs honor their historical missions and create spaces for Black faculty (Howard University Newsroom Staff, 2021).

Persistent in the denial of tenure for Black faculty is the institutional determination that the service, teaching, and research of Black faculty is a less than, illegitimate, and unworthy contribution based on white normative standards. Despite the important turn of events for Nikole Hannah-Jones, denying Black faculty tenure is common, evidenced in the cases of Natasha B. Barnes, Cornel West, and Paul C. Harris (Zahneis, 2021). The reality for many Black faculty is that denied tenure results in extreme stigmatization, seen in Valeria Sinclair-Chapman's (2019) recount of the violence directed toward her via silencing, invisibility, dismissal, and public belittlement in a hostile space that has failed to promote Black women from assistant to associate professor. She states that the tenure and promotion processes are highly politicized and hierarchical: "It also matters how the department is ranked (or aspires to be ranked), who heads the department, what the dean wants, what the financial situation is like, what has occurred politically in the previous year, and so on" (Sinclair-Chapman, 2019, p. 52). Like *Carpenter*, Sinclair-Chapman (2019) speaks to how the department valued her teaching, not her scholarship. Thus, a discrepancy emerges between professed ideas of teaching and service and actual tenure processes that penalize Black faculty for engaging in the latter areas (Wood, Hilton, & Nevarez, 2015).

The Black Tax—Teaching, Mentoring, and Service

Black faculty labor is penalized in the tenure process. Walter Allen et al. (2002) identify two obstacles: the tremendous weight of teaching and service responsibilities, and rigid research and publication expectations. Such obstacles result from the extreme undergraduate-to-Black-faculty ratio and what Griffin, Bennett, and Harris (2013) describe as the "Black tax," or the cost of increased service and mentorship demands. Faculty of Color and Black faculty specifically have greater advising and mentoring responsibilities, including advising student groups and supervising theses and dissertations "in areas where they are among the few faculty with expertise" (Allen et al., 2002, p. 193; Griffin, 2020; Guillaume & Apodaca, 2020; Stanley, 2006; Turner, 2002). In addition, there is a frequent expectation for Black faculty to serve in committees on issues of campus climate and the recruitment of Faculty and Students of Color, yet "more often than not, work on such fronts is viewed as avocation, not vocation; it seldom 'gets counted' on measures of academic career advancement" (Allen et al., 2002, p. 193). Institutions position mentorship and service demands as the wrong use of time, separate from the currency of tenure—research (Sinclair-Chapman, 2019), yet they place extra demands on Black faculty, particularly Black women, to engage in such work (Carter Andrews, 2015; Griffin et al., 2013; Kelly & Winkle-Wagner, 2017; Porter et al., 2020). This pattern is observed across institutional types, as Black women faculty at HBCUs receive disproportionate mentorship and service burdens (Ricks, 2012). The words *caretaker* and *nurturer* in scholarship characterize the service tax placed on Black women in HWIs (Dancy II, Edwards, & Davis, 2018; Griffin & Reddick, 2011). Linking to the colonial order, T. Elon Dancy, II, Kirsten T. Edwards, and James Earl Davis (2018) detail how Black women are called upon to "clean up behind" via promotion after scandals (p. 183). Adding granularity to the gendered experiences of Black faculty is necessary, given the group-differentiated vulnerability to economic and social exploitation within the academy.

Race and Gender: Misogynoir in the Professoriate

Within the hierarchical structure of faculty ranks and prestige, the interlocking nature of racism, sexism, classism, and heterosexism shapes minoritized faculty's experiences in academia. However, research on the experiences of Black faculty with minoritized gender and/or sexual identities is limited, particularly focused on Black queer, nonbinary, or trans faculty (Bonner et al., 2015; Haynes et al., 2020; Story, 2017). Scholars have documented how Black women face vast disparities within the faculty ranks and across tenure status (Croom, 2017; Croom & Patton, 2012; Gregory, 2001), and are directly affected by misogynoir, the unique experience of anti-Black racist misogyny (Bailey, 2021). While Black men encounter their challenges, gendered differences in power, opportunity structure, and labor affect Black women's entrance and longevity within the field (Croom, 2017; Kelly & Winkle-Wagner, 2017; Priest, 2008; Young & Hines, 2018). For instance, Black women earn doctorates in larger numbers than Black men—8,807 and 4,588, respectively, in 2015–2016 (Snyder, de Brey, & Dillow, 2019)—however, fewer Black women enter academia due to inequitable access, racist and sexist environments in their graduate programs and the lack of mentoring support (Croom, 2017).

Black women faculty are challenged to constantly prove their worth due to being perceived as less qualified by their colleagues and students (Collins, 1998; Kelly, Gayles, & Williams, 2017). In a study of Women of Color faculty, Chavella T. Pittman (2010) found white male students consistently "(1) challenged their authority, (2) questioned their teaching competency, and (3) disrespected their scholarly expertise" (p. 187), as well as leveraged intimidation and threats "directed at both their persons and their careers" (p. 191). Harsh evaluations from students are common (Posselt et al., 2020; Stanley, 2006), and despite notions of teaching as generally less impactful on tenure review, Black women report greater harm to tenure and promotion prospects and the necessity to abide by a different set of standards (Griffin et al., 2013).

Jemimah L. Young and Dorothy E. Hines (2018) describe a process of *spirit-murdering*, the violence enacted against Black women faculty, both actions against the body and the cumulative effect of hostile racialized spaces, "an analogy to the killings of black women by police" (p. 19). The authors describe how white students must "have the last word" against Black women faculty, applying labels including "reverse racists" and seeking to dehumanize via verbal assaults (p. 21). Young and Hines (2018) further show the "denigration of course content" in which "white students often struggle to comprehend the relevance of cultural and racial diversity courses and see it as an academic requirement that has little meaning and worth," a pattern extending to white faculty (p. 21–22). Black women faculty are also widely presumed to be incompetent, and any "poor academic performance or absences are often attributed to *our* perceived lack of pedagogical training and methods for promoting class engagement" (Young & Hines, 2018, p. 22). Demands to see Black women's doctorates as proof of their qualifications and the equating of professors to white show the routine educational violence that attempts to deny Black women humanity (Mustaffa, 2017; Young & Hines, 2018).

The issue goes beyond their viability as scholars and faculty and must account for how higher education predisposes Black women to extreme exhaustion, isolation, exploited labor, and premature death. Myisha Priest (2008) presents an account of the numerous Black women who have transitioned after battling cancer and other serious illnesses. Underscored in noting the deaths of Sherley Anne Williams and Sylvia Boone, the first Black women faculty to be tenured at UC San Diego and Yale, respectively, is the relationship between the political struggle in and out of the academy and how "death is becoming an occupational hazard of Black female intellectual life" (Priest, 2008, p. 116–117). In order to mitigate the negative impact of getting to and through academia, much is to be explored about the ways Black women are continuously marginalized by systems that relegate them into lower-level faculty positions, disproportionately overload them with departmental responsibilities, discredit the rigor of their work, and create environments in which their colleagues and students disregard them.

Methodology

The present study utilizes institutional data from the Integrated Postsecondary Education Database System (IPEDS) to examine the tenure status of full-time Black faculty. The survey requires degree-granting institutions to complete 12 interrelated surveys, including the human resource or fall staff survey. For the fall staff survey, institutions report the number of full-time instructional staff, by faculty and tenure status, academic rank, race/ethnicity, and gender. We descriptively analyzed a subsample of institutions based on the top 20 states with the largest Black populations (see Allen et al., 2018).

According to the 2015 US Census Bureau, the 20 states with the largest Black populations are Florida, Texas, New York, Georgia, California, North Carolina, Illinois, Maryland, Virginia, Ohio, Pennsylvania, Louisiana, Michigan, South Carolina, New Jersey, Alabama, Tennessee, Mississippi, Missouri, and Indiana (table 7.1). Many of these states are places where the legality of operating racially segregated higher education systems (e.g., *Ayers*

Table 7.1. Largest Black Population by State: List of States, Institution Name, and Institution Type

State	Number of State Total	Percent	Institution Name	Institution Type
Florida	3,401,179	17.3	University of Florida	Flagship
			Florida A&M University	HBCU
			Florida Atlantic University	BSI
Texas	3,390,604	12.8	University of Texas at Austin	Flagship
			Texas Southern University	HBCU
			University of Houston, Downtown	BSI
New York	3,344,602	17	SUNY, Albany	Flagship
			CUNY, Medgar Evers College	BSI
			CUNY, City College	BSI
Georgia	3,212,824	32.1	University of Georgia	Flagship
			Savannah State University	HBCU
			Georgia State University	BSI
California	2,710,216	7.1	University of California, Berkeley	Flagship
			University of California, Los Angeles	Flagship
			California State University, Dominguez Hills	BSI
North Carolina	2,241,952	22.8	University of North Carolina at Chapel Hill	Flagship
			North Carolina A&T State University	HBCU
			University of North Carolina at Charlotte	BSI
Illinois	1,972,360	15.3	University of Illinois-Urbana Champaign	Flagship
			Chicago State University	BSI
			Southern Illinois University, Carbondale	BSI
Maryland	1,848,257	31.2	University of Maryland, College Park	Flagship
			Morgan State University	HBCU
			University of Maryland, Baltimore County	BSI
Virginia	1,717,174	20.8	University of Virginia	Flagship
			Norfolk State University	HBCU
			Old Dominion University	BSI
Ohio	1,585,347	13.7	The Ohio State University	Flagship
			Central State University	HBCU
			Cleveland State University	BSI
Pennsylvania	1,561,343	12.2	Pennsylvania State University, University Park	Flagship
			Lincoln University	HBCU
			Temple University	BSI
Louisiana	1,528,695	33.1	Louisiana State University	Flagship
			Southern University and A&M College	HBCU
			Northwestern State University of Louisiana	BSI
Michigan	1,509,779	15.2	University of Michigan, Ann Arbor	Flagship
			Michigan State Uni.	BSI
			Wayne State University	BSI
South Carolina	1,367,604	28.6	University of South Carolina, Columbia	Flagship
			South Carolina State University	HBCU
			Francis Marion University	BSI
New Jersey	1,314,132	14.8	Rutgers University, New Brunswick	Flagship
			Kean University	BSI
			Rutgers University, Newark	BSI
Alabama	1,312,584	27.2	University of Alabama	Flagship
			Alabama State University	HBCU
			University of Alabama Birmingham	BSI
Tennessee	1,150,035	17.7	University of Tennessee	Flagship
			Tennessee State University	HBCU
			Middle Tennessee State University	BSI
Mississippi	1,136,159	38	University of Mississippi	Flagship
			Jackson State University	HBCU
			University of Southern Mississippi	BSI
Missouri	764,195	12.6	University of Missouri	Flagship
			Lincoln University	HBCU
			University of Missouri St. Louis	BSI
Indiana	678,881	10.3	Indiana University Bloomington	Flagship
			Indiana State University	BSI
			Indiana University Purdue University Indianapolis	BSI

Note: Historically Black College and University (HBCU), Black-Serving Institution (BSI)
Source: U.S. Census Bureau, American Fact Finder Total Population 2011-2015 American Community Survey.
Authors' calculations

v. Fordice, 1999; *Kenneth Adams et al. v. Elliot L. Richardson, Individually, and as Secretary of the Department of Health, Education and Welfare, et al.*, 1973; *United States v. Fordice*, 1992) and race-conscious policies (e.g., *Fisher v. University of Texas at Austin*, 2013, 2016; *Gratz v. Bollinger*, 2003; *Grutter v. Bollinger*, 2003; *Regents of the University of California v. Bakke*, 1978; California's Proposition 209 and Michigan's Proposal 2) have been contested.

To capture a more comprehensive depiction of Black faculty at public four-year institutions, we identified three institutions in each of the 20 sampled states. We selected colleges across three institutional types: state flagship universities, Black-serving institutions (BSIs), and historically Black colleges and universities. While highly resourced institutions, flagships have denied access to Black folks and continue to be the primary targets for anti–affirmative action challenges. Next, we identified the BSI and HBCUs (where present) that enrolled the most Black students in their respective states. Black-serving institutions are HWIs with greater representations of Black students, providing access to a four-year education. HBCUs are critical in the enrollment and degree completion for Black students and key spaces for Black faculty. Reporting the Black composition by three diverse institutional types assists in describing the current status of the Black professoriate and identifies areas to broaden participation.

We looked at Black faculty in higher education based on gender and tenure status. For the purposes of reporting, IPEDS defines faculty as "persons identified by the institution as such and typically those whose initial assignments are made for the purpose of conducting instruction, research or public service as a principal activity" and includes personnel across various academic ranks and individuals that currently primarily serve in administrative roles (NCES, 2018a). Tenure status constitutes three categories: tenure, tenure-track, and not on tenure track or no tenure system. Regarding social characteristics, gender in this data set reproduces the male and female binary where reporting unknown or nonconforming gender identities at the institutions' discretion but must comply and adhere to male and female categories for "completeness." The racial classification in IPEDs denotes Black as those "having origins in any of the black racial groups of Africa" only. This omits individuals who are Latinx and/or selected two or more racial categories (NCES, n.d. a, n.d. b). Thus, this data set essentializes race and gender by imposing categories that may not accurately reflect respondents' self-definitions (Allen, Jones, & McLewis, 2019). While the operational definitions of race, ethnicity, and gender in the data set do not necessarily reflect the authors' politics, we are limited by institutional decisions.

Findings

In this chapter, we examine the current status of full-time Black instructional staff at public, four-year institutions. Our analysis compares how the representation of Black faculty varies based on tenure status (tenure, tenure-track, not on tenure track/no tenure system) and institutional type (flagship, Black-serving institutions, and historically Black colleges and universities). Our findings provide insights into where full-time Black faculty are and illuminate the bleak reality: Black people and their Blackness are mostly not welcomed in the professoriate.

LOCATING BLACK FACULTY IN THE ACADEMY

Black faculty are grossly underrepresented in the academy. Representing 7.74% of all full-time instructional staff, there were 5,913 Black faculty members out of 76,407 total faculty in our sample of 60 institutions (table 7.2). Our findings place the majority of Black academics at historically Black colleges and universities and a few Black-serving institutions. Except for Lincoln University in Missouri, Black Americans comprise more than 40% of the instructional staff at HBCUs and two BSIs: Chicago State University and CUNY, Medgar Evers College. HBCUs are vanguards in hiring and advancing Black college faculty, with proportions as large as 72.53% at Southern University and A&M College (table 7.2). However, mirroring the sparse demographics of the Black student population, Black faculty are vastly underrepresented at flagship institutions. The composition of Black faculty on these campuses ranges from 3.27% at the University of California, Los Angeles, to 7.12% at the University of Mississippi, with the highest percentage (m= 4.45) (table 7.2). Similar patterns were observed at Black-serving institutions.

The racial demographics of faculty at BSIs resembles the scant representation of Black faculty at flagship institutions. Black faculty range from 4.13% at Indiana State University to 12.12% at Georgia State University (see table 7.2). Chicago State University and CUNY, Medgar Evers College, are again anomalies with 41.8% and 66.28%, respectively. Black faculty represent less than 5% of instructional staff at Indiana State University (4.13%), Francis Marion University (4.33%), Michigan State University (4.41%), Indiana University Purdue University Indianapolis (4.42%), University of Southern Mississippi (4.57%), and Northwestern State University of Louisiana (4.97%). Overall, Black faculty are heavily concentrated

Table 7.2. Numbers and Percentages of Black Full-Time Instructional Staff by Gender, 2017

	Full-Time Instructional Staff						
	All Staff			Black Faculty			
	T	W	M	T	%	W	M
Florida							
University of Florida	2,613	961	1,652	94	3.60	48	46
Florida A&M University	552	266	286	377	68.30	203	174
Florida Atlantic University	824	366	458	55	6.67	33	22
Texas							
University of Texas at Austin	2,637	1,070	1,567	96	3.64	43	53
Texas Southern University	418	198	220	287	68.66	151	136
University of Houston, Downtown	362	173	189	43	11.88	28	15
New York							
SUNY, Albany	660	274	386	29	4.39	19	10
CUNY, Medgar Evers College	172	77	95	114	66.28	52	62
CUNY, City College	589	226	363	47	7.98	23	24
Georgia							
University of Georgia	2,033	803	1,230	104	5.12	53	51
Savannah State University	205	96	109	88	42.93	47	41
Georgia State University	1,155	561	594	140	12.12	105	35
California							
University of California, Berkeley	1,648	588	1,060	62	3.76	25	37
University of California, Los Angeles	3,522	1,339	2,183	115	3.27	60	55
California State University, Dominguez Hills	354	194	160	36	10.17	21	15
North Carolina							
University of North Carolina at Chapel Hill	1,951	898	1,053	110	5.64	66	44
North Carolina A&T State University	445	188	257	222	49.89	115	107
University of North Carolina at Charlotte	1,079	517	562	75	6.95	49	26
Illinois							
University of Illinois Urbana-Champaign	2,283	864	1,419	102	4.47	54	48
Chicago State University	189	100	89	79	41.80	55	24
Southern Illinois University, Carbondale	995	389	606	54	5.43	28	26
Maryland							
University of Maryland, College Park	1,830	692	1,138	98	5.36	52	46
Morgan State University	460	202	258	206	44.78	104	102
University of Maryland, Baltimore County	548	262	286	33	6.02	18	15
Virginia							
University of Virginia	2,283	862	1,421	97	4.25	48	49
Norfolk State University	247	122	125	143	57.89	85	58
Old Dominion University	839	382	457	53	6.32	35	18
Ohio							
The Ohio State University	3,908	1,612	2,296	151	3.86	68	83
Central State University	98	34	64	47	47.96	18	29
Cleveland State University	541	249	292	30	5.55	18	12

	All Staff			Black Faculty			
	T	W	M	T	%	W	M
Pennsylvania							
Pennsylvania State University, University Park	2,773	1,121	1,652	103	3.71	54	49
Lincoln University	97	39	58	43	44.33	17	26
Temple University	2,253	906	1,347	125	5.55	65	60
Louisiana							
Louisiana State University	1,334	497	837	55	4.12	29	26
Southern University and A&M College	233	104	129	169	72.53	86	83
Northwestern State University of Louisiana	302	180	122	15	4.97	13	2
Michigan							
University of Michigan, Ann Arbor	6,559	2,590	3,969	228	3.48	107	121
Michigan State University	2,724	1,095	1,629	120	4.41	52	68
Wayne State University	1,643	693	950	123	7.49	69	54
South Carolina							
University of South Carolina, Columbia	1,701	742	959	93	5.47	60	33
South Carolina State University	133	64	69	88	66.17	51	37
Francis Marion University	208	109	99	9	4.33	7	2
New Jersey							
Rutgers University, New Brunswick	3,233	1,456	1,777	129	3.99	83	46
Kean University	333	183	150	31	9.31	16	15
Rutgers University, Newark	555	201	354	41	7.39	18	23
Alabama							
University of Alabama	1,435	647	788	93	6.48	58	35
Alabama State University	224	114	110	132	58.93	76	56
University of Alabama Birmingham	2,336	947	1,389	146	6.25	98	48
Tennessee							
University of Tennessee, Knoxville	1,567	692	875	62	3.96	29	33
Tennessee State University	363	163	200	147	40.50	81	66
Middle Tennessee State University	911	434	477	65	7.14	33	32
Mississippi							
University of Mississippi	1,797	814	983	128	7.12	84	44
Jackson State University	370	171	199	230	62.16	130	100
University of Southern Mississippi	678	331	347	31	4.57	22	9
Missouri							
University of Missouri, Columbia	1,827	754	1,073	67	3.67	29	38
Lincoln University	106	50	56	19	17.92	9	10
University of Missouri St. Louis	421	225	196	26	6.18	17	9
Indiana							
Indiana University Bloomington	2,038	805	1,233	85	4.17	33	52
Indiana State University	460	213	247	19	4.13	10	9
Indiana University Purdue University Indianapolis	2,353	1,010	1,343	104	4.42	56	48
Total	76,407	31,915	44,492	5,913		3,216	2,697

Source: Authors' calculations based on data from National Center for Education Statistics

T: Total; W: Women; M: Men

at HBCUs and marginally represented at flagship universities and most BSIs.

Few and Far Between: Underrepresentation of Black Faculty with Tenure

The number of Black faculty with tenure at HWIs and Black-serving institutions is sparse. For example, some flagship campuses have as few as 14 Black tenured faculty, such as the case at the University of Missouri, Columbia (see table 7.3). Similarly, there were 16 Black tenured faculty at SUNY, Albany; 24 at the University of Tennessee, Knoxville; and 27 at Louisiana State University. Overall, Black tenured faculty constituted 5% or less of tenured faculty at 18 out of 21 sampled public flagships and less than 3.64% of all instructional staff for all sampled public flagships (see table 7.3). This pattern mirrors the persistently low proportions of Black students at flagships (Allen et al., 2018).

While more Black students attend and graduate from Black-serving institutions compared to flagship universities (Allen et al., 2018), Black tenured faculty are severely underrepresented at these colleges. We expected to observe a greater presence of Black faculty at campuses with a representative Black student population but were struck with the relatively low number of Black faculty holding tenured appointments at Black-serving institutions. For instance, at Francis Marion University in South Carolina, more than 47% of enrolled undergraduates are Black, and yet the university has the fewest Black faculty appointed to tenure, a mere 3 (see table 7.3). Similar patterns are observed at Georgia State University, where Black students constitute 40.9% of the undergraduate population (Allen et al., 2018), and 6.74% of tenured faculty; 30.4% of undergraduates and 2.74% of tenured faculty at Northwestern State University; and 30.3% of undergraduates and 3.39% of tenured faculty at the University of Southern Mississippi. Of the Black-serving institutions in this study, two were exemplars in having a Black tenured faculty that reflected the racial demographic of the student population: Chicago State University and CUNY, Medgar Evers College. Comparatively, Black faculty with tenure are much better represented at historically Black colleges and universities.

Reflecting the racial demographic of the Black students they serve, HBCUs award tenure to more Black faculty than other colleges and universities. In our sample of selected 14 HBCUs, Black faculty accounted for

Table 7.3. Numbers and Percentages of Black Full-Time Instructional Staff by Tenure Status and Gender, 2017

	Total Instructional Staff				Total Black Faculty						Black Women Faculty						Black Men Faculty					
	Total	T	TT	NTT	T	1	TT	2	NTT	3	T	1	TT	2	NTT	3	T	1	TT	2	NTT	3
Florida																						
University of Florida	2613	1524	486	603	45	1.72	17	0.65	32	1.22	18	0.69	12	0.46	18	0.69	27	1.03	5	0.19	14	0.54
Florida A&M University	552	290	118	144	192	34.78	78	14.13	107	19.38	79	14.31	50	9.06	74	13.41	113	20.47	28	5.07	33	5.98
Florida Atlantic University	824	415	164	245	25	3.03	7	0.85	23	2.79	16	1.94	4	0.49	13	1.58	9	1.09	3	0.36	10	1.21
Texas																						
University of Texas at Austin	2637	1514	326	797	60	2.28	14	0.53	22	0.83	26	0.99	6	0.23	11	0.42	34	1.29	8	0.30	11	0.42
Texas Southern University	418	188	46	184	113	27.03	32	7.66	142	33.97	46	11.00	25	5.98	80	19.14	67	16.03	7	1.67	62	14.83
University of Houston, Downtown	362	164	78	120	14	3.87	14	3.87	15	4.14	10	2.76	7	1.93	11	3.04	4	1.10	7	1.93	4	1.10
New York																						
SUNY, Albany	660	370	188	102	16	2.42	9	1.36	4	0.61	9	1.36	7	1.06	3	0.45	7	1.06	2	0.30	1	0.15
CUNY, Medgar Evers College	172	107	49	16	74	43.02	27	15.70	13	7.56	30	17.44	16	9.30	6	3.49	44	25.58	11	6.40	7	4.07
CUNY, City College	589	436	123	30	33	5.60	13	2.21	1	0.17	16	2.72	6	1.02	1	0.17	17	2.89	7	1.19	0	0.00
Georgia																						
University of Georgia	2033	1220	391	422	74	3.64	18	0.89	12	0.59	35	1.72	10	0.49	8	0.39	39	1.92	8	0.39	4	0.20
Savannah State University	205	45	84	76	23	11.22	33	16.10	32	15.61	6	2.93	17	8.29	24	11.71	17	8.29	16	7.80	8	3.90
Georgia State University	1155	475	262	418	32	2.77	41	3.55	67	5.80	18	1.56	36	3.12	51	4.42	14	1.21	5	0.43	16	1.39
California																						
University of California, Berkeley	1648	1126	235	287	42	2.55	10	0.61	10	0.61	13	0.79	5	0.30	7	0.42	29	1.76	5	0.30	3	0.18
University of California, Los Angeles	3522	1480	244	1798	61	1.73	12	0.34	42	1.19	26	0.74	6	0.17	28	0.80	35	0.99	6	0.17	14	0.40
California State University, Dominguez Hills	354	147	85	122	11	3.11	8	2.26	17	4.80	5	1.41	4	1.13	12	3.39	6	1.69	4	1.13	5	1.41

Table 7.3. Continued.

	Total Instructional Staff			Total Black Faculty					Black Women Faculty					Black Men Faculty				
	Total	TT	NTT	T	1	TT	2	NTT	3	T	1	TT	2	NTT	3	T	1	TT	2	NTT	3

	Total	TT	NTT	T	1	TT	2	NTT	3	T	1	TT	2	NTT	3	T	1	TT	2	NTT	3
North Carolina																					
University of North Carolina at Chapel Hill	1951	1032	618	52	2.67	24	1.23	34	1.74	32	1.64	13	0.67	21	1.08	20	1.03	11	0.56	13	0.67
North Carolina A&T State University	445	261	79	128	28.76	46	10.34	48	10.79	56	12.58	29	6.52	30	6.74	72	16.18	17	3.82	18	4.04
University of North Carolina at Charlotte	1079	525	340	31	2.87	19	1.76	25	2.32	17	1.58	12	1.11	20	1.85	14	1.30	7	0.65	5	0.46
Illinois																					
University of Illinois Urbana-Champaign	2283	1282	521	55	2.41	29	1.27	18	0.79	25	1.10	16	0.70	13	0.57	30	1.31	13	0.57	5	0.22
Chicago State University	189	91	82	22	11.64	10	5.29	47	24.87	15	7.94	7	3.70	33	17.46	7	3.70	3	1.59	14	7.41
Southern Illinois University, Carbondale	995	435	387	21	2.11	8	0.80	25	2.51	6	0.60	6	0.60	16	1.61	15	1.51	2	0.20	9	0.90
Maryland																					
University of Maryland, College Park	1830	1108	434	40	2.19	23	1.26	35	1.91	18	0.98	13	0.71	21	1.15	22	1.20	10	0.55	14	0.77
Morgan State University	460	216	135	89	19.35	46	10.00	71	15.43	43	9.35	24	5.22	37	8.04	46	10.00	22	4.78	34	7.39
University of Maryland, Baltimore County	548	295	147	19	3.47	6	1.09	8	1.46	9	1.64	5	0.91	4	0.73	10	1.82	1	0.18	4	0.73
Virginia																					
University of Virginia	2283	1048	823	48	2.10	19	0.83	30	1.31	19	0.83	9	0.39	20	0.88	29	1.27	10	0.44	10	0.44
Norfolk State University	247	124	42	72	29.15	38	15.38	33	13.36	43	17.41	24	9.72	18	7.29	29	11.74	14	5.67	15	6.07
Old Dominion University	839	419	246	22	2.62	13	1.55	18	2.15	8	0.95	9	1.07	18	2.15	14	1.67	4	0.48	0	0.00
Ohio																					
The Ohio State University	3908	1824	1453	64	1.64	29	0.74	58	1.48	29	0.74	9	0.23	30	0.77	35	0.90	20	0.51	28	0.72
Central State University	98	54	12	30	30.61	13	13.27	4	4.08	9	9.18	6	6.12	3	3.06	21	21.43	7	7.14	1	1.02
Cleveland State University	541	313	115	19	3.51	3	0.55	8	1.48	8	1.48	3	0.55	7	1.29	11	2.03	0	0.00	1	0.18

	Total Instructional Staff				Total Black Faculty						Black Women Faculty						Black Men Faculty					
	Total	T	TT	NTT	T	1	TT	2	NTT	3	T	1	TT	2	NTT	3	T	1	TT	2	NTT	3
Pennsylvania																						
Pennsylvania State University, University Park	2773	1313	431	1029	50	1.80	19	0.69	34	1.23	22	0.79	13	0.47	19	0.69	28	1.01	6	0.22	15	0.54
Lincoln University	97	54	36	7	27	27.84	14	14.43	2	2.06	8	8.25	7	7.22	2	2.06	19	19.59	7	7.22	0	0.00
Temple University	2253	709	277	1267	41	1.82	12	0.53	72	3.20	17	0.75	3	0.13	45	2.00	24	1.07	9	0.40	27	1.20
Louisiana																						
Louisiana State University	1334	701	281	352	27	2.02	9	0.67	19	1.42	13	0.97	4	0.30	12	0.90	14	1.05	5	0.37	7	0.52
Southern University and A&M College	233	135	64	34	95	40.77	47	20.17	27	11.59	40	17.17	32	13.73	14	6.01	55	23.61	15	6.44	13	5.58
Northwestern State University of Louisiana	302	146	106	50	4	1.32	10	3.31	1	0.33	4	1.32	8	2.65	1	0.33	0	0.00	2	0.66	0	0.00
Michigan																						
University of Michigan, Ann Arbor	6559	2140	650	3769	90	1.37	35	0.53	103	1.57	33	0.50	18	0.27	56	0.85	57	0.87	17	0.26	47	0.72
Michigan State University	2724	1415	455	854	54	1.98	22	0.81	44	1.62	18	0.66	13	0.48	21	0.77	36	1.32	9	0.33	23	0.84
Wayne State University	1643	724	194	725	36	2.19	9	0.55	78	4.75	17	1.03	3	0.18	49	2.98	19	1.16	6	0.37	29	1.77
South Carolina																						
University of South Carolina, Columbia	1701	781	332	588	34	2.00	22	1.29	37	2.18	19	1.12	17	1.00	24	1.41	15	0.88	5	0.29	13	0.76
South Carolina State University	133	76	28	29	45	33.83	20	15.04	23	17.29	23	17.29	13	9.77	15	11.28	22	16.54	7	5.26	8	6.02
Francis Marion University	208	117	58	33	3	1.44	3	1.44	3	1.44	2	0.96	3	1.44	2	0.96	1	0.48	0	0.00	1	0.48
New Jersey																						
Rutgers University, New Brunswick	3233	1335	363	1535	39	1.21	16	0.49	74	2.29	24	0.74	10	0.31	49	1.52	15	0.46	6	0.19	25	0.77
Kean University	333	189	44	100	20	6.01	0	0.00	11	3.30	10	3.00	0	0.00	6	1.80	10	3.00	0	0.00	5	1.50
Rutgers University, Newark	555	304	97	154	20	3.60	5	0.90	16	2.88	10	1.80	3	0.54	5	0.90	10	1.80	2	0.36	11	1.98

Table 7.3. Continued.

	Total Instructional Staff				Total Black Faculty							Black Women Faculty							Black Men Faculty						
	Total	T	TT	NTT	T	1	TT	2	NTT	3		T	1	TT	2	NTT	3		T	1	TT	2	NTT	3
Alabama																									
University of Alabama	1435	584	365	486	34	2.37	28	1.95	31	2.16		21	1.46	13	0.91	24	1.67		13	0.91	15	1.05	7	0.49
Alabama State University	224	108	64	52	56	25.00	36	16.07	40	17.86		35	15.63	18	8.04	23	10.27		21	9.38	18	8.04	17	7.59
University of Alabama Birmingham	2336	819	529	988	39	1.67	39	1.67	68	2.91		21	0.90	28	1.20	49	2.10		18	0.77	11	0.47	19	0.81
Tennessee																									
University of Tennessee, Knoxville	1567	818	313	436	24	1.53	27	1.72	11	0.70		9	0.57	14	0.89	6	0.38		15	0.96	13	0.83	5	0.32
Tennessee State University	363	219	113	31	88	24.24	44	12.12	15	4.13		48	13.22	26	7.16	7	1.93		40	11.02	18	4.96	8	2.20
Middle Tennessee State University	911	509	174	228	34	3.73	9	0.99	22	2.41		14	1.54	7	0.77	12	1.32		20	2.20	2	0.22	10	1.10
Mississippi																									
University of Mississippi	1797	603	330	864	45	2.50	22	1.22	61	3.39		26	1.45	13	0.72	45	2.50		19	1.06	9	0.50	16	0.89
Jackson State University	370	186	64	120	104	28.11	38	10.27	88	23.78		53	14.32	27	7.30	50	13.51		51	13.78	11	2.97	38	10.27
University of Southern Mississippi	678	295	173	210	10	1.47	6	0.88	15	2.21		8	1.18	1	0.15	13	1.92		2	0.29	5	0.74	2	0.29
Missouri																									
University of Missouri, Columbia	1827	735	238	854	14	0.77	27	1.48	26	1.42		5	0.27	11	0.60	13	0.71		9	0.49	16	0.88	13	0.71
Lincoln University	106	52	22	32	12	11.32	1	0.94	6	5.66		4	3.77	1	0.94	4	3.77		8	7.55	0	0.00	2	1.89
University of Missouri St. Louis	421	191	57	173	12	2.85	7	1.66	7	1.66		6	1.43	5	1.19	6	1.43		6	1.43	2	0.48	1	0.24
Indiana																									
Indiana University Bloomington	2038	1011	368	659	34	1.67	22	1.08	29	1.42		13	0.64	9	0.44	11	0.54		21	1.03	13	0.64	18	0.88
Indiana State University	460	244	106	110	10	2.17	8	1.74	1	0.22		5	1.09	5	0.01	0	0.00		5	1.09	3	0.65	1	0.22
Indiana University Purdue University Indianapolis	2353	788	385	1180	31	1.32	20	0.85	53	2.25		15	0.64	10	0.42	31	1.32		16	0.68	10	0.42	22	0.93
Total	76407	35829	12831	27747	2659		1236		2018			1233		731		1252			1426		505		766	

Source: Authors' calculations based on data from National Center for Education Statistics

1: Percent Tenured; 2: Percent Tenure-Track; 3: Percent Non-Tenure-Track

T: Total Tenured Faculty; TT: Total Tenure-Track Faculty; NTT: Total Non-Tenure-Track Faculty more than 40% of tenured faculty at 13 institutions and more than 50% at 10 institutions (see table 7.3). The proportion of Black faculty with tenure appointments was the largest at Southern University and A&M College with 70.37%, followed by Florida A&M University and Texas Southern University with 66.21% and 60.11%, respectively. While tenure appointments for Black faculty are in as few as single digits at HWIs, some HBCUs boast well over 100. For example, in 2017, there were 104 Black faculty with tenure at Jackson State University, 113 at Texas Southern University, and 128 at North Carolina A&T University.

The Road Less Traveled: Black Faculty on the Tenure Track

While the percentage of Black faculty with tenure is small, the proportion on the tenure track is even smaller. For instance, of those who are full-time instructional staff, Black Americans represent 1.73% of tenured faculty and .34% of tenure-track faculty at the University of California, Los Angeles (see table 7.3). Although this finding reflects broader trends of fewer faculty on tenure track (12,831) than with tenure (35,829), it also vividly depicts the numerical representation and degree of marginalization for Black ladder faculty, especially at HWIs (see table 7.3).

Across institutional types, however, there were fewer than 50 Black faculty on tenure track at all sampled college campuses, with the exception of Florida A&M University with 78 (see table 7.3). Particularly at flagship institutions, we observe relatively few Black faculty on the tenure track at campuses such as SUNY, Albany, and Louisiana State University, with 9, and the University of California, Berkeley, with 10. Strikingly, our findings indicate there are even fewer at Black-serving institutions. In our sample of 25 Black-serving institutions, the number of Black faculty on tenure track was in the single digits at 13 institutions, with Kean University having zero. A similar pattern was observed at Lincoln University, a historically Black college in Missouri. However, when compared to their institutional counterparts, the majority of our sampled historically Black institutions had more than 30 Black faculty members on the tenure track. While Black faculty in tenure-track positions are better represented at HBCUs than at other institutional types, they do not constitute the majority of tenure track faculty at HBCUs. In fact, Black faculty account for 50% or more of those on tenure track at only 6 HBCUs.

Black Faculty Not on the Tenure Track

Resembling the imbalance of Black faculty in the academy across faculty status, Black faculty comprise a smaller proportion of full-time institutional staff in non-tenure-track positions. Black faculty represented less than 5% of non-tenure-track faculty at 14 flagship institutions: University of California, Los Angeles; University of Tennessee, Knoxville; University of Michigan, Ann Arbor; University of Texas at Austin; University of Georgia; University of Missouri, Columbia; Pennsylvania State College, University Park; University of Illinois Urbana-Champaign; University of California, Berkeley; University of Virginia; SUNY, Albany; The Ohio State University; Indiana University Bloomington; and Rutgers University, New Brunswick. Black faculty also represented less than 5% of non-tenure-track faculty at 5 Black-serving institutions: Indiana University–Purdue University Indianapolis; Indiana State University; Northwestern State University of Louisiana; CUNY, City College; and University of Missouri–St. Louis (see table 7.3). However, while the racial composition is comparable across faculty status within institutional types, we observed higher concentration in non-tenure-track positions.

Black faculty are more concentrated in non-tenure-track positions compared to tenure-track. In our sample, 2,018 Black faculty members are in non-tenure-track positions and 1,236 are ladder faculty (see table 7.3). Particularly at HBCUs, non-tenure-track faculty are a considerable portion of the faculty population. Black non-tenure-track faculty comprise 33.97% of full-time instructional staff at Texas Southern University, 23.78 at Jackson State University, and 19.38% at Florida A&M University (see table 7.3). Exceptions include North Carolina A&T State University and Savannah State University, where the size of tenure-track and non-tenure-track populations are comparable. Southern University and A&M College and Tennessee State University hire more tenure-track than non-tenure-track faculty.

At flagship institutions where the proportion of Black non-tenure-track faculty was greater than 1%, the proportion of Black faculty on the tenure track was lower. For example, at the University of Mississippi, tenure-track Black faculty represent 1.22% of all instructional staff, while Black faculty with non-tenure-track positions represent 3.39% (see table 7.3). This trend is even more apparent at Black-serving institutions (exception CUNY, Medgar Evers). At Chicago State University, 5.29% of full-time instructional staff are Black faculty on the tenure track, while non-tenure-track Black faculty comprise 24.87%. Similar proportional differences in faculty classification were observed at Wayne State University, where .55% of Black faculty are on the tenure track compared to 4.75% of non-tenure-track Black faculty, and at Temple University, with Black faculty on tenure track representing .53% of instructional staff and 3.20% of non-tenure-track faculty. Put another way, the counts of Black instructional staff by faculty status show Black faculty are much more frequently in non-tenure-track positions. Temple University, for example, has 2,253 full-time instructional staff members, and of those, 41 Black faculty are tenured, 12 are on the tenure track, and 72 are in non-tenure-track positions. Thus, a pattern is evident of institutions positioning Black faculty among non-tenure-track roles.

Teaching at the Intersection: Race and Gender Demographics of Black Faculty

Considering race and gender differences, Black men and women are both severely underrepresented in the academy. Gender does, however, correlate with tenure status. Black men are more likely to hold tenured appointments at 15 out of 21 flagship institutions (see table 7.3). For instance, tenured appointments are held by 13 Black women and 29 Black men at the University of California, Berkeley. Similarly, at the University of Michigan, Ann Arbor, there were 33 Black women and 57 Black men with tenured appointments. This trend was also observed at 12 out of 25 Black-serving institutions and 9 out of the 14 historically Black colleges and universities. Comparing tenured faculty status across institutional types, Black women are more likely to be on tenure track than Black men. However, Black women are discernibly concentrated in non-tenure-track positions. This fact was most noticeable at institutions where there were twice or more Black women in non-tenure-track positions compared to Black men. Exemplars of this pattern include Florida A&M University, where 74 Black women and 33 Black men are in non-tenure-track positions; Georgia State University with 51 and 16; Rutgers University, New Brunswick, with 49 and 25; University of Mississippi with 45 and 16; Chicago State University with 33 and 14; University of California, Los Angeles, with 28 and 14; Savannah State University with 24 and 8; University of Alabama with 24 and 7; and Old Dominion with 18 and 0, respectively. These patterns discredit the myth that Black women are advantaged and confirm racial disparities affect both Black women and Black men in the professoriate.

Summary, Discussion, and Conclusion

Seeing through the Smog of Anti-Blackness

Findings of this study indicate a persistent problem in US higher education: Black faculty are severely underrepresented. College faculty are primarily white cis-men, and changes to this portrait are grim. We found Black faculty constituted a small proportion of full-time instructional staff at both flagship institutions *and* Black-serving institutions, regardless of faculty status (i.e., tenured, tenure-track, not on tenure system). This problem reflects patterns of Black student exclusion at flagships. Moreover, even though Black-serving institutions serve a greater proportion of Black students (Allen et al., 2018), Black faculty are dismally represented on these campuses. Black-serving institutions, many of which are minority-serving institutions, are unique colleges with missions and environments that serve underrepresented students (Parker, 2012). Thus, it is peculiar how Black college faculty recruitment and retention are undermined. Yet these findings reflect higher education's predisposition in which anti-Black racism and the exclusionary, white-centered practices are normalized. Lori Patton Davis (2016) describes how "the lack of racial diversity among higher education faculty and leaders is an unsurprising, long-standing trend that is commonplace in the academy" (p. 323). The lack of Black faculty at historically white colleges evokes the degree to which the status quo remains unchallenged and unchanged.

Despite the anti-Black climate of academe, historically Black colleges and universities continue to be beacons of hope. The contributions of HBCUs enrolling and graduating Black undergraduate and graduate students is matched with their dedication in hiring Black faculty. Representing approximately 2% of colleges (Snyder, de Brey, & Dillow, 2019), these institutions overwhelmingly employ more Black college faculty compared to the single digits reported by HWIs. In fact, Howard University, a historically Black college in Washington, DC, has the most full-time Black faculty in the nation. This accomplishment confirms the importance of historically Black colleges and is reflective of their unique mission and legacy, as refuges for Black folks who have been systematically denied opportunity in white spaces (Allen et al., 2020; Mobley, 2017). Further, it begs the question: if historically Black colleges and universities can effectively employ Black faculty, what prevents historically white institutions from doing the same?

Supply-side theory has been utilized to explain the underrepresentation of Black faculty at flagships and HWIs. Divorced from such contentions is how the recruitment, hiring, and advancement of Black college faculty members is stifled by anti-Black dispositions and practices that deny access and success in the professoriate. As articulated by Charles R. Lawrence III (2015), "When people of color come to the academy, a place where inequality is institutionalized and rationalized, we trespass on white property" (p. 9). Discriminatory practices inhibit broader representation of Black college faculty. In fact, studies have found there is an assumption applicants of color will be highly recruited (Tuitt, Sagaria, & Turner, 2007; White-Lewis et al., 2021), and thus resources should not be wasted trying to recruit them. This false assumption indicates the continuous real tensions between diversity paradigms and anti-Blackness in the professoriate.

BENEFITS OF DIVERSITY AT THE EXPENSE OF BLACK FACULTY

While *Grutter* ruled that diversity is an educational benefit, recognizing the benefits of a diverse professoriate has not extended to the hiring and promotion of Black faculty. Equity is impeded by color-blind ideologies that are in fact *raced*, and that actively protect whiteness (Harris, 1993) to render Blackness as unqualified (Mustaffa, 2017). In the faculty hiring process, factors including selectivity of graduate program, innovation, and visibility of research are deemed fair and race-neutral measures (Matthew, 2016; White-Lewis, 2020), while the lack of qualified Black applicants is alleged. Walter R. Allen and colleagues (2000) describe their experiences witnessing discussions of the qualifications of Black faculty applicants: "All too often, recognizing and valuing diversity are perceived in such meetings as special pleadings to recruit and hire unqualified professors. Rarely are African American candidates for collegiate faculty positions seen as especially competitive for their value in presenting profiles different from the mainstream in their research, backgrounds, and race; yet, this is an important part of what they have to offer" (p. 126). Anti-Blackness routinely abounds in reviews of Black applicants and in the evaluation of their merits and credentials. Critical race theory rejects claims of meritocracy (Delgado & Stefancic, 2017), noting how academic pillars of teaching, research, and service are far from neutral and often leveraged instead to devalue Black faculty energies and creativity—especially as pertains to tenure status.

Despite professed ideals of diversity, we found Black faculty are more likely to be in non-tenure-track positions, and across HWIs, Black faculty are largely excluded from the tenure process altogether. Faculty status reflects the hierarchy and prestige of academe, where tenure is the promise of an indefinite position and long-term institutional investment—benefits largely connected to academic freedom (AAUP, n.d.). Thus, barring access to tenure poses severe consequences for Black academics. Anti-Blackness at work in higher education is visible in how research and scholarship produced by Black faculty are considered illegitimate (Allen et al., 2002; Porter et al., 2020; Settles et al., 2021); teaching evaluations are weaponized as an attack (Griffin et al., 2013; Haynes et al., 2020; Stanley, 2006); Black women are routinely challenged by both white students and faculty to prove their qualifications and the importance of their work (Collins, 1998; Kelly, Gayles, & Williams, 2017; Pittman, 2010; Young & Hines, 2018); and the increased service demands placed on Black faculty, especially Black women (Griffin et al. 2013; Priest, 2008). Although teaching, research, and service are the currencies to access promotion and tenure, we see a paradox where Black faculty (especially women) are burdened with the "invisible labor" of diversity work and yet penalized in the tenure process (as seen in *Carpenter*). Higher education as a public good and tenure as the promise of academic freedom in service of the public interest warrants the need to address the ongoing lack of tenured and tenure-track Black faculty. Rarely are the fruits of academia bestowed on Black academics.

Reimagining an Academy with Black Faculty Included

Critics of the diversity rationale ask, "Who benefits?" and contend this paradigm serves white interests (Allen et al., 2018; Harris, Barone, & Patton, 2015). Nicola Rollock (2018) terms *racial gesture politics* the "words, policies or behaviours, which ostensibly address racial disparities but in reality maintain a racially inequitable status quo" (p. 324). Professed commitments to diversity are overshadowed when anti-Blackness takes precedence. This fact is evident in the allocation of resources and the disinvestment in supporting institutions that primarily serve Black and other racially diverse students. Compared to historically white and land grant institutions, HBCUs are severely underfunded (Allen et al., 2020; Allen & Esters, 2018), and their faculty receive lower salaries (Womble, 2018), which "reflects a sordid commitment to the elimination of Black enterprise. It also undergirds the relationship of trauma between Blackness and the educational system," (Dancy II, Edwards, & Davis, 2018, p. 188). Moreover, the disenfranchisement of Black faculty limits the extension of diversity as an educational benefit to *all* students.

Faculty of Color foster positive campus climates and contribute to undergraduate and graduate education (Hurtado et al., 2012). Black college faculty particularly enhance learning environments by thoroughly enriching pedagogical techniques (Umbach, 2006), exposure to diverse perspectives and research (Milem, 2003), guidance and advocacy for student-activists (Stokes & Miller, 2019), and providing academic and professional support and mentorship for students and faculty with diverse backgrounds (Allen & Joseph, 2018; Cole & Griffin, 2013). For Black women, co-mentorship is a form of community building and resistance to marginalization (Allen & Joseph, 2018; Baldwin & Johnson, 2018; Fries-Britt & Kelly, 2005). However, the scarcity of Black women faculty at HWIs also creates a mentorship void for Black women in graduate programs seeking connection-based shared experiences (Patton & Harper, 2003). Thus, we see the marginalization of Black women profoundly reflected across our findings.

Facing challenges of anti-Black racism similar to those of their male counterparts, Black women are uniquely affected by the confluence of racism, patriarchy, and other dominant systems of power. Our findings conclude Black women are less likely to hold tenured appointments. Being employed without tenure status places Black women in a vulnerable position of excessively laboring for less benefit while combating the scourge of anti-Black gendered racism. For Black women in academic settings, there is a constant struggle under the burdens of hypervisibility and invisibility, exacerbated more for Black femmes (Story, 2017), "students, other faculty, and staff all see us and don't see us, while consequently seeking to place our identities and racialized gender performances within their own designated understandings of what blackness and femininity mean to them" (p. 414). This problem occurs at both historically white and Black institutions (Ricks, 2012).

While Black faculty are tremendous assets to the university, the lack of Black faculty is reflective of institutional failure to combat racism, and imposes additional service demands and diversity work on the relatively few (Fries-Britt et al., 2011; Harris, Barone, & Patton, 2015). They are often overloaded beyond "normal" expectations while being devalued and unrewarded. Imploring Black faculty to serve as *diversity mules* is a form of objectification and is grounded in the thinking of numerical diversity as a solution. Numerical representation is insufficient if the campus climate and institutional culture remain unaddressed: "The hiring of a few minorities and women—particularly when a faculty is under pressure from students or civil rights agencies—is not a departure from, but an adherence to, this power-preserving doctrine" (Bell, 1993, p. 374). Further, the absence of Black faculty "illuminates the systemic racism that exists within higher education and affirms White students' stereotypical beliefs and racial narratives about who are authority figures and who are not" (Parker & Neville, 2019, p. 898). Higher education institutions miss the opportunity to actively challenge systemic racism on their campuses and create learning environments that equip students to be change agents. Instead, the promise of diversity remains a distant, unfulfilled dream, and anti-Blackness continues to be entrenched and valorized.

As we reimagine an academy with Black faculty, we do not define inclusion as tokenism. Our findings show the extreme underrepresentation of Black faculty at flagships and at many Black-serving institutions. With fewer than 10 Black faculty at many public universities, and even fewer with tenure, the significance of the catastrophic lack of Black college faculty cannot be overstated. Isolation, hostile racist campus climates, and service demands placed upon Black faculty, especially Black women, exact negative costs on their professional, physical, emotional, mental, and spiritual well-being (Carter Andrews, 2015; Priest, 2008; Young & Hines, 2018). The exclusion of Black faculty betrays the premise of public higher education as a public good. For example, Gregory Price and Rhonda Sharpe (2018) describe how the absence of Black faculty in economics departments denies the creation of knowledge to "inform public policies that would reduce racial inequality and improve the living standards of black Americans" (p. 1). At stake are influencing and preparing future generations for democratic citizenship, generating research that informs policy, and transforming society to become more just. Therefore, incremental changes to broaden Black participation in the professoriate will not suffice.

Recommendations

Efforts to increase the representation of Black college faculty challenge institutions to create conditions where Black faculty can thrive. This requires eradicating the reproduction of anti-Black ideologies and practices. This requires abandoning myths of Black lack, such as the supply-side theory (Griffin, 2019; Myers & Turner, 2004), deficit beliefs about merit and qualifications (Allen et al., 2000; Griffin, 2020; Tuitt, Sagaria, & Turner, 2007; White-Lewis, 2020), and white cis-male logic that undergirds the tenure and promotion review process (Haynes et al., 2020). Further, institutions are charged with interrogating organizational dimensions that undermine Blackness and direct educational violence onto Black faculty, especially Black women (Mustaffa, 2017). Colleges and universities "must shift from a discourse of preservation to one of transformation" (Fries-Britt et al., 2011, p.

29) to adequately address hostile climates that propagate racism and sexism, as well as homophobia and xenophobia. Recourse requires more than mere statements, it will require the embodiment of social justice ideas and change (Moreno et al., 2013; Moreno Report Implementation Committee, 2021). This requires action and correction to cease institutional participation in, and maintenance of, anti-Blackness and misogynoir. Action is investing in the recruitment and retention of Black faculty, including, but not limited to, facilitating opportunities for mentorship and professional development (Jones, Hwang, & Bustamante, 2015), providing resources and support for research (Griffin et al., 2013), limiting demands for entry-level faculty (Griffin, 2020; Kelly, Gayles, & Williams, 2017), and ensuring departmental and institutional cultures are conducive for faculty success.

BLACK LIFE MAKING IN THE ACADEMY

Occupying the space as outsiders within (Collins, 1986), Black faculty are uniquely positioned to advance and transform the academy. This is evident in the production of scholarship that shifts our discourse and challenges knowledge rooted in racism and white supremacy (Collins, 1986; Patton, 2016). Further, the personal biographies and cultural wealth of Black faculty are sources to resist the racist, heteronormative ethos of academia and cultivate their own spaces. Building off the scholarship of Black geographers and Black feminists, Jalil Bishop Mustaffa (2017) describes how "manifestations of anti-Black violence are disrupted due to practices of *Black life-making*," a term to describe "the creative spaces of possibility and freedom Black people produce when practicing self-definition, self-care, and resistance" (p. 712). We extend this discourse and consider how Black faculty might be empowered to practice Black life making inside and outside the university.

Across institutions, Black faculty are enacting Black life making and disrupting anti-Blackness. For example, HBCU presidents provide counternarratives to the anti-Black, deficit frames such as lacking intelligence, discipline, or morality compared to their non-Black counterparts that question the continued necessity of HBCUs. They describe HBCUs' contributions in advancing student success, innovation, and leadership. (Williams et al., 2019). In addition, Evette Allen and Nicole Joseph (2018) describe the Sistah Network, a communal space for Black women graduate students, faculty, and staff at an HWI. The collective centers on academic achievement, mentorship, and emotional support in which participants are empowered and affirmed: "Such an act is powerful because it disrupts oppression, isolation, and positions Black women in a positive light" (Allen & Joseph, 2018, p. 164).

#BlackFacultyMatter

Where the university may have only a few Black faculty, digital spaces and hashtag activism are venues for Black life making (Bailey, 2021; Jackson, 2016; Williams, 2015). Digital spaces serve as counterspaces and mediums for minoritized faculty to advocate, mobilize, collaborate, and accentuate their existence and contributions to the field. In particular, social media is a mechanism for Black academics to build community (Johnson et al., 2018) and challenge the exclusionary practices of citation politics (Hancock, 2016; Williams & Collier, 2022,). This work has been orchestrated particularly by Black women.

Founded by Drs. Joan Nicole Collier and Brittany Marie Williams in 2016, #CiteASista™ is a digital counterspace that "exists to uplift, center, and literally task people with properly crediting Black womxn. It exists to honor Black womxn's contributions upon which new concepts are formed, irrespective of spatial constraints (Williams & Collier, 2022, p. 100). Similarly, #CiteBlackWomen (2017) is a "movement dedicated to highlighting the expertise of Black women scholars (organically and academically trained) who are often undercut and undermined" (Smith et al., 2021, p. 12). Other digital counterspaces, including #BlackandHooded, #BlackWomenPhD, and #BlackMalePhDs, depict Black people with advanced degrees and are spaces to celebrate community and challenge the scarcity of "qualified" Black faculty myths of supply-side theory. This collective portrayal of the diversity within academe challenges the racist, heteronormative imagination of who is dominantly perceived as intellectuals—cis white men. Thus, digital spaces dispel the hegemonic conceptions of who "looks" and "acts" like a professor to showcase counternarratives of minoritized faculty, as well as other knowledge producers (Pritchard, 2015; Story, 2017).

Embedded in the ethos of public higher education are notions of colleges and universities as the great equalizers. However, the promise of higher education continues to be throttled by anti-Black racism and the failure to disrupt white supremacy. There are few guarantees Black people will reap the educational benefits. The insidious impact of anti-Blackness on US colleges and universities (Allen et al., 2020; Allen et al., 2018; Mustaffa, 2017) and the global higher education enterprise (Rollock, 2018) urgently demands transformative change. Restricting access to the professoriate denigrates the ideals of public education and hinders improving the quality of life for marginalized people and communities. The absence of Black faculty undermines the potential to create necessary institutional changes on our way to an equitable society. This is a risk we simply cannot afford.

References

Adams. v. Richardson, 356 F. Supp. 92, DDC (1973).
Adams v. Bell, 711 F.2d 161, DC Cir. (1983).
African American Policy Forum. (2021). Welcome to the #TruthBeTold campaign. Retrieved from https://www.aapf.org/truthbetold
Allen, B. C. M., & Esters, L. T. (2018). *Historically Black land-grant universities: Overcoming barriers and achieving success: CMSI Research Brief.* Retrieved from https://cmsi.gse.upenn.edu/content/historically-black-land-grant-universities-overcoming-barriers-and-achieving-success
Allen, E. L., & Joseph, N. M. (2018) The Sistah Network: Enhancing the educational and social experiences of Black women in the academy. *NASPA Journal about Women in Higher Education, 11*(2), 151–170.
Allen, W., Jones, C., & McLewis, C. (2019). The problematic nature of racial and ethnic categories in higher education. In L. L. Espinosa, J. M. Turk, M. Taylor, & H. M. Chessman (Eds.), *Race and ethnicity in higher education: A status report* (13–20). American Council on Education.
Allen, W. R., DeVost, A., and Mack, C. (2020). Hidden in Plain Sight: Historically Black colleges and universities in America. *la società contemporanea / The Color Line and the History of Sociology*, Paolo Parra Saiani (Ed.), Quaderni di sociologia, Nuova Serie, *64*(83), 25–46.
Allen, W. R., Epps, E. G., Guillory, E. A., Suh, S. A., Bonous-Hammarth, M. (2000). The Black academic: Faculty status among African Americans in U.S. higher education. *The Journal of Negro Education, 69*(1/2), 112–127.
Allen, W. R., Epps, E. G., Guillory, E. A., Suh, S. A., Bonous-Hammarth, M., Stassen, M. L. A. (2002). Outsiders within: Race, gender, and faculty status in US higher education. In W. A. Smith, P. G. Altbach, & K. Lomotey (Eds.), *The Racial Crisis in American Higher Education: Continuing Challenges for the 21st Century* (189–220). New York, NY: SUNY Press.
Allen, W. R., McLewis, C. C., Jones, C. M., & Harris, D. (2018). From Bakke to Fisher: African American students in US higher education over 40 years. *RSF: The Russell Sage Foundation Journal of the Social Sciences, 4*(6), 41–72.
American Association of University Professors. (n.d.). *Tenure*. Retrieved from https://www.aaup.org/issues/tenure
Ayers v. Fordice, 40 F. Supp. 2d 382 (1999).
Bailey, M. (2021). *Misogynoir transformed: Black women's digital resistance*. NYU Press.

Baldwin, A. N., & Johnson, R. (2018). Black women's co-mentoring relationships as resistance to marginalization at a PWI. In O. N. Perlow, D. I. Wheeler, S. L. Bethea, & B. M. Scott (Eds.), *Black women's liberatory pedagogies: Resistance, transformation, and healing within and beyond the academy* (pp. 125–140). Palgrave Macmillan.

Bell, D. A. (1993). Diversity and academic freedom. *J. Legal Educ*, *43*(3), 371–379.

Berrey, E. (2015). *The enigma of diversity: The language of race and the limits of racial justice.* University of Chicago Press.

Bilimoria, D., & Buch, K. K. (2010). The search is on: Engendering faculty diversity through more effective search and recruitment. *Change: The Magazine of Higher Learning, 42*(4), 27–32.

Bonner, F. A., II, Marbley, A. F., Tuitt, F., Robinson, P. A., Banda, R. M., & Hughes, R. L. (2015). *Black faculty in the academy: Narratives for negotiating identity and achieving career success.* Routledge.

Carpenter v. Board of Regents of the University of Wisconsin System, 728 F.2d 911, 7th Cir. (1984).

Carter Andrews, D. J. (2015). Navigating raced-gender microaggressions: The experiences of tenure-track Black female scholars. In F. A. Bonner II, A. F. Marbley, F. Tuitt, P. A. Robinson, R. M. Banda, & R. L. Hughes (Eds.), *Black faculty in the academy: Narratives for negotiating identity and achieving career success* (pp. 79–88). Routledge.

#CiteASista. (2016). *About us.* Retrieved from https://citeasista.com/about/

#CiteBlackWomen. (2017). *Our story.* Retrieved from ttps://www.citeblackwomen-collective.org/

Civil Rights Act of 1964 § 7, 42 USC. § 2000e et seq. (1964).

Cole, D., & Griffin, K. A. (2013). Advancing the study of student-faculty interaction: A focus on diverse students and faculty. In *Higher education: Handbook of theory and research* (561–611). Springer.

Collins, P. H. (1986). Learning from the outsider within: The sociological significance of Black feminist thought. *Social Problems, 33*(6), S14–S32.

Collins, P. H. (1998). *Fighting words: Black women and the search for justice.* University of Minneapolis Press.

Commodore, F., Gasman, M., Conrad, C., & Nguyen, T. H. (2018). Coming together: A case study of collaboration between student affairs and faculty at Norfolk State University. *Front. Educ., 3*, 39. doi: 10.3389/feduc.2018.00039

Corbin, N. A., Smith, W. A., & Garcia, J. R. (2018). Trapped between justified anger and being the strong Black woman: Black college women coping with racial battle fatigue at historically and predominantly white institutions, *International Journal of Qualitative Studies in Education, 31*(7), 626–643.

Crenshaw, K., Gotanda, N., Peller, G., & Thomas, K. (1995). Introduction. In K. Crenshaw, N. Gotanda, G. Peller, & K. Thomas (Eds.), *Critical race theory: The key writings that informed the movement* (xiii–xxxii). The New Press.

Croom, N. N. (2017). Promotion beyond tenure: Unpacking racism and sexism in the experiences of Black womyn professors. *The Review of Higher Education, 40*(4), 557–583.

Croom, N., & Patton, L. (2012). The miner's canary: A critical race perspective on the representation of Black women full professors. *Negro Educational Review, 62*(1), 13–39.

Dancy II, T. E., Edwards, K. T., & Earl Davis, J. (2018). Historically white universities and plantation politics: Anti-Blackness and higher education in the Black Lives Matter era. *Urban Education, 53*(2), 176–195.

Dei, G. J. S. (2017). Towards a [re] theorization of blackness, anti-blackness, and black solidarities. In George J. Sefa Dei (Ed.), *Reframing blackness and black solidarities through anti-colonial and decolonial prisms* (pp. 31–63). Springer.

Delgado, R., & Stefancic, J. (2017). *Critical race theory: An introduction* (3rd ed.). NYU Press.

Dumas, M. J., & ross, k. m. (2016). "Be real black for me" imagining BlackCrit in education. *Urban Education, 51*(4), 415–442.

Espinosa, L. L., Turk, J. M., Taylor, M., & Chessman, H. M. (2019). *Race and ethnicity in higher education: A status report.* American Council on Education.

Ethridge, G., Andrews, A., Thomas, A. A., & Boston, Q. (2018). Mentorship across faculty lines: Implications for lack of mentorship at historically Black colleges and universities. In C. S. Conway (Ed.), *Faculty mentorship at historically Black colleges and universities* (35–57). IGI Global.

Fisher v. University of Texas, 570 US (2013).

Fisher v. University of Texas, 579 US (2016).

Fries-Britt, S., & Kelly, B. T. (2005). Retaining each other: Narratives of two African American women in the academy. *The Urban Review, 37*(3), 221–242.

Fries-Britt, S. L., Rowan-Kenyon, H. T., Perna, L. W., Milem, J. F., & Howard, D. G. (2011). Underrepresentation in the academy and the institutional climate for faculty diversity. *Journal of the Professoriate, 5*(1), 1–34.

Gratz v. Bollinger, 539 US 244 (2003).

Gregory, S. T. (2001). Black faculty women in the academy: History, status and future. *The Journal of Negro Education, 70*(3), 124–138.

Griffin, K. A. (2019). Redoubling our efforts: How institutions can affect faculty diversity. In L. L. Espinosa, J. M. Turk, M. Taylor, & H. M. Chessman (Eds.), *Race and ethnicity in higher education: A status report* (pp. 273–280). Washington, DC: American Council on Education.

Griffin, K. A. (2020). Institutional barriers, strategies, and benefits to increasing the representation of women and men of color in the professoriate. In L. W. Perna (Ed.), *Higher education: Handbook of theory and research* (Vol. 35, pp. 1–73). Springer Nature.

Griffin, K. A., Bennett, J. C., & Harris, J. (2013). Marginalizing merit? Gender differences in Black faculty D/discourses on tenure, advancement, and professional success. *The Review of Higher Education, 36*(4), 489–512.

Griffin, K. A., Perez II, D., Holmes, A. P., & Mayo, C. E. (2010). Investing in the future: The importance of faculty mentoring in the development of students of color in STEM. *New Directions for Institutional Research, 2010*(148), 95–103.

Griffin, K. A., & Reddick, R. J. (2011). Surveillance and sacrifice: Gender differences in the mentoring patterns of Black professors at predominantly White research universities. *American Educational Research Journal, 48*(5), 1032–1057.

Grutter v. Bollinger, 539 US 306 (2003).

Guillaume, R. O., & Apodaca, E. C. (2022). Early career Faculty of Color and promotion and tenure: The intersection of advancement in the academy and cultural taxation. *Race Ethnicity and Education, 25*(4), 546–563.

Hancock, A. M. (2016). *Intersectionality: An intellectual history*. Oxford University Press.

Hannah-Jones, N., & NAACP Legal Defense and Educational Fund, Inc. (2021, May 27). Statements regarding Nikole Hannah-Jones. Retrieved from https://www.naacpldf.org/press-release/statements-regarding-nikole-hannah-jones/

Harper, S. R., & Simmons, I. (2019). *Black students at public colleges and universities: A 50-state report card*. University of Southern California, Race and Equity Center.

Harris, C. I. (1993). Whiteness as property. *Harvard Law Review, 106*(8), 1707–1791.

Harris, J. C., Barone, R. P., & Patton, L. D. (2015). Who benefits? A critical race analysis of the (d) evolving language of inclusion in higher education. *Thought & Action, 21,* 21–38.

Harris, J. C., & Patton, L. D. (2019). Un/doing intersectionality through higher education research. *The Journal of Higher Education, 90*(3), 347–372.

Haynes, C., Taylor, L., Mobley Jr., S. D., & Haywood, J. (2020). Existing and resisting: The pedagogical realities of Black, critical men and women faculty. *The Journal of Higher Education, 91*(5), 698–721.

Howard University Newsroom Staff. (2021, July 5). Two iconic American writers join Howard to create a center to help educate the next generation of Black journalists. Office of University Communications. Retrieved from https://newsroom.howard.edu/newsroom/article/14641/two-iconic-american-writers-join-howard-create-center-help-educate-next

Hurtado, S., Alvarez, C. L., Guillermo-Wann, C., Cuellar, M., & Arellano, L. (2012). A model for diverse learning environments. In J. C. Smart & M. B. Paulsen (Eds.), *Higher education: Handbook of theory and research* (41–122). Springer.

Jackson, S. J. (2016). (Re) imagining intersectional democracy from Black feminism to hashtag activism. *Women's Studies in Communication, 39*(4), 375–379.

Jayakumar, U. M., Howard, T. C., Allen, W. R., & Han, J. C. (2009). Racial Privilege in the professoriate: An exploration of campus climate, retention, and satisfaction. *The Journal of Higher Education, 80*(5), 538–563.

Johnson, J. M., Boss, G., Mwangi, C. G., & Garcia, G. A. (2018). Resisting, rejecting, and redefining normative pathways to the professoriate: Faculty of Color in higher education. *The Urban Review, 50*(4), 630–647.

Jones, B., Hwang, E., & Bustamante, R. M. (2015). African American female professors' strategies for successful attainment of tenure and promotion at predominately white institutions: It can happen. *Education, Citizenship and Social Justice, 10*(2), 133–151.

Kayes, P. E. (2006). New Paradigms for Diversifying Faculty and Staff in Higher Education: Uncovering Cultural Biases in the Search and Hiring Process. *Multicultural Education, 14*(2), 65–69.

Kelly, B. T., Gayles, J. G., & Williams, C. D. (2017). Recruitment without retention: A critical case of Black faculty unrest. *The Journal of Negro Education, 86*(3), 305–317.

Kelly, B. T., & Winkle-Wagner, R. (2017). Finding a voice in predominantly white institutions: A longitudinal study of Black women faculty members' journeys toward tenure. *Teachers College Record, 119*(June), 1–36.

Kelly, B. T., & Fries-Britt, S. (Eds.). (2022). *Building mentorship etworks to support Black women: A guide to succeeding in the Academy*. Routledge.

Kezar, A., & Bernstein-Sierra, S. (2016). Contingent faculty as nonideal workers. *New Directions for Higher Education, 2016*(176), 25–35.

Ladson-Billings, G., & Tate, W. F. (1995). Toward a critical race theory of education. *Teachers College Record, 97*(1), 47–68.

Lawrence III, C. R. (2015). Passing and trespassing in the academy: On whiteness as property and racial performance as political speech. *Harv. J. Racial & Ethnic Just., 31*(7), 7–30.

Liera, R. (2020). Moving beyond a culture of niceness in faculty hiring to advance racial equity. *American Educational Research Journal, 57*(5), 1954–1994.

Light, P. (1994). "Not like us": Removing the barriers to recruiting minority faculty. *Journal of Policy Analysis and Management, 13*, 164–180.

Matthew, P. A. (Ed.). (2016). *Written/unwritten: Diversity and the hidden truths of tenure*. UNC Press Books.

McLewis, C. C. (2021). The Limits of choice: A Black feminist critique of college "choice" theories and research. In L. W. Perna (Ed.), *Higher education: Handbook of theory and research, 36* (105–160). Springer.

Milem, J. F. (2003). The educational benefits of diversity: Evidence from multiple sectors. In M. J. Chang, D. Witt, J. Jones & K. Hakuta (Eds.), *Compelling interest: Examining the evidence on racial dynamics in colleges and universities* (pp. 126–169). Stanford University Press.

Mobley Jr., S. D. (2017). Seeking sanctuary: (Re) claiming the power of historically Black colleges and universities as places of Black refuge. *International Journal of Qualitative Studies in Education, 30*(10), 1036–1041.

Moreno, C., Jackson-Triche, M., Nash, G., Rice, C., & Suzuki, B. (2013). *Independent investigative report on acts of bias and discrimination involving faculty at the University of California, Los Angeles*. UCLA Office of the Chancellor.

Moreno Report Implementation Committee. (2021). *Final report: Moreno report implementation committee*. Retrieved from https://ucla.app.box.com/s/j286jtajiuh7egrayxz0dwdor7rrrl3g

Mustaffa, J. B. (2017). Mapping violence, naming life: A history of anti-Black oppression in the higher education system. *International Journal of Qualitative Studies in Education, 30*(8), 711–727.

Myers, Jr., S. L., & Turner, C. S. (2004). The effects of Ph.D. supply on minority faculty representation. *The American Economic Review, 94*(2), 296–301.

National Center for Education Statistics, Integrated Postsecondary Education Data System (IPEDS). (2018a). *2018–2019 survey materials: Glossary*. US Department of Education. Retrieved from https://surveys.nces.ed.gov/ipeds/Downloads/Forms/IPEDSGlossary.pdf

National Center for Education Statistics, Integrated Postsecondary Education Data System (IPEDS). (2018b). Full-time faculty in degree-granting postsecondary institutions, by race/ethnicity, sex, and academic rank: Fall 2015, fall 2016, and fall 2017. US Department of Education. Table 315.20. Spring 2016 through spring 2018 human resources component, fall staff section

National Center for Education Statistics, Integrated Postsecondary Education Data System (IPEDS). (n.d.-a). Definitions for new race and ethnicity categories. US Department of Education. Retrieved from https://nces.ed.gov/ipeds/report-your-data/race-ethnicity-collecting-data-for-reporting-purposes

National Center for Education Statistics, Integrated Postsecondary Education Data System (IPEDS). (n.d.-b). Collecting race and ethnicity data from students and staff using the new categories. US Department of Education. Retrieved from https://nces.ed.gov/ipeds/report-your-data/race-ethnicity-collecting-data-for-reporting-purposes

Ndemanu, M. T. (2017). Antecedents of college campus protests nationwide: Exploring Black student activists' demands. *Journal of Negro Education 86*(3), 238–251. Retrieved from https://doi.org/10.7709/jnegroeducation.86.3.0238

Parker, T. L. (2012). The role of minority-serving institutions in redefining and improving developmental education. *Southern Education Foundation*. Retrieved from https://files.eric.ed.gov/fulltext/ED529085.pdf

Parker, T. L., & Neville, K. M. (2019). The influence of racial identity on white students' perceptions of African American faculty. *The Review of Higher Education, 42*(3), 879–901.

Patton, L. D. (2016). Disrupting postsecondary prose: Toward a critical race theory of higher education. *Urban Education, 51*(3), 315–342.

Patton, L. D., & Harper, S. R. (2003). Mentoring relationships among African American women in graduate and professional schools. *New Directions for Student Services, 2003*(104), 67–78.

Pittman, C. T. (2010). Race and gender oppression in the classroom: The experiences of women Faculty of Color with white male students. *Teaching Sociology, 38*(3), 183–196.

Porter, C, J., Moore, C. M., Boss, G. J., Davis, T. J., & Louis, D. A. (2020). To be Black women and contingent faculty: Four scholarly personal narratives. *The Journal of Higher Education, 91*(5), 674–697.

Posselt, J., Hernandez, T. E., Villarreal, C. D., Rodgers, A. J., & Irwin, L. N. (2020). Evaluation and decision making in higher education: Toward equitable repertoires of faculty practice. *Higher Education: Handbook of Theory and Research, 35*, 1–63.

Price, G. N., & Sharpe, R. V. (2018). Is the economics knowledge production function constrained by race in the USA? *Journal of the Knowledge Economy, 11*(2), 1–16.

Priest, M. (2008). Salvation is the issue. *Meridians: feminism, race, transnationalism, 8*(2), 116–122.

Pritchard, S. B., Koh, A., & Moravec, M. (2015, August 10). We look like professors, too. *Inside Higher Ed.* https://www.insidehighered.com/views/2015/08/10/essay-explains-new-hashtag-campaign-draw-attention-diversity-professors-and-their.

Porter, C. J., Moore, C. M., Boss, G. J., Davis, T. J., & Louis, D. A. (2020). To be Black women and contingent faculty: Four scholarly personal narratives. *The Journal of Higher Education, 91*(5), 674–697.

Regents of the University of California v. Bakke, 438 US 265 (1978).

Ricks, S. A. (2012). Lifting as we climb: A Black woman's reflections on teaching and learning at one southern HBCU. *Journal of Curriculum Theorizing, 28*(3), 10–21.

Rivera, L. A. (2017). When two bodies are (not) a problem: Gender and relationship status discrimination in academic hiring. *American Sociological Review, 82*(6), 1111–1138.

Rogers, I. H. (2012). *The Black campus movement: Black students and the racial reconstitution of higher education, 1965–1972*. Palgrave MacMillan.

Rollock N. (2018). The heart of whiteness: Racial gesture politics, equity and higher education. In J. Arday & H. S. Mirza (Eds.), *Dismantling Race in Higher Education*. Palgrave Macmillan.

Scott v. University of Delaware, 455 F. Supp. 1102, D. Del. (1978).

Settles, I. H., Jones, M. K., Buchanan, N. T., & Dotson, K. (2021). Epistemic exclusion: Scholar(ly) devaluation that marginalizes faculty of color. *Journal of Diversity in Higher Education, 14*(4), 493.

Sinclair-Chapman, V. (2019). Rebounding on the tenure track: Carving out a place of your own in the academy. *PS: Political Science & Politics, 52*(1), 52–56.

Smith, C. A., Williams, E. L., Wadud, I. A., Pirtle, W. N., & Cite Black Women Collective. (2021). Cite black women: A critical praxis (a statement). *Feminist anthropology, 2*(1), 10–17.

Smith, W. A. (2004). Black faculty coping with racial battle fatigue: The campus racial climate in a post-civil rights era. In D. Cleveland (Ed.), *A long way to go: Conversations about race by African American faculty and graduate students* (pp. 171–190). Peter Lang.

Snyder, T. D., de Brey, C., & Dillow, S. A. (2019). *Digest of education statistics 2017* (53rd ed.). US Department of Education, National Center for Education Statistics.

Stanley, C. A. (2006). Coloring the academic landscape: Faculty of Color breaking the silence in predominantly White colleges and universities. *American Educational Research Journal, 43*(4), 701–736.

Stokes, S., & Miller, D. (2019). Remembering "The Black Bruins": A case study of supporting student activists at UCLA. In D. L. Morgan & C. H. F. Davis III (Eds.), *Student Activism, Politics, and Campus Climate in Higher Education* (pp. 143–163). Routledge.

Story, K. A. (2017). Fear of a Black femme: The existential conundrum of embodying a Black femme identity while being a professor of Black, queer, and feminist studies. *Journal of lesbian studies, 21*(4), 407–419.

Tuitt, F. A., Sagaria, M. A. D., & Turner, C. S. V. (2007). Signals and strategies in hiring faculty of color. In J. C. Smart (Ed.), *Higher education: Handbook of theory and research* (pp. 497–535). Springer.

Turner, C. S. V. (2002). Women of Color in academe: Living with multiple marginality. *The Journal of Higher Education, 73*(1), 74–93.

Turner, C. S. V., González, J. C., & Wood, J. L. (2008). Faculty of Color in academe: What 20 years of literature tells us. *Journal of Diversity in Higher Education, 1*(3), 139–168.

Turner, C. S. V., Gonzalez, J. C., & Wong (Lau), K. (2011). Faculty Women of Color: The critical nexus of race and gender. *Journal of Diversity in Higher Education, 4*(4), 199–211.

Turner, C. S. V., & Myers, S. L. (2000). The nature and extent of minority faculty representation. *Faculty of Color in Academe: Bittersweet Success.* Allyn & Bacon.

Umbach, P. D. (2006). The contribution of Faculty of Color to undergraduate education. *Research in Higher Education, 47*(3), 317–345.

US Census Bureau, Population Division. Annual Estimates of the Resident Population by Sex, Race, and Hispanic Origin for the United States: April 1, 2010 to July 1, 2019 (NC-EST2019-SR11H). Retrieved from https://www2.census.gov/programs-surveys/popest/tables/2010-2019/national/asrh/nc-est2019-sr11h.xlsx

United States v. Fordice, 505 US 717 (1992).

Ware, L. (2000). People of Color in the academy: Patterns of discrimination in faculty hiring and retention. *Boston College Third World Law Journal, 20*(1), 55–76.

White-Lewis, D., O'Meara, K. Culpepper, D., Templeton, L., & Anderson, J. (2021). *One foot out the door: Interrogating the "risky hire" narrative in STEM faculty careers*. Paper presented at the virtual annual meeting of the American Educational Research Association.

White-Lewis, D. K. (2020). The façade of fit in faculty search processes. *The Journal of Higher Education, 91*(6), 833–857.

Wilder, J., Osborne-Lampkin, L. T., & Jackson, E. N. (2015). Rearticulating Black Faculty Diversity Efforts in the Age of "Postracialism" and Obama. *Western Journal of Black Studies, 39*(3), 174–185.

Williams, B. M., & Collier, J. N. (2022). Citations are currency: How #CiteASista leverages online platforms to center Black womxn. In B. Turner-Kelly & S. Fries Britt (Eds.), *Building mentorship networks to support Black women: A guide to succeeding in the academics* (pp. 100–116). Routledge.

Williams, K. L., Burt, B. A., Clay, K. L., & Bridges, B. K. (2019). Stories untold: Counter-narratives to anti-Blackness and deficit-oriented discourse concerning HBCUs. *American Educational Research Journal, 56*(2), 556–599.

Williams, S. (2015). Digital defense: Black feminists resist violence with hashtag activism. *Feminist Media Studies, 15*(2), 341–344.

Womble, C. C. (2018). Faculty salary (in) equity: A Review of the Literature. *Trends in Diversity, 1*(1), 1–29.

Wood, J. L., Hilton, A. A., & Nevarez, C. (2015). Faculty of Color and white faculty an analysis of service. *Journal of the Professoriate, 8*(1), 85–109.

Young, J. L., & Hines, D. E. (2018). Killing my spirit, renewing my soul: Black female professors' critical reflections on spirit killings while teaching. *Women, Gender, and Families of Color, 6*(1), 18–25.

Zahneis, M. (2021, July 16). When tenure denials go public. *The Chronicle of Higher Education*. Retrieved from https://www.chronicle.com/article/when-tenure-denials-go-public

Chapter 8

African American Faculty and Administrators in Higher Education

From Recruitment to Retention

NA LOR AND JERLANDO F. L. JACKSON

With unprecedented demographic changes in the United States, colleges and universities are enrolling an increasingly diverse student body. Today an estimated 45% of undergraduate and graduate students are non-White, compared to only 34% in 1996 (US Census, 2018). As the number of students of color entering college is expected to rise, there is a similar need to address faculty and staff diversity (Jackson & Flowers, 2003; Phillips, 2002). It has been argued that employing a diverse workforce is paramount if colleges and universities are to remain relevant to a student body that is more racially and ethnically diverse than ever before (Assenoh, 2003; Brown, 2004). Yet, in contrast to the student population, the racial composition of the higher education workforce remains disproportionately White.

African Americans are especially noted as underrepresented in the higher education workforce. According to the US Census (2018), African Americans make up 13% of the overall US population, constituting 40.1 million people. As of 2016, African Americans represent 11% of the student body, 6% of academic faculty, and 13% of student affairs administrators (Kena et al., 2016). These numbers set forth substantial progress since the 1980s, when African

American faculty and staff at predominantly White institutions (PWIs) were "so rare that they could be individually identified" (Wolfe & Dilworth, 2015, p. 668). Over the years, the increasing visibility of African Americans in the higher education workforce can be attributed, in part, to legislative initiatives such as Executive Order 11246 that prohibit employment discrimination (Lewis, 2016), a climbing number of African Americans attaining advanced degrees (McFarland et al., 2018), faculty cluster hires that bolster affirmative action (Kelly, Gayles, & Williams, 2009), and growing commitment to institutional diversity (Cabrera et al., 1999; Holmes et al., 2000).

As more African Americans are entering the higher education workforce each year, research evinces the beneficial impacts on student outcomes. For instance, African American administrators are said to play an important role in "warming up a chilly climate" on campus (Wolfe & Dilworth, 2015). The visibility of African American faculty on college campuses has been linked to enrollment among African American students (Allen et al., 2000; Darden, Kamel, & Jacobs, 1998; Kulis, Chong, & Shaw, 1999). An increase in the representation of African American faculty and staff is further shown to boost the academic success of African American undergraduate students (Cole & Barber, 2003; Umbach, 2006). Overall, a more racially and ethnically diverse faculty and staff is believed to foster intercultural competence among all students, particularly at PWIs (Madyun et al., 2013).

Despite these advancements, extant studies reveal that African Americans recurringly face racial bias and systemic barriers. African American faculty describe their experiences as alienating and lacking in support and mentorship (Allen et al., 2002). African American administrators often find themselves in hostile working environments that limit opportunities for advancement toward leadership positions (Wolfe & Dilworth, 2015). Incidents of hidden or sometimes explicit racism and discrimination (Griffin, Bennett, & Harris, 2011; Turner, Myers, & Cresswell, 1999) leave faculty and staff with feelings of oppression (Jackson & O'Callaghan, 2009; Wolfe & Dilworth, 2015) and isolation, which in turn influences attrition (Harper & Hurtado, 2007; Pittman, 2012; Turner, Gonzalez, & Wood, 2008). For these reasons, higher education diversity initiatives to attract African Americans to their institutions have been referred to as a "bait and switch" approach (Kelly, Gayles, & Williams, 2017). That is, colleges and universities are successively recruiting African American faculty and staff, but concerns are mounting over whether pathways toward retention are sufficient.

This chapter examines the state of the African American workforce in higher education using national data. The purpose of this chapter is to examine changes in African American employment in higher education institutions across (a) geographical regions, (b) institution type and sector, and (c) position, rank, age, gender, and degree credentials over time. Specifically, we seek to answer: what progress has been made in the recruitment and retention of African American faculty and administrators in the higher education workforce?

We begin with a descriptive analysis of the most recent Integrated Postsecondary Education Data System (IPEDS) 2017 faculty level data (Ginder, Kelly-Reid, & Mann, 2018) and the National Association of Student Personnel Administrators (NASPA) Salary Tool 2014 administrative level data. We compare these data with prior data sets using the National Study of Postsecondary Faculty (NSPOF) 1999 and NASPA Salary Tool 1999 to better understand changes over time. We focus on both faculty and administrators to provide a holistic perspective on African American leaders in higher education. To guide our descriptive analysis of the data we employ social closure theory. We discuss the findings in relation to extant literature on the topic of African American faculty and administrators. We conclude with implications and recommendations for policy and practice.

The Data

The IPEDS 2017 data on full-time instructional staff provides information on faculty at degree-granting institutions of all levels and sectors. The IPEDS data include all institutions that participate in the Federal Student Aid program, along with any institution not eligible for Federal Student Aid who requests participation in IPEDS, including for-profit and non-degree-granting institutions. Data on full-time instructional staff are collected each fall and released a few months later. In IPEDS 2017, faculty (N = 720,331) refer to individuals who hold joint appointments. Therefore, faculty includes anyone whose original appointment involved conducting research, teaching, and/or public service. Faculty represents professors at all academic ranks, instructors/lecturers, and any administrator who previously or concurrently holds a research, teaching, and/or service position. Faculty can also include chancellors/presidents, provosts, vice provosts, deans, directors, associate deans, assistant deans, and department chairs.

The NASPA Salary Tool includes information on vice presidents for student affairs (VPSAs) and/or chief student affairs officers from 850 institutions. Data are collected through a survey by the NASPA Research and Policy Institute. Individuals who hold a VPSA position by the Higher Education Directory are eligible for participation. Survey participants

(N = 868) constitute over 39 student affairs areas, such as academic advising, admissions, international student services, and orientation. Throughout this chapter, we refer to VPSAs as administrators broadly.

The NASPA Salary Tool uses IPEDS institutional characteristics data to match respondents to institutions using IPEDS IDs and the Higher Education Directory. The survey captures higher education administrators from all levels and sectors: 28% located at public institutions; 43% private, not-for-profit institutions; 2% private for-profit institutions, 27% two-year institutions, and less than 1% private, not-for-profit, two-year institutions.

To better understand the shifting patterns among African American faculty and administration over the last nearly two decades, we further draw a comparison between IPEDS 2017 and the NSPOF 1999 as well as NASPA Salary Tool 2014 and NASPA Salary Tool 1999. The NSPOF 1999 (N = 17,600 respondents) uses a nested sample of the same 960 IPEDS institutions and faculty. What follows is a description of the theoretical framework we use to better understand the data in the changing landscape of African Americans in the higher education workforce.

Theoretical Framework

Social closure theory posits that collective groups of people aim to limit opportunities and restrict resources to select individuals with whom they share certain social traits or physical attributes, closing off access to all others (Parkin, 1979). In other words, groups seek to maintain a set of exclusionary practices in order to preserve a position of privilege, what is also referred to as exclusionary closure (Parkin, 1979). In the context of the American higher education system, colleges and universities were historically built to serve White, middle-class men. Participation in the higher education workforce among women and racial/ethnic minorities, in turn, is thought to be a form of what is called usurpationary closure, when groups excluded from the system seek to gain a greater share of resources by pushing back against exclusionary practices (Parkin, 1979).

As faculty and administrators of color are increasingly entering the higher education workforce, they are also gaining access to a space that, putatively, enables them to contest dominant White male ideologies, methodologies, and leadership styles that perpetuate inequality and systemic oppression. Thus, inclusion of racial and ethnic minorities in the higher education landscape is, putatively, a threat to the system and resources historically controlled by White men. Subsequently, African Americans are let into the academy, but their participation is limited to the roles and services White male higher education leaders see fit. We take the position that the recurring challenges African American leaders face in the academy can be attributed to social closure (Parkin, 1979). This theoretical perspective guides our data analysis and interpretation of the findings.

Geography of African Americans in Higher Education

Given the exclusion of African Americans in the higher education system prior to the 1970s, historically Black colleges and universities (HBCUs) were the primary institution that served African American students, faculty, and administrators (Anderson, 2002; Jackson & Daniels, 2007; Wolfe & Dilworth, 2015). In 1999, approximately 43% of African American faculty were employed in the Southeast region (e.g., Alabama, Arkansas, Florida, Georgia, Kentucky, Louisiana, Mississippi, North Carolina, South Carolina, Tennessee, Virginia, and West Virginia), where HBCUs are most prevalent. As of 2017, African American faculty in the Southeast is down a striking 25 percentage points as African American faculty are now more dispersed across the United States (see table 8.1).

Table 8.1. Percentage Distribution of Regions among Faculty by Race and Year, 1999 and 2017

	All races/ ethnicities 1999	All races/ ethnicities 2017	African American 1999	African American 2017
UW Service School	—	.9	—	.5
New England	5	8	6	5
Mideast	13	16	16	27
Great Lakes	17	19	14	11
Plains	9.3	11	2	4
Southeast	26	9	43	18
Southwest	10	11	6	14
Rocky Mountains	6	11	1	15
Far West	14	11	12	5
Outlying area	—	3	—	2

Source: US Department of Education, National Center for Education Statistics; National Study of Postsecondary Faculty, 1999 (NSPOF:99); Integrated Postsecondary Higher Education Data System (IPEDS). Author created.

Geographical Mobility among Faculty

Today, a majority of African American faculty can be found in the Mideast (e.g., Delaware, District of Colombia, Maryland, New Jersey, New York, and Pennsylvania), where we observe an 11 percentage point increase in the share of African American faculty since 1999. This area, which is home to some of the original colonial colleges and the first HBCUs, is now where one out of every four African American faculty are employed.

The US region with the lowest share of African American faculty is the Plains (4%). The Plains (e.g., North Dakota, South Dakota, Nebraska, Kansas, and Oklahoma) are recognized as having areas with high concentrations of rural areas, low population density, and fewer higher education opportunities. Therefore, the low representation of African American faculty may be attributed to an overall low number of faculty due to "education deserts," or geographical locations where there are very few colleges (Hillman, 2019). Nonetheless, the share of African American faculty in the Plains increased from 2% in 1999 to 4% in 2017, suggesting that colleges and universities in this area are effectively attracting and recruiting African American faculty.

In contrast, in areas such as New England (e.g., Maine, Vermont, New Hampshire, Massachusetts, Connecticut, and Rhode Island), we observe a decrease in faculty that are African American and, simultaneously, a slight increase in all faculty. Although New England is rural, it is also recognized as having many urban centers. Moreover, there is a long history of higher education and a sizeable concentration of colleges and universities in these states, including half of the eight Ivy League institutions. This makes the education desert explanation for the decrease in African American faculty in this location less plausible.

The same pattern of a rise in all faculty but a fall in African American faculty is also observed in the Great Lakes (e.g., Wisconsin, Michigan, Illinois, Indiana, and Ohio), another area with a plethora of colleges and universities. We find the regions of both New England and Great Lakes have a considerable share of states that are relatively more White than other parts of the United States (see figure 8.1). Although the percentage point changes in these two regions are small, with a difference of only one to three percentage points, the rise in all full-time faculty but a decline in African American faculty is noteworthy, nonetheless.

What Contributes to African American Faculty Mobility?

Increases in the share of African Americans across the different US regions can be attributed, in part, to successful recruitment of African Americans into

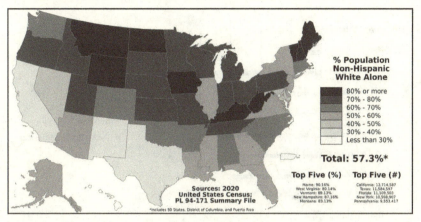

Figure 8.1. Percentage of non-Hispanic White population by state. *Note:* US Census 2020 data. From Wikimedia Commons 2021.

the faculty workforce by colleges and universities. For example, the region with the most significant percentage change increase in African American faculty is the Rocky Mountains (e.g., Colorado, Idaho, Montana, Utah, and Wyoming), whose share of African American faculty was 1% in 1999 but grew 15 percentage points in 2017. In contrast to all full-time faculty (11%) in this area, African American faculty (15%) are overrepresented. Regions like the Rocky Mountains where there were previously very few African Americans demonstrate that attracting and/or recruiting African Americans into the faculty workforce is attainable.

Yet we observe a decrease in the share of African American faculty in New England, the Great Lakes, and the Far West, which indicates that faculty are leaving their academic positions due to attrition/relocation or, alternately, they are concluding their tenure via retirement. Since a majority of African American faculty are in the lower ranks of their tenure (see figure 8.2), the latter explanation is less likely, which points to poor attrition as a key contributor to geographic mobility.

Extant studies demonstrate a relationship between PWIs and low retention among African American faculty (Kelly, Gayles, & Williams, 2017). A study on faculty job satisfaction finds that 23% of African American faculty reported satisfaction with their jobs compared to 37% of White faculty (Allen et al., 2002). A negative racial climate is linked to lower job satisfaction among African American faculty, but this relationship is not found among other race/ethnic groups (Jayakumar et al., 2009). The

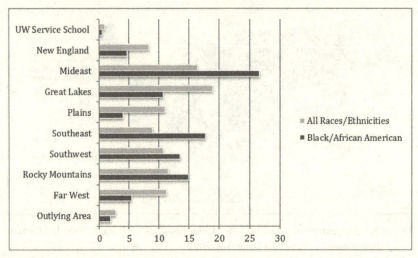

Figure 8.2. Percentage distribution of faculty by race, 2017. Author created.

same institutions where African American faculty perceive a negative racial climate and lower job satisfaction also happen to be the institutions with high retention rates among White faculty (Jayakumar et al., 2009), all of which influences attrition. Thus, as the number of African American faculty at PWIs is rising (Modica & Mamaseishvili, 2010), equal attention toward both recruitment and retention is pertinent.

Colleges and universities are known to sometimes add an additional faculty line reserved for hiring a faculty of color to diversify, but it has been noted that this approach may be more beneficial to the institution than to the faculty of color (Kelly, Gayles, & Williams, 2017). As social closure theory posits, African American faculty are let into the academy, but they encounter structural issues and racial discrimination that impede their ability to fully participate. This "bait and switch" recruitment approach is not sustainable and further leads to concerns over a recruitment process that portrays African Americans as an "institutional commodity" (Kelly, Gayles, & Williams, 2017).

Geographical Mobility among Administrators

Unlike the geographic shift of African American faculty toward the northeastern regions of the United States over the years, we observe little change

African American Faculty and Administrators in Higher Education | 217

in mobility among African American administrators. Most African American administrators (38%) are employed in NASPA Region III (e.g., Alabama, Florida, Kentucky, Louisiana, Mississippi, North Carolina, Tennessee, Texas, and Virginia), where we observe a six percentage point increase from 32% in 1999 to 38% in 2014 (see table 8.2).

Only two other increases in the share of African American administrators are observed during this time period. In Region VI (e.g., California and Arizona), we observe a five percentage point increase from 8% in 1999 to 13% in 2014, where the share of African American administrators (13%) in this area nearly doubles that of all full-time faculty (7%). Likewise, we observe a 1 percentage point increase in Region V (e.g., Alaska, Washington, Oregon, Idaho, Montana, Nevada, and Utah), from 3% in 1999 to 4% in 2014. No other increases in the share of African American administrators are observed.

We find that African American administrators are underrepresented in all other NASPA regions, apart from Regions III and VI. Interestingly, the most significant decreases in the share of African American administrators are observed in Region I (e.g., Maine, Vermont, New Hampshire, Massachusetts, Connecticut, and Rhode Island); Region IV-E (e.g., Illinois, Indiana, Iowa, Minnesota, Ohio, and Wisconsin); and Region IV-W (e.g., North Dakota, South Dakota, Nebraska, Kansas, Missouri, Arkansas, Oklahoma, New Mexico, Colorado, and Wyoming). Notably, NASPA Regions I and IV-E have considerable overlap with regions of New England and the

Table 8.2. Percentage Distribution of Region among Administrators by Race and Year, 1999–2014

	All races/ ethnicities 1999	All races/ ethnicities 2014	African American 1999	African American 2014
Region I	9	8	6	3
Region II	16	19	16	15
Region III	25	25	32	38
Region IV-E	22	22	21	17
Region IV-W	16	12	14	11
Region V	7	6	3	4
Region VI	6	7	8	13

Source: NASPA Salary Tool, 1999, 2014. Author created.

Great Lakes, where we observed a decline in African American faculty but an increase in all faculty. Taken together, we find similar patterns in the geographic mobility of both African American faculty and administrators in the higher education workforce. This finding further provides evidence for social closure in the American higher education system: colleges and universities restrict access and limit resources to reinforce a closed system that maintains a privileged position among a group of gatekeepers.

What Contributes to African American Administrator Lack of Mobility?

Increases in the share of African American administrators across the NASPA regions are most apparent where there are higher concentrations of African Americans in the population, including the Southeast (Region III), the Southwest (Region VI), and the Mideast (Region II). For example, the states with the largest African American populations include the District of Colombia, Mississippi, Louisiana, Georgia, and Maryland (US Census, 2018), and are in these same NASPA regions. This suggests that colleges and universities may not be effectively attracting and recruiting African American administrators to areas outside of these regions and/or they are unable to retain African American administrators at PWIs once recruited.

As other scholars have noted, the transition into the workforce at PWIs is especially tumultuous among African American administrators (Gardner, Barrett, & Pearson, 2014; Kelly, Gayles, & Williams, 2017; Wolfe & Dilworth, 2015). Upon entering the academy, ongoing workplace challenges are reported (Kulis, Chong, & Shaw, 1999). Incidents of implicit or sometimes explicit racism and discrimination (Griffen, Bennett, & Harris, 2011; Turner, Myers, & Cresswell, 1999) leave staff with feelings of oppression (Jackson & O'Callaghan, 2009; Wolfe & Dilworth, 2015), exclusion, and isolation (Harper & Hurtado, 2007; Pittman, 2012; Turner, Gonzalez, & Wood, 2008). African American administrators often find themselves in hostile working environments that limit opportunities for advancement toward leadership positions (Wolfe & Dilworth, 2015). Subsequently, racial and ethnic bias are believed to influence attrition (Turner, Meyer, & Cresswell, 1999). As the literature suggests, nominal changes in the geographical location of African American administrators can be attributed to poor retention in predominantly White spaces, states, and institutions, and/or a lack of opportunity for African American leaders in these areas altogether.

Nominal changes in geographical location of African American administrators might also be attributed to satisfaction with one's current location/institution as well as a desire to work toward the goal of "community uplift": the idea that educated African Americans should aim to give back to the African American community and the colleges themselves should not be separated from the community (Du Bois, 1968; Wendling, 2018). In which case, a stable concentration of African American administrators in Regions II, III, and VI over the years would be explained by a commitment among African American administrators to serve African American students, institutions of higher education, and surrounding communities. Although it's important to note, African American administrators can self-select into the regions where they work; but ultimately, colleges and universities control who they attract and employ at their institution.

Overall, African American administrators are overrepresented in Regions III and VI, but representation is low in all other NASPA regions of the United States (see figure 8.3), which indicates that there is much more work to be done in diversifying the higher education workforce and including African Americans in that process. To better understand African American patterns of employment, what follows next is exploration of how African American faculty and administrators fare across institution type, sector, and size.

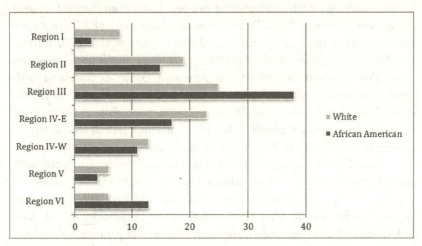

Figure 8.3. Regional distribution of administrators by race, 2014. Author created.

Patterns of Employment across Institutional Characteristics

There are approximately 2,902 two-year institutions, 1,932 four-year institutions, and 1,808 less-than-two-year institutions in the United States (including for-profit and non-degree-granting institutions). An estimated 101 are HBCUs; 50% of these are public institutions, and the other 50% are private nonprofit institutions. Each university varies significantly in type, size, sector, and admissions policies, as well as in their ability to recruit and retain African Americans. In this section, we examine patterns of African American employment across institutional characteristics.

Growing Faculty Participation in the Private Sector and Two-Year Institutions

Although a majority of African American faculty are employed at four-year institutions, we find the share of African American faculty at two-year institutions increased eight percentage points from 1999 to 2017. This percentage change is small, but an increase in the share of faculty at two-year institutions among all faculty is not observed, which makes the relationship between African American faculty and two-year institutions especially noteworthy.

This finding suggests that African Americans, in comparison to their counterparts, may be more inclined to work at two-year institutions (including for-profit institutions and non-degree-granting institutions). African American faculty report higher job satisfaction at two-year institutions than at four-year institutions (Flowers, 2005). Furthermore, a similar share of African American students at two-year institutions (24%) (Hussar et al., 2020) mirrors the African American faculty distribution at these institutions. Research shows that representation of African American faculty is correlated with enrollment among African American students (Darden, Kamel, & Jacobs, 1998; Kulis, Chong, & Shaw, 1999). Likewise, poor representation of an African American student body is thought to mirror a lack of representation among African American faculty (Allen et al., 2000).

According to Carnegie classifications, which is often associated with prestige, more than one in three African American faculty (38%) is employed at a doctorate-granting university (see tables 8.3 and 8.4). While this is an impressive achievement, when compared to all full-time faculty (51%), African American faculty are underrepresented at doctorate-granting universities. Prior research has raised concerns over the participation of African American faculty at more prestigious institutions (Jackson & Daniels, 2007), and

Table 8.3. Percentage Distribution of Institutional Control and Institutional Type among Faculty by Race and Year, 1999 and 2017

	All races/ethnicities 1999	All races/ethnicities 2017	African American 1999	African American 2017
Public	66	50	61	37
Private	34	44	39	55
Four-year	86	84	81	73
Two-year	14	16	19	27

Source: US Department of Education, National Center for Education Statistics; National Study of Postsecondary Faculty (NSPOF), 1999; Integrated Postsecondary Higher Education Data System (IPEDS), 20. Author created.

Table 8.4. Percentage Distribution of Carnegie Classification among Faculty by Race and Year, Fall 2017

	All races/ethnicities	African American
Doctorate-granting university	51	38
Master's colleges	10	25
Baccalaureate colleges	5	11
Associates colleges	10	14
Special focus institution	23	12
Tribal college	.8	.1

Source: National Center for Educational Statistics; Integrated Postsecondary Higher Education Data System (IPEDS). Author created.

this concern is still relevant today. Although African American faculty are overrepresented at master's colleges, baccalaureates colleges, and associates colleges, representation of African American faculty at doctorate-granting universities remains low.

At the lowest end of what is considered a prestigious college or university are, perhaps, for-profit institutions. At for-profit institutions, an estimated one in 10 faculty (Taylor et al., 2020) and one in three students (Hussar et al, 2020) is expected to be African American. Although for-profit institutions are key sites of education for African American students and of employment for African American faculty (Hussar et al., 2020), due to the disproportionate enrollment of African Americans at for-profit institutions and the many accusations of these institutions as substantial contributors to unequal college debt among African American students, for-profit institutions are considered a growing problem by many higher education constituents.

Growing Administrator Participation at Research Institutions and Two-Year Institutions

According to Carnegie classification, we find the largest share of African American administrators (35%) at associates colleges, or what is comparable to two-year institutions (see tables 8.5 and 8.6). African American administrators are overrepresented when compared to all full-time faculty at these institutions. At master's colleges and baccalaureate colleges, African American administrators are underrepresented. However, at the Carnegie classification of doctoral-granting university, African American administrators are once again overrepresented. More than one in every five African

Table 8.5. Percentage Distribution of Institution Sector among Administrators, 2014

	All races	White	African American
Public, four-year	27	26	40
Private, four-year	42	46	25
Public, two-year	28	26	33
No response	3	3	2

Source: NASPA Salary Tool, 2014. Author created.

Table 8.6. Percentage Distribution of Institution Type among Administrators, 2014

	All races	White	African American
Doctoral-granting university	14	13	23
Master's colleges	26	26	22
Baccalaureate colleges	23	25	17
Associates colleges	30	29	35
No response	8	8	4

Source: NASPA Salary Tool, 2014. Author created.

American administrators works at a doctorate-granting university, which is almost twice than that of the share of White administrators.

Taken together, these findings suggest two predominant pathways among African American faculty and administrators. The first is employment at a community college (e.g., associates college), and the second is employment at a research institution (e.g., doctorate-granting university). Considering that African Americans report higher retention rates, higher levels of job satisfaction, and a better racial climate at more prestigious and/or selective research institutions (Jayakumar et al., 2009), the fact that most African American faculty are employed at private institutions (55%) and most African American administrators are employed at public four-year institutions (40%) is not surprising. However, unlike their counterparts, a considerable share of African American faculty and administrators are also employed at two-year institutions.

We speculate what may be driving African Americans in the higher education workforce toward two very different institution types could be the African American student population. Like African American faculty (55%), a larger share of African American students (57%) are enrolled at private institutions than public institutions (Hussar et al., 2020). Likewise, as previously noted, the share of African American student enrollment at two-year institutions (24%) reflects that of African American faculty employment at two-year institutions (27%) (Hussar et al., 2020). Relatedly, student enrollment at HBCUs is surging (Edwards, 2019; "Enrollment Surges," 2018), creating a demand for faculty and administrators in regions where HBCUs are more widespread. Accordingly, the trends in parallel enrollment among students and employment among faculty and administrators circle back to the idea of community uplift that African Americans utilize their education and skillsets to uplift African American students and communities.

Changing Representation of Higher Education Leaders in the Academy

In 1999 African Americans made up 4% of the full-time faculty workforce and 8% of all higher education administrators. Today, African Americans constitute 6% of the full-time faculty and 13% of administrators. In this section we highlight some of the accomplishments and setbacks of African Americans in the higher education workforce.

African American Faculty

African American females are said to face a double barrier in the academy, but in recent years, the number of African American female faculty entering the higher education workforce is rising. As of 2017, at the ranks of assistant professor, roughly 7,162 are African American females and only 4,345 are African American males. At the rank of associate professor, the African American faculty gender distribution is slightly in favor of females, with an estimated 4,857 African American females and 4,300 African American males. At the level of full professor, however, the tables turn in favor of males: an estimated 4,127 are African American males compared to only 2,809 African American females (see table 8.7).

Across the academic ranks of full professor, associate professor, assistant professor, and instructor/lecturer, we see that African American males are equally distributed across academic tenure ranks (see table 8.8). This is not the case among African American females, where we observe a larger share of faculty in the middle of their tenure and a smaller share at the lowest ranks and highest ranks, respectively. This bell curve–like effect might be explained by the later age of retirement expected among male faculty as compared to female faculty (Yakoboski, 2015). That is, if African American females retire sooner than their African American male counterparts, they might appear to be in the earlier or middle stage of their career.

By count alone, African American female faculty outnumber African American male faculty (Jackson & Daniels, 2007). Also, at the lower academic ranks, African American female faculty consistently outnumber

Table 8.7. Total African American Men and Women by Academic Rank, 2017

	Full professor	Associate professor	Assistant professor	Instructor/ lecturer	Other rank/ NA
African American men	4,127	4,300	4,345	3,424	3,236
African American women	2,809	4,857	7,162	5,618	5,583

Source: National Center for Educational Statistics; Integrated Postsecondary Higher Education Data System (IPEDS), 2017. Author created.

Table 8.8. Percentage Distribution of Academic Rank by Race and Gender, 2017

	Full professor	Associate professor	Assistant professor	Instructor/ lecturer	Other rank/ NA
All races/ethnicities men	28	20	20	15	19
All races/ethnicities women	16	19	24	21	20
African American men	21	22	22	18	17
African American women	11	19	28	22	21

Source: National Center for Educational Statistics; Integrated Postsecondary Higher Education Data System (IPEDS), 2017. Author created.

African American male faculty. African American female faculty also tend to earn lower salaries, earn tenure at a slower promotion rate, and report the lowest levels of overall job satisfaction (Allen et al., 2002; Jayakumar, et al., 2009). Thus, a rise in female faculty is a remarkable milestone. Although it is important to note African American male faculty as a group are consistently underrepresented (see table 8.9), making up only 22% of all African American assistant professors in 2017. Hence, the possibility of a creeping deficit in African American males entering the faculty tenure track pipeline should not be overlooked either. Efforts to ensure that the higher education workforce does not induce a reverse problem of poor representation among African American male faculty is pertinent (see table 8.10).

Table 8.9. Percentage Distribution of Gender by Race and Year, 1999 and 2017

	All races/ ethnicities 1999	All races/ ethnicities 2017	African American 1999	African American 2017
Male	63	54	47	43
Female	37	46	53	57

Source: National Center for Educational Statistics; Integrated Postsecondary Higher Education Data System (IPEDS), 2017; National Study of Postsecondary Faculty (NSPOF), 1999. Author created.

Table 8.10. Percentage Distribution of Academic Rank by Race and Year, 1999 and 2017

	All races/ ethnicities 1999	All races/ ethnicities 2017	African American 1999	African American 2017
Full professor	37	22	19	15
Associate professor	20	19	27	20
Assistant professor	8	22	16	25
Instructor/lecturer	13	17	14	20
Other ranks/NA	22	19	24	19

Source: National Center for Educational Statistics; National Study of Postsecondary Faculty (NSPOF), 1999; Integrated Postsecondary Higher Education Data System (IPEDS), 2017. Author created.

African American Administrators

In 1999 African Americans made up only 8% of all higher education administrators compared to 13% of higher education administrators today. It has been pointed out that having lower degree credentials than competitors in the pool of applicants can be a setback for African Americans in the job market (Allen et al., 2002; Jackson & Daniels, 2007; Turner & Myers, 2000). In recent years, 40% of African American administrators hold a PhD degree and another 28% of African American administrators hold an EdD degree (see table 8.11), which makes African Americans highly competitive candidates in the higher education administration job market.

Table 8.11. Percentage Distribution of Highest Educational Credential Attained among Administrators by Race and Year, 1999 and 2014

	All races/ ethnicities 1999	All races/ ethnicities 2014	African American 1999	African American 2014
Male	50	49	45	52
Female	49	47	55	47
Doctorate degree	27	32	31	40
Master's/professional degree	54	38	63	31
Bachelor's degree or less	20	—	15	—
EdD	—	22	—	28

Source: NASPA Salary Tool, 1999, 2014. Author created.

Table 8.12. Salaries of Student Affairs Administrators by Race, 2014

	White	Black
25th percentile	$95,750	$97,397
Median	$120,000	$139,500
Average	$126,395	$150,056
75th percentile	$150,000	$190,000

Source: NASPA Salary Tool, 2014. Author created.

Table 8.13. Age of Students Affairs Administrators by Race, 2014

	White 2014	African American 2014
Under 40	7	8
40–49	26	38
50–59	40	31
60–65	20	8
Older than 66	4	8
No response	2	8

Source: NASPA Salary Tool, 2014. Author created.

Table 8.14. Years in Student Affairs Administrative Position by Race, 2014

	White	African American
New in 2013	3	4
1–2 years	22	29
3–5 years	26	31
6–9 years	21	18
10–14 years	16	6
15–19 years	6	10
More than 20 years	6	3

Source: NASPA Salary Tool, 2014. Author created.

Commensurate with qualifications, African American administrators, on average, receive a higher salary than White administrators (see table 8.12). The median salary for African American administrators is $140,000 in contrast to only $120,000 for White administrators. At the 75th percentile of the salary distribution, African Americans earn an average of $190,000, which is

$40,000 more than White administrators. Taken together, African Americans are younger (see table 8.13), with fewer years of experience in their current roles (see table 8.14), but on average, African American administrators are more qualified and earn higher salaries, which reflect their qualifications.

Notably, interest in the study of education at the doctoral level among African Americans is growing. In 2018 alone a striking 40% of PhD degrees conferred to all African Americans was in an education related field (e.g., education administration, educational leadership, and higher education evaluation and research) (National Center for Science and Engineering Statistics, 2020). Thus, we expect to see more African American faculty and administrator participation in coming years, which further evinces the idea that giving back to community is especially important among African American leaders.

Recurring Challenges from Recruitment to Retention

Despite the achievements of African American faculty and administrators, as an aggregate group African Americans remain underrepresented in the higher education workforce. Faculty representation is adequate in the higher education landscape at large, but at prestigious institutions in particular, African Americans are no more visible today than they were nearly two decades ago. Administrators are, on average, better educated and better paid, but they are unequally dispersed across the United States, with respect to region and institution characteristics.

It has been pointed out that a lack of diversity might be due to a shortage of eligible job candidates (Allen et al., 2002), but roughly 35,274 PhD degrees were conferred to US citizen and permanent resident graduate students in 2019 (National Center for Science Engineering Statistics, 2020). An estimated 7% of these PhD recipients were African American. Although the respective share of African American doctorate recipients is small, it amounts to an average of 2,273 PhD degrees that are conferred to African Americans each year (National Center for Science and Engineering Statistics, 2020). Thus, African American doctorate recipients are certainly out there and available to fill open faculty and administrative positions.

While some attribute the lack of African American representation to a K–16 pipeline problem, others argue that the issue is rooted in a racially hostile and oppressive work environment (Allen et al., 2002; Jayakumar et al., 2009). Similarly, we argue that social closure in the American higher education system contributes to the deficiency of African American participation in the higher education workforce that is manifested in a recruitment and retention problem.

As social closure theory posits, African Americans are let into the academy, but to what extent they can participate in the higher education system is controlled by a dominant group, White males. Upon arriving at the institution, African American leaders often take on extraneous roles and responsibilities related to diversity and inclusion, which, in turn, can take away from the primary roles and responsibilities they were originally recruited to do (Griffin, 2012; Jackson & Daniels, 2007). These extraneous demands are referred to as cultural taxation (Joseph & Hirshfield, 2011) and are further believed to affect African American females and males differently (Griffin, Bennett, & Harris, 2011; Jackson & O'Callaghan, 2009).

Furthermore, poor socialization into the academy (Kosoko-Lasaki, Sonnino, & Voytko, 2006) and lack of a mentors are believed to be among the greatest concerns African Americans experience in the academy (Jackson & O'Callaghan, 2009; Patton, 2009; Tillman, 2001). Conflicts such as invalidation of research study topic (Pittman, 2012), stressful interactions with students in the classroom (Pittman, 2012), biased student evaluations (Smith & Hawkins, 2011), and issues regarding compensation (Ryan, Healy, R., & Sullivan, 2012; Walker, Reason, & Robinson, 2003) all add up to racial battle fatigue among faculty of color (Arnold, Crawford, & Khalifa, 2016). For these reasons, among others, participation in the higher education workforce can be viewed as discouraging by many African Americans (Jackson, 1991), which, in turn, leads to low retention, particularly at PWIs.

To some extent, African Americans certainly self-select into the regions, institutions, roles, and/or positions they desire, but ultimately, in the role of the "gatekeeper," White higher education leaders have power over who they choose to include or exclude in hiring decisions and, with that, the potential to monopolize opportunities. Likewise, African Americans in the higher education workforce have the autonomy to leave a job they are unsatisfied with, but White higher education leaders are in a position of privilege that can perpetuate exclusionary boundaries or create inclusive practices that improve racial climate and foster a more equitable work environment.

Conclusion

In this chapter we have reviewed patterns of African American participation in the higher education workforce, and we argued that the path from recruitment to retention for African Americans is met with systemic challenges and racial bias that is made more visible through the lens of social closure theory. Notwithstanding, we also document the progress of African American leaders in the higher education workforce. We found that African American faculty and administrators are more dispersed across parts of the United States where there was once nominal African American representation prior. Among faculty, there are more African American female faculty entering the ranks of assistant and associate professor than ever before. Among administrators, African Americans are employed at more prestigious universities, hold higher degree credentials, and receive a higher salary than their counterparts.

While HBCUs were once thought to be the primary opportunity for African American faculty and staff (Jackson & Daniels, 2007; Wilson, 1989), this is changing. Seasoned professors are completing their tenure, and senior student affairs administrators are stepping down. Opportunities are increasing for a potentially more diverse faculty body and administrative staff to enter the academy. As this chapter demonstrates, African Americans are ascending leaders in the changing higher education landscape.

Recommendations

Based on our descriptive analysis of African Americans in the higher education workforce, coupled with supporting literature, we propose the following recommendations to disrupt processes of social closure and, in turn, improve the recruitment and retention of African Americans.

- Diversify the student body in aiming to diversify faculty and staff. African American representation in the faculty and administrative workforce is associated with African American representation in the student body. A rise in one is often correlated with an increase in the other, whereas scarcity of one often results in a shortage of the other. If colleges and universities aim to recruit African American faculty and administrators, then, correspondingly, recruitment and enrollment of African American students is pertinent.
- Address the African American faculty gender gap. The recurring underrepresentation of African American males in faculty positions suggests that African American men are at a disadvantage in the academic job market. There is a need to address the

gender imbalance by recruiting and retaining African American males in the faculty. This calls for disaggregating African American males and females in hiring decisions and providing each with the necessary support to facilitate excellence in their assigned tasks and roles.

- Enact rather than espouse diversity. Espousing diversity and enacting diversity are different objectives. The former is exemplified by recruiting African Americans into leadership positions as a diversity commodity (Kelly, Gayles, & Williams, 2017). The latter amounts to developing purposeful strategies and actionable steps toward successful retention of African American faculty and administrators. Espousing diversity rather than enacting diversity calls for equal emphasis on both recruitment and retention.

- Redistribute the onus of "representing" diversity to all faculty and administration. University administrators often hold African American leaders and their non–African American colleagues to different standards. The same administrations expect African Americans to represent and to foster institutional diversity, without sufficient resources or support for attending to problems of racism and discrimination on campus. Colleges and universities can aim to cultivate a shared responsibility toward embodying diversity, equity, and inclusion among all faculty and staff. This, in turn, redistributes the weight placed upon the shoulders of African American leaders, enabling them to attend to tangential priorities.

- Socialize African American leaders toward full participation. Systematic practices of exclusion prevent African Americans from fully participating in the higher education system. African American leaders perpetually feel marginalized, excluded, and invalidated. Thus, the socialization of African American leaders through formal and informal orientation, training, support, professional development, mentorship, and networking opportunities that facilitate full participation in university life is pertinent.

- Situate community at the core. As community uplift is integral to the pursuit of higher education among African American leaders, holding this expectation for all faculty and staff also serves as one way to integrate African American culture into the academy. Schools and departments can implement policies and practices that reward faculty for community-engaged partnerships, community-engaged scholarship, academic advising, and student and/or faculty mentorship. Embedding these values and practices into the system is a way to reward African American leaders for student-centered activities and diversity-focused services that often demand their time. Rewarding these values and practices further invites all academic leaders to connect research to surrounding communities and to prioritize mentorship that aims to uplift others.

References

Allen, W. R., Epps, E. G., Guillory, E. A., Suh, S. A., and Bonous-Hammarth, M. (2000). The Black academic: Faculty status among African Americans in US higher education. *Journal of Negro Education, 69*(1–2), 112–127.

Allen, W. E., Epps, E. G., Guillory, E. A., Suh, S. A., Bonous-Hammarth, M., & Stassen, M. (2002). Outsiders within: Race, gender, and faculty status in US higher education. In W. A. Smith, P. G. Altbach, & K. Lomotey (Eds.), *The racial crisis in American higher education* (pp. 189–220). State University of New York Press.

Anderson, J. D. (2002). Race in American higher education: Historical perspectives on current conditions. In W. A. Smith, P. G. Altbach, & K. Lomotey (Eds.), *The racial crisis in American higher education* (pp. 3–21). State University of New York Press.

Arnold, N. W., Crawford, E. R., & Khalifa, M. (2016). Psychological heuristics and faculty of color: Racial battle fatigue and tenure/promotion. *Journal of Higher Education, 87*(6), 890–919. https://doi.org/10.1353/jhe.2016.0033

Assenoh, A. N. (2003). Trouble in the promised land: African American studies program and the challenges of incorporation. *Journal of Black Studies, 34*(1), 52–62.

Brown, L. I. (2004). Diversity: The challenge for higher education. *Race Ethnicity and Education, 7*(1), 21–34.

Cabrera, A. F., Nora, A., Terenzini, P. T., Pascarella, E. T., & Hagedorn, L. S. (1999). Campus racial climate and adjustment of students to college. *The Journal of College Student Development, 35,* 98–102.

Cole, S., & Barber, E. (2003). *Increasing faculty diversity: The occupational choices of high-achieving minority students.* Harvard University Press.

Crenshaw, K. Mapping the margins: Intersectionality, identity politics, and violence against women of color. *Stanford Law Review, 43*(6), 1241–1299.

Domingue, A. D. (2015). "Our leaders are just we ourself": Black women college student leaders' experiences with oppression and sources of nourishment on a predominantly White college campus. *Equity and Excellence in Education, 48*, 454–472.

Du Bois, W. E. B. (1968). *The souls of Black folk: Essays and sketches*. A. G. McClurg (Ed.). Johnson Reprint.

Edwards, B. (2019, March 18). *HBCU enrollment on the rise amid increasing racial tensions*. Retrieved from https://www.essence.com/news/hbcu-enrollment-on-the-rise-amid-increasing-tensions/

Enrollment surges at a number of historically black colleges and universities. (2018, September 30). *The Journal of Blacks in Higher Education*. https://www.jbhe.com/2018/09/enrollment-surges-at-a-number-of-historically-black-colleges-and-universities/

Epps, E. G. (1989). Academic culture and the minority professor. *Academe, 75*(5), 23–26.

Flaherty, C. (2015). Demanding 10 percent. *Inside Higher Ed*. Retrieved from https://www.insidehighered.com/news/2015/11/30/student-activists-want-more-black-faculty-members-how-realistic-are-some-their-goals

Flowers, L. A. (2005). Job satisfaction differentials among African American faculty at 20-year and 4-year institutions, *Community College Journal of Research and Practice, 29*(4), 317–328.

Fountaine, T. P. (2012). The impact of faculty-student interaction on Black doctoral students attending historically Black institutions. *The Journal of Negro Education, 81*, 136–147.

Gardner, L., Barrett, T. G., & Pearson, L. C. (2014). African American administrators at PWIs: Enablers of and barriers to career success. *National Association of Diversity Officers in Higher Education, 7*(4), 235–251.

Gasman, M., Kim, J., & Nguyen, T. H. (2011). Effectively recruiting faculty of color at highly selective institutions: A school of education case study. *Journal of Diversity in Higher Education, 4*, 212–222.

Ginder, S.A., Kelly-Reid, J.E., & Mann, F.B. (2018). Enrollment and employees in postsecondary institutions, fall 2017; and Financial statistics and academic libraries, fiscal year 2017: First look (Provisional Data) (NCES 2019-021rev). US Department of Education. National Center for Education Statistics. Retrieved from http://nces.ed.gov/pubsearch

Griffin, K. A. (2012). Black professors managing mentorship: Implications of applying social exchange frameworks to analyses of student interactions and their influence on scholarly productivity. *Teachers College Record, 114*(5), 1–37.

Griffin, K. A., Bennett, J. C., & Harris, J. (2011). Analyzing gender differences in Black faculty marginalization through a sequential mixed-methods design. *New Directions for Institutional Research, 2011*(151), 45–61.

Guillory, R. M. (2001). Strategies for overcoming the barriers of being an African American administrator on a predominantly White university campus. In

L. Jones (Ed.), *Retaining African Americans in higher education: Challenging paradigms for retaining students, faculty, and administrators* (pp. 111–123). Stylus Publishing.

Haizlip, B. N. (2012). Addressing the underrepresentation of African Americans in counseling and psychology programs. *College Student Journal, 46*(1), 214–222.

Harper, S. R., & Hurtado, S. (2007). Nine themes in campus racial climates and implications for institutional transformation. *New Directions for Student Services, 120,* 7–24.

Hillman, N. (2019, May 21). Place matters: A closer look at education deserts. Retrieved from https://www.thirdway.org/report/place-matters-a-closer-look-at-education-deserts

Holmes, S. L., Ebbers, L. H., Robinson, D. C., & Mugenda, A. G. (2000). Validating African American students at predominantly White institutions. *Journal of College Student Retention: Research, Theory, & Practice, 2,* 41–58.

Huggins-Hoyt, K. Y. (2018). African American faculty in social work schools: A citation analysis of scholarship. *Research on Social Work Practice, 28*(3), 300–308.

Hussar, B., Zhang, J., Hein, S., Wang, K., Roberts, A., Cui, J., Smith, M., Bullock Mann, F., Barmer, A., & Dilig, R. (2020). *The Condition of Education 2020* (NCES 2020-144). US Department of Education. National Center for Education Statistics. Retrieved from https://nces.ed.gov/pubsearch/pubsinfo.asp?pubid=2020144

Jackson, J. F. L. (2001). A new test for diversity: Retaining African American administrators at predominantly White institutions. In L. Jones (Ed.), *Retaining African Americans in higher education: Challenging paradigms for retaining Black students, faculty, and administrators* (pp. 93–109). Stylus.

Jackson, J. F. L. (2002). Retention of African American administrators at predominantly White institutions: Using professional growth factors to inform the discussion. *College and University, 78*(2), 11–16.

Jackson, J. F. L. (2003). Engaging, retaining, and advancing African Americans in student affairs administration: An analysis of employment status. *NASAP Journal, 6*(1), 9–24.

Jackson, J. F. L. (2004). Engaging, retaining, and advancing African Americans to executive-level position: A descriptive and trend analysis of academic administrators in higher and postsecondary education. *Journal of Negro Education, 73*(1), 4–20.

Jackson, J. F. L., & Daniels, B. D. (2007). A National Progress Report of African Americans in the administrative workforce in higher education. In J. Jackson (Ed.), *Strengthening the African American educational pipeline: Informing research, policy, and practice.* University of New York Press.

Jackson, J. F. L., & Flowers, L. A. (2003). Retaining African American student affairs administrators: Voices from the field. *College Student Affairs Journal, 22*(2), 125–136.

Jackson, J. F. L., & Leon, R. (2010). Enlarging our understanding of glass ceiling effects with social closure theory in higher education. In J. E. Smart (Ed.) *Higher Education: Handbook of Theory and Research* (pp. 351–379). Springer.

Jackson, J. F. L., & O'Callaghan, E. M. (2009). Ethnic and racial administrative diversity—understanding work life realities and experiences in higher education. *ASHE Higher Education Report, 35*(3), 1–95.

Jackson, J. F. L., Parish, W. P. P., & Contreras, C. (2018). Applying an engagement, retention, and advancement model for administrators of color in higher education. In J. F. L. Jackson, L. J. Charleston, & C. Gilbert (Eds.), *Advancing Equity and Diversity in Student Affairs*. Information Publishing.

Jayakumar, U. M., Howard, T. C., Allen, W. R., & Han, J. C. (2009). Racial privilege in the professoriate: An exploration of campus climate, retention, and satisfaction. *The Journal of Higher Education, 80*(5), 539–563.

Joseph, T. D., & Hirshfield, L. E. (2011). "Why don't you get somebody new to do it?" Race and cultural taxation in the academy. *Ethnic and racial studies, 34*(1), 121–141.

Kelly, B. T., Gayles, J. G., & Williams, C. D. (2017). Recruitment without retention: A critical case of Black faculty unrest. *Journal of Negro Education, 86*(3), 305–317.

Kena, G., Hussar W., McFarland J., de Brey C., Musu-Gillette, L., Wang, X., Zhang, J., Rathbun, A., Wilkinson-Flicker, S., Diliberti M., Barmer, A., Bullock Mann, F., & Dunlop Velez, E. (2016). *The condition of education 2016* (NCES 2016-144). US Department of Education, National Center for Education Statistics. Retrieved from http://nces.ed.gov/pubsearch

Kosoko-Lasaki, O., Sonnino, R. E., & Voytko, M. L. (2006). Mentoring for women and underrepresented minority faculty and students: Experience at two institutions of higher education. *Journal of the National Medical Association, 98*(9), 1449.

Kulis, S., Chong, Y., & Shaw, H. (1999). Discriminatory organizational context and Black scientists on postsecondary faculties. *Research in Higher Education, 40*(2), 115–147.

Lewis, C. (2016). Gender, race, and career advancement: When do we have enough cultural capital? *The Negro Educational Review, 67*(1–4), 106–132.

Libresco, L. (2015). *Here are the demands from students protesting racism at 51 colleges*. FiveThirtyEight. Retrieved from https://fivethirtyeight.com/features/here-are-the-demands-from-students-protesting-racism-at-51-colleges/

Madyun, N., Williams, S. M. McGee, E. O., & Milner, H. R., IV. (2013). On the importance of African American faculty in higher education: Implications and recommendations. *Educational Foundations, 27*(3–4), 65–84.

McFarland, J., Hussar, B., Wang, X., Zhang, J., Wang, K., Rathbun, A., Barmer, A., Forrest Cataldi, E., & Bullock Mann, F. (2018). *The condition of education 2018* (NCES 2018-144). US Department of Education. National Center for

Education Statistics. Retrieved from https://nces.ed.gov/pubsearch/pubsinfo.asp?pubid=2018144

Modica, J. L., & Mamiseishvili, K. (2010). Black faculty at research universities: Has significant progress occurred? *Negro Educational Review, 61*(1–4), 107–122.

National Association of Student Personnel Administrators (NASPA). (1999). NASPA salary tool [Data file]. Retrieved from https://census.naspa.org/salary-intro

National Association of Student Personnel Administrators (NASPA). (2014). NASPA salary tool [Data file]. Retrieved from https://census.naspa.org/salary-intro

National Center for Science and Engineering Statistics. (2020). *Doctorate recipients from US universities: 2019*. Special Report NSF: 21-308. National Science Foundation. Retrieved from https://ncses.nsf.gov/pubs/nsf21308/data-tables

Parkin, F. (1979). *Marxism and class theory: A bourgeois critique*. Columbia University Press.

Patton, L. (2009). My sister's keeper: A qualitative examination of mentoring experiences among African American women in graduate and professional schools. *The Journal of Higher Education, 80*, 510–537.

Payton, F. C., & Yarger, L. (2018). (Text)mining microaggressions literature: Implications impacting black computing faculty. *Journal of Negro Education, 87*(3), 217–229.

Perna, L. W., Gerald, D., Baum, E., & Milem, J. (2007). The status of equity for Black faculty and administrators in public higher education in the South. *Research in Higher Education, 48*(2), 193–228.

Phillips, R. (2002). Recruiting and retaining a diverse faculty. *Planning for higher education, 30*(4), 32–39.

Pittman, C. T. (2012). Racial microaggressions: The narratives of African American faculty at a predominantly White university. *Journal of Negro Education, 81*, 82–92.

Ross, H. H., & Edwards, W. J. (2016). African American faculty expressing concerns: Breaking the silence at predominantly White research-oriented universities. *Race, Ethnicity, and Education, 19*(3), 461–479.

Ryan, J. F., Healy, R., & Sullivan, J. (2012). Oh, won't you stay? Predictors of faculty intent to leave a public research university. *Higher Education, 63*, 421–437.

Siegel, D. J., Barrett, T. G., & Smith, T. H. (2015). To stay or to go: A comparison of factors influential in the decisions of African American faculty to remain at two elite Southern research universities. *Journal of Negro Education, 84*(4), 593–607.

Smith, D. G. (1991). The challenge of diversity: Alienation in the academy and its implications for faculty. *Journal on Excellence in College Teaching, 2*, 129–137.

Smith, B. P., & Hawkins, B. (2011). Examining student evaluations of Black college faculty: Does race matter? *The Journal of Negro Education*, 149–162.

Strauss, V. (2015). It's 2015. Where are all the Black college faculty? "Answer Sheet." *The Washington Post.* Retrieved from https://www.washingtonpost.com/news/answer-sheet/wp/2015/11/12/its-2015-where-are-all-the-black-college-faculty/

Taylor, M. Turk, J. M., Chessman, H. M., & Espinosa, L. L. (2020). Race and ethnicity in higher education: 2020 supplement. *American Council on Education.*

Tillman, L. C. (2001). Mentoring African American faculty in predominantly White institutions. *Research in Higher Education, 42*(3), 295–325.

Turner, C. (2003). Incorporation and marginalization in the academy: From border toward center for faculty of color? *Journal of Black Studies, 34*(1), 112–125.

Turner, C. S. V., Gonzalez, J. C., & Wood, J. L. (2008). Faculty of color in academe: What twenty years of literature tells us. *Journal of Diversity in Higher Education, 1*(3), 139–168.

Turner, C. S. V., & Myers, S. L., Jr. (2000). Faculty of color in academe: Bittersweet success. Allyn & Bacon.

Turner, C. S. V., Myers, S. L., & Cresswell, J. W. (1999). Exploring underrepresentation: The case of faculty of color in the Midwest. *Journal of Higher Education, 70*(1): 27–59.

Umbach, P. (2006). The contribution of faculty of color to undergraduate education. *Research in Higher Education, 47,* 317–345.

US Census Bureau. (2018). QuickFacts, United States. Retrieved from http://census.gov/quickfacts/fact/table/UW/PST045218

US Census Bureau. (2000). Newsroom Archive. Retrieved from https://www.census.gov/newsroom/releases/archives/census_2000/cb01cn176.html

US Census Bureau (2021). 2020 census state redistricting data (Public Law 94-171) summary file.

US Department of Education. National Center for Education Statistics. (2002). 1999 National Study of Postsecondary Faculty (NSOPF:99) Methodology Report, NCES 2002-154, by Sameer Y. Abraham, Darby Miller Steiger, Margrethe Montgomery, Brian D. Kuhr, Roger Tourangeau, Bob Montgomery, and Manas Chattopadhyay. Project Officer Linda J. Zimbler.

Villalpando, O., & Delgado Bernal, D. (2002). A critical race theory analysis of barriers that impede the success of faculty of color. In W. A. Smith, P. G. Altbach, & K. Lomotey (Eds.), *The racial crisis in American higher education* (pp. 243–270). State University of New York Press.

Walker, D. A., Reason, R. D., & Robinson, D. C. (2003). Salary predictors and equity issues for student affairs administrators at public and private institutions: From dean to director of security. *Journal of Student Affairs Research and Practice, 40*(2), 320–338.

Wendling, L. A. (2018). Higher education as a means of communal uplift: The educational philosophy of W. E. B. Du Bois. *The Journal of Negro Education, 87*(3), 285–293.

Wolfe, B. L., Dilworth, P. P. (2015). Transitioning normalcy: Organizational culture, African American administrators, and diversity leadership in higher education. *Review of Educational Research, 85*(4), 667–697.

Yakoboski, P. J. (2015). Understanding the faculty retirement (non)decision: Results from the faculty career and retirement survey. *Trends and Issues, TIAA Institute (June 2015)*, 1–11.

Chapter 9

Asian American Faculty Discrimination
Why Does It Matter?

ROBERT T. TERANISHI, ROSE ANN RICO EBORDA GUTIERREZ,
AND ANNIE LE

In 2012, the University of California, Los Angeles (UCLA) established a commission to study racial bias and discrimination against faculty members. Widely known as the Moreno Report (Moreno, 2013), the impetus for this study was a group of concerned faculty members who approached the executive vice chancellor about incidents of racial bias and/or discrimination in the university. The "Moreno Report," as it was called, was presented to Executive Vice Chancellor and Provost Scott Waugh. It was authored by Hon. Carlos Moreno (Ret.). The outcome was an external review team charged with investigating perceived racial bias and discrimination through interviews with staff and faculty and an examination of current policies and procedures in place to handle these incidents. Indeed, they found that faculty and staff were experiencing instances of racial tension and hostility in the workplace, and that the university could set in place better organizational structures and mechanisms to address these issues.

Though the findings from this report may be intuitive given the challenges associated with the historical vestiges of discrimination and bias in higher education, the substance of this report deserves closer consideration and attention. Namely, how is it that Asian American faculty, who made up half of the complaints in the Moreno Report, become peripheral to issues surrounding campus racial climate? Specifically, while the report demonstrates that faculty of color matter, it raises questions about the discrimination Asian American faculty experience in academia that rarely gets addressed, even when incidents are blatant. For example, the report highlighted an instance in "Department A" of overt racial and gender discrimination when a faculty recounted that another faculty member had mentioned, "I thought Asian women were supposed to be submissive" (Moreno, 2013, 13).

As further context for this chapter, while quantitative data show Asian American faculty being numerically well represented in academia (Espinosa et al., 2019; Turner, Myers, & Creswell, 1999), interviews reveal that structural diversity or numerical representation do not indicate that an institution has reached goals of diversity, inclusion, and equity (Cho, 1996; Huang, 2013; Hurtado et al., 1998; Jayakumar et al., 2009; Turner, Myers, & Creswell, 1999; Yeung, 2013). In addition, Kimberly Griffin (2019) notes that "while Asian American faculty experience marginalization in the academy and are not equally represented across all ethnic subgroups or in all disciplines, they are not usually considered underrepresented in the professoriate" (p. 273). Thus, diversifying the faculty does not suffice when a historically marginalized community such as Asian Americans continue to experience discrimination and systemic racism in the professoriate (Nakanishi, 1993).

This chapter examines the discrimination that faculty of color experience through the lens of Asian Americans and sheds light on the role and function of faculty of color in higher education. We focus on Asian American faculty because their numerical representation in studies have created a false perception that they have reached parity with White faculty, which conceals and exacerbates their negative experiences. This chapter is divided into three sections. The first addresses why faculty of color matter, not just representationally but because of the value, assets, and skills they bring to an institution. The second attends to the significance of the campus climate being a consistent factor in retaining faculty of color. The third dives into a discussion about the unique needs, challenges, and contributions of Asian American faculty. Finally, implications are discussed to ground us in understanding why Asian American faculty deserve attention within the overall faculty of color community to ensure their inclusion in future research, practice, and policy.

Faculty of Color Matter

The role of higher education as a public good has been written about extensively. Research has shown that access to higher education leads to more social mobility and contributes to a greater workforce and more robust economy (Abel & Deitz, 2014; Harrison, 2017; Kurtzleben, 2014). This outcome is evident in the increase in college participation rates. According to the National Center for Education Statistics (McFarland et al. (2018), every racial group, except for American Indian/Alaska Native young adults, experienced an increase in college enrollment from 2000 to 2017. In addition, a report by the Pew Research Center (Fry & Cilluffo, 2020) found that the percentage of students of color in colleges grew from 29% to 47% between 1996 and 2016 (for public and private nonprofit colleges as well as for-profit colleges).

Given the changing racial demography of students attending colleges, universities have made public commitments to diversity and racial inclusion, and one of those strategies include hiring more faculty of color. Faculty members shape the curriculum, produce intellectual thought, and ultimately play a pivotal role in students' academic and social experiences on campus. For example, Sharon Lee (2002) wrote, "Faculty are key to the quality of higher education. They determine course content and standards of performance and educate the next generation of workers and leaders. Faculty also conduct research that advances knowledge in all fields. Research on whether and how the nation's faculty are changing because of larger demographic trends and how nontraditional—in this case, racial minority—faculty are treated can inform policy makers about the responsiveness of higher education to larger social and demographic changes" (p. 696). Diversifying faculty has been the center of debates, discussions, and priorities of higher education institutions. While historically, the professoriate has been predominantly White men, recent statistics show that the demographics are beginning to shift toward a better reflection of the growing diversity among college students (Heilig et al., 2019; Osei, 2019). Even then, a host of literature rightfully criticizes the overall low number of faculty of color, especially when it comes to higher rank academic positions (Bustillos & Siqueiros, 2018; Espinosa et al., 2019).

Hiring practices aside, a racially diverse faculty also matters beyond numerical representation. Research has shown that having faculty members who mirror the student demographic is essential because students can feel more comfortable seeing themselves represented in classes taught by professors who share similar backgrounds and identities (Antonio, 2002). This emotional connection can foster more mentoring relationships between faculty and students and promote advocacy by faculty of color for students of color (Abdul-Raheem, 2016; Allen, 2013). Studies have also shown that having a diverse faculty exposes students to a wide range of intellectual thought and perspectives and curricula (Hurtado, 2001; Neville & Parker, 2017; Vargas, Villa-Palomino, & Davis, 2019). Indeed, US Supreme Court Justice Sandra Day O'Connor supported this notion regarding affirmative action when she said, "The skills needed in today's increasingly global marketplace can only be developed through exposure to widely diverse people, cultures, ideas, and viewpoints" (*Grutter v. Bollinger*, 2003).

Campus Climate Matters

Historically, higher education institutions in the United States have predominantly enrolled White students and employed White faculty, staff, and administrators (McCoy, 2014) because of the ways these institutions were designed to function and serve elite White men (Thelin, 2019). As the student demography in colleges and universities continues to change and grow to be more racially and ethnically diverse (National Center for Education Statistics, 2017), higher education institutions have responded by giving attention to diversifying the professoriate to reflect the students that they serve (Gasman, Kim, & Nguyen, 2011; Sgoutas-Emch et al., 2016). Yet we know from research that increasing an institution's compositional or numerical racial and ethnic diversity does not equate to racial inclusion (Wingfield, 2016). Recruiting and hiring faculty of color is an important initial step to redressing systemic racism on college campuses. However, more intentional efforts need to be made by higher education institutions to retain faculty of color and ultimately achieve a campus climate with inclusion and racial equity in mind (Davis, 2002; Hurtado et al., 1998).

The literature on campus climate has primarily focused on students, but an emerging body of literature has set their attention to examining campus climate for faculty (Fries-Britt et al., 2011; Hall & Sandler, 1982; Mayhew et al., 2006; Turner, Myers, & Creswell, 1999, 2008). In the last decade, scholars have consistently documented negative experiences and a "chilly climate" (Turner, Myers, & Creswell, 1999) from faculty of color working at historically White institutions (Garvey & Rankin, 2018; Jayakumar et al., 2009; Poloma, 2014; Victorino, Nylund-Gibson, & Conley, 2013). Understanding what contributes to a chilly climate, or in other words, a hostile racial campus climate, for faculty of color is critical because having a supportive work environment is one of the single most important factors in determining faculty success in academia (Spann, 1990). Characteristics of a chilly climate include being held to higher standards than White peers, which works in tandem with denial of promotion and tenure, tokenization, an expectation to handle affairs concerning minorities, devaluation of research regarding racial and ethnic minorities, nonexistent reward systems for service and mentorship activities, and a lack of resources and collegial mentorship (Carlos, 2016; Jayakumar et al., 2009; Turner, Myers, & Creswell, 1999).

Needs, Challenges, and Contributions

More recently, scholars have given context in examining the challenges of faculty of color in academia in a growing digital age where information is readily accessible on the Internet amid a sociopolitical climate in which racial tensions have been brought to the forefront in national discourse (Grande, 2017). In Sandy Grande's (2017) article in *Inside Higher Ed*, she mentions that faculty members, and more specifically faculty of color, have "suffered a backlash for speaking out against injustices," which have resulted in a denial of opportunities for professional development and advancement in academia. As a result, faculty of color have often felt isolated, alienated, and othered at their universities, which consequently leads to high levels of turnover; the "revolving door effect" makes apparent the amount of faculty of color who are hired at higher education institutions and a disproportionate number of those who remain (Carter & O'Brien, 1993; Harper, 2012; Pittman, 2012). Additionally, faculty of color also have felt tokenized or expected to be the spokesperson for the group to which they belong (Carlos, 2016). For example, in the past year, as the COVID-19 pandemic began, many Asian American faculty have been called to lead listening spaces, serve on institutional task forces, speak on panels and webinars, and take on more research activity to historically contextualize and address the current forms of anti-Asian racism. In contrast, prior to COVID-19, Asian American faculty and research about the racialized experiences of Asian Americans were not often included in the discourse on race and racism on college campuses.

Identifying mechanisms that contribute to low retention rates with a specific focus on the campus climate for faculty of color can begin to address issues beyond recruitment with the vision of cultivating a more supportive environment that will actually retain them and support the advancement of their career development in academia. Thus, the institution needs to make a consistent effort in cultivating a climate of inclusion on campus, which is important for the career trajectory of faculty of color.

Implications for the Inclusion of Asian American Faculty

To be sure, there is an increase in awareness about the importance of hiring and sustaining faculty of color. However, there remains a significant gap in the literature about how and where Asian American faculty fit into this call to action. While a growing body of research has been conducted on Asian American students (Hune, 2002), little is known about the experiences of Asian American faculty. In fact, data on Asian American faculty can have methodological shortcomings. For example, research on Asian American faculty may not discern between specific subethnic groups. Elsewhere, scholars have written on the political and theoretical irresponsibility of not disaggregating data within the Asian American community (Lee, 2015; National Commission on Asian American and Pacific Islander Research in Education, 2013). Under the panethnic identity of Asian Americans, disparities within various subethnic groups are masked, creating further inequality for the subcommunities, such as Southeast Asians and in some instances Pacific Islanders, that warrant greater attention in policy and practice.

Additionally, another conflation is between *Asian Americans*—perhaps those who earned their degrees in the United States—and *Asians*—those who earned their degrees outside of the United States (Kim, Twombly, & Wolf-Wendel, 2012). For example, a study compared the salary of White and Asian American faculty to test if there was a glass ceiling for the latter group, and only 18% of the sample had been born in the United States (Lee, 2002). It is not clear for those who are born outside of the United States where they earned their degree or whether they are considered international scholars.

The conflation of Asian and Asian American faculty statistically presents an inaccurate and misleading portrayal that further conceals the underrepresentation of Asian Americans in the ranks of the professoriate in academia. In the 1990s, the US Equal Employment Opportunity Commission reported that 40% of Asian and Asian American faculty in higher education were international scholars (Carter & O'Brien, 1993). These questions of the data help to represent the conflation of international Asians and Asian Americans, which has important implications for how both Asians and Asian Americans are discussed within this context. Specifically, data that include international scholars may exaggerate statistics that may be trying to represent information about Asian Americans. Nicholas Hartlep's (2014) research on professors of education holding an endowed or a distinguished chair/professorship shed light on this stance. He concluded that while Asian American faculty may be considered "model minorities," the first Asian American endowed professor of education was not granted until 2005, nearly 150 years after the first endowed chair was granted. Further, Asian American faculty made up only 2% of endowed professors of education. Even outside the field of education, where Asian American professors may have more representation, they are still not receiving as many endowed positions as White faculty. Given that endowed professorships are one of the most prestigious ranks in higher education, the underrepresentation of Asian American faculty points to how their unique set of challenges cannot be overlooked.

This challenge is consistent with other research that suggests that Asian American faculty are not immune to racial discrimination and bias. For example, in 1989, Sucheng Chan (1989), then a professor in the history department as well as chair of the Asian American studies department at the University of California, Santa Barbara, wrote a reflection piece in the *Magazine of Higher Learning* on what it is like to be an Asian American faculty member. She speculates her reasons on the challenges Asian Americans face: "Asian Americans lack 'leadership' qualities, American style. If foreign-born, the Asian candidate is said to be either insufficiently assertive or too rigidly authoritarian. If American-born, the candidate supposedly lacks self-esteem or is too militant" (p. 50). She then lays out the types of power one must navigate when working in a collegiate institution and advises other Asian American staff and faculty on dealing with racism.

Another article examined faculty hiring practices of Asian American law professors during affirmative action (Yen, 1996). The author found that such hiring practices exclude Asian Americans yet have higher rates of Black and Latino faculty being hired. Indeed, discrimination experienced by faculty of color in the workplace plays out in distinct ways for different racial and ethnic communities. Asian American faculty prove to be a unique population to examine, as their forms of discrimination are less quantifiable given an aggregated portrait in descriptive statistics without a critical explanation of the nuances and limitations in the data.

Yan and Museus (2013) found that Asian American and Pacific Islander faculty had the "lowest levels of satisfaction with employment and instructional activity" (p. 259). Additionally, the pervasive narrative of the model minority myth that assumes that Asian Americans are successful and do not encounter discrimination in the professoriate further renders this community invisible and excludes their consideration for support (Cho, 1996). Sumi Cho (1996) points out that generational status matters in distinguishing the discrimination experienced by Asian American faculty and Asian international scholars who teach in the United States. For example, Asian international faculty and first-generation Asian American immigrants experience discrimination in receiving negative evaluations due to their accents (Cho, 1996; Huang, 2013). Asian American faculty are assumed to be foreigners, with colleagues and students questioning their ability to speak and understand English well (Huang, 2013; Turner, Myers, & Creswell, 1999). One of Caroline Turner and colleagues' (1999) participants stated that when this occurs, "They've already superimposed on me that I don't belong here" (p. 44).

Shirley Hune and Kenyon Chan (1996) found that Asian Pacific American faculty experience a chilly climate and glass ceiling in their workplace more often than other faculty since their issues are made invisible. The climate is more salient in particular academic departments for Asian American faculty, as demonstrated in the Moreno Report. Physical isolation as "one of the only few" intensifies feelings of being an outcast in departments such as the arts, humanities, social sciences, and applied fields. Even when Asian American faculty have greater representation in science, technology, mathematics, and engineering, fields in which Asian American faculty may have more colleagues and senior faculty they can turn to for support, they still express a lack of connection to the department and other colleagues (Huang, 2013).

Consider the extent to which collegial support and mentorship within a field matter for faculty when undergoing the tenure process. For example, Belinda Huang's (2013) research revealed the undeniable racism during a faculty's review process when the chair of the department said, "I don't know if it's because you are Indian or if it's because of the work that makes you arrogant" (p. 274). Likewise, Asian American faculty have described their ideas being scrutinized, feeling the need to legitimize their research, and justifying their need for resources in terms of their work (Huang, 2013; Yeung, 2013) that have resulted in racial battle fatigue (Chikkatur, 2019; Smith, 2004; Sato, 2019). Although racial battle fatigue was conceptual-ized from the experiences of Black faculty at historically White universities (Smith, 2004), this framework has been useful in validating the racialized and politicized experiences of faculty of color, including Asian Americans, Latinos, and Native Americans (Hartlep & Ball, 2019). More specifically, Asian American faculty have been able to name the psychological stress to their mind and the physiological responses of their body when experiencing racism in the academy (Chikkatur, 2019; Cho & Men, 2019; Sato, 2019).

One landmark tenure case for Asian American faculty and faculty of color in general involved Don Nakanishi in the 1980s. This case was significant for a few reasons. First, it helped bring attention to the need for a broader and more comprehensive view on scholarship, which too often does not value research on inequality or communities of color (e.g., it lacks broad appeal). When Nakanishi was denied tenure from the Graduate School of Education at the University of California, Los Angeles, some speculated that it was due to his research on the decline of admissions of Asian American applicants. Second, he received criticism about his research agenda, which focused on the "access, representation and influence of Asian Pacifics in the major social, educational and political institutions in this country" (Gordon, 1988). Third, his interdisciplinary work in education and political science was considered risky in traditional scholarship at the time. Nakanishi filed a grievance that pointed out how he was the only Asian American faculty in the school of education and claimed that the tenured review process was plagued by racial bias (Rojas, 2016).

Finally, it is notable that Professor Nakanishi's case resulted in the mobilization of a number of communities who, recognizing that a lack of appreciation of Nakanishi and his work as a lack of appreciation for the work and contributions of many faculty of color, stepped up to fight on his behalf. Gann Matsuda (1990) chronicles the details of Nakanishi's tenure case that lasted from December 1986 to June 1989. Dale Minami (1990), Nakanishi's lawyer, recounts that after his initial reading of procedural irregularities in Nakanishi's tenure review, they needed to approach the case with a legal-political strategy rather than a lawsuit that would be drawn out for years. The multiracial and cross-generational organization and mobilization of different groups across the state and country to advocate for Nakanishi's tenured case demonstrates Nakanishi's impact outside academia.

Important to recognize is the fact that students were critical in this battle and were vital to organizing rallies, forums, demonstrations, and candlelight vigils (Katayama, 1990; Matsuda, 1990; Minami, 1990). In addition, student leaders lobbied UCLA undergraduate and graduate student governing boards to pass resolutions, in addition to working alongside professors and administrators to submit petitions demanding explanations. Their conviction and continued effort in pressuring the university to respond were complementary to the public attention broadcasted in media such as the *Daily Bruin*, a student newspaper, and the *Los Angeles Times*. Even the Asian Pacific American alumni group sent letters, and two individuals, then president Ernest Hiroshige and Stewart Kwoh, made explicit that they would resign from the chancellor-appointed Community Advisory Board if Nakanishi's tenure were denied (Minami, 1990).

It is also notable that Nakanishi received endorsements from 27 California state legislators through letters, public hearings, lobbying UCLA officials, and legislative aides (Minami, 1990). Local government officials and leaders from Los Angeles Unified School District also met with Chancellor Charles Young to advocate on behalf of Nakanishi (Matsuda, 1990; Minami, 1990). Community and labor organizations from other racial and ethnic communities, including Latinos, Blacks, and Jewish folks, also partook in the fight that demonstrated that Nakanishi's academic work, service to the community, and relationships went beyond the Asian American community (Minami, 1990; Nakanishi, 1990). The legal-political strategy proved to be successful, and Nakanishi was granted tenure on May 25, 1989.

Finally, with tenure, Professor Nakanishi was appointed director of the UCLA Asian American Studies Center, which eventually became the largest and most prominent program of its kind. After his passing in 2016, he was celebrated as a pioneer and left behind a legacy for community-based scholars. UCLA released a statement that lauded Professor Nakanishi for "gain[ing] national recognition for establishing Asian American studies as a viable and relevant field of scholarship, teaching, community service and public discourse" (Rojas, 2016).

While cases of racism and discrimination against Asian American faculty such as Professor Nakanishi's tenure case are significant lessons for the field, it is also important to recognize when they are compounded by sexism. Upon closer look at the numbers, three-quarters of Asian American and Pacific Islander faculty appear to be male across all ethnic groups (Hune & Chan, 1997; Yan & Museus, 2013). While Asian American men hold 7% across the board for assistant, associate, and full professorships, Asian American women represent only 6%, 4%, and 2%, respectively (Hune et al., 2019). Compared to their White counterparts, Asian American women faculty experienced a more drastic decline in rank from assistant to full professor (Hune et al., 2019). In Huang's (2013) qualitative study of Asian

American faculty that interviewed men and women, a salient theme for Asian American faculty who were women was feeling pressured to balance work and family. A recent quantitative study finds that Asian American men faculty reported the highest level of perceived work-life balance compared to Latino men and Asian American, Black, and Latina women faculty (Szelényi & Denson, 2019). That is not to say that Asian American men faculty who are more family-centered and egalitarian in their approach to familial responsibilities do not feel a similar pressure to women. Even in Katalin Szelényi and Nida Denson's (2019) analyses, the highest averages of reported work-life balance among Asian American men were located at the midpoint between "neither agree nor disagree" and "somewhat agree," which suggests that further exploration into these responses is needed. Departments and institutions need to rethink their structure to consider the personal and familial responsibilities that faculty of color are pressured to manage along with the professional obligations to conduct research and engage in service all around (Denson, Szelényi, & Bresonis, 2018).

Conclusion

Many lessons can be learned about discrimination against faculty of color that is informed by perspectives from the Asian American experience. First, Asian Americans are a case-in-point for demonstrating the difference between compositional diversity or representation and the meaningful engagement of faculty of color to promote a positive campus climate. For example, despite a greater numerical representation of Asian American faculty in many colleges and universities, it is questionable if they are recognized for the value, assets, and skills they bring to these institutions. Additionally, Asian American faculty are often not included in broader diversity efforts on college campuses, which neglect to recognize instances of discrimination and harassment as faculty of color. Also, Asian American faculty have a unique racialized experience in higher education, and their unique needs and challenges are too often overlooked.

Second, there is a need to be more critical of our notions of "representation" regarding Asian Americans in higher education. In many ways, Asian American faculty are conflated with international scholars from Asia (Carter & O'Brien, 1993), some of whom stay in the United States, and others of whom do not. For example, Asian and Asian Americans comprise 8% of the professoriate when US citizenship is accounted for, but Asian

Americans make up only 3% of all full-time faculty (Carter & O'Brien, 1993). Thus, there is a need to more carefully track Asian American faculty in a meaningful way. This concern is a particularly salient issue when comparing Asian and Asian American faculty across different disciplines and fields where there are more international faculty from Asia in STEM fields relative to the humanities and social sciences.

Third, it is also notable to consider the unique contribution of Asian American faculty, particularly within the context of COVID-19. Asian and Asian American professors experienced additional challenges during the global pandemic due to the rise in anti-Asian hate crimes and violence. In an interview with *Diverse Issues in Higher Education*, Dr. Madeline Hsu, professor at the University of Texas at Austin stated, "There has been a sharp ticking-up of requests to give talks to educate people very quickly about Asian American history. . . . A lot of people have been writing op-ed pieces in order to produce quick, easily digestible publications" (Stewart, 2021). She added that Asian and Asian American faculty "have been approached by their institutions to conduct emotional, counseling support on campus" in addition to feeling "overwhelmed because of so many sudden demands on them." During this time, it is crucial for institutions to demonstrate their support for Asian American faculty by sending statements of solidarity and by providing resources and funding research centers and academic departments that have been engaging with issues surrounding the Asian American community. Their research and impact on the Asian American community, for example, is critical for this large and growing population. They are raising awareness about the Asian American community in ways that help understand their unique needs, challenges, and contributions and how and why it is relevant to broader issues in our society. Moreover, for the critical mass of Asian American students in many colleges and universities, Asian American faculty are critical for providing a place to turn when they want to pursue similar lines of inquiry that may resonate with them.

Finally, a focus on Asian American faculty discrimination shows the importance of broad and inclusive coalitions regarding advocacy. This is because advocacy for the needs and challenges faced by Asian American faculty does not exist without the inclusion of other communities of color. Put another way, there is a lack of recognition that discrimination against Asian American faculty exists, not to mention the need to include them in broader institutional efforts to address racial climate for faculty of color. Yet through broad, cross-racial, and multigenerational coalitions, we can shed light on and bring attention to the unique needs and challenges of Asian

American faculty. These are lessons that are relevant to any marginalized and vulnerable population that is being overlooked and underserved.

References

Abdul-Raheem, J. (2016). Faculty diversity and tenure in higher education. *Journal of Cultural Diversity, 23*(2), 53–56.

Abel, J. R., & Deitz, R. (2014). Do the benefits of college still outweigh the costs? *Current Issues in Economics and Finance, 20*(3), 1–12.

Allen, A. L. (2013). The role model argument and faculty diversity. In S. M. Cahn (Ed.), *The affirmative action debate* (pp. 169–183). Routledge.

Antonio, A. L. (2002) Faculty of color reconsidered. *The Journal of Higher Education, 73*(5), 582–602.

Bustillos, L. T., & Siqueiros, M. (2018). Left out: How exclusion in California's colleges and universities hurts our values, our students, and our economy. Retrieved from https://collegecampaign.org/wp-content/uploads/2018/03/2018-Left-Out-Executive-Summary-Final.pdf

Carlos, S. (2016). Campus climate and coalition building for faculty of color. In B. Taylor (Ed.), *Listening to the voices: Multi-ethnic women in education* (pp. 69–78). University of San Francisco.

Carter, D. J., & O'Brien, E. (1993). *Employment and hiring patterns for faculty of color.* American Council on Education.

Chan, S. (1989). Beyond affirmative action. *Change: The Magazine of Higher Learning, 21*(6), 48–52.

Chikkatur, A. (2019). When you name a problem, you become the problem: (En)countering Whiteness at a small, liberal arts college as a South Asian American tenured professor. In N. D. Hartlep and D. Ball (Eds.), *Racial battle fatigue in faculty: Perspectives and lessons from higher education* (pp. 70–83). Routledge.

Cho, A., & Men, S. P. (2019). Navigating weird comments, stereotypes and microaggressions as Southeast Asian American faculty as a predominately White community college. In N. D. Hartlep & D. Ball (Eds.), *Racial battle fatigue in faculty: Perspectives and lessons from higher education* (pp. 57–69). Routledge.

Cho, S. (1996). Confronting the myths: Asian Pacific American faculty in higher education. *Ninth Annual APAHE Conference Proceedings* (pp. 31–56). APAHE.

Davis, L. R. (2002). Racial diversity in higher education: Ingredients for success and failure. *The Journal of Applied Behavioral Science, 38*(2), 137–155.

Denson, N., Szelényi, K., & Bresonis, K. (2018). Correlates of work-life balance for faculty across racial/ethnic groups. *Research in Higher Education, 59,* 226–247.

Espinosa, L. L., Turk, J. M., Taylor, M., & Chessman, H. M. (2019). *Race and ethnicity in higher education: A status report.* American Council on Education.

Fries-Britt, S. L., Rowan-Kenyon, H. T., Perna, L. W., Milem, J. F., & Howard, D. G. (2011). Underrepresentation in the academy and the institutional climate for faculty diversity. *The Journal of the Professoriate, 5*(1), 1–34.

Fry, R., & Cilluffo, A. (2020, May 30). A rising share of undergraduates are from poor families, especially at less selective colleges. Pew Research Center's Social and Demographic Trends Project. https://www.pewresearch.org/social-trends/2019/05/22/a-rising-share-of-undergraduates-are-from-poor-families-especially-at-less-selective-colleges/

Garvey, J. C., & Rankin, S. (2018). The influence of campus climate and urbanization on queer-spectrum and trans-spectrum faculty intent to leave. *Journal of Diversity in Higher Education, 11*(1), 67–81.

Gasman, M., Kim, J., & Nguyen, T-H. (2011). Effectively recruiting faculty of color at highly selective institutions: A school of education case study. *Journal of Diversity in Higher Education, 4*(4), 212–222.

Gordon, L. (1988, December). Tempest over tenure at UCLA: Professor's fight for permanent position raises racial issue. Retrieved from https://www.latimes.com/archives/la-xpm-1988-12-20-me-634-story.html

Grande, S. (2017, July 14). Academic blackballing. *Inside Higher Ed.* https://www.insidehighered.com/advice/2017/07/14/academics-who-speak-out-against-injustice-are-experiencing-backlash-essay

Griffin, K. A. (2019). Redoubling our efforts: How institutions can affect faculty diversity. In L. L. Espinosa, J. M. Turk, M. Taylor, & H. M. Chessman (Eds.), *Race and ethnicity in higher education: A status report* (pp. 273–279). American Council on Education.

Grutter v. Bollinger, 539 US 306 (2003).

Hall, R. M., & Sandler, B R. (1982). *The classroom climate: A chilly one for women?* Association of American Colleges.

Harper, S. R. (2012). Race without racism: How higher education researchers minimize racist institutional norms. *The Review of Higher Education, 36*(1), 9–29.

Harrison, D. F. (2017). The role of higher education in the changing role of work. *Educause Review, 52*(6), 8–9.

Hartlep, N. D. (2014, May). A model minority? A national look at Asian-Americans and endowed professors of education. Retrieved from https://diverseeducation.com/article/63996/

Hartlep, N. D., & Ball, D. (2019). *Racial battle fatigue in faculty: Perspectives and lessons from higher education.* Routledge.

Heilig, J. V., Flores, I. W., Barros Souza, A. E., Barry, J. C., & Monroy, S. B. (2019). Considering the ethnoracial and gender diversity of faculty in United States college and university intellectual communities. *Hispanic Journal of Law and Policy*, 2019, 1–31.

Huang, B. L. (2013). From revolving doors and chilly climates to creating inclusive environments for pre-tenure Asian American faculty. In S. D. Museus, D. C.

Maramaba, & R. T. Teranishi (Eds.), *The misrepresented minority: New insights on Asian Americans and Pacific Islanders, and the implications for higher education* (pp. 266–280). Stylus.

Hune, S. (2002). Demographics and diversity of Asian American college students. *New Directions for Student Services, 2002*(97), 11–20.

Hune, S., & Chan, K. S. (1997). Special focus: Asian Pacific American demographic and educational trends. In D. J. Carter & R. Wilson (Eds.), *Minorities in higher education: Fifteenth annual status report* (pp. 39–67). American Council on Education.

Hune, S., Noh, E., Junn, J., Mai'a, K., Pham, C. M., Yee, M., & Takeyama, A. (2019). *Fight the tower: Asian American women scholars' resistance and renewal in the academy*. Rutgers University Press.

Hurtado, S. (2001) Linking diversity and educational purpose: How diversity affects the classroom environment and student development. In G. Orfield (Ed.), *Diversity challenged: Evidence on the impact of affirmative action* (pp. 187–203). Harvard Education Publishing Group and The Civil Rights Project at Harvard University.

Hurtado, S., Milem, J. F., Clayton-Pedersen, A. R., & Allen, W. R. (1998). Enhancing campus climates for racial/ethnic diversity through educational policy and practice. *Review of Higher Education, 21*(3), 279–302.

Hurtado, S., Milem, J. F., Clayton-Pedersen, A. R., & Allen, W. R. (1999). *Enacting diverse learning environments: Improving the campus climate for racial/ethnic diversity in higher education*. ASHE-Eric Higher Education Report, Vol. 26, No. 8. The George Washington University, Graduate School of Education and Human Development.

Jayakumar, U. M., Howard, T. C., Allen, W. R., & Han, J. C. (2009). Racial privilege in the professoriate: An exploration of campus climate, retention, and satisfaction. *The Journal of Higher Education, 80*(5), 538–563.

Katayama, M. (1990). Doing the right thing: The critical role of students in the tenure campaign. *Amerasia Journal, 16*(1), 109–117.

Kim, D., Twombly, S., & Wolf-Wendel, L. (2012). International faculty in American universities: Experiences of academic life, productivity, and career mobility. In Y. J. Xu (Ed.), *Refining the focus on faculty diversity in postsecondary institutions* (pp. 27–46). Wiley.

Kurtzleben, D. (2014, February 11). Study: Income gap between young college and high school grads widens. *US News & World Report*. https://www.usnews.com/news/articles/2014/02/11/study-income-gap-between-young-college-and-high-school-grads-widens

Lee, S. J. (2015). *Unraveling the "model minority" stereotype: Listening to Asian American youth*. Teachers College Press.

Lee, S. M. (2002). Do Asian American faculty face a glass ceiling in higher education? *American Educational Research Journal, 39*(3), 695–724.

Llamas, J. D., Nguyen, K., & Tran, A. G. (2021). The case for greater faculty diversity: Examining the educational impacts of student-faculty racial/ethnic match. *Race Ethnicity and Education, 24*(3), 375–391.

Matsuda, G. (1990). "Only the beginning": Continuing our battle for empowerment. *Amerasia Journal, 16*(1), 159–169.

Mayhew, M. J., Grunwald, H. E., & Dey, E. L. (2006). Breaking the silence: Achieving a positive campus climate for diversity from the staff perspective. *Research in Higher Education, 47*(1), 63–88.

McCoy, D. L. (2014). A phenomenological exploration of the experiences of first-generation students of color at one "extreme" predominately White institution. *College Student Affairs Journal, 32*(1), 155–169.

McFarland, J., Hussar, B., Wang, X., Zhang, J., Wang, K., Rathbun, A., Barmer, A., Forrest Cataldi, E., & Bullock Mann, F. (2018). *The condition of education 2018* (NCES 2018-144). US Department of Education. National Center for Education Statistics. Retrieved from https://nces.ed.gov/pubsearch/pubsinfo.asp?pubid=2018144

Minami, D. (1990). Guerrilla war at UCLA: Political and legal dimensions of the tenure battle. *Amerasia Journal, 16*(1), 81–107.

Moreno, C. (2013, October 15). Independent investigative report on acts of bias and discrimination involving faculty at the University of California, Los Angeles. University of California, Office of the President. http://www.ucop.edu/moreno-report/external-review-team-report-10-15-13.pdf

National Center for Education Statistics. (2017). Percentage of 18- to 24-year-olds enrolled in degree-granting postsecondary institutions, by level of institution and sex and race/ethnicity of student: 1970 through 2015. Retrieved from https://nces.ed.gov/programs/digest/d16/tables/dt16_302.60.asp

National Commission on Asian American and Pacific Islander Research in Education. (2013). *iCount: A data quality movement for Asian Americans and Pacific Islanders in higher education.* Author.

Nakanishi, D. (1990). Why I fought. *Amerasia Journal, 16*(1), 139–158.

Nakanishi, D. T. (1993). Asian Pacific Americans in higher education: Faculty and administrative representation and tenure. *New Directions for Teaching and Learning, 53*, 51–59.

Neville, K. M., & Parker, T. L. (2017). A breath of fresh air: Students' perceptions of interactions with African American faculty. *Journal of College Student Development, 58*(3), 349–364.

Osei, Z. (2019, May). Low-Income and minority students are growing share of enrollments, and two other takeaways from new study. Retrieved from https://www.chronicle.com/article/Low-IncomeMinority/246346

Pittman, C. T. (2012). Racial microaggressions: The narratives of African American faculty at a predominantly White university. *The Journal of Negro Education, 8*(1), 82–92.

Poloma, A. W. (2014). Why teaching faculty diversity (still) matters. *Peabody Journal of Education, 89*(3), 336–346.

Rojas, L. B. (2016, March). UCLA professor Don Nakanishi was considered a pioneer in Asian American studies. Retrieved from https://www.scpr.org/news/2016/03/23/58817/ucla-professor-don-nakanishi-was-considered-a-pion

Sato, T. C. (2019). Ignored, pacified, and deflected: Racial battle fatigue for an Asian American non-tenure track professor. In N. D. Hartlep & D. Ball (Eds.), *Racial battle fatigue in faculty: Perspectives and lessons from higher education* (pp. 84–98). Routledge.

Sgoutas-Emch, S., Baird, L., Myers, P., Camacho, M., & Lord, S. (2016). We're not all White men: Using a cohort/cluster approach to diversify STEM faculty hiring. *Thought & Action, 32*(1), 91–107.

Smith, D. G. (1991). The challenge of diversity: Alienation in the academy and its implications for faculty. *Journal on Excellence in College Teaching, 2*, 129–137.

Smith, W. A. (2004). Black faculty coping with racial battle fatigue: The campus racial climate in a post-civil rights era. In D. Cleveland (Ed.), *Broken silence: Conversations about race by African Americans at predominantly White institutions* (pp. 171–190). Peter Lang.

Spann, J. (1990). *Retaining and promoting minority faculty members: Problems and possibilities.* The University of Wisconsin System.

Stephen, C. O. L. E., Barber, E. G., & Cole, S. (2009). *Increasing faculty diversity: The occupational choices of high-achieving minority students.* Harvard University Press.

Stewart, P. (2021, May 13). Ending the hate: Scholars call for academia to address anti-Asian bias with structural change. *Diverse Issues in Higher Education, 38*(4), 14–18.

Szelényi, K., & Denson, N. (2019). Personal and institutional predictors of work-life balance among women and men faculty of color. *The Review of Higher Education, 43*(2), 633–655.

Thelin, J. (2019). *A history of American higher education* (3rd ed.). Johns Hopkins University Press.

Turner, C. S. V., Gonzálesz, J. C., & Wood, J. L. (2008). Faculty of color in academe: What 20 years of literature tells us. *Journal of Diversity in Higher Education, 1*(3), 139–158.

Turner, C. S. V., Myers, S. L., Jr., & Creswell, J. W. (1999). Exploring underrepresentation: The case of faculty of color in the Midwest. *The Journal of Higher Education, 70*(1), 27–59.

Umbach, P. D. (2006). The contribution of faculty of color to undergraduate education. *Research in Higher Education, 47*(3), 317–345.

Vargas, N., Villa-Palomino, J., & Davis, E. (2020). Latinx faculty representation and resource allocation at Hispanic-serving institutions. *Race Ethnicity and Education, 23*(1), 39–54.

Victorino, C. A., Nylund-Gibson, K., & Conley, S. (2013). Campus racial climate: A litmus test for faculty satisfaction at four-year colleges and universities. *The Journal of Higher Education, 84*(6), 769–805.

Wingfield, A. H. (2016, September). Faculty of color and the changing university. Retrieved from https://www.insidehighered.com/advice/2016/09/09/more-faculty-color-can-and-should-be-top-ranks-universities-essay

Yan, W., & Museus, S. D. (2013). Asian American and Pacific Islander faculty and the glass ceiling in higher education. In S. D. Museus, R. T. Teranishi, & D. C. Maramba (Eds.), *The misrepresented minority: New insights on Asian Americans and Pacific Islanders, and the implications for higher education* (pp. 249–265). Stylus.

Yen, A. C. (1996). Statistical analysis of Asian Americans and the affirmative action hiring of law school faculty. *Asian Law Journal, 3,* 39–54.

Yeung, F. P. (2013). Struggles for professional and intellectual legitimacy: Experiences of Asian and Asian American female faculty members. In S. D. Museus, D. C. Maramaba, & R. T. Teranishi (Eds.), *The misrepresented minority: New insights on Asian Americans and Pacific Islanders, and the implications for higher education* (pp. 281–293). Stylus.

PART 4
LEADERSHIP DOES MATTER

Chapter 10

HBCU Activism

The Evolving Role of HBCUs in Resolving Racial Tensions and Advancing Racial Conciliation in Higher Education

IVORY A. TOLDSON, BIANCA M. MACK, AND TEMPLE R. PRICE

Historically Black colleges and universities (HBCUs) have played a prominent role in advancing Black social progress and racial conciliation in higher education in the United States and American society. They have used education as a "vehicle" for fighting against racial bias, discrimination, and oppression (Crewe, 2017, p. 360). Serving as the "pipeline" to education for the people who gained freedom from slavery, HBCUs performed a three-dimensional function (Stevenson, 2007, p. 99): first, to promote civil rights; second, to improve Black people's opportunities in the post-slavery period; and third, to offer Black students opportunities equal to those that were provided to their White peers (Stevenson, 2007). Historically Black colleges and universities have played an indelible role in establishing Black people's intellectual, cultural, and spiritual development.

As defined in the Higher Education Act of 1965, HBCUs are historically Black colleges and universities that gained accreditation before 1964 and whose primary responsibility was, and still is, educating Black Americans (Toldson, 2014). The first HBCUs were Cheyney University, founded in

1837 (Crewe, 2017), followed by Lincoln University (1854) and Wilberforce University (1856). At present, the number of HBCUs slightly exceeds 100, which accounts for nearly 3% of postsecondary schools (Toldson, 2014).

Since their foundation, HBCUs have experienced various levels of demand and have served different purposes depending on the prevailing social issues in the nation. However, an undoubted fact about HBCUs is that they have always pursued the noble mission of making the lives of Black Americans richer in terms of the opportunities they received and the knowledge they gained. This chapter comprises several sections divided chronologically, with each depicting the development and functioning of HBCUs in different periods of Black consciousness movements. Finally, the chapter summarizes the role of HBCUs in establishing Black movements and the general development of African Americans' quest for equality since the beginning of the 20th century.

HBCUs during Reconstruction and Post-Reconstruction (1862–1900)

During the periods of reconstruction and post-reconstruction, the first HBCUs emerged and developed their agendas. The newly emancipated Black people endeavored to obtain legal recognition as US citizens. At the same time, they had to resist the terroristic actions of hostile White Southerners. During those periods, HBCUs lacked both the legal and financial support to be competitive. One of the greatest developments occurred in 1862, implementing the first Morrill Land Grant Act (Harper, Patton, & Wooden, 2009). The act helped to start the educational movement in mechanical arts and agriculture. In addition, the new law promoted developing areas that had not previously received sufficient attention. Despite the considerable achievements accessible through the first act, the second Morrill Act of 1890 endowed equal funds for Black universities and colleges in 17 states.

Although the act's purpose was beneficial, educational facilities did not receive the promised funds. As a result, instead of focusing on agricultural and mechanical arts, many HBCUs concentrated on training Black students to become teachers (Craig, 1992). Since many graduates of facilities based on the 1890 act became teachers, more qualified high school educators entered the Black community. As a result, more African American parents sent their children to school, which gave a start to new student generations

(Craig, 1992). Further, the general development of education equality gave way to more HBCUs.

The second Morrill Act supported the segregation of White and Black educational facilities. As a result, HBCUs established during the 1890s and 1900s were of much lower quality than White colleges and universities opened under the first Morrill Act of 1862 (Harper, Patton, & Wooden, 2009). In 1896, with the *Plessy v. Ferguson* court case ruling that racial segregation could continue on the condition that educational establishments received equal accommodations, many Black people believed the situation would improve (Harper, Patton, & Wooden, 2009). However, even after *Plessy v. Ferguson*, Black colleges received 26 times less funding than White colleges. In addition, the per-pupil expenditure rate for White students was four times higher than that for their Black counterparts.

Despite some deficiencies, the Morrill Acts presented a considerable opportunity to cultivate Black education. About 90% of African Americans who received a university degree in the first decades of the 1900s were graduates of HBCUs. Despite the poor financial conditions of HBCUs prior to the 1900s, these institutions served as the means of enhancing quality of life not only for Black people but also for other underserved populations (Crewe, 2017). The prevailing ideology of the 1862–1900 period was that of "racial uplift" (Crewe, 2017, p. 361). This ideology suggested that African Americans were accountable for their race's welfare, which encouraged young people to receive education and use it as a tool to be used against attempts to limit their civil and political rights.

The first HBCUs were more than merely educational establishments: they were also places aimed at bolstering the African American community through intellectual development. For example, the mission of Morehouse College, founded in 1867, was to resist Jim Crow laws aimed at discriminating against Black people and promoting segregation (Jensen, 2017). The educational process at the college had a profound effect on developing Black religious and educational opportunities. Three decades before the establishment of Morehouse College, Cheyney University opened. About one-fifth of African Americans were illiterate (Crewe, 2017). Cheyney University became the most significant driving force in the foundation of a new life position for post-abolitionist Black citizens in the reconstruction era.

The idea of racial uplift, which prevailed in the vision of the first HBCUs, gave way to racial advocacy. The latter included such pivotal notions as social justice, empowerment, cultural development, diversity, and inclusion (Crewe, 2017). The initial aim of the educational process of HBCUs between 1863 and 1900 was resisting oppression. By receiving education, students of HBCUs could pursue the goal of removing systemic restrictions that were widespread in the African American community.

Mission statements of the first HBCUs founded between 1865 and 1869 included such aspects as providing high-quality education, cultivating creativity and social responsibility, and developing a society in which all citizens could have their needs satisfied (Crewe, 2017). Although some White educational institutions also aimed to resolve race issues, this endeavor's unanimity was present only in HBCUs. Further, improving the attitude of society toward the race question was an institutional purpose and a personal one (Crewe, 2017). Both faculty members and students realized that the future of their race depended upon their efforts. Therefore, the first universities' and colleges' missions incorporated antidiscrimination efforts and established equal opportunities in the future.

HBCUs during the New Negro Movement (1900s–1940s)

HBCUs helped during the New Negro movement with significant accomplishments in the spheres of education and art. In the 1900s–1940s, there was a heightened feeling of Black people's cultural contribution to the nation's development. Historically Black fraternities and sororities formed in colleges and universities, and HBCU leadership transitioned from White charities to Black Americans. A renaissance of African American scholarship emerged at HBCUs during this period, and HBCUs started evolving into entities that were fertile for civil rights movements.

The New Negro movement emerged as a response to the post-reconstruction terror regime and the harsh effect of the *Plessy v. Ferguson* case. As a result of these affects, African Americans initiated a justice-seeking movement of self-assertion and resistance (Dodson, 2016). The New Negro movement paved the way for the civil rights movement that inspired Black people to fight for their rights and equality. HBCUs played a major role in this process since their students became the most critical participants within these movements (Barrett, 2017). Because of the New Negro movement, a new generation of African American people appeared who spared no effort to validate their identity as human beings and prove that they could do much more than the US government expected of them (Dodson, 2016).

The debate between W. E. B. Du Bois and Booker T. Washington during the early 20th century on social and economic issues highlighted conflicting beliefs about self-preservation within the Black community. Washington's more conservative philosophy of self-help and having a laissez-faire disposition toward segregation was a point of contention with Du Bois. Du Bois responded with a philosophy of education and active pursuit of civil rights through the agitation of the political system.

During the New Negro movement era, the development of the Niagara movement led to the creation of the National Association for the Advancement of Colored People (NAACP) in 1908. The NAACP made contributions to education and the arts through the magazine called *The Crisis*. The magazine, spearheaded by Du Bois, incorporated the first periodical for Black youth in America called *The Brownies Book*. It was distributed on Black college campuses during the Harlem Renaissance era. This periodical focused on political, social, economic, educational, moral, and ethical issues and the Du Bois philosophy of "The Talented Tenth" and the rise of Black colleges.

Black colleges were a "ready-made" hub for activism and involvement with local NAACP chapters (Barrett, 2017). Some of the earliest HBCU activism inspired by NAACP literature occurred at Fisk University, Morgan State University, and Howard University. Influenced by the writings in *The Crisis* and similar periodicals, students at HBCUs rejected the ideas of White philanthropists having control over the conditions of Black colleges, and in 1925 Fisk University students protested poor campus conditions (Rogers, 2010).

Protests began in February and lasted until the resignation of President Fayette Avery McKenzie two months later. The Fisk Strike influenced students on other HBCU campuses to assert their existence as men and women who did not need White paternalism on- or off-campus (Lamon, 1974). Similar protests ensued in the 1920s–1940s at Morgan State University and Howard University (Barrett, 2017).

Morgan State College and Howard University played a significant role in developing the New Negro movement and Black art. These and other educational establishments became centers of African Americans' cultural and intellectual life from the 1900s until the 1940s. Because of considerable cultural development, Black people could establish a new unique community of artists (Dodson, 2016). In addition, Morgan State College became one of the centers of the New Negro movement because of its student activism. Specifically, in 1939, many Morgan students became members of the

NAACP and participated in the first National Youth Conference (Barrett, 2017). Also, many of these young people were representatives of the City-Wide Young People's Forum, which originated in 1931.

As scholars consider the forum to have been a catalyst for the Youth and College Division of the NAACP, HBCUs played a vital role in developing African American people's cultural and civil rights movements (Barrett, 2017). The forum also catalyzed other significant student organizations, such as the Student Nonviolent Coordinating Committee.

Scholars usually relate the New Negro movement to the Harlem Renaissance explosion of the 1920s. There is a common opinion that these two terms are synonymous and that the upheaval of the Harlem Renaissance was the heart of the New Negro movement (Dodson, 2016). It is possible to justify such an association by the Harlem Renaissance's outstanding effect on cultural and artistic landscapes both in the United States and worldwide. Although it became popular in the 1900s until the 1940s, the term *New Negro movement* emerged earlier—in the 1890s. Initially, the movement was a reaction of African Americans to White Americans' post-reconstruction violation of Black people's rights, image, and dignity (Dodson, 2016). In the beginning, the New Negro movement pursued activist and intellectual goals rather than artistic and literary ones. Apart from that, the movement asserted coordinated group activity and self-regulating operations. At the turn of the 20th century, Black people established more organizations protecting their rights and ratifying their humanity than at any other point of history until the late 1960s (Dodson, 2016).

Apart from the NAACP (founded in 1909), such organizations as the National Association of Colored Women (1895), the Niagara movement (1905), the National Urban League (1910), and the Association for the Study of Negro Life and History (1915) appeared (Dodson, 2016). The *Plessy v. Ferguson* case, the main impetus for the development of these organizations, made African Americans rise in defense of their race to eliminate the unfair effect of segregation. Within ten years following *Plessy v. Ferguson*, the New Negro movement developed into a national Black movement aimed to resist post-reconstruction terrorism. Both local and national associations created by African Americans from the 1900s until the 1940s helped to bolster the rights and social position of Black people (Dodson, 2016).

Initially, Howard University seemed incompatible with the New Negro movement because of its dependence on federal funding and its White leadership who considered the university as their institution that they magnanimously ran for African American students (Dodson, 2016). Hence, the founders viewed it as their duty to sustain their leadership and give the best "colonial" education to Blacks, none of whom could become the university's leader (Dodson, 2016, p. 992). However, under the pressure of the nascent movement, Howard University underwent considerable changes. The university selected its last White president in 1918, Dr. James Stanley Durkee. In 1919, racial confrontations gave way to the growing need for African Americans to defend their rights. By the end of Durkee's presidency, about two-thirds of the university's faculty was African American (Dodson, 2016). The New Negro movement activists succeeded in enabling Black people to take control of Howard and altering its curriculum. Particularly, courses were to reflect African American history and culture.

Gradually, other universities started following the ideas pursued by the New Negro movement activists. HBCUs became places where Black people could meet their cultural and spiritual needs as well as develop in intellectual and artistic dimensions. Educational programs became adjusted to cover the most relevant topics of African American life. The movement helped Black people discover their identity and show it to other nations that had been underestimating them for many centuries.

HBCUs during the Civil Rights Movement (1940s–1960s)

The lengthy period of slavery and Jim Crow laws did not remain unnoticed in US society. Due to frequent racist attacks, African Americans felt that their race was devalued. The most prominent response to such unfair treatment from the 1940s until the 1960s was the civil rights movement. The movement started as the opposition to Jim Crow laws, which supported segregation (Clayton, 2018). The civil rights movement relied on young people whose enthusiasm and energy inspired others. HBCUs played a crucial role in the civil rights movement of the 1950s and 1960s. In particular, they provided intellectual leadership, foot soldiers, and secure places to meet and plan (Williamson, 2004). In addition, political and economic independence from the state allowed their students to participate in various activities without worrying about legislative punishment. Still, their position of privacy did not protect them entirely from the state's exasperation, especially when colleges' and universities' goals contradicted state interests (Williamson, 2004).

The most typical arguments against HBCUs' participation in the civil rights movement was that they should promote constitutionally protected freedoms. Another opinion was that HBCUs should ignore political affairs and concentrate on educational purposes. There were frequent debates over the educational establishments' role in the movement. The most committed activists underwent severe punishment but did not refuse to follow their ideals (Williamson, 2004). The civil rights movement was inevitable because of unfairness between the rights of White and Black people living in the United States. By 1950, only 2.3% of African Americans had a high school certificate. Also, nearly 70% of Blacks aged 25 and older did not have an education level higher than the seventh grade (Williamson, 2004). The pivotal moment in this movement was the *Brown v. Board of Education* case, which proclaimed segregation illegal. However, many universities and colleges continued treating White and Black students unequally. Hence, the movement's activists continued working hard to pursue their goals.

While private HBCUs had comparative independence to participate in movements, public establishments did not relish such a prospect. For instance, Southern colleges and universities were under the control of states, which refused to support Black schools because they participated in the processes destroying the social order (Williamson, 2004). However, despite different obstacles, HBCUs became essential centers of civic engagement of the time. The primary aim of higher education is promoting academic achievement and cultivating citizenship and positive qualities in students (Gasman, Spencer, & Orphan, 2015). Unlike historically White colleges and universities, which were not interested in civil engagement much, HBCUs focused on this goal from the beginning of their existence. Early on in the development of HBCUs, there was insufficient support for civil participation and liberal arts. However, with their development and growth, these institutions became centers of community life within the African American population (Gasman, Spencer, & Orphan, 2015). Because of mass discrimination, HBCUs occupied a much more important place in establishing Black culture than White colleges and universities did in promoting White culture.

Along with universities, churches played a significant role in promoting interests pursued by the civil rights movement. The most prominent leader of the movement, Martin Luther King Jr., was a Baptist minister who advocated the nonviolent means of proving one's point (Clayton, 2018). There were few public places where people could gather and discuss their strategies, but the Black church was among such venues. Many students were active in the church, so they arranged their meetings and plans there. In the civil rights movement, the combination of efforts made by HBCUs and the church aided in reaching considerable results. Black colleges and universities included the same dimensions as White institutions: research, teaching, and public service (Gasman, Spencer, & Orphan, 2015). However, the difference was that Black colleges and universities performed one more function, which White establishments lacked: the search for social justice for their students and other people. Since social justice is the basis of civic engagement and the development of democracy, this feature made HBCUs more focused on these issues than White colleges and universities.

Finally, it is necessary to mention the movement within the movement that developed in the 1950s. Whereas Black people lacked the rights and freedoms that White people had, there was also inequality among the members of the Black community. Specifically, African American women experienced worse treatment than men in terms of access to education. Thus, when the civil rights movement evolved into a full-scale struggle, Black women confronted those who, in their opinion, were accountable for the oppression they experienced (Jean-Marie, 2006).

The *Brown v. Board of Education* case, which was prominent for African American education, gave a start to women's pursuit of education and increased their chances for engaging in professional careers. HBCUs served as a "repository of hope" for universal education for every individual (Jean-Marie, 2006, p. 87). The participation of HBCU students in the civil rights movement helped promote the educational, civic engagement, and spiritual goals of African American youth. Moreover, women started a campaign to gain equal rights in education and work. The ideals of democracy and equality, which dominated in the 1940s through the 1960s, received considerable support and encouragement with the help of the civil rights movement.

HBCUs during the Black Power Movement (1960s–1970s)

More intense activist activity marked the next period in the existence of HBCUs and the lives of African Americans. Students took part in demonstrations, which brought about conflicts with law enforcement. Many Black students became victims of assaults and murders, such as the students at Southern University and Jackson State University. The movement involved African Americans and poor people from other ethnic groups who disagreed with the capitalist structure of the country. People strived to gain Black liberation and equality by any means. The Black Panther Party was the most popular and influential organization during this period. Its members challenged the police's violent treatment of African Americans and engaged in many social programs to enhance Black lives.

One of the pivotal episodes during the 1960s and 1970s was the initiation of sit-ins. These activities presupposed resistance to support segregation in public places and transportation. During that period, with Jim Crow laws facilitating segregation, students became some of the most ardent participants of sit-ins to dismantle separate facilities. The first sit-in occurred in February 1960, when four African American students of North Carolina A&T College in Greensboro, North Carolina, sat in at the store's lunch counter, in disobedience of Jim Crow laws (Franklin, 2003). It was an inspiring decision, and many students followed the example, ready to sacrifice their lives for social justice. Thus, with the first sit-in, a new stage in the struggle for Black freedom in the United States began.

At the end of the 1950s and the beginning of the 1960s, Black activists attempted to desegregate various establishments and the public transportation system. Prior to the initiation of sit-ins in the 1960s, African American students undertook measures to ignite the spirit of freedom and equality. The first endeavors were unsuccessful, ending in the arrest of the participants. For instance, the arrest of some Florida A&M University students followed their refusal to move to the rear part of the bus (Franklin, 2003). Nevertheless, many of such sit-ins received support from church activists and other community members. What differentiated the 1950s and the 1960s protests was that the latter initiated a new phase in the struggle for freedom that involved both Black and White students.

Black women activists played a significant role in the movement for racial equality. One of the most compelling examples is the involvement of African American female students of Bennett College in the 1960 sit-in movement in Greensboro, North Carolina (Flowers, 2005). When the Supreme Court declared segregation in education illegal, Black students hoped they would receive better opportunities and freedoms in education and other spheres of life. However, when the expected changes did not occur, they created change for themselves. The women of Bennett College joined students from North Carolina A&T in protesting for equality by organizing sit-ins. Nearly 40% of Bennett College students were arrested during the sit-in movement for expressing their position (Flowers, 2005). Women arranged marches, sit-ins, and pickets to defend their right to social justice.

During the Black power movement, the Black studies movement emerged, which gave way to developing a separate scholarly discourse and developing into a separate academic discipline in subsequent decades. A prominent phase in the evolution of the Black studies movement was in 1968, when three critical events happened. The first was the occupation of the bursar's building of the Northwestern University for 40 hours, when 90 African American students demanded more efforts to recruit Black students, improved housing conditions, a more culturally inclusive curriculum, and enhanced student facilities (Fenderson, Stewart, & Baumgartner, 2011). Their goal, however, was putting an end to segregation, which was abolished de jure but de facto prevailed in the university. Introducing Black studies courses was another important goal.

The second significant event happened at Yale University in New Haven, Connecticut, just a few days from the previous one. On May 9 and 10, the Black Student Alliance arranged a two-day symposium called "Black Studies in the University" (Fenderson, Stewart, & Baumgartner, 2011). They invited university administrators, White educational power brokers, and Black activist scholars and named the event "educational experience for professional educators" (Fenderson, Stewart, & Baumgartner, 2011, p. 3). Although there were many objections to implementing Black studies among the participants, the symposium was a starting point for the future Black studies model.

The third event was the publication of the "Special Report on Student Unrest at Black Colleges" in *Jet*, the key magazine of Black society. Although the article covering Black students' revolt bore a less significant meaning than the previous two events, it was rather important due to attracting the public's attention to the increased political activity of African American students.

Student-led political activism continued into the 1970s and did not come without casualty. For example, in 1972, students at Southern University advocated for a better curriculum and more funding for students. One thousand students organized a peaceful sit-in at the administrative building and simultaneously asked for the release of students arrested from protesting the night before. The school president, George Leon Netterville, informed students he would advocate for the arrested protesters, but soon after, the national guard and police officers arrived at the school. Law enforcement killed Denver Smith and Leonard Brown in the chaos. Nevertheless, students requested better learning conditions, but they were not isolated from past protests at HBCUs or more recent demonstrations for racial equality (Aiello, 2012).

The increase in the political activity of African American students reflected both academic and social injustices. Two years before the Southern University killings, Jackson State University mourned the murders of Phillip Gibbs and James Earl Green. Historians credit the Jackson State University protest to the influence of Kent State's antiwar protest. This linkage, however, has distracted from the crux of the Jackson University protest, which led to the racial killings of Gibbs and Green (Chura, 2019). The murders of the Jackson State student and the 17-year-old occurred at the culmination of protests and miniriots that began in 1963. Black students protested law enforcement and racial harassment by White locals. These on-campus protests from 1963 until 1972 were a student-led response to social discrimination and the killings of Black political leaders of the time, such as Medgar Evers, Malcolm X, and Dr. King (Chura, 2019).

The aftermath of the desegregation protests involved far more than allowing Blacks to use the same facilities as Whites. There were other outcomes that ignited people's belief in the possibility of gaining equality and inspired them to pursue such a goal. Specifically, sit-ins inspired many people to oppose segregation, so HBCU students' actions had an effect on the entire country's life as well as their own (Biggs & Andrews, 2015). Protesters could disrupt the country's economic stability by interfering with the regular process of producing and distributing goods. By arranging protests, activists gained major changes at the state and federal policy levels. It is conceivable to conclude that HBCUs' initiation of the Black Power movement led to considerable positive changes in African Americans' civil rights protection.

HBCUs during the Afrocentric Movement (1980s–2000s)

The philosophy of Afrocentrism originated in the Temple University School of Scholars. The term *Afrocentricity* emerged in 1970 and became popularized in the 1980s (Chawane, 2016). The premise of the Afrocentric movement was that Black people should reclaim their pride and dignity through a connection to Africa as their homeland. Afrocentricity presupposes that Black people in America should have an African viewpoint. The supporters of this movement argued that by viewing themselves as central figures of their history, African Americans could inhabit their nation as participants and agents rather than being "marginal and on the periphery" of economic and political dimensions (Chawane, 2016, p. 78). The movement's viability became a key debate topic both among Black and White scholars of the time.

The concept of Afrocentricity had received many definitions depending on the scholars' focus and beliefs. Some considered Afrocentricity to be the approach in which African values and interests occupied the dominant position, and thus viewed it as a new historical perspective (Chawane, 2016). Others defined Afrocentricity as an intellectual movement emphasizing Africans' achievement and cultural heritage. One more approach was to view Afrocentricity as a metamorphosis of values and beliefs, signifying that African people should take pride in their contribution to civilization's development (Chawane, 2016). What was similar in these definitions was the focus on African culture's centrality. In the area of academia, Afrocentricity presupposed the theory, ideology, and method that educators should use to attain the needed change. In relation to the civil rights movement and other pivotal movements involving Black students, Afrocentrism served the function of explaining intellectual colonialism that had given way to the political and social oppression of African Americans.

Racial identity played a crucial role in establishing Black students' values and beliefs in the last few decades of the 20th century. A probable reason for such a connection was that the conceptualization of ethnic identity evolution occurred during African Americans' rebellious struggle for civil rights (Cokley, 2005). Although Afrocentric beliefs positively related to Black identity and internationalization attitudes, scholars admitted that it was not always possible to identify the conceptual divergences between ethnic and racial identity and Afrocentric values (Cokley, 2005). Thus, some researchers viewed the development of Afrocentrism as the revelation of a crisis in the intellectual evaluation of culture and race. Stanley Crouch (1995) referred to Afrocentrism as "another of the clever but essentially simple-minded hustles" (p. 77). The scholar argued that the Afrocentric approach had hardly any intellectual substance to offer, being a collection of discontinuous actions and ideals. However, despite some criticism, many historians considered the Afrocentric movement as a significant element of the civil rights movement.

In the 1980s through the 2000s, HBCUs became places where the ideas of Afrocentrism found their most prominent reflection. The Afrocentric movement focused on the bolstering of Black students' understanding of their cultural origin and heritage. Although its significance underwent some criticism, the movement played a vital role in shaping Black students' identity and increasing their dedication to the purpose of gaining social equality. Probably the most significant idea of the Afrocentric movement was that African Americans should receive favorable treatment not only because of their humanity but also because of their contributions to the development of civilizations. Slavery and other crucial though negative social processes started before the initiation of the United States as an independent country. Hence, the advocates of Afrocentricity emphasized the value of Black intellectual and spiritual functions in the United States. HBCUs played a prominent role in establishing the Afrocentric movement. Students who had always been the moving power of social movements actively participated in the establishment of Afrocentrism.

One important factor in integrating Afrocentrism and student life was hip-hop music. HBCUs and hip-hop culture are inextricably linked, and hip-hop in the 1980s and 90s was a vehicle for self-expression and burgeoning nationalism (Decker, 1993). Analysis by journalism students at the University of Maryland Philip Merrill College of Journalism revealed that in the 1980s and 1990s, many of the songs that topped the hip-hop charts had plain political themes (O'Connor, 2018). In addition, a variety of socially engaged acts gave hip-hop listeners at HBCUs multiple entry points to pro-Black thought.

Afrocentric scholars brought prominence to Africana studies at HBCUs. Gregory Carr at Howard University, Kobi Kambon of Florida Agricultural and Mechanical University, and Imari Obadele at Prairie View A&M University were influential professors who lent their expertise at Black colleges. While most Africana studies programs in the United States are at primarily White institutions, Black perspectives influenced departments throughout Black universities (Challenor, 2002). This focus on Black and African studies helped provide HBCU students with historical and theoretical grounding for their movements.

The Black Lives Matter Movement (2010s–Present)

With the advancement of technology and Internet access, modern social movements can engage more participants and spread information about their plans and achievements to vast numbers of people. Because of these technological advancements and the extensive spread of information, there has been a 10% increase in HBCU enrollment since 2013 (Gasman, 2013). The increase in HBCU enrollment happened in the wake of the murder of Trayvon Martin and the creation of the Black Lives Matter movement.

The most prominent movement to focus on African Americans' fight for equality started in 2013 with the Twitter hashtag #BlackLivesMatter. It emerged after a White man, George Zimmerman, was not prosecuted for murdering a Black teenager, Trayvon Martin, in Florida (Banks, 2018). Although Martin was unarmed, his murderer was acquitted, which raised a wave of protests from the African American community. Media reflected nonviolent demonstrations by Black Lives Matter activists as violent riots and referred to the group as racist and "anti-law enforcement" (Banks, 2018, p. 709). However, the righteousness of the motives that aroused Black people's quest to gain justice and the desire to thrive in Black spaces is palpable.

Being a grassroots organization, Black Lives Matter evolved from a hashtag into a complex network with about 30 branches in the United States and worldwide. The movement employs strategies favored by the civil rights movement activists and focuses on nonviolent action to draw the public's attention to police abuse and the killings of Black people (Clayton, 2018). In addition, the Black Lives Matter movement pursues goals similar to those important to activists in previous decades resisting systematic oppression and racism (Clayton, 2018). Despite a long history of civil rights activism, the Black Lives Matter movement remains necessary, since many inequality problems were not resolved during previous movements.

Black Lives Matter started in 2013, but it gained the pinnacle of its development in 2014 after a Black teenager, Michael Brown, was killed by a white police officer, Darren Wilson. The growing number of similar cases of unjustified violence against unarmed African Americans led to the bolstering of the movements' activists' ideas about the need to defend their cause (Banks, 2018). After Trayvon Martin's murder, three women, Alicia Garza, Opal Tometi, and Patrisse Cullors, created Tumblr and Twitter accounts for the movement, where they encouraged users to share the hashtag "BlackLivesMatter" (Banks, 2018). The initial tweets reflected the impetus for the movement's initiation; the women considered that Black liberation actions in the United States focused on heterosexual and cis-gendered men and paid little attention to women and the LGBTQ community. The Black Lives Matter movement concentrates on inequality and aims at increasing the level of inclusiveness for all African American individuals.

Critics of the Black Lives Matter movement and other young millennial organizers have suggested that young activists are too oppositional, particularly in response to left-leaning or democratic legislators. In 2015, protesters were criticized for interrupting Hillary Clinton at a rally held at Clark Atlanta University during her second presidential campaign. The presence of the late Representative John Lewis, a legendary figure from the midcentury civil rights movement, evoked a contrast in approach between the 1960s and the 21st century. Representative Lewis was seen attempting to speak to the young protesters, apparently on Clinton's behalf, as he had introduced her at the event (Williams & Lowery, 2015). This development led CNN anchor Don Lemon to admonish the students, saying on-air,

"If you don't respect him (Rep. John Lewis), who asks you to have some manners at least and listen to Secretary Clinton, then I don't know who you will listen to" (Darcy, 2020). He added, "Listen, I know Black Lives Matter was formed out of anger. But now they are at the table. And their tactics need to change. . . . They need to grow up and start listening."

Dewey Clayton (2018) describes two key differences between the civil rights movement and the tactics enacted by Black Lives Matter (BLM). The first is that while the 1960s featured a few central male leaders, BLM leadership is more diffuse, in part with the help of social media. Second, respectability, or alignment with middle-class values, was a prominent aspect of midcentury activism. During the civil rights movement, demonstrators were encouraged to wear "Sunday's best" attire for protests and to conduct themselves with respectable decorum. In addition, young protestors underwent training to learn how to resist the urge to lash out at law enforcement or hostile bystanders. This structure stands in stark contrast to young people protesting in the 2010s, who have been condemned for their dress and presentation. For example, one op-ed by a former civil rights protester, published in *The Washington Post*, castigated youth protesters for their sagging pants and use of profanity (Reynolds, 2015).

One thing that seems to remain consistent is HBCUs' status as a refuge for Black students. During more transparent expressions of hate facilitated by the Trump White House, enrollment at HBCUs rose as students sought safe haven. Breanna Edwards (2019) noted, "The most recent federal data shows that in fall 2017, enrollment into these historical Black universities and colleges was up to 298,138, a 2.1% increase from 2016, an increase that came although enrollment has continued to decline across all US colleges and universities" (p.1). Students interviewed by the Black publication *Essence* expressed concern for their comfortability that factored into their school choice (Edwards, 2019).

Since HBCUs continue to have a significant effect on students' identity development, it is necessary to understand the care-related reasons for young people's choices of educational establishments. According to Debbie Van Camp, Jamie Barden, and Lloyd Sloan (2009), the less racial centrality and contact, the more likely that Black students will join care-oriented clubs to promote racial identity. Therefore, it is viable to assume that for many young people the formation of identity, which later finds reflection in distinct movements, likely occurs at HBCUs. Since the Black Lives Matter movement originated among youth, it is possible to draw connections between the movement's start and HBCUs' cultivation of racial identity.

Summary and Conclusions

HBCUs may have started as institutions for meeting Black students' educational needs, but they have become much more than that. Established in the period following the Civil War and until 1964, these colleges and universities have not been limited to opportunities for Black students to get an education. They enrich African Americans' knowledge of their own culture and identity, enhance their understanding of their race's significance, and bolster their self-pride. They have given the world many ardent activists of social movements who were not afraid to sacrifice their lives for the sake of other people's freedom. Many of the active participants of the New Negro movement, the civil rights movement, the Black Power movement, the Black studies movement, and the Afrocentric movement were HBCU students. Although at present, there is better access to education for Black students, the politics of HBCUs still inspire modern youth to arrange protests and defend their compatriots' right to life and equality. The Black Lives Matter movement is an excellent example of such inspiration.

HBCUs need to reconsider some of their practices to comply with modern political and social processes. For instance, these institutions should reimagine the capacity of their campus environments to interrupt marginalizing actions and respect other socially disenfranchised groups (Njoku, Butler, & Beatty, 2017). In addition, HBCUs should add research to their agenda, since this dimension is currently underrepresented in their mission statements (Stevenson, 2007). However, even despite some criticism and failures, it is an undisputed fact that HBCUs have played a significant role in forming many generations of Black activists. The latter include civil rights defenders and leaders of their ethnicity who inspire the many minds of people of African American descent and other origins. The beneficial effect of HBCUs' functioning is evident through the achievements in the civil rights sphere and the improved position of the African American population in the United States.

References

Aiello, T. (2012). Violence is a classroom: The 1972 Grambling and Southern riots and the trajectory of Black student protest. *Louisiana History: The Journal of the Louisiana Historical Association, 53*(3), 261–291.

Arroyo, A., & Gasman, M. (2014). An HBCU-based educational approach for black college student success: Toward a framework with implications for all institutions. *American Journal of Education, 121*(1), 57–85.

Banks, C. (2018). Disciplining black activism: Post-racial rhetoric, public memory and decorum in news media framing of the Black Lives Matter movement. *Continuum: Journal of Media & Cultural Studies, 32*(6), 709–720. doi:10.1080/10304312.2018.1525920

Barrett, S. R. (2017). "We bring thee our laurels whatever they may be": A concise history of morgan state college student-led protest (Order No. 10639164). Available from ProQuest Dissertations and Theses Global; Social Science Premium Collection (2007561351). Retrieved from https://login.ezproxy.lib.utah.edu/login?url=https://www.proquest.com/dissertations-theses/we-bring-thee-our-laurels-whatever-they-may-be/docview/2007561351/se-2

Biggs, M., & Andrews, K. T. (2015). Protest campaigns and movement success: Desegregating the US South in the early 1960s. *American Sociological Review, 80*(2), 416–443. doi: 10.1177/0003122415574328

Challenor, H. (2002). African Studies at historically Black colleges and universities. *African Issues, 30*(2), 24–29. doi:10.2307/1535085

Chawane, M. (2016). The development of Afrocentricity: A historical survey. *Yesterday & Today* (16), 78–99.

Clayton, D. M. (2018). Black Lives Matter and the civil rights movement: A comparative analysis of two social movements in the United States. *Journal of Black Studies, 49*(5), 448–480. doi:10.1177/0021934718764099

Closson, R. B., & Henry, W. J. (2008). Racial and ethnic diversity at HBCUs: What can be learned when whites are in the minority?*Multicultural Education, 15*(4), 15–19.

Cokley, K. O. (2005). Racial(ized) identity, ethnic identity, and Afrocentric values: Conceptual and methodological challenges in understanding African American identity. *Journal of Counseling Psychology, 52*(4), 517–526.

Craig, L. A. (1992). "Raising among themselves": Black educational advancement and the Morrill Act of 1890. *Agriculture and Human Values, 9*(1), 31–37.

Crewe, S. E. (2017). Education with intent—the HBCU experience. *Journal of Human Behavior in the Social Environment, 27*(5), 360–366. doi:10.1080/10911359.2017.1318622

Crouch, S. (1995). The Afrocentric hustle. *The Journal of Blacks in Higher Education* (10), 77–82. doi:10.2307/2962771

Darcy, O. (2020, June 18). CNN host Don Lemon gives stern five-word piece of advice to Black Lives Matter Movement. *TheBlaze*. https://www.theblaze.com/news/2015/10/30/cnn-host-don-lemon-gives-stern-five-word-piece-of-advice-to-black-lives-matter-movement

Decker, J. (1993). The state of rap: Time and place in hip hop nationalism. *Social Text* (34), 53–84. doi:10.2307/466354

Dodson, H. (2016). Howard University, the New Negro movement, and the making of African American visual arts in Washington, DC: Part 1. *Callaloo, 39*(5), 983–998. doi:10.1353/cal.2016.0138

Douglas, T.-R. M. O. (2012). HBCUs as sites of resistance: The malignity of materialism, Western masculinity, and spiritual malefaction. *The Urban Review, 44*(3), 378–400. doi:10.1007/s11256-012-0198-1

Edwards, B. (2019). HBCU enrollment on the rise amid increasing racial tensions. *Essence*. Retrieved from https://www.essence.com/news/hbcu-enrollment-on-the-rise-amid-increasing-tensions/

Fenderson, J., Stewart, J., & Baumgartner, K. (2011). Expanding the history of the Black studies movement: Some prefatory notes. *Journal of African American Studies, 16*(1), 1–20. doi:10.1007/s12111-011-9200-3

Flowers, D. B. (2005). The launching of the student sit-in movement: The role of black women at Bennett College. *Journal of African American History, 90*(1/2), 52–63.

Franklin, V. P. (2003). Patterns of student activism at historically black universities in the United States and South Africa, 1960–1977. *The Journal of African American History, 88*(2), 204–217. doi:10.2307/3559066

Gasman, M. (2013). The changing face of historically black colleges and universities. *Penn Graduate School of Education*. Retrieved from https://repository.upenn.edu/cgi/viewcontent.cgi?article=1396&context=gse_pubs

Gasman, M., Spencer, D., & Orphan, C. (2015). "Building bridges, not fences": A history of civic engagement at private black colleges and universities, 1944–1965. *History of Education Quarterly, 55*(3), 346–379. doi:10.1111/hoeq.12125

Harper, S. R., Patton, L. D., & Wooden, O. A. (2009). Access and equity for African American students in higher education: A critical race historical analysis of policy efforts. *Journal of Higher Education, 80*(4), 389–414.

Hope, E. C., Keels, M., & Durkee, M. I. (2016). Participation in Black Lives Matter and deferred action for childhood arrivals: Modern activism among Black and Latino college students. *Journal of Diversity in Higher Education, 9*(3), 203–215.

Jean-Marie, G. (2006). Welcoming the unwelcome: A social justice imperative of African-American female leaders at historically black colleges and universities. *Educational Foundations, 20*(1), 85–104.

Jensen, K. E. (2017). Pedagogical personalism at Morehouse College. *Studies in Philosophy and Education, 36*(2), 147–165.

Lamon, L. C. (1974). The Black community in Nashville and the Fisk University student strike of 1924–1925. *The Journal of Southern History, 40*(2), 225–244.

Njoku, N., Butler, M., & Beatty, C. C. (2017). Reimagining the historically Black college and university (HBCU) environment: Exposing race secrets and the binding chains of respectability and othermothering. *International Journal of Qualitative Studies in Education, 30*(8), 783–799. doi:10.1080/09518398.2017.1350297

O'Connor, A. (2018) The evolution of conscious hip-hop. *Capital News Service*. Retrieved from https://cnsmaryland.org/interactives/fall-2018/rap-politics/index.html

Reynolds, B. (2015, August 24). I was a civil rights activist in the 1960s. But it's hard for me to get behind Black Lives Matter. *The Washington Post*. Retrieved from https://www.washingtonpost.com/posteverything/wp/2015/08/24/i-was-a-civil-rights-activist-in-the-1960s-but-its-hard-for-me-to-get-behind-black-lives-matter

Rogers, I. H. (2010). *The black campus movement: An afrocentric narrative history of the struggle to diversify higher education, 1965–1972*. Temple University.

Stevenson, J. M. (2007). From founding purpose to future positioning: Why historically black colleges and universities must maintain but modify mission. *Jackson State University Researcher, 21*(3), 99–102.

Toldson, I. A. (2014). 60 years after *Brown v. Board of Education*: The Impact of the Congressional Black Caucus on the education of Black people in the United States of America (Editor's Commentary). *The Journal of Negro Education, 83*(3), 194–198. https://doi.org/10.7709/jnegroeducation.83.3.0194

Van Camp, D., Barden, J., & Sloan, L. R. (2009). Predictors of Black students' race-related reasons for choosing an HBCU and intentions to engage in racial identity—Relevant behaviors. *Journal of Black Psychology, 36*(2), 226–250. doi:10.1177/0095798409344082

Williams, V., & Lowery, W. (2015). Black Lives Matter protesters attempt to interrupt Clinton speech in Atlanta. *The Washington Post*. Retrieved from https://www.washingtonpost.com/news/post-politics/wp/2015/10/30/black-lives-matter-protesters-attempt-to-interrupt-clinton-speech-in-atlanta/

Williamson, J. A. (2004). "This has been quite a year for heads falling": Institutional autonomy in the civil rights era. *History of Education Quarterly, 44*(4), 554–576.

Chapter 11

Exploring the Latinx-Servingness of Faculty at Hispanic-Serving Institutions

CHERYL CHING

Over the past two decades, the population of Latinx college students in the United States has more than doubled, from 1.4 million in 2000 to 3.4 million in 2018 (Hussar et al., 2020). This demographic trend is paralleled by a growing number of Hispanic-serving institutions (HSIs). HSIs are federally designated, degree-granting public or private not-for-profit colleges and universities with undergraduate, full-time equivalent enrollments of at least 25% Latinx students. According to *Excelencia* in Education (2020), there were 280 HSIs in 2008; by 2018, that figure rose to 539, an increase of 93%. With 17% of US higher education institutions currently designated as HSIs and two-thirds of all Latinx undergraduates enrolled in HSIs (*Excelencia* in Education, 2020), the question of what it means to be a "Hispanic-serving institution" is critically important.

According to those who study in HSIs, *enrolling* Latinx students is not tantamount to *serving* them (Contreras, Malcom, & Bensimon, 2008; G. Garcia, 2017). The distinction between Latinx-enrolling and Latinx-serving HSIs has motivated a body of scholarship that seeks to understand how HSIs foster the educational experiences, outcomes, and successes of Latinx students. To date, the evidence is mixed, with research suggesting positive (e.g., Cuellar, 2014), negative (e.g., Contreras, Malcom, & Bensimon, 2008), and neutral (e.g., Fosnacht & Nailos, 2016) benefits for Latinx students at

HSIs, relative to non-HSIs. Some research has focused on achieving equity in academic outcomes such as retention and graduation for Latinx students as a metric for "Latinx-servingness" (e.g., Contreras, Malcom, & Bensimon, 2008). Other research has proposed that HSIs must advance equity in nonacademic outcomes such as academic self-concept (Cuellar, 2014). And still others have stated that we must cultivate campus cultures and structures that resist the racialization of Latinx students and instead reflect, be responsive to, and validate them (e.g., G. Garcia, 2017). Based on a systematic review of HSI scholarship, Garcia, Núñez, and Sansone (2019) argue that Latinx-servingness is a multidimensional concept premised on equitable outcomes (academic, nonacademic) and experiences (validating, racialized), as well as on having the organizational structures (e.g., hiring practices, curriculum, pedagogy) and capacity to mine academic student needs.

Ultimately, Latinx-servingness matters at HSIs, primarily since so few originated with the express purpose of educating Latinx students; instead, most are predominately white institutions (PWIs) that evolved into HSIs as their student population became compositionally more Latinx (Contreras, Malcom, & Bensimon, 2008). For some, this outcome could be the result of intentional efforts to recruit and retain Latinx students. For others, geography is the primary driver; as the proportion of Latinx people in the communities in which they are located increased, so did the proportion of Latinx students on their campuses. Either way, as Frances Contreras, Lindsey Malcom, and Estela Bensimon (2008) observe, HSIs have a "manufactured identity that is highly variable," "unplanned," and "unstable" (p. 74). They differ from historically Black colleges and universities (HBCUs) and tribal colleges and universities (TCUs), founded for Black and Native American students, respectively, and remain committed to these students' advancement. For HSIs, then, being Latinx-serving is not a given (G. A. Garcia, 2019). With most being PWIs that crossed the enrollment threshold of 25% Latinx for one reason or another, the only guarantee is that these institutions are eligible to apply for grants from the Hispanic-Serving Institutions Division of the US Department of Education. Whether HSIs create and enact a Latinx-serving culture and how they go about doing so will likely depend on the commitments and actions of the practitioners they employ. What practices do they enact? What programs do they develop? What structures and policies do they implement? What ideas and frameworks do they use to guide their work? Moreover, in what ways do efforts center the needs and affirm the potential of Latinx students, if at all?

In this chapter, I present an exploratory study of practitioners who have a hand in shaping Latinx-servingness at HSIs: faculty. My focus on faculty is premised on several observations from the extant scholarship. First, research has consistently shown that faculty influence the achievement, learning, development, and sense of belonging of students in general (Hurtado & Carter, 1997; Pascarella & Terenzini, 2005) and Latinx students in particular (Cole & Espinoza, 2008; Einarson & Clarkberg, 2010; Lundberg & Schreiner, 2004). Second, while Latinx students at HSIs desire faculty who express interest in them, understand Latinx culture, and use asset-based, culturally relevant, and validating approaches (Garcia & Okhidoi, 2015; Maestas, Vaquera, & Zehr, 2007; Medina & Posadas, 2012), they routinely confront those who do not exhibit these characteristics (Dayton et al., 2004; Gooden & Martin, 2014). Third, the variability in how faculty support Latinx students could partly stem from when faculty arrived at HSIs and why they teach there. Finally, faculty who achieve tenure tend to stay. Therefore, many professors may have arrived before their institution became an HSI (Dowd et al., 2013). As such, their practices could be more suited to white than to Latinx students. Moreover, the decision to join the faculty at an HSI may have nothing to do with an institution being an HSI. Instead, the decision could turn on factors such as needing a job or being attracted to another institutional identity, such as a community college or research university (Hurtado & Ruiz, 2012). This factor contrasts with faculty at HBCUs, many of whom are committed to the education of Black students (Greene & Oesterreich, 2012).

Prior scholarship suggests that what faculty think and how they approach their commitments to Latinx students can affect whether and in what ways Latinx-servingness is enacted at an HSI. Building on this idea, I examined what ten faculty at two exemplary four-year HSIs—Southeastern University (SEU) and Western University (WU), both pseudonyms—do to support Latinx students and what informs the thinking and motivation behind their actions. I focused on how they (1) describe their role in educating and supporting Latinx students, (2) articulate what they have done and are willing to do on these students' behalf, and (3) frame the "why" of their actions. The data for my analysis came from interviews conducted for a more extensive study on how HSIs advance the access and success of Latinx students in science, technology, engineering, and mathematics (STEM). A detailed discussion of the original study's methods, including the sampling procedures, can be found in Estela Bensimon et al. (2019) and Dowd et al. (2010). The HSIs were exemplary on two dimensions: (1) having a solid track record in graduating Latinx students with STEM degrees, and (2) having policies, programs, and practices that benefit Latinx students and other groups underrepresented in STEM. The faculty were chosen based on two reputational factors: (1) they were known to go above and beyond for Latinx students, and (2) they were considered to be "in the know" about their institution's Latinx-serving efforts. While most were STEM faculty, the sample also included professors of education, English, and psychology. Only two faculty members were female, both Latina; the male participants included three Latino and five white faculty members. When the interviews took place, three-quarters of the faculty had been at their institutions for at least a decade, ranging from three to 40 years. Several were in administrative positions at the time of data collection, ran programs at the universities, and were faculty. In what follows, I first describe the context and structures of Latinx-servingness at the two HSIs to situate what faculty do to support Latinx students.

Contexts and Structures of Servingness at Southeastern University and Western University

While located in different states, SEU and WU are in cities in agricultural regions with significant Latinx populations. Both are the go-to four-year state institutions in their areas, whether for students who matriculate directly from high school or transfer from a neighboring community college. As a participant from WU stated, "We are really important in this community because we are the only university here." In interviews, faculty shared how their institutions are committed to serving their communities, for example, by maintaining—and repairing when needed—relationships with local high schools and community colleges. This partnership is done by collaborating with school and county districts on grant opportunities and initiatives and bringing parents, families, and students to campus for programs and celebrations. Although Latinx students comprised the largest racial/ethnic group for both, the proportions differed, with SEU being roughly 90% Latinx and WU approximately 40% Latinx at the time of data collection. At the faculty level, SEU and WU were both overwhelmingly white.

Garcia, Núñez, and Sansone (2019) propose that one dimension of Latinx-servingness is what they call "structures of serving," which encompass a range of policies, procedures, and practices that HSIs use to enhance institutional capacity to respond to the needs of Latinx students and foster their success. These structures include:

- diversity and strategic plans that prioritize Latinx students
- hiring practices that increase the compositional diversity of practitioners
- curricula and pedagogical approaches that are culturally relevant and asset-based for Latinx-students
- cocurricular programs for Latinx and other minoritized students
- initiatives that strengthen engagement with the Latinx community
- decision-making processes that center Latinx needs

In the interviews, the faculty described several such structures at their institutions. For example, SEU (1) sponsors a week-long conference that aims to attract Latinx students from the region into STEM fields; (2) holds a "Latina day" for Latina students and their mothers that features Latina speakers who have "made it big"; (3) opens the campus up to the community for a Saturday of celebration; and (4) recruits faculty who have "fire in their belly to teach" and who routinely involve Latinx students in research and publication opportunities. Similar structures existed at WU. In addition, participants spoke of (1) open houses in which they engaged the parents of prospective Latinx students; (2) colleagues who "are attuned with Hispanic culture" even if they are not Latinx and "go that extra mile"; and (3) using their HSI grant to smooth the transfer pathway from the local community college where many Latinx students start their college educations. They also spoke of senior administrators who have (1) worked to improve college-going in the region, (2) focused on diversifying the racial/ethnic makeup of campus leaders, and (3) directed resources toward a new student recreational center despite faculty objection and budget cuts because it was what students desired and what Latinx students in particular needed.

Faculty Acts of Servingness

While a good portion of the interviews focused on programmatic and institutional-level efforts to advance Latinx students in STEM, there were ample moments when the ten faculty spoke about their individual-level actions. They recalled specific Latinx students they helped, mused about why Latinx students need support, and described their background and experiences. This insight offers a hint as to why they approach teaching, mentoring, and relationship-building with Latinx students in the ways that they do. For example, Jim (all names are pseudonyms), a white professor of English at WU, spoke of a Latina student he spent 20 minutes with prior to the interview. This Latina was a straight-A student who was the first in her family to go to college and whose parents he had met. Jim said, "It's important for me for someone like that to succeed." Although he did not explain why this particular Latina's success is critical to him, Jim offered insights into his thinking at several points during the interview. In his mind, some of the Latinx students in his courses are among "the brightest in our county." Many, however, are first-generation college students and may not fully grasp the opportunities available to them, may find higher education "an alien experience," and may not "see themselves as special as we do." Many have to work to support their families by taking on jobs that undercut their focus on being full-time students. These ideas undergird Jim's efforts to (1) follow up with students if they are not doing well in class, (2) hold extra office hours, (3) provide students his home and mobile phone numbers, (4) connect students with campuses resources, (5) speak with them about nonacademic matters such as balancing school work and their jobs, and (6) involve himself in a wide range of cocurricular activities. They push him to make the college experience for Latinx students life-changing, as his own was decades earlier. They result in him making statements such as, "This is my life. This is what I do."

Examined at a microersonal level, Jim's thoughts, motivations, and actions are unique; what and why he does what he does stems from his particular complex of experiences, tendencies, and ways of looking at and understanding the world. Indeed, this can be said of every one of the other nine participants. At the same time, taking a few steps back from their cases, I detected patterns in the Latinx-focused actions they reported, even as the thinking and motivations behind these actions varied. These actions generally were from faculty helping Latinx students navigate two arenas: college generally and STEM specifically. With the latter, participants also worked with others outside their universities, often through outreach programs and in conversations with prospective employers, to broaden opportunities and establish better supports for Latinx students.

NAVIGATING COLLEGE

For most participants, helping Latinx students make sense of college was a routine act of servingness. Specifically, the faculty helped Latinx students navigate the academic (e.g., course taking) and nonacademic (e.g., relationships with faculty) dimensions of college life. In several cases, this support required careful negotiation between students' first-generation college status and the need to work on the one hand, and the norms of academia, on the other. For example, Sofia, a Latina professor of psychology at WU, saw herself as an academic parent—as she said, "I feel like I'm their mom and dad"—who is proactive in mentoring Latinx students. Similar to Jim, she noted that the majority of students who attend WU, across race/ethnicity, are the first in their families to attend college. Consequently, many of them do not have family members with the experiences to help them navigate postsecondary education. Of Latinx students in particular she said that parents are supportive of their children's higher education goals, "but there's no knowledge. What do you do in your first year of college? How do you get into graduate school? What was it like for mom and dad? They are very supportive, but they don't have a clue." Unlike Jim, who is motivated by memories of his life-changing college experience, Sophia's actions are informed by her experience as a first-generation Latina college student. Her parents were supportive of her educational pursuits and proud that she earned a doctorate, but they had little understanding of what this achievement entailed and what it means to be a researcher and a professor. Sofia's acts of guidance are further informed by a difference she has detected between her first-generation white and Latinx students.

White students "don't have a problem demanding this is what I need and I need it now" and "seem to have picked up on you're here for me," she said. With Latinx students, she explained, "I have to ask them. I have to train them to ask." Sofia did not elaborate on why she thinks white students behave in this way. However, she offered that the behavior of Latinx students has to do with culture: "It's the culture of you don't make any waves. You don't cause any trouble. You don't go in and ask for things. . . . Hispanics are collectivistic. It's good for the group. You're not going to make any waves."

Like Sofia, Lara, a Latina professor of education at SEU, takes on the task of training—or in her words, "coaching"—Latinx students on how to engage with professors. She is known as someone who understands and listens to Latinx students, especially when they have challenges with faculty. Lara does not resolve these challenges directly but instead helps students figure out what to do. Students, she explained, are sometimes too passive, potentially fearful of the faculty, or, in the other extreme, too aggressive. For those who are passive, she helps them see why it is crucial to speak to their professors about the issues they are facing in the course; for those who are aggressive, she helps them communicate in ways that are "assertive" and "takes responsibility for what they're saying." She brainstorms with students about what their message should be, has them write down what they will say, and encourages them to practice their speech before meeting with their professor. In Lara's mind, this situation is one of the students not knowing how and not being taught how to engage the faculty. As she explained, "So, that's why someone like me in this position can understand that and does not see that as a deficit, but sees it as, 'I just need to teach you how.' " To Lara, "someone like me" is a person who was instilled with a strong sense of ethnic identity and culture, who has never felt "inferior because I was Hispanic," and who was raised by parents who prioritized education for their daughters so that they could take care of themselves. This personal history underlies Lara's approach with Latinx students and the belief that they can resolve their problems with a bit of help and coaching from someone who understands who they are.

Most Latinx students in the study were first-generation college students. So, the notion that family is a significant part of their lives and culture resonated across the interviews. For the most part, the family was seen as challenging student progression and success in college because of the financial and caretaking responsibilities they had to shoulder. Jim, for instance, shared how he often has "long talks" with students about the number of hours they work outside of school. If the number is high—say, 30 hours—and the student is attending WU full-time, Jim tells the student that it is "time to talk to mom and dad and come to some agreement on this." While this guidance makes practical sense and is a solution to the problem of working too many hours, it cuts against the commitment to family. According to Sofia and Lara, faculty need to understand that family is, in effect, a nonnegotiable. "Family definitely comes first," Sofia said. "I can't knock them for taking care of the family." Armando, a Latino professor of physics and dean of science and engineering at WU, shared Sofia's and Lara's sentiments. He recalled a Latino student who worked at his parents' accounting firm while attending school. Unfortunately, the student was not doing well nor progressing academically, and for this reason, he landed in

Armando's office. In contrast to Jim, who counsels students to explain to their parents that they cannot work so many hours, Armando recognized that such an approach is "almost like advising them to be against their family." Thus with the student, Armando emphasized that focusing on college is not only about advancing his personal goal of becoming a doctor but also about what he "can do for [his] family in the long term." Armando advised the student to reduce his coursework, "to just take one class and get an A," and then to "take two classes, and you get two A's." The student took Armando's advice, which "motivated him to see that he could succeed" while maintaining his family commitments.

Navigating STEM

As the original study focused on STEM, the faculty spoke extensively about it and about their efforts to promote Latinx success in these fields. Like participants' guidance on navigating college, their guidance around STEM also touched on academic and nonacademic matters. For Thomas, a white professor of chemistry at WU, one area of advice is on course taking. As chemistry courses build on one another, grasping the material in previous courses is key to success in subsequent ones. Unfortunately, this piece of information is not always apparent to students. So, Thomas strives to make this clear and help students reconcile their desire to finish their degree as quickly as possible because of college costs. He asks questions such as "Do you want to take these courses and not do well and risk having to take even more time or risk in fact completely giving up on your dreams?" and "Do you just want to get through here as quickly as possible and have a piece of paper at the end or do you actually do well?" Admittedly, this kind of questioning has worked with some students but not all.

Thomas's actions benefit students who are already in a STEM major. However, at both SEU and WU, participants cited two precollege barriers that could stymie interest in STEM without guidance and intervention: family and K–12 schooling. Again, Latinx students' first-generation college status factored in participant thinking. For instance, Nathan, a white professor of geology at WU, said, "They come from a background where, you know, their parents probably didn't go to college. So, what does a physicist do, or a chemist, or even a biologist for that matter, or a geologist? So, I think that's probably the biggest barrier." The Latina and Latino faculty echoed this idea, stating a lack of Latinx role models and representation in STEM, with Lara and Sofia underscoring the even more limited representation of

Latinas. Lara noted that at SEU, there are only three Latina STEM faculty, a fact that can discourage Latinas from aspiring to STEM majors and careers "because they don't see anybody who is in those fields." The second barrier that participants referenced had to do with the extent to which the sciences are taught well in elementary, middle, and high schools. Several faculty commented that K–12 teachers might not have sufficient training in STEM to make the subjects come alive for students. In contrast, others added that the culture of testing has resulted in limited science curricula at the secondary level.

Several participants spoke extensively about efforts to address these barriers. This work involved outreach to middle and high schools and parents, often within the context of an outreach program. For example, Elliot, a white professor of education at WU, was involved in a partnership between the university and local school district that brought racially minoritized students in the sixth grade to campus for a day of science. Elliot also consults on improving science education with other school districts that serve a large Latinx population. At WU, Armando has visited high schools and engaged leaders in building stronger STEM programs. During a visit to one of the largest high schools in the district, he observed, "I see there is no sense of STEM, period. . . . It's not that they don't have the classes and a staff, but it's not up to the level that it needs to be and promoted." Making sure not to focus on the deficits he perceived in the school's science curriculum and teachers, he framed the conversation with the principal around opportunity and whether the education students receive will enable them to have real choices about the careers they can pursue in the future. Armando has also spoken with Latinx parents about their children pursuing a STEM degree. In talking with them, he has heard responses such as, "My kid is smart, but not smart enough to go into these high-difficult fields." For Armando, this is a misconception that comes from parents not understanding the richness of STEM and from not knowing people who work in these fields. As a result, he has focused on providing information about STEM to the Latinx community through one-on-one conversations and events such as "parents night" at the university, which he believes is "the number one way to empower them to make decisions for themselves."

In addition to the kind of outreach that Elliot and Armando have done, participants' perceptions of the barriers facing Latinx students in STEM have propelled those running research labs to actively recruit Latinx students. The clearest example was Sofia, who recalled a Latino student who was clearly "picking up on key things" but sat in the back of the classroom, never made eye contact, and did not participate. She invited him to join her lab, where she works with students one-on-one, providing them with holistic support that fosters a sense of belonging in STEM. Attending to "the little things that other students at other universities take for granted," her work is not only about training students how to research. She also helps them study for a class, manage time, balance academic and personal responsibilities, prepare and print a poster for a presentation, hone speaking skills, and write a personal statement for graduate school.

Moreover, she wants to understand the lack of self-esteem and confidence she notices in her Latinx students. Some of them "don't even know how to give eye contact," and others continue to question their ability even when they are at the point of applying to graduate programs. Thus, providing ongoing positive reinforcement and affirmation is critical. As she shared, "I don't know how many times I had to bring [students] in and talk about not about the research, but about I am so proud of you. Look at where you've come. You can do it. . . . They really need the reinforcement from somebody."

A final set of participant actions focused on the futures of Latinx students beyond their time at the university. In some cases, these efforts entailed participants helping students balance graduate education and career options with personal and family considerations. In other cases, they involved participants assisting prospective employers to make sense of who Latinx students are, what they need, and what assets they will bring to the job. As an example of the former, Elliot at WU shared that he has struggled to get Latinx students who excel academically to plan and consider a five- or ten-year plan for their future. "Sometimes it's really hard to get them to think about the value of continuing their education for the long-term payoff," he explained, when faced with the option of a job that could earn them "$40,000 a year next year" as a secretary—knowing that such a salary is a "carrot" that is hard to pass up given the need of many Latinx students to support their families financially. Elliot maintains that if students show potential in math or science, they should become doctors, not secretaries. He routinely speaks with students about career options and what it means to finish their bachelor's and possibly pursue a master's degree for a "better payoff and a higher quality of life down the road."

According to some participants, part of the challenge with Latinx students pursuing further opportunities in STEM has to do with a hesitancy to leave their families and the local community. As Armando said, "For them, you know, moving 5 miles is a long distance, and parents also do not like to get rid of their kids." He added that finding the right opportunities in STEM typically necessitates moving around the country. Lara acknowledged that reluctance to leave the community is an issue with Latinx students; however, she added that going elsewhere could also mean trading "an environment that is so caring, so warm, so supportive" for one of loneliness and isolation. Undergirding Lara's point is the experience of valedictorians from local high schools who go to Harvard or Yale, face "culture shock," and return after a semester. In her mind, Latinx students not wanting to leave is "not necessarily the whole story." Lara's SEU colleague Oliver, a white professor of physics and dean of science and engineering, operates from a similar perspective, one that was instilled after a "straight A" Latino physics major came back from a summer internship elsewhere in the state and returned a "C or D student." Oliver learned that the student could not meet his boss' expectations, which "devastated" him. This student's experience is one of several he shared during the interview that has convinced him that as much as Latinx students need coaching on navigating college and STEM successfully, the employers who want to hire them also need to be coached. Oliver explained,

> I just had several meetings with [company name] in [city], and they say, will the kids from the [region where SEU is located] leave the [region]? And I say darn right they will, but you got to provide a support system there. I want you to hire at least two. Financial barriers are the biggest barriers our kids face. I want you to give 'em some travel money upfront. And I want you to help 'em find a place to live. Ideally, put 'em with an employee family. If they're Hispanic, that's even better, but any family will work so that they can have a big brother, big sister to kinda take care of 'em and mentor 'em a little bit and tell 'em about the corporate culture.

Along with coaching employers on the practical forms of support, Oliver has shared ideas that he believes will help them make sense of who Latinx students are. Specifically, he has told them that Latinx students being the first in their families to attend college means they have a "tremendous work ethic" and a willingness to figure out how to do things even when they might not know how. He has also explained that their strong family ties "doesn't mean that they won't go and they won't perform well" and that "their loyalty to their family, that bleeds over into their loyalty to their employer."

Conclusion

This chapter aimed to showcase the actions of 10 faculty members working at two Hispanic-serving institutions who are considered "exemplary" in their Latinx-servingness. The focus on practitioners and, in this case, faculty is premised on the idea that their commitments and actions are crucial for making HSIs places where Latinx students can succeed academically, develop personally, imagine future possibilities, are affirmed, and feel like they belong. Using data from a broader study on supporting Latinx students in STEM at HSIs, I show that participants' Latinx-servingness is grounded, first and foremost, in a holistic approach to Latinx students. That is, they do not see Latinx students only as bodies in a classroom but as people with full lives, with families, with hopes and ambitions, and with challenges that must be navigated. They understand that the opportunities and inequalities facing Latinx students, particularly in STEM, are part of a more extensive ecology that includes what happens before, during, and after college. Notably, this recognition of systemic barriers that Latinx students experience, especially prior to college, are not reasons to give up but instead to (1) step up, (2) do more with students, high schools, parents, and prospective employers, (3) make themselves available, and (4) be proactive in their support. These acts of servingness more or less align with Laura Rendón's (1994) concept of "validation," which she describes as "an enabling, confirming and supportive process initiated by in- and out-of-class agents that fosters academic and interpersonal development" (as cited in Rendón Linares & Muñoz, 2011, p. 17). Key to validation, and specifically to validating acts, are faculty's initiation of contact with students, and their acting in authentic, caring, and nonpatronizing ways to enhance student learning, feelings of self-worth, and motivation to succeed. These elements were present in the faculty's attempts to help Latinx students navigate the norms of college and STEM, in their efforts to bolster students' confidence and self-esteem, and in their sincere belief in students' potential. SEU's and WU's strong record in achieving equitable outcomes for Latinx students in STEM suggests that a validation approach to enacting servingness is promising, and that using Rendón's framework could be a productive way of organizing and designing faculty development initiatives at HSIs.

I also demonstrate that faculty's acts of servingness are very much tied to their conceptions on how they (1) think about Latinx students, (2) believe students need to succeed in college and STEM, (3) understand Latinx culture, and (4) make sense of their histories, both personal and professional.

Even when participants acted in a similar vein, for example, being proactive and initiating contact with students, there were differences in the thinking behind their actions. A clear example of this were Jim and Armando, who spoke of actions associated with helping Latinx students balance academic and work responsibilities. While Jim's advice was for students to tell their parents that they cannot work so many hours and still succeed in school, Armando framed school as a means of simultaneously fulfilling personal and family goals and counseled the student to proceed slowly but steadily with coursework. Because he was Latino Armando clearly understood family as a vital part of Latinx culture and a nonnegotiable one. This is not to say that Jim does not appreciate the significance of family. Instead, his way into this aspect of Latinx culture—indeed, all aspects—is more learned than experienced; that is, he gets it secondhand, from what he is told and from what he observes, not from growing up in the culture. I raise this point not to suggest that one way of thinking is better than the other, but to highlight that (1) the way faculty members think matters when it comes to serving Latinx students, (2) differences in perspective can lead to different actions, and (3) the actions are undertaken may not be culturally validating despite the best intentions.

Relatedly and finally, the faculty's conceptions of Latinx students and culture tended toward a deficit framing, focusing on (1) what students lacked (e.g., not knowing how to balance school and work), (2) what their families could not provide (e.g., STEM role models), and (3) how families can stymie their progression (e.g., by needing support, financial and otherwise). Bensimon (2005) suggests that deficit thinking can lead to inaction if faculty think that little can be done to address these challenges. This type of thinking was not the case with faculty in this study. Despite the deficit framing, participants worked to support Latinx students and remove barriers facing them. In this way, they can be considered "institutional agents" who are "high-status," "non-kin" individuals who use their power, knowledge, access to resources, and the like to create opportunities and mitigate inequities for, as well as empower, minoritized students (Stanton-Salazar, 2011, p. 1067). At the same time, however, the deficit framing has consequences for the kind of actions undertaken. Starting with what Latinx students lack is more likely for acts of servingness to be compensatory (Yosso, 2005). For example, Lara's helping Latinx students speak with faculty is about resolving a lack (i.e., that students do not know how to engage professors) and addressing the professor in a language that the professor can understand. In this case, Lara is not asking the student, not the professor, to change. I do not want to suggest that efforts such as Lara's are inherently wrong or flawed. Indeed, the coaching she provides is valuable and should impart students with skills that will help them navigate similar situations in the future. My point, rather, is that a student deficit framing directs the locus of change on students and stymies change in other areas. For example, Oliver offered a few affirmative, asset-based interpretations of Latinx students' families and first-generation college status. With asset-based conceptions as a starting point, he sought a change in how employers should support and treat Latinx students and highlighted what companies would gain with them on staff. Ultimately, as crucial as it is to examine how faculty enact servingness, it is equally essential to interrogate the conceptions that undergird their actions to more fully understand whether, how, and why they are Latinx serving.

References

Bensimon, E. M. (2005). Closing the achievement gap in higher education: An organizational learning perspective. *New directions for higher education, 2005*(131), 99–111.

Bensimon, E. M., Dowd, A. C., Stanton-Salazar, & Dávila, B. A. (2019). The role of institutional agents in providing institutional support to Latinx students in STEM. *The Review of Higher Education, 42*(4), 1695–1727.

Cole, D., & Espinoza, A. (2008). Examining the academic success of Latino students in science technology engineering and mathematics (STEM) majors. *Journal of College Student Development, 49*(4), 285–300. https://doi.org/10.1353/csd.0.0018

Contreras, F. E., Malcom, L. E., & Bensimon, E. M. (2008). Hispanic-serving institutions: Closeted identity and the production of equitable outcomes for Latino/a students. In M. Gasman, B. Baez, & C. S. V. Turner (Ed.), *Understanding minority-serving institutions* (pp. 71–90). SUNY Press.

Cuellar, M. (2014). The impact of Hispanic-serving institutions (HSIs), emerging HSIs, and non-HSIs on Latina/o academic self-concept. *The Review of Higher Education, 37*(4), 499–530. https://doi.org/10.1353/rhe.2014.0032

Dayton, B., Gonzalez-Vasquez, N., Martinez, C. R., & Plum, C. (2004). Hispanic-serving institutions through the eyes of students and administrators. *New Directions for Student Services, 2004*(105), 29–40. https://doi.org/10.1002/ss.114

Dowd, A. C., Malcom, L. E., & Macias, E. E. (2010). *Improving transfer access to STEM bachelor's degrees at Hispanic-serving institutions through the America COMPETES Act.* https://cue.usc.edu/publications/briefs-reports-papers/

Dowd, A. C., Sawatzky, M., Rall, R. M., & Bensimon, E. M. (2013). Action research: An essential practice for 21st century assessment at HSIs. In M. R. T. Palmer,

D. C., & Gasman, M. (Ed.), *Fostering success of ethnic and racial minorities in STEM: The role of minority serving institutions* (pp. 149–167). Routledge.

Einarson, M. K., & Clarkberg, M. E. (2010). Race differences in the impact of students' out-of-class interactions with faculty. *The Journal of the Professoriate, 3*(2), 101–134.

Excelencia in Education. (2020). *Hispanic-serving institutions (HSIs): 2018–2019.* Excelencia in Education. https://www.edexcelencia.org/research/publications/hispanic-serving-institutions-hsis-2018-19

Fosnacht, K., & Nailos, J. N. (2016). Impact of the environment: How does attending a Hispanic-serving institution influence the engagement of baccalaureate-seeking Latina/o students? *Journal of Hispanic Higher Education, 15*(3), 187–204. https://doi.org/10.1177/1538192715597739

Garcia, G. (2017). Defined by outcomes or culture? Constructing an organizational identity for Hispanic-serving institutions. *American Educational Research Journal, 54*(Supp. 1), 111S–134S.

Garcia, G. A. (2019). *Becoming Hispanic-serving institutions: Opportunities for colleges and universities.* Johns Hopkins University Press.

Garcia, G. A., & Okhidoi, O. (2015). Culturally relevant practices that "serve" students at a Hispanic serving institution. *Innovative Higher Education, 40*(4), 345–357. https://doi.org/10.1007/s10755-015-9318-7

Garcia, G. A., Núñez, A. M., & Sansone, V. A. (2019). Toward a multidimensional conceptual framework for understanding "servingness" in Hispanic-serving institutions: A synthesis of the research. *Review of Educational Research, 89*(5), 745–784.

Gooden, S. T., & Martin, K. J. (2014). Facilitating college success among emerging Hispanic-serving institutions: Multiple perspectives yield commonly shared diversity goals. *Journal of Public Management & Social Policy, 20*(1), 1–28.

Greene, D., & Oesterreich, H. A. (2012). White profs at Hispanic-serving institutions: Radical revolutionaries or complicit colonists? *Journal of Latinos and Education, 11*(3), 168–174. https://doi.org/10.1080/15348431.2012.686351

Hurtado, S., & Carter, D. F. (1997). Effects of college transition and perceptions of the campus racial climate on Latino college students' sense of belonging [Empirical]. *Sociology of Education, 70*(4), 324–345.

Hurtado, S., & Ruiz, A. (2012). *Realizing the potential of Hispanic-serving institutions: Multiple dimensions of institutional diversity for advancing Hispanic higher education.* Higher Education Research Institute.

Hussar, B., Zhang, J., Hein, S., Wang, K., Roberts, A., Cui, J., Smith, M., Mann, F. B., Barmer, A., & Dilig, R. (2020). *The condition of education 2020* (NCES 2020-144). National Center for Education Statistics. https://nces.ed.gov/pubsearch/pubsinfo.asp?pubid=2020144

Lundberg, C. A., & Schreiner, L. A. (2004). Quality and frequency of faculty-student interaction as predictors of learning: An analysis by student race/

ethnicity. *Journal of College Student Development, 45*(5), 549–565. https://doi.org/10.1353/csd.2004.0061

Maestas, R., Vaquera, G. S., & Zehr, L. M. (2007). Factors impacting sense of belonging at a Hispanic-serving institution. *Journal of Hispanic Higher Education, 6*(3), 237–256. https://doi.org/10.1177/1538192707302801

Medina, C. A., & Posadas, C. E. (2012). Hispanic student experiences at a Hispanic-serving institution: Strong voices, key message. *Journal of Latinos and Education, 11*(3), 182–188. https://doi.org/10.1080/15348431.2012.686358

Pascarella, E. T., & Terenzini, P. T. (2005). *How college affects students: A third decade of research* (Vol. 2). Jossey-Bass.

Rendón Linares, L. I., & Muñoz, S. M. (2011). Revisiting validation theory: Theoretical foundations, applications, and extensions. *Enrollment Management Journal, 5*(2), 12–33.

Stanton-Salazar, R. D. (2011). A social capital framework for the study of institutional agents and their role in the empowerment of low-status students and youth. *Youth & Society, 43*(3), 1066–1109. https://doi.org/10.1177/0044118X10382877

Yosso, T. J. (2005). Whose culture has capital? A critical race theory discussion of community cultural wealth. *Race Ethnicity and Education, 8*(1), 69–91. https://doi.org/10.1080/1361332052000341006

Chapter 12

Black Women Faculty Engendering Brave (Online) Spaces for Black/Students of Color and Themselves

M. BILLYE SANKOFA WATERS, MOUNIRA MORRIS, AND CHERESE CHILDERS-MCKEE

Many curricula across disciplines in higher education have begun to advertise "social justice" as a recruitment and retention tool for issues of diversity, inclusion, agency, and "fixing a gap" (Gutiérrez, 2008; Ladson-Billings, 2006; Muhammad, 2020; Ochoa, 2013; Sanders, 1997). This move is likely attributed to data that lean into the rapid "Browning" of America; the visibility of movements such as #BlackLivesMatter, #NoDAPL, #abolishICE, #metoo; and the dismantling of white, patriarchal, heteronormative, colonial, terrorist systems (hooks, 2004; Love, 2019; Taylor, 2016). This dismantling gained international momentum during the onset of the COVID-19 pandemic in May 2020, when one police officer publicly executed George Floyd while others looked on. Professional development invitations for social justice interventions went out like Atlanta club flyers for MLK weekend, and university diversity, equity, and inclusion office communications were lit up like 911 call centers. At the same time, it can not be ignored that the presidential administration took time to pen an executive order *prohibiting* "divisive concepts," which are implicitly and explicitly aligned with critical race theory, culturally relevant teaching, abolitionist education, and the very nature of diversity, equity, and inclusion departments, at the base. Therefore, in 2020, the social justice advertisements (quite literally, if you look at the commercials of major corporations that began to color logos in red, black, and green and insert the Black Lives Matter hashtag) became more than a clarion call for neoliberals and tokenized diversity—but a poignant life-or-death call to action for Black (and Asian American Pacific Islander) folx around the world. This call would prove even more difficult—beyond historical and cultural resistance and a Trump executive order—because folx were now confined to their homes, some with access to resources, some with no access at all.

Moreover, while we (Billye, Mounira, and Cherese) have been teaching online for several years, these events are an acute marking of a different trajectory. Online delivery for a social justice curriculum has always felt clumsy at best because of the desire to incorporate tactile learning and create physical community with folx. Nevertheless, we braved the space because so many of our institutions have moved toward this platform. Thus, we acknowledge the impact of 2020 on social justice curricula while we assert that voice, community, and action do not and *should* not be sacrificed in online delivery.

We identify two primary challenges for creating, implementing, and sustaining a critical social justice curriculum: (1) the efforts conventionally fall on the shoulders of the faculty of the global majority (Berk, 2017; Lomax, 2015; Matthew, 2016; Mowatt, French, & Malebranche, 2013), and (2) the curriculum is designed to interrogate the so-called other but does not require the student to interrogate themselves. This interrogation is especially relevant for students who have been taught color-blind and meritocracy ideologies (Banks, 1991; Delpit, 2006; Gay, 2014; Ladson-Billings, 1995; Milner, 2007; Stanfield, 1985). This autoethnographic, Black feminist contribution addresses these issues of labor and curriculum by highlighting the work of three Black women full-time faculty members in a large, predominantly White graduate school of education (referred to herein as New Commonwealth University). We have designed and facilitated foundational 12-week social justice courses and workshops for undergraduate and graduate students, in addition to preparing other faculty members to teach these courses to maintain the integrity and rigor of social justice praxis.

This chapter (1) provides vignettes of each contributor's positionality as Black women in higher education; (2) discusses labor practices for those called to this work in terms of a Black feminist framework; and, finally, (3) suggests three cornerstones to create and model brave spaces. The goal of this work is to build practices of self-care for those who choose to engage in this work.

Birth of My Calling: Why We Came and Why We Stay

We—Billye, Mounira, and Cherese—met in 2017 along our respective paths as faculty in higher education. Shaped since birth from the Midwest, the East, and the South, there was an immediate kinship among us that was grounded in social justice and equity, resilience and excellence, and hip-hop and Black girlhood. We all found ourselves in a school of education where we continue to leverage our lived experiences and privileges to engender culturally relevant pedagogies. As Black women, we are sensitive to the needs of those who share the same intersectional identities because of a history of "otherness" in higher education. Even now, we still move as the first-few-only (Hill-Collins, 1990/2009) and are resolved in our stance to both hold space and pass the mic. We believe we are submerged in the trend of Black and Latino/a/x students enrolling in online programs—with "social justice" marketing strategies—due to access and flexibility. We witness and advocate for a disproportionate number of brilliant Black and Latino/a/x students who are rendered disabled (Withers et al., 2019) by their respective institutions because various forms of cultural wealth (Yosso, 2005)—especially navigational and linguistic—are not acknowledged and cultivated for them to thrive. We have over 25 years of experience working in various capacities in education, as junior faculty, directors, and most certainly as othermothers (Hill-Collins, 2009). We teach undergraduate and graduate-level social justice courses and are committed to teaching students across all races, ethnicities, and identities because, in short, "Black" texts are not just for "Black" courses. We employ seminal texts and materials from W. E. B. Du Bois (1903) to Derrick Bell's 1992 C-SPAN talk "Faces at the Bottom of the Well" to TED Talks with Chris Emdin (2013), Jamila Lyiscott (2014), and Brittney Cooper (2016), and require our students to keep reflexivity journals and do community walks. We speak explicitly about violent oppression and the need for joy, and show up as multifaceted human beings.

There is a shared narrative among us that schooling has primarily been a space to foster citizenship, a strong work ethic, and discipline. To this end, there were persistent curricula in our development that promoted character education, meritocracy and competition, respect for authority, and fluency in White intellectualism. Adherence to such programming was ostensibly the road to personal accomplishment, social success, and family financial stability: the American dream. However, our strong Black identities always troubled this Eurocentric curriculum and created a sense of responsibility to open up a different kind of educational space.

Billye. This responsibility was true even for Billye, who attended predominately Black primary and secondary schools in Chicago.

> *I'm incredibly proud of the learning spaces from which I come. I had strong teachers in every grade up through high school who pushed me. In fifth grade, Mrs. Franklin sent us home with what seemed like a half-inch thick, xeroxed packet of Black inventors that we had to memorize for the year. Beyond rote memorization, it was an early encyclopedia of Black excellence for me. In high school, Mr. Rehak made sure that we didn't just get Greek and classic mythology in our Honors English class. He made us analyze everything from* The Bluest Eye *to* Hollywood Shuffle. *However, we were always concerned with tests. As early as kindergarten, even to get into the school of my parents' choice, I was taught to pass the tests, and even though the Black texts were important, they were never integrated into the "standards."*
>
> *Of course, most of us had to learn how to be bilingual in this way. But as I began to move through higher education, the Black texts were often supplemental at best. I was hungry for a Black-centered curriculum and blessed that while I was in undergrad, my college finally offered Black world studies as a minor for the first time. This strengthened me for sure; however, when I entered one of my first courses in graduate school—a cultural studies course—it was clear that if I did not quote from White male authors, I would not be heard in the class. That space was hostile and deflating. I had to perform my wobbly knowledge of White intellectualism to literally earn a "pass."*
>
> *Frustrated with the shallow social justice agenda of the academy, I sat in the office of one of my mentors to discuss simply completing coursework and returning to Chicago to work "on the ground." I decided to attend graduate school only after working in various*

urban elementary schools because I wanted to learn more about how to teach teachers. Specifically, I wanted to have a grounded understanding in the culturally relevant ways I was educated so that I could better equip teachers ready to enter urban classrooms to teach Black children and work with Black families. She listened and shared a personal narrative of her trajectory as a child of Brown (desegregation) and now as a tenured Black woman at a "very high research activity" institution. She noted the number of committees where she sat as the first and the only—the exhaustion, blowback, microaggressions, and blatant violence she experienced by simply advocating for Black and Latinx students. This was especially true of her work on a high-profile case that involved Black athletes. Her labor was unpaid and often seen as "getting in the way" of her tenure portfolio. However, she simply said to me, "I just always wonder what further damage would have been done to those Black men if I hadn't been in the room." She reminded me of what Denise Taliaferro Baszile claimed earlier: "My work in the academy is activism." And I resolved to stay. Over the next couple of semesters, I gained more tools, language, and strength not only to persist but also to make room for others.

Mounira. Mounira, who grew up in Dorchester, Massachusetts, claims that she "never struggled being in this black body."

My neighborhood was comprised of individuals from the African diaspora—Southern Great Migration Blacks, Caribbean Blacks, West African Blacks—and we embraced one another. It wasn't until I entered high school that Black became "heavy." I enrolled and excelled in honors courses where I was often the only Black student and subsequently felt the need to represent all Black students. I invested a significant number of hours studying and preparing for my courses because I couldn't disappoint my ancestors, family, and community. I wanted to be clear that I earned every bit of my space. One day, I was accused of cheating on a math exam. My teacher stated, "You definitely cheated because Blacks are incapable of succeeding in math." It was imperative to channel my hurt, anger, and frustration into something larger than myself.

During my graduate and doctoral studies, my research solely focused on individual and institutional experiences of Black students at predominantly white institutions. The participants in my dissertation study were Black, female doctoral students or recent degree completers. The findings, such as lack of mentoring, support, and faculty of color, mirrored my doctoral journey. My participants' stories, coupled with the accusation I faced in high school, fired me up to examine interpersonal and institutional racism, especially in higher education.

Cherese. From a rural community in the South, Cherese shares "memories of dirt roads, hot summers, lots of trees, and the freedom to roam and explore all of nature."

> I was fiercely protected by a strong Black mother, parents who as teenagers had experienced the first waves of desegregation, a church family with a rich history, and a community of folks with hard-working, blue-collar values. While most in my family didn't have the opportunity to go to college, I always had models of Black people who were teachers, principals, and professors—strong advocates of education. From the beginning, I was told I was special and that I would work hard and achieve.
>
> As free and protected as we felt in our neighborhood, I knew early on that school, and the surrounding White community, viewed me and my community as less than. Some of my earliest memories are of the KKK marching through downtown, seeing a burnt cross in someone's yard, being terrified that they would come and drag me out of my bed one night and take me away. These were the family members of my classmates who I went to school with every day. My father comforted me by assuring me that in my neighborhood, we protected each other and that the KKK was afraid to come anywhere near where we lived. In school, the few Black kids from my neighborhood were automatically relegated to the slow-learner classes. We weren't invited to participate in the academically gifted program and were routinely treated differently than everyone else. Because my mother constantly advocated on my behalf, the school soon learned that she was a force to be reckoned with and that they needed to recognize my talents and abilities. The systems of prejudice remained, though—and as a result, in K–12, I was often the only Black student in honors and advanced classes.
>
> I matriculated through an undergraduate program at an elite private university and experienced much of the same. While

I've received strong content education throughout my life, my educational journey has always been bifurcated. Education on Black struggle and Black excellence rested in the realm of home, church, and community. I was taught that school was where you go to get book smarts that were important in helping you to navigate the white world, code-switch, and get a good job, but that all of these things were useless without an understanding of who you were and where you came from.

It wasn't until graduate school when I began to learn about the social context of education, critical pedagogy, social justice, and gender studies that the two parts of me—home and school education—began to merge. It was a painful yet healing journey to reconcile these pieces of myself as I became equipped with the historical understanding, the language, and the authority to speak out loudly about them.

Most of us are taught that education is the path to freedom, and it provides us a seat at the table. For our ancestors and generations before us who were tortured and murdered for learning, we understand and honor these teachings. We are the children of the landmark Supreme Court cases such as Oliver Brown et al. v. Board of Education of Topeka *(1954) and have been afforded the privilege of integrated magnet schools, exposure to extracurricular activities beyond academic learnings, and access to top-tier educational resources from which our parents and grandparents were banned. Because of this integration, exposure, and access, our generation has the skills and ability to not only pull up a seat at the proverbial table but to build our own tables as well. In this way, we can create a new social order. This is arguably the responsibility of our generation and, thus, why we "stay" in higher education.*

Labor Practices

When the quarter or semester begins, the first textbook our students see is us. Our bodies are read as raced and gendered, specifically Black and female—at the intersections of invisible and hypervisible, packed with all the controlling images between Mammy, "Real Atlanta Housewife," and #blackgirlmagic (Crenshaw, 1991; Davis, 1981; Hill-Collins, 2004; Mowatt, French, & Malebranche, 2013; Sankofa Waters, 2015). Oftentimes the initial response of a student is, "I was nervous to take your class, and I'm hoping you won't spend the entire time lecturing as a Black woman about how horrible I have been as a White person, especially when you don't know what I've been through." Or the pendulum swings the other way. We have students who enroll in our classes because they saw our locked hair or our big hoop earrings and immediately felt comfortable. We have students who have rarely if ever had a Black or Black female instructor—one that looked like them or someone with whom they shared a close kinship. They are so eager for learning and mentorship that their weight feels heavy even as their expectations are incredibly fragile. We carry them both.

We practice the same diplomacy and care poured into us, perhaps exhausting ourselves with exacting the measurements and sometimes balancing too much space for willful ignorance or at times not enough space for genuine vulnerability. We test ourselves against the Black feminist tenets: (1) lived experience as a criterion for meaning, (2) use of dialogue to assess knowledge claims, (3) ethic of care, and (4) ethic of personal responsibility (Hill-Collins, 1989/1995). We look to the work of Cynthia B. Dillard (2000, 2008; Okpalaoka & Dillard, 2011), who challenges us to re/member who we are with great respect to the cultural mores of wisdom, healing, and reciprocity. In practice, this looks like creating a curriculum rooted in examining positionality beyond a biographical sketch. This practice asks each person to reflexively respond to at least five core questions. First, why are you here? Second, who sent for you in your intended research site? Third, what are the assets of the space you intend to claim for research? Fourth, how will you work with collaborators and build resources? Finally, where do you have the potential to cause harm? This looks like centering each conversation around a set of "critical community agreements" and revisiting those agreements at least three times throughout the course, especially when they are violated. This looks like negotiating and renegotiating your personal boundaries to make sure you are both healthy and fully present. When you exercise this *ethic of care,* you have to let the people in. This is true for a range of courses, but especially true for social justice courses.

We have been responsible for designing and teaching social justice courses across institutions and levels. However, this does not mean that we *teach* social justice. Social justice is a practice and lived experience. At best, we share historical texts, prominent ideologies, and contemporary praxis. This experience allows us to understand better our individual and collective ability to leverage our privileges *toward justice.* Our definitions of this work are not absolute; they overlap, are nuanced, and have various tensions between them. We also make a critical observation. With conventionally marginalized intersectional identities, we are held responsible, too often, for this instruction and teaching others *how* to teach these courses. Still, the central themes are clear, especially regarding the educational foundation of our work. We employ practices of community wealth and protest, freedom dreaming, and decolonization and abolitionist teaching (Bettez, 2011; Dillard, 2000; Hilliard, 1997; hooks, 2003; Kelley, 2003; Love, 2019; Milner, 2007; Stovall, 2016; Taylor, 2016; Yosso, 2005).

WE DON'T TEACH IN A VACUUM

Billye began her professional career in higher education as a remote faculty member amid the 2012 Chicago teachers' strike and on the cusp of 500 murders, including one of her former students, Hadiya Pendleton. These events were transformative and traumatic, because Chicago was not just the foundation for her educational career; Chicago was *home*. Here, Billye offers the following:

> *As a brand new faculty member at New Commonwealth, I was charged with designing and teaching the first course focused on social justice and equity as a new program requirement. Additionally, I was the first Black woman, full-time faculty member. I note being the "first, Black" not as a credential but to emphasize the responsibility I inherited—to design and teach anti-racist, anti-sexist curricula through perpetual spaces of both resistance and affirmation. Every piece of my material and lecture was drenched with intense urgency as I worked to balance the communal and political spaces exploding around me. My goals were to be authentic and practical, and every quarter grew with intensity as I addressed student concerns such as "I thought this course would help me find a solution, and now I feel worse" and "Why do we need to read texts from the 1900s?" But I was clear. There was no way we could ever talk about the onslaught of injustices broadcast daily, that range from state-sanctioned violence to oil spills and fracking, without talking about their historical roots. Often students have wanted a quick fix toward salvation but rarely look at the trajectory of complicity, especially when unearned privileges have to be examined (and sacrificed).*
>
> *When I taught the social justice and equity course in spring 2015, it was an acutely wild ride. This quarter was heavy with both*

public violence and celebration. In just five months, we witnessed the aggressive attack on Dajerria Becton and the teens in McKinney, Texas; the death of Freddie Gray and the Baltimore uprisings (on the heels of the highly publicized cases of Mike Brown and Tamir Rice); the Charleston 9 shooting; the Haitian deportation from the Dominican Republic; the monumental rulings of the Supreme Court on health care and same-sex marriage; and the confirmation of Loretta Lynch—through and beyond the election of Donald Trump. This was aligned with a painstaking examination (and oftentimes introducing) interlocking systems of racism, capitalism, and patriarchy—every day. In our social justice course for that quarter, the personal was always political. One week after the course ended, a student emailed me to say, "This has indeed been such a historical moment in the history of our country, and I can't imagine a safer, more stimulating place to be at that time than in your class." While I was obviously pleased that the student found both safety and stimulation, there were others that felt antagonized and unsupported.

One, in particular, immigrated to this country as a child to escape abject poverty. Aja introduced herself as an orthodox conservative living in a "pungently liberal" American city. She anticipated that she would not agree with her classmates but was steadfastly committed to social change at the heart of every word she expressed on the discussion boards. She noted in an individual email that she'd felt attacked during the course because she didn't find allies for her positions and questioned if it had to do with her ethnicity and/or academic ability. I assured her that our class was a place of learning and free from the retribution of "disagreeing with the professor." I welcomed her ideas—especially as a woman with lived experiences across countries—and assured her that the only power she needed to be concerned with during the quarter was her own and the students with whom she worked to affect change with/for. I communicated that her voice, silence, frustrations, and even grades were hers to own, even though she consistently resisted through the final week. I rested in my labor of simply planting a robust seed that she could water in her own time and capacity. However, the unseen learning curve was that it was I who needed to adjust my righteous assumption—that a person of color exploring strategies to leverage privilege and enact justice is an inherently affirming act.

Harmonize Our Voices

Our work to affirm and to be affirmed has a strong legacy. We have shared many laughs when we talk about the length of our dissertation acknowledgments sections and joked that they read something like the book of Genesis. This comes from the intense desire to honor those who have come before us and to honor those who continue to walk beside us. More importantly, acknowledging the histories and sacrifices of those who have paved our roads compels us to walk taller and with greater purpose for those to come. We have a responsibility to mentor. Cherese captures it when she says, "My mentors' words stay with me when I am giving critical feedback to my students while loving and affirming them; meeting them where they are, but pushing them to do more; being available to them, while still maintaining work/life balance and practicing self-care." In this way, we talk about mentoring as a natural act of service and often privilege it above our formal obligations to teach and research. Operating in social justice courses organically opens the door for mentoring relationships because we are in community, wrestling with tough ideas and practices together. When the 12 weeks have concluded, we have agreed to organize critical race community groups, invited students to publish and present with us, advocated for students individually, and agreed to chair their research committees. We do this to water the seeds that have been planted in us and build larger communities.

Cherese shares,

> *After having taught in face-to-face settings for over 15 years, I was initially unsure of how to cultivate relationships online with students all over the country and the world. One of the interesting aspects of this doctoral program is that it's not as siloed and discipline-specific as many education programs. Students are studying a variety of topics related to all facets of education—some more interesting to me personally than others. It presents an interesting challenge as a mentor—a higher degree of intellectual flexibility and acuity. When you're not an expert on your students' topics or the body of literature that they're engaging with, it takes more work to manage their research projects.*
>
> *Last quarter, I saw a discussion board post that immediately piqued my interest. Adrian worked in an urban high school with Black and Latinx students and was describing his critical lens,*

relationship building with his students, and social justice. I emailed him to let him know he was speaking my "love language" and that we had similar research interests. He quickly responded about how much he appreciated my use of the term "love language," and there began our mentor/mentee relationship. My walls of protection warned me not to get too close, but this continues to be a process of building trust and mutual respect. When I look at him, I see a former version of myself—one from my ESL teacher life, a life I miss sometimes—the love for a people and a culture that is not yours by birth but that you feel very much a part of, navigating positionality as a border crosser, and the messy chaos of high school life. Adrian enjoys saying that he and I are working together to "harmonize" our voices.

Exhaustion

We are advocates, sometimes architects, for social justice in our respective departments and classrooms, and while we have read empirical data that informs us of the long-term effect of racial battle fatigue, microaggressions, whitesplaining, mansplaining, and Beckery, we feel the exhaustion in our bones. We have come into these learning spaces excited to design and teach. However, we have often found (1) we are the only ones called, and (2) we are the first ones called into the principal's office when a complaint against "social justice" is submitted. Unfortunately, our responses as the first-few-only are usually to pay the "Black-tax" and continue to overperform, thus becoming complicit in our own fractures and tears. To mitigate this, Mounira states, "It is imperative for me to share experiences with colleagues within and outside of my department. It is not only validating but a time to receive constructive criticism on my pedagogy."

When Mounira was offered a teaching role at New Commonwealth, she was "honored and privileged to be provided an opportunity to give back." She was asked to teach a required masters-level course that focused on race and ethnicity in education. However, she admits to being nervous teaching students for the first time to uncover "deep-rooted emotions around race." She feared that they might not be receptive to the direction nor the course materials. The latter proved to be true when students questioned texts such as *Why Are All the Black Kids Sitting Together in the Cafeteria?* (Tatum, 1997) and "White Privilege: Unpacking the Invisible Knapsack" (McIntosh, 1989). The overarching goal was for students to develop critical and analytical lenses, but their pushback was basic. By the end of the course, she felt it had been a holistic success but wondered "if the responses would have been the same had the instructor been a White and/or male scholar." This is a nagging question of our triple consciousness that we tease out in conversation to develop strategies not just to fortify our teaching but to make sure our souls stay intact.

Cherese shares how her experiences with this type of resistance presented her with the opportunity to fiercely claim self. She had dreams of a tenure-track faculty position but was geographically bound and ultimately accepted a staff position, "the one where you are told you are 'just like faculty' because you are doing faculty work but do not get the money or the credit." She told herself it was a solid stepping-stone and dove into honors education and course development concerning community engagement and social justice. Her position was new and became a great space for creativity. She was excited to teach courses with topics that spanned race, gender, sexuality, disability, ageism, and more. One course in particular required students to develop a social justice project alongside a community organization. Cherese offers below her excitement:

> *Through readings and discussions, students learned about topics like the history of the community surrounding their university, redlining, gentrification, race relations, activism, and more. From a creative perspective, creating the courses was a wonderful experience; actually, facilitating and managing the resistance I faced from students was exhausting. As the university "crème of the crop," my students were highly intelligent, conscientious, and hardworking. Many of them were also white, raised in conservative communities, and had very little experience with any type of diversity. For most, I was their first Black teacher, and they were suspicious of my feminist, people of color–centric views. I routinely received complaints that my classes were great, but I talked about too much "Black stuff" and "gay stuff."*
>
> *At that point in my career, I only knew one way to teach—just as I had approached my role as an ESL teacher, it was an embodied experience for me. So I threw my whole self into my instruction, trying to love my students into embracing new perspectives. When they rejected me and my views, I understood this as a part of the process and hoped that the seed had been planted that might someday be watered by someone else—but this and other experiences in my "faculty, but not really faculty" role ate away little by little at*

> *my confidence and my spirit. I couldn't find community among my coworkers, couldn't find anyone who spoke my "language," couldn't find a space to be my authentic self, couldn't really find anyone who cared about the issues that I was passionate about. Those critical, philosophical, radical, "fuck the system" conversations that were so common in graduate school came to a screeching halt as I tried my best to embrace my new life.*

Conversations with Mounira opened us up to understand "counterspace" (Ong, Smith, & Ko, 2018; West & Jones, 2019) as a useful weapon she developed and accessed, especially in leadership positions. She explains that this is a space where she does not have to explain who she is culturally, racially, or otherwise, but she instead relaxes her double (and often) triple consciousness. As a result, she does not have to always filter or think twice about misinterpretations of her Black and gendered body.

> *Before pursuing a career at New Commonwealth, I accepted administrative positions requiring me to develop policies and practices addressing diversity and inclusion. I have often been the "only one" or "one of few" in my higher education career. Fortunately, I have had amazing colleagues who serve as part of my support system and allies. But my Black woman identity is critical to who I am. I created spaces for underrepresented communities to "exhale" or temporarily escape from the hostile environment around them, which is part of my self-care. It was a space where students, faculty, and staff shared their common experiences and presented coping mechanisms to navigate the landscape of their predominantly white institutions. These professional experiences reaffirmed my calling to serve as a mentor and advisor to marginalized communities and to teach how to create a more inclusive environment. In addition to developing strategies to navigate higher education, we find opportunities to coauthor and/or copresent our work.*

We embody the ubiquitous phrase "To whom much is given, much is required."

To this end, we repeat patterns of pushing and embracing. Every step of the way, we tell each other, "We do this for our students" and declare that we are "involved in work [our] soul must have" (Walker, 1983, p. 241). We are an endless cycle of proverbs and anthems that we use to affirm ourselves and one another. And when Billye finished preparing her promotion dossier, she called us to say, "How on Earth did I get all of this done?!" One of us jokingly used the word "magic," but each part of our work comprises flesh and blood. When we espouse the notion that what we do is *super*natural, it binds us to unhealthy labor practices and continuously bends a curve toward bad precedent. Billye simply responded, "It's time to give myself a break!"

"but some of us are *brave*": Synthesis

On the first day of the social justice and equity course required for the doctoral students in our program, Billye traditionally opens with, "This is not a Tylenol course. In other words, do not expect to pop in a book about social justice and feel better." We are aware that while some of our students are enrolled as a requirement to meet the institution's respective mission, many of them are there because of a genuine hunger to understand and operate as change agents. Many of them are there for the same reasons that we are: to "hold the pole" and operate as co-conspirators to disrupt violence and oppression.[1] Or they are there to ensure that the people in their classrooms, school districts, nonprofits, and any other learning space are met with critical educators. These are people who have high expectations, are culturally competent, critique the social order, and exercise an ethic of care steeped in reflexivity and reciprocity, not salvation. Some of them are there to build Village. One of our key operational guides for this work comes from Loyce Caruthers and Jennifer Friend (2014). They posit critical pedagogy in online spaces as a "thirdspace." There are four salient concepts:

1. knowledge (truth) is socially constructed, culturally mediated, and historically situated;

2. understanding the relationship between knowledge and power means critiquing the dominant curriculum, the instrumental use of knowledge, and its discourses and discursive practices;

3. helping educators acknowledge that curriculum is a form of cultural politics and must be examined within the larger capitalist social order;

4. and critiquing the social reproduction function of schooling entails illuminating how schools "transmit the status and class positions of the wider society." (p. 10)

We work from the premise that social justice is not simply about differences. Instead, we operate from a rich critique of social structures: who gets to build, operate, protect, regenerate, exclude, and receive benefits from them—and, most importantly, who am I in this structure (with all my multiple/intersectional identities)? Such a process requires critical self-awareness, investment, and risk from each of us—student and teacher—throughout our 12-week journey together. And so many of us have been asked to shift our language from creating "safe" spaces wherein people can hide in silence and group-think rather than "brave" spaces where people can fully share themselves with the trade-off of critique, affirmation, or growth (or, hopefully, all three). We tell them that their "silence will not protect [you]" (Lorde, 1984).

Design Effectively

To effectively design our social justice courses, we lean on the "use of dialogue to assess knowledge claims" (Hill-Collins, 1990/2009). In this way, we take a step back so that there is no laser focus on us as the instructor but rather on the community and the norms they set with one another. Early on, we establish small pods of four to five students who spend the quarter in peer review and deep reflection on the materials. Silvia Bettez (2011) takes her lead from Paulo Freire's assertion about creating critical communities among graduate students in social justice courses: "In critical community building there must be, at a minimum, an attempt to question dominant norms and a goal to further one another's critical thinking, particularly around issues of power, oppression, and privilege" (p. 81). Creating small groups in which students alternate stages with one another are important for this goal because we have found that when *we* as Black women center every class discussion, the students are usually responding directly to us as raced and gendered bodies rather than taking up their own positionalities and the diverse bodies among them. This community design does not absolve us of teaching by any means but instead redistributes agency.

Moreover, neither is this simply "group work"; rather it is an intentional facilitation of dialogue to tease out big and small concepts of the week's materials. This includes prompts such as "Given the materials that explore constructions of knowledge and community, spend time this week considering your definition of leadership and social justice both as individual terms as well as spaces of practice and change" and "How do the authors investigate power as it relates to institutionalized oppression?" Because students are leveraging their various areas of expertise without directing thoughts about leadership and social justice to us for knee-jerk reaction or academic points, they make substantial progress in assessing their own knowledge claims. We operate in the proverb: iron sharpens iron.

SET BOUNDARIES

By definition, boundaries are markers to note limitations. These markers can be physical, verbal, or emotional; however, the key is knowing what you need to *protect* so that you know what you need to limit. Here we lean on our "lived experience as criterion for meaning" (Hill-Collins, 1990/2009) to assert that our histories and knowledges of self are what validate our work. Moreover, they set our boundaries—or rather, the terms to protect ourselves. For example, knowledge of self means I cannot say "yes" to every question and maintain a holistic, healthy life balance, even if the questions appear urgent. Knowing self means that I know when I say "no," I am relieving my ego and body from believing that I am capable of doing *everything*. Knowing self means that we are unbothered with words such as *selfish* and *unapologetic* because we are comfortable with what we contribute and do not owe anyone any more than that. For some of us, this looks like a clear and bold statement in the syllabus that we will not communicate via email, phone, text, or otherwise from Friday at 5 p.m. until Monday at 9 a.m. or on weekdays after 5 p.m. It may also look like directing a colleague to the same social justice resources we have researched and incorporated rather than handholding them through one-on-one lessons. We set boundaries so that others honor our time and bodies and as a model for them to honor their own.

RE/IMAGINE SPACE

Along our journey to higher education, we have often been rigorously trained to speak with authority and cite empirical evidence. This runs counter to how we live in the fullness of our everyday lives. In this way, we lean on Cynthia Dillard (2008), who coaches us to understand that our lived experiences "are inspirational, breathing new life into the work of teaching, researching, and living. They are memories that transform; a place within and without that feeds our ability to engage new metaphors and practices in our work" (pp. 90–91). We then take personal accountability (Hill-Collins, 1990/2009) for our space by enacting our imagination and creativity. Mounira demonstrates this in her examples of creating places to "exhale." Cherese shares this in her story of Adrian. Billye recalls that in many one-on-one conversations with her students, they simply wanted to know more about *her*, which made her aware of how she restrained herself as a critical community member—to maintain professionalism. So she began to perform poetry with her students. We offer no prescriptions here but room for dialogic engagement as creative human beings with dynamic narratives. We are constantly reinventing our social justice learning spaces to freely share truths. We are constantly reminded not to forget our joy in this work.

We know that we have to enact both safety and bravery in our social justice courses, especially those online. There are privileges we have to be willing to sacrifice, and perhaps small bits of privacy. Sometimes our students, especially Black/students of color, do not readily recognize any privilege to leverage. When we comb through Du Bois's classic *The Souls of Black Folk* (1903) and make alignments with "The Case for Reparations" (Coates, 2014), we are aware that we hit decades of racial trigger points. These conversations can swing from flat to explosive. In the latter, our students tend to spend a great deal of time explicating the historical oppression that can simply become exhausting and deflating. We do not take for granted that, like us, our students have a range of experience across identities, geographies, and generations. Their release is real and necessary. In fact, we write this chapter to honor *them*. We show up in each other's space with the intention to not leave the same way that we came in. Therefore, as curriculum creators, instructors, and community members sharing these learning spaces, we have to consciously and actively balance the narratives. This does not mean sharing a viral video of officers handing out ice cream or critiquing editorials of forgiveness featuring Brandt Jean. It means that we take responsibility to resist deficit-based narratives and use our respective privileges to design effectively set boundaries and to re/imagine space.

Note

1. "Hold the pole" is a reference to the relationship between Bree Newsome and James Tyson, who were strangers before committing and training to remove the Confederate flag from the South Carolina state capital in 2015. While Newsome climbed the flagpole, Tyson held its base to keep the police from tasing it, thus

electrifying/killing her. Bettina Love (2019) refers to this as an ultimate act of a "coconspirator."

References

Bensimon, E. M. (2005). Closing the achievement gap in higher education: An organizational learning perspective. *New directions for higher education, 2005*(131), 99–111.

Bensimon, E. M., Dowd, A. C., Stanton-Salazar, & Dávila, B. A. (2019). The role of institutional agents in providing institutional support to Latinx students in STEM. *The Review of Higher Education, 42*(4), 1695–1727.

Banks, J. A. (1991). Teaching multicultural literacy to teachers. *Teaching Education, 4*(1), 133–142. https://doi.org/10. 1080/1047621910040118

Baszile, D. T. (2009). Deal with it we must: Education, social justice, and the curriculum of hip hop culture. *Equity & Excellence in Education, 42*(1), 6–19. doi.org/10.1080/

Bell, D. (1992, September 24). Book discussion on "Faces at the Bottom of the Well." C-SPAN. Retrieved from http://www.c-spanvideo.org/program/34630-1

Berk, R. A. (2017). Microaggressions trilogy: Part 1. Why do microaggressions matter? *The Journal of Faculty Development, 31*(1), 63–112.

Bettez, S. C. (2011). Building critical communities amid the uncertainty of social justice pedagogy in the graduate classroom. *Review of Education, Pedagogy, and Cultural Studies, 33*(1), 76–106.

Caruthers, L., & Friend, J. (2014). Critical pedagogy in online environments as thirdspace: A narrative analysis of voices of candidates in educational preparatory programs. *Educational Studies, 50*(1), 8–35.

Coates, T. (2014). The case for reparations. *The Atlantic*. Retrieved from http://www.theatlantic.com/features/archive/2014/05/the-case-for-reparations/361631/

Cooper, B. (2016, October). The racial politics of time: Brittney Cooper at TEDWomen 2016. TEDx Talks. Retrieved from https://www.ted.com/talks/brittney_cooper_the_racial_politics_of_time

Crenshaw, K. (1991). Mapping the margins: Intersectionality, identity politics, and violence against women of color. *Stanford Law Review (43)*6, 1241–1299.

Davis, A. (1981). *Women race & class*. Random House.

Delpit, L. (2006). *Other people's children: Cultural conflict in the classroom* (Rev. ed.). New Press.

Dillard, C. B. (2000). The substance of things hoped for, the evidence of things not seen: Examining and endarkened feminist epistemology in educational research and leadership. *International Journal of Qualitative Studies in Education, 13*(6), 661–681.

Dillard, C. B. (2008). Re-membering culture: Bearing witness to the spirit of identity in research. *Race and Ethnicity in Education, 11*(1), 87–93.

Du Bois, W. E. B. (1903). *The souls of Black folk.* Bantam Books.

Emdin, C. (2013, March 7). Empowering children through urban education: Christopher Emdin at TEDxColumbiaSIPA. TEDx Talks. Retrieved from https://www.youtube.com/watch?v=ouudXr-csZg

Gay, G. (2014). Culturally responsive teaching principles, practices, and effects. In H. R. Milner IV & K. Lomotey (Eds.), *Handbook of urban education* (pp. 353–372). Routledge.

Gutiérrez, R. (2008). A "gap-gazing" fetish in mathematics education? Problematizing research on the achievement gap. *Journal for Research in Mathematics Education, 39*(4), 357–364.

Hill-Collins, P. (1995). The social construction of Black feminist thought. In B. Guy-Sheftall (Ed.), *Words of fire: An anthology of African American feminist thought* (pp. 338–357). The New Press. (Original work published 1989)

Hill-Collins, P. (2004). Get your freak on: Sex, babies and images of Black femininity. In P. Hill-Collins (Ed.), *Black sexual politics: African Americans, gender, and the new racism* (pp. 119–148). Routledge.

Hill-Collins, P. (2009). Black feminist thought: Knowledge, consciousness, and the politics of empowerment. Routledge. (Original work published 1990)

Hilliard, A. G. III (1997). *SBA: The reawakening of the African mind.* Makare Publishing.

hooks, b. (1984). *Feminist theory: From margin to center.* South End.

hooks, b. (1993). *Teaching community: A pedagogy of hope.* Routledge.

hooks, b. (2004). *The will to change: Men, masculinity, and love.* Washington Square Press.

Kelley, R. D. G. (2003). *Freedom dreams: The Black radical imagination.* Beacon Press.

Ladson-Billings, G. (1995). Toward a theory of culturally relevant pedagogy. *American Educational Research Journal, 32*(3), 465–491. doi.org/10.3102/00028312032003465

Ladson-Billings, G. (2006). From the achievement gap to the education debt: Understanding achievement in US schools. *Educational Researcher, 35*(7), 3–12.

Lomax, T. (2015, May 18). Black women's lives don't matter in academia either, or why I quit academic spaces that don't value Black women's life and labor. *The Feminist Wire.* Retrieved from https://thefeministwire.com/2015/05/black-womens-lives-dont-matter-in-academia-either-or-why-i-quit-academic-spaces-that-dont-value-black-womens-life/

Lorde, A. (1984). *Sister outsider.* Crossing Press.

Love, B. (2019). *We want to do more than survive: Abolitionist teaching and the pursuit of educational freedom.* Beacon Press.

Lyiscott, J. (2014, June 24). 3 ways to speak English. TEDx Talks. Retrieved from https://www.ted.com/talks/Jamila_lyiscott_3_ways_to_speak_english/up-next

Matthew, P. A. (2016, November 23). What is faculty diversity worth to a university? *The Atlantic*. Retrieved from https://www.theatlantic.com/education/archive/2016/11/what-is-faculty-diversity-worth-to-a-university/508334/

McIntosh, P. (1989). White privilege: Unpacking the invisible knapsack. *Peace and Freedom Magazine* (July/August), 10–12.

Milner, H. R. (2007). Race, culture, and researcher positionality: Working through dangers seen, unseen, and unforeseen. *Educational Researcher*, *36*(7), 388–400. doi.org/ 10.3102/0013189X07309471

Mowatt, R. A., French, B. H., & Malebranche, D. A. (2013). Black/female/body hyper visibility and invisibility: A Black feminist augmentation of feminist leisure research. *Journal of Leisure Research*, *45*(5), 664–660.

Muhammad, G. (2020). *Cultivating genius: An equity framework for culturally and historicallyresponsive literacy*. Scholastic, Inc.

Ochoa, G. L. (2013). *Academic profiling: Latinos, Asian Americans, and the achievement gap*. University of Minnesota Press.

Okpalaoka, C. L., & Dillard, C. B. (2011). Our healing is next to the wound: Endarkened feminism, spirituality, and wisdom for teaching, learning, and research. *New Directions for Adult and Continuing Education*, *131*, 65–74. doi:10.1002/ace.422

Ong, M., Smith, J. M., & Ko, L. T. (2018). Counterspaces for women of color in STEM higher education: Marginal and central spaces for persistence and success. *Journal of Research in Science Teaching*, *55*(2), 206–245.

Sanders, M. G. (1997). Overcoming obstacles: Academic achievement as a response to racism and discrimination. *The Journal of Negro Education*, *66*(1), 83–93.

Sankofa Waters, B. (2015). *We can speak for ourselves: Parent involvement and ideologues of Black mothers in Chicago*. Sense Publishers.

Stanfield, J. H. (1985). The ethnocentric basis of social science knowledge production. *Review of Research in Education*, *12*(1), 387–415.

Stovall, D. O. (2016). *Born out of struggle: Critical race theory, school creation, and the politics of interruption*. SUNY Press.

Tatum, B. (1997). *"Why are all the Black kids sitting together in the cafeteria?" and other conversations about race*. Basic Books.

Taylor, K.Y. (2016). *From #BlackLivesMatter to Black liberation*. Haymarket Books.

Walker, A. (1983). *In search of our mothers' gardens: Womanist prose*. Harcourt Brace & Company.

Weis, L., & Fine, M. (2012). Critical bifocality and circuits of privilege: Expanding critical ethnographic theory and design. *Harvard Educational Review* *82*(2), 173–201.

West, N. M., & Jones, T. B. (2019). Architects of change in the Ivory Tower: Recasting the role of Black women engaged in higher education professional counterspaces. In U. Thomas (Ed.), *Navigating micro-aggressions toward women in higher education* (pp. 23–72). IGI Global.

Withers, A. J., Ben-Moshe, L., Brown, L. X. Z., Erickson, L, da Silva Gorman, R., Lewis, T. A., McLeod, L., & Mingus, M. (2019). Radical disability politics. In R. Kinna and U. Gordon (Eds.), *Routledge handbook of radical politics* (pp. 178–193). Routledge.

Yosso, T. J. (2005). Whose culture has capital? A critical race theory discussion of community cultural wealth. *Race Ethnicity and Education, 8*(1), 69–91.

Chapter 13

Diversity Leadership at the University of Michigan

From Desegregation to Diversity, Equity, and Inclusion

PHILLIP J. BOWMAN, JAMILLAH B. WILLIAMS,
ANGELA EBREO, AND NIA D. HOLLAND

As we move further into the 21st century, the University of Michigan (UM) remains a national leader in innovative diversity, equity, and inclusion (DEI) strategies. As a significant UM priority, the current DEI strategic planning agenda is among the most comprehensive in the nation. In consultation with the UM president and the provost, a chief diversity officer coordinates a decentralized DEI process in collaboration with all unit leaders in the campus community. The UM's comprehensive DEI strategic planning process includes a set of five-year plans at both the campus and specific unit levels, annual progress reports, periodic digital progress updates, and an annual campus-wide summit. In addition, the annual DEI summit features a national keynote speaker, progress highlights, and multiple events to actively engage all campus leaders, faculty, staff, and students. Current DEI leaders build on a solid legacy in which UM has often been viewed as a national exemplar for innovative diversity initiatives in higher education (Duderstadt, 2015; Gurin, Lehman, & Lewis, 2004; Perry, 2007). However, current DEI strategic initiatives build directly on the transformative agenda of UM leaders who during the early 2000s helped to shift national policy from an *affirmative action* to a *benefits of diversity* agenda.

In June 2003, UM diversity leaders were thrust into the epicenter of a national debate about affirmative action when the US Supreme Court affirmed their benefits-of-diversity legal strategy to support the use of race as a factor in university admissions in two historic cases (*Gratz v. Bollinger*, 539 US 244 [2003] and *Grutter v. Bollinger*, 539 US 306 [2003]). These two landmark cases placed UM at the center of a national paradigm shift in strategic diversity policy with widespread historical and societal implications (Gurin, Lehaman, & Lewis, 2004; Gurin, Nagda, & Lopez, 2004; Jayakumar & Garces, 2015; Perry, 2007). Rather than the earlier focus on strong affirmative action enforcement to promote racial justice, the strategic diversity leadership team led by UM President Lee Bollinger promoted a new business case for diversity to promote excellence in higher education, corporations, and other major social institutions (Herring, 2009; Page, 2007, 2017).

In a rapidly diversifying nation, it is vital to better understand this *evolution* from affirmative action to a business case for diversity during the Bollinger era within the historical context of shifting societal policies, higher education desegregation, and the ongoing story of diversity leadership at the UM and beyond. DEI values have been deeply intertwined in the fabric of the UM throughout its 200-year history (Duderstadt, 2015; Gurin, Lehman, & Lewis, 2004; Gurin, Nagda, & Lopez, 2004). Founded in 1817, UM has often led the way in making higher education accessible to all. For example, UM was one of the first universities in the nation to admit women, in 1870, long before it defended race-conscious admission policies at the US Supreme Court in 2003. Analysis of the historical diversity triumphs and tribulations at UM can serve as a platform to better understand how these past experiences continue to shape the university's present and future. Historically, the evolution of racial/ethnic diversity policies at UM and other historically white colleges and universities (HWCUs) have reflected broader societal-level shifts from chattel slavery, legal segregation, desegregation, civil rights, affirmative action, and anti–affirmative action to contemporary DEI strategies (Anderson, 2002; Bowman & Betancur, 2010; Feagin & Feagin, 2011).

Since its founding in 1817, UM diversity policies have evolved from less to more inclusive and equitable in response to related shifts in broader societal racial/ethnic diversity policies (Boyd, 1971; Duderstadt, 2015). However, it was not until the 1950s that landmark national desegregation policy prompted leaders at UM and other HWCUs to develop transformative campus racial/ethnic diversity policies (Peterson et al., 1978; Teddlie & Freeman, 2002). From the 1950s to the present, a succession of UM Presidents and their leadership teams have evolved innovative campus diversity strategies that respond to shifting national racial/ethnic policies. In addition to national policy shifts, strategic diversity leaders at the UM have also addressed related shifts in campus-level diversity challenges (Allen, 1982, 1985; Peterson et al., 1978). Since the 1950s, UM leaders' primary campus diversity challenges have been a diversifying student population, campus climate issues, and student activism (Smith, Altbach, & Lomotey, 2002).

Within a historical context, this chapter further clarifies the evolving story of diversity leadership at UM, a national exemplar for innovative responses to broader racial/ethnic policy shifts in American society since the 1950s. First, the following section provides a conceptual framework to understand better the major racial/ethnic diversity policy shifts in American society that required strategic responses from leaders at the UM and other HWCUs. Next, we examine how sociopolitical and campus challenges since the 1950s required UM leaders to shift from legal segregation to more equitable and inclusive campus diversity policies. Finally, we highlight a series of seven UM diversity leadership teams from the 1950s to the present, focusing on how their strategic priorities have evolved from desegregation, affirmative action, and multiculturalism to current DEI strategic planning agendas.

Historical Shifts in Societal Diversity Policies

Figure 13.1 provides a *conceptual framework* for a more systematic understanding of historical shifts in multilevel racial/ethnic policies in the United States that have shaped the *evolving strategic diversity* story at the UM and beyond (Bowman & Betancur, 2010). As noted in a special *New York Times* 1619 Project series, *chattel slavery* systematically excluded African Americans from higher education and other societal opportunities from early British *colonization* to the 1865 emancipation of slaves following the American Civil War. Therefore, from 1817 to 1865, the UM and other HWCUs were systematically burdened by blatant society-wide legacies of chattel slavery, Eurocentric privilege, white supremacy, and institutionalized racism (Anderson, 2002; Feagin & Feagin, 2011). For example, the landmark Dred Scott Supreme Court decision in 1857 essentially ruled that Blacks, slave or free, were not US citizens and "had no rights which the white man was bound to respect."

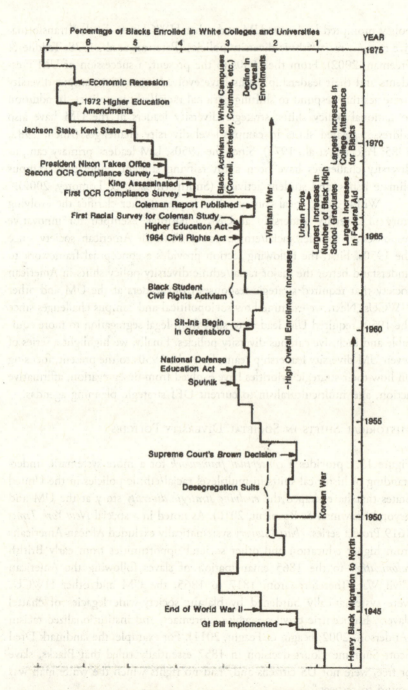

Figure 13.1. Percentage of Blacks enrolled in white colleges and universities.

Between 1865 and 1954, the national sociopolitical context for diversity policy at UM and other HWCUs shifted from chattel slavery to legal segregation (Bowman & Betancur, 2010; Feagin & Feagin, 2011). Legal racial segregation was systematically codified into law in 1896 with the *Plessy v. Ferguson* Supreme Court case. Guided by the "separate but equal" provision of the *Plessy v. Ferguson* decision, a separate public system of historically Black colleges and universities (HBCUs) was established to complement a number of existing private HBCUs (Anderson, 1988, 2002; Boyd, 1971). Historian James Anderson (1988) describes how these public and private HBCUs helped legitimize legal segregation and the restricted access of African Americans to the UM and other HWCUs.

Despite systematic legal restrictions against Blacks prior to the 1950s, UM and a few other northern public universities developed more "inclusive" merit-based diversity policies that went beyond White Anglo-Saxon Protestant (WASP) males (Bowman, St. John, & Kreger Stillman, 2011; Feagin & Feagin, 2011). For example, the UM was among the first public universities to admit Catholics, Jews, women, and others based on academic merit rather than ethnicity, gender, or elite family sponsorship. Moreover, while HWCUs in the South practiced a more strict form of racial segregation, UM and some other liberal northern universities admitted a very small number of Black students before the 1950s (Anderson, 1988; Teddlie & Freeman, 2002). Following World War II, the small number of Black students at HWCUs briefly increased from less than 1% in 1943 to 3% in 1953, spurred by the GI Bill (Anderson, 1993; Peterson et al., 1978). However, the few Black students admitted to HWCUs during the legal segregation era faced blatant racial isolation and discrimination within a campus racial climate characterized by anti-Black, deficit-based stigma, and WASP assimilation rather than multiculturalism empowerment (P. J. Bowman, 2013; Bowman & Betancur, 2010; Feagin & Feagin, 2011).

From Desegregation to Affirmative Action: Sociopolitical and Campus Diversity Challenges

Zelda Gamson and Charles Arce (1978) provided an insightful summary of the unprecedented increase in Black student enrollment within HWCUs from 1940 to 1975, along with related sociopolitical and campus determinants. Racial/ethnic diversity at UM and other HWCUs significantly increased following the landmark 1954 *Brown v. Board* Supreme Court case and 1958 National Defense Education Act (Boyd, 1971; Peterson et al., 1978; Sedlacek, 1987). Although Brown legalized desegregation in 1954, the Great Migration and racial justice activism in both the South and the North spurred the unprecedented enrollment of Black students in HWCUs after 1967 (Astin et al., 1975; Gurin & Epps, 1975). Black enrollment in HWCUs was facilitated by the Great Migration of African Americans from the Jim Crow South to higher-paying jobs in northern and western cities. As Blacks migrated to northern urban centers, the UM and other HWCUs became more accessible to them. In addition to Black urban migration, the access of Black students to northern HWCUs was also enhanced by financial aid, the 1964 Civil Rights Act, and especially Black political activism.

Black Student Activism and Affirmative Action

During the late 1960s and 1970s, Black student activism at HWCUs had a compelling impact on diversity policies at the federal, state, local, and university levels. As Black student activism shifted from civil rights to Black Power agendas, strategic diversity leadership at HWCUs faced demands to shift campus diversity policies from Eurocentric assimilation to multi-culturalism and empowerment strategies (Blauner, 1972; Peterson et al., 1978). From 1967 to 1975, Black student activism at northern HWCUs had transformative effects on Black enrollment, institutional diversity policies, and campus programs (Astin et al., 1975; Forgianni, 1973; Peterson et al., 1978). This growing Black student activism in HWCUs helped to transform early affirmative action policies to boost further Black enrollment and institutional racial/ethnic diversity (Bowen & Bok, 1998; Catlin, Seeley, & Talburtt, 1974; Rai & Critzer, 2000).

Federal affirmative action policies were first formalized in 1961 by Executive Order 10925 that mandated "affirmative action" to ensure that government employers "did not discriminate against any employee or applicant for employment because of race, creed, color, or national origin" (Peterson et al., 1978). However, the expansion of employment-focused affirmative action policies to enforce diversity in higher education did not occur until 1967, when the US Department of Education's Office of Civil Rights implemented an accountability system with regular compliance surveys. Between 1967 and the late 1970s, strong affirmative action policies combined with Black student activism at HWCUs to boost Black enrollment to historically high levels (Centra, 1970; Sedlacek, 1987). At UM and other HWCUs, the demands of early Black student activists resulted in unprecedented Black student enrollment levels and major programmatic transformations, including Black studies, academic support programs, and Black cultural centers (Blassingame, 1973; Record, 1973; Rojas, 2007).

Anti–Affirmative Action Backlash: From the Reagan Era to the Michigan Diversity Defense

From the 1960s to the 1980s, Black student activism and strong affirmative action policies helped to transform HWCUs from exclusive bastions of White privilege to increasingly diverse campus communities (Peterson et al., 1978; Rai & Critzer, 2000; Winkle-Wagner & Locks, 2014). However, a conservative anti–affirmative action movement gained momentum in the 1980s and continues ongoing legal efforts to abolish race-conscious affirmative action policies (Jayakumar & Garces, 2015; Smith, Altbach, & Lomotey, 2002). Moreover, during the two Ronald Reagan presidential terms between1980 and 1988, the anti–affirmative action movement began to gain greater political legitimation as an official government-based backlash to earlier civil rights–era affirmative action and diversity policies.

Throughout the 1990s, the anti–affirmative action movement continued to gain momentum at both the federal and state levels with sharp retrenchments in affirmative action at the University of Texas (Hopwood Case), University of California (Proposal 209), and beyond (Jayakumar & Garces, 2015; Smith, Altbach, & Lomotey, 2002). In 2003, the UM became the epicenter of the national anti–affirmative action debate when it was targeted in two landmark Supreme Court lawsuits (*Gratz v. Bollinger* and *Grutter v. Bollinger*) and a state-level ballot initiative banning affirmative action (Michigan Civil Rights Initiative [2006] and *Schuette v. Coalition to Defend Affirmative Action* [2014]). In response, UM leaders developed a new strategic "benefits of diversity" defense for affirmative action that was argued in several lower court cases and eventually in the Supreme Court (Gurin, Lehman, & Lewis, 2004; Gurin, Nagda, & Lopez, 2004). In addition, since the Bollinger era, diversity leadership teams at UM have gone beyond affirmative action to develop innovative benefits of diversity and inclusion strategies that promote excellence in higher education, corporations, and other major social institutions (Gurin, Lehman, & Lewis, 2004; Gurin, Nagda, & Lopez, 2004); Page, 2017; Winkle-Wagner & Locks, 2014).

Evolution of Strategic Diversity Leadership at Michigan

The Bollinger era (1996–2001) shift from affirmative action lawsuits to diversity strategy needs to be better understood within the shifting historical context of UM diversity policy from the 1950s to the present. In the *Gratz* and *Grutter* lawsuits, the UM diversity leadership developed a legal strategy beyond the historical rationale for affirmative action to promote racial justice. In contrast, UM leaders advanced a new business case for affirmative action to promote the benefits of diversity for excellence in higher education and society (Gurin, Lehman, & Lewis, 2004; Gurin, Nagda, & Lopez, 2004; Page, 2007, 2017). By 2003, the *Gratz* and *Grutter* lawsuits reached the US Supreme Court, which placed UM at the center of a national paradigm shift in strategic diversity policy in higher education, corporations, and other major social institutions (Herring, 2009; Perry, 2007; Phillips, 2014). Despite the landmark national impact of Bollinger's diversity leadership, his tenure represents only one of several significant eras in UM's evolving story of strategic diversity leadership since the 1950s.

Going beyond the historic affirmative action cases in Michigan, we further clarify the broader and still evolving UM story of strategic diversity leadership. The seven presidential eras at UM since the 1950s include the Hatcher (1951–1967), Fleming (1968–1979), Shapiro (1980–1987), Duderstadt (1988–1996), Bollinger (1996–2001), Coleman (2002–2014), and Schlissel (2014–2002) eras. Drawing from UM archives, we highlight how diversity leadership teams developed innovative agendas to address shifting sociopolitical and campus challenges during each of these presidential eras. For example, during each of these seven eras, a UM diversity leadership team has made the campus a national exemplar for innovative institutional diversity strategies that are more inclusive and equitable (Duderstadt, 2015; Gurin, Lehman, & Lewis, 2004; Gurin, Nagda, & Lopez, 2004; Perry, 2007).

Before 1951, during the Hatcher era, there was no strategic need for a diversity leadership team at the UM nor the other HWCUs because of exclusionary historical racial/ethnic diversity policies in the United States. Prior to the 1950s, non-White access to UM was systematically restricted by chattel slavery and various Eurocentric legal segregation provisions, including the US Supreme Court *Dred Scott* and *Plessy* decisions (Bowman & Betancur, 2010; Feagin & Feagin, 2011). However, beginning with the *Brown* desegregation decision in 1954, UM relied on a succession of strong diversity leadership teams to address shifting sociopolitical effectively and campus challenges. Since the 1950s, the specific challenges and priorities for UM's strategic diversity leadership teams have evolved from early desegregation to the current DEI strategies.

For each of the seven successive UM presidential eras beginning with Hatcher, we first present the core campus diversity leaders and then highlight how their strategic priorities have evolved from desegregation, affirmative action, and multi-culturalism to DEI strategic planning agendas. During each era, core campus diversity leaders have included the UM president, the provost, and a chief diversity leader.

HATCHER ERA (1951–1967): LEGAL SEGREGATION TO DESEGREGATION STRATEGIES

From 1951 to 1967, Harlan Hatcher served as UM's eighth president, with Marvin Niehuss (1951–1962), Roger Heyns (1962–1965), and Allan Smith (1965–1967) providing senior leadership as provosts. During his 17-year tenure Hatcher led the UM through the end of legal segregation in the United States and new desegregation policies (Anderson, 2002; Boyd, 1971). In 1954, the landmark *Brown v. Board of Education* decision reversed the 1896 *Plessy v. Ferguson* court decision and codified desegregation into national law. Although Hatcher did not appoint a formal UM chief diversity leader, both Hobart Taylor Jr. and Albert Wheeler played important diversity leadership roles. While serving as the executive vice chairman of the President's Committee on Equal Employment Opportunity, and with a law degree from the UM, Taylor worked closely with US Presidents John F. Kennedy and Lyndon B. Johnson on the Executive Order 10925 of 1963 that codified affirmative action.

Because the national president's committee did not include higher education admissions, Taylor decided to work closely with UM President Hatcher and Provost Heyns to design a novel affirmative action admissions initiative at UM called the Opportunity Awards Program. With Taylor's leadership, the innovative UM-based program became a national model and increased Black student enrollment from 0.5% in 1964 to 3% by 1970. Along with Taylor, Albert Wheeler also provided Hatcher with strategic consultation on the program and on other early UM desegregation strategies, including residence halls desegregation and a visiting student program with the Tuskegee Institute (an HBCU). Wheeler earned a doctor of public health degree from UM in 1944 and became the first African American to earn tenure at the UM in 1959. He was also an active leader in the Ann Arbor Black community and became the first Black mayor of Ann Arbor in 1975.

FLEMING ERA (1968–1979): CIVIL RIGHTS TO BLACK POWER AND BAM I ACTIVISM

Robben Fleming served as the 9th president of the UM from 1968 to 1979. During the 11-year Fleming era, three UM senior leaders served as provost, including Allan Smith (1968–1974), Frank Rhodes (1974–1977), and Harold Shapiro (1977–1979). Fleming was faced with developing strategic UM responses to increasingly strident Black student activism and the related sociopolitical challenges (Astin et al., 1975; Forgianni, 1973; Peterson et al., 1978). During the Fleming era, Black student activism at UM was fueled by the turbulent national shift from a Southern-based civil rights movement to a northern-based Black Power movement in the late 1960s and 1970s (Blauner, 1972; Morris, 1984; Peterson et al., 1978). In addition to this national Black Power shift, Black UM student activists with families in the Detroit area were also inspired by the city's strong legacy of Black political activism (Duderstadt, 2015; Kerner Commission, 1968; Meier & Rudwick, 2007).

President Fleming increasingly relied on more expert diversity leadership to manage related challenges as Black student activism heightened. In 1970, Fleming hired William Cash as special assistant to the president to help manage new racial/ethnic challenges. With a PhD in guidance and counseling from the UM, Cash was among the first tenured Black professors at the university (School of Education). However, as a special assistant to the president, Cash's expertise in more conciliatory human relations strategies often proved insufficient to address the increasingly strident demands of more militant Black student activists. In addition to Cash, Fleming also hired Henry Johnson in 1972 as the vice president for student services. Johnson was the first African American to hold this central administrative position at UM.

During the Fleming era, two early episodes of Black student activism at UM—the 1968 administrative building takeover and the 1970 Black action movement (BAM) strike—had significant consequences for transformative institutional diversity (Duderstadt, 2015; Lewis, 2004; Perry, 2007). BAM activists not only "demanded" a sharp increase in Black student enrollment (10%) but strategic institutional changes as well, including Black studies (Center for Afroamerican and African Studies), an academic support program (Coalition for the Use of Learning Skills, now the Comprehensive Studies Program), and a Black cultural center (William Monroe Trotter House).

SHAPIRO ERA (1980–1987): MANAGING RACIAL TENSIONS AND DEVELOPING STRATEGIC DIVERSITY RESPONSES AT THE UNIVERSITY OF MICHIGAN

After serving as provost, Harold Shapiro took office as UM's 10th president in 1980 and served until 1987, when he departed to become president at Princeton University. During Shapiro's seven years as president, both Billy Frye (1980–1986) and James Duderstadt (1986–1987) served as provost and vice president for academic affairs. Among Shapiro's many accomplishments, a major legacy was developing strategic UM responses to growing sociopolitical backlash against race-based affirmative action at the federal, state, and campus levels (Rai & Critzer, 2000; Smith, Altbach, & Lomotey, 2002). Shapiro faced unique UM campus racial tensions exacerbated by conservative ideologies to reverse civil rights–era policies in higher education and other major social institutions during the 1980s Reagan revolution (Altbach, Lomotey, & Rivers, 2002; Teddlie & Freeman, 2002).

Shapiro struggled to develop a strategic diversity leadership team to effectively manage growing UM campus conflicts between conservative anti–affirmative action forces and a resurgent BAM-II group of Black student activists (Allen, 1982; 1985; Duderstadt, 2015). In 1981, President Shapiro and Provost Frye appointed Harold Johnson as the first Black dean at UM (School of Social Work) and later as special counsel to the president. Among his many accomplishments as dean (1981–1993), Johnson provided the leadership necessary to move the School of Social Work to the number one ranking in the nation. However, despite his many accomplishments as dean, Johnson recalled, "There were people who certainly resented the fact that I was black and dean, including some members of my faculty, and they tried to make life difficult for me" (Bicentennial StoryCorps, 2018).

In addition to Johnson, Shapiro recruited Professor Niara Sudarkasa in 1981 as the new associate vice president for academic affairs. Sudarkasa earned her PhD in anthropology from Columbia University and was the first Black woman to earn tenure at UM as an associate professor in 1969 and full professor in 1976. Professor Sudarkasa was also the first Black female director of the UM Center for Afroamerican and African Studies as a Pan-African expert on African, Caribbean, and Black American cultural ties. While serving as associate vice president from 1981 to 1986, Sudarkasa supported strategic institutional responses to growing campus racial conflicts and black student activism. As UM's associate vice president, Sudarkasa helped translate growing student activism into innovative diversity initiatives by building on her earlier experience as a trusted young Black professor working with 1970 BAM leaders. From 1986 to 1998, Sudarkasa served as the first female president of Lincoln University, the oldest HBCU in the United States.

Duderstadt Era (1988–1996): Michigan Mandate to Legal Opposition

James Duderstadt became UM's 11th president in 1988 after serving as interim president and provost from 1986 to1988. Challenged by the anti–

affirmative action movement, President Duderstadt developed a more proactive diversity agenda that emphasized multiculturalism and linked diversity to academic excellence and global competitiveness (Duderstadt, 1990, 2015; Janssens et al., 2010). Duderstadt's (1990) proactive multicultural agenda was clearly articulated in the "Michigan Mandate: A Strategic Linking of Academic Excellence and Social Diversity."

The Michigan Mandate's goal was to diversify the UM and reshape academic programs to prepare students for the global economy and the information age. This bold mandate was Duderstadt's major legacy demonstrating strategic leadership and institutional transformation based on a future vision linking knowledge, globalization, and pluralism. From 1988 to 1996, Duderstadt worked with three provosts to advance the Michigan Mandate process, including Charles Vest (1989–1990), Gilbert Whitaker (1990–1995), and J. Bernard Machen (1995–1997). In addition to these provosts, Duderstadt also worked closely with chief diversity leaders, deans, and other critical stakeholders on Michigan Mandate goal setting, planning, implementation, monitoring, and evaluation.

As chief diversity leaders, Charles Moody (vice provost for the Office of Minority Affairs, 1988–1993) and Lester Monts (senior vice provost for academic affairs and senior counselor to the president for diversity, 1993–1996) played central administrative roles in the Michigan Mandate process. Vice Provost Moody helped plan strategies to change UM's "corporate culture" based on extensive leadership experience as a professor, program director, and administrator in the School of Education. Senior Vice Provost Monts and Associate Vice Provost John Matlock worked closely with Duderstadt on implementing the Michigan Mandate the better to diversify all areas of academic affairs at the UM. In addition, Rhetaugh Dumas played a pivotal leadership role as the first Black woman to serve as dean at UM (School of Nursing) from 1981 to 1996. After three terms as Dean, Dumas served as vice provost for health affairs in 1996 to provide strategic leadership on critical institutional diversity priorities in several UM health professional schools, including the Schools of Medicine, Nursing, Pharmacy, and Public Health.

The many successes of the Michigan Mandate are clearly documented in the report "A 50 Year History of Social Diversity at the University of Michigan" (Duderstadt, 2015). This report documents the success of the Michigan Mandate in making significant progress toward three major goals: (a) to recognize that diversity and excellence are complementary and compelling goals for the university and to make a firm commitment to their achievement; (b) to commit to the recruitment, support, and success of members of historically underrepresented groups among our students, faculty, staff, and leadership; and (c) to build on the UM campus an environment that nourishes and sustains diversity and pluralism and values and respects the dignity and worth of every individual.

Despite the documented successes between 1988 and 1996, Duderstadt's Michigan Mandate also aroused growing multilevel sociopolitical resistance (Duderstadt, 2015). This resistance was rooted in growing national anti–affirmative action legal opposition and cross-racial campus climate tensions and ideological differences (Bowman & Smith, 2002; Natour, Locks, & Bowman, 2011). For example, a bitter debate emerged at UM over a proposal for mandatory courses dealing with race and ethnicity. Despite administrative support, the UM faculty narrowly voted down a proposal to mandate such a course requirement, and the effort antagonized many White alumni. President Duderstadt said, "They question whether we're ceasing to be their university"; they "fear that we're eliminating opportunities for their own children and grandchildren" (Wilkerson, 1990). In addition to campus-level resistance, the Michigan Mandate also attracted growing national anti–affirmative action opposition that became a major challenge for the subsequent Bollinger presidential era at UM.

BOLLINGER ERA (1996–2001): ANTI–AFFIRMATIVE ACTION LAWSUITS TO DIVERSITY LEGAL STRATEGY

From 1996 to 2001, during Lee Bollinger's tenure as UM's 12th twelfth president, legal opposition to affirmative action at the national level shifted to the UM campus. Perhaps the most visible legacy of Bollinger's UM presidency are the two UM affirmative action lawsuits and the related benefits of diversity legal strategy. The two affirmative action lawsuits—*Gratz v. Bollinger* and *Grutter v. Bollinger*—reflect tensions between (a) the growing national opposition to affirmative action, and (b) the reinforcement of UM's strong campus commitment to diversity by the Michigan Mandate process during the preceding Duderstadt years (Duderstadt, 1990, 2015; Gurin, Lehman, & Lewis, 2004; Gurin, Nagda, & Lopez, 2004; Perry, 2007). As a legal scholar, Bollinger organized a diversity leadership team to develop an effective legal strategy to defend race-based affirmative action in higher education. Bollinger worked closely with Provost Nancy Cantor (1997–2001), Vice Provost Lester Monts (1996–2014), vice president for student life E. Royster-Harper (1999–2020), and other key UM experts to develop a new benefits of diversity legal strategy to support the use of race as a factor in university admissions.

The need for a new diversity legal strategy on the UM campus was driven by historic shifts in anti–affirmative action court cases across the nation. Increasingly, courts were rejecting the historical racial injustice and past discrimination rationales for race-targeted college admissions and supporting more conservative anti–affirmative action agendas at the University of California (*Regents of the University of California v. Bakke*), University of Texas (*Hopwood v. Texas*), and beyond (Jayakumar & Garces, 2015; Smith, Altbach, & Lomotey, 2002). Thus, in contrast to the historical racial justice argument, Bollinger's UM leadership team developed a new business case for affirmative action to promote diversity and excellence in higher education, corporations, and other major social institutions (Gurin, Lehman, & Lewis, 2004; Gurin, Nagda, & Lopez, 2004; Herring, 2009; Perry, 2007).

As UM provost from 1997 to 2001, Nancy Cantor emerged as a key member of Bollinger's UM leadership team that developed the new diversity legal strategy (Cantor & Engot, 2014; Gurin, Lehman, & Lewis, 2004; Gurin, Nagda, & Lopez, 2004). Cantor was a pivotal player as a social psychological expert with strong skills in collaborating with deans, faculty, students, and staff members (Gurin, Lehman, & Lewis, 2004; Gurin, Nagda, & Lopez, 2004; Gurin et al., 2002; Gurin, Nagda, & Lopez, 2004). Cantor worked especially closely with fellow UM psychologist Patricia Gurin, a key expert witness in the Supreme Court affirmative action lawsuits. In collaboration with Cantor and Gurin, several other UM scholars helped develop a compelling benefits of diversity legal strategy that was theory-driven, evidence-based, and relevant to higher education and other major social institutions.

COLEMAN ERA (2002–2014): AFFIRMATIVE ACTION BAN TO INSTITUTIONAL DIVERSITY STRATEGY

After serving as the president of the University of Iowa for seven years, Mary Sue Coleman was selected to replace Lee Bollinger in 2002 as UM's 13th president and its first female president. Between 2002 and 2014, she worked closely with three provosts, including Paul N. Courant (2002–2005), Teresa Sullivan (2006–2010), and Philip Hanlon (2010–2013). President Coleman faced two significant diversity challenges upon her arrival at UM in 2002—first, to manage the growing legal opposition to affirmative action, and subsequently to develop a more proactive institutional diversity agenda (Gurin, Lehman, & Lewis, 2004; Gurin, Nagda, & Lopez, 2004).

In the *Grutter* lawsuit, the Supreme Court supported UM's law school affirmative action admission strategy that used race along with other factors to obtain "the educational benefits that flow from a diverse student body" (Allen & Solorzano, 2001). However, in the *Gratz* lawsuit, the Supreme Court ruled that UM's undergraduate admissions system that awarded points based on race was unconstitutional (Gurin, Lehman, & Lewis, 2004; Gurin, Nagda, & Lopez, 2004; Perry, 2007). In 2006, President Coleman was further hindered when a state ballot initiative passed by a 58% majority to ban affirmative action in Michigan (Natour, Locks, & Bowman, et al., 2011). This growing national and state affirmative action opposition was deeply rooted in an increasingly conservative American racial ideology that reinforced campus racial climate tensions at the UM and beyond (Bowman & Smith, 2002; Tatum, 2017).

Despite restrictions on affirmative action, President Coleman worked closely with the UM Provost Office and Senior Vice Provost Lester Monts on several innovative strategies to promote the benefits of diversity throughout the UM campus. First, Ted Spencer, associate vice provost and executive director of undergraduate admissions, was authorized to become a national leader in innovative "holistic review" processes that maintain academic excellence and a diverse student body consistent with federal and state laws. Second, Laurita Thomas was appointed as the associate vice president and chief human resource officer to promote the core values of diversity in all aspects of UM's central resource operations, including both academic and business units. In addition, Vice Provost Monts also worked closely with campus diversity leaders to advance two major innovative institutional diversity initiatives: (a) innovative diversity research and training initiatives; and (b) the National Center for Institutional Diversity. These two proactive diversity initiatives not only went beyond defending affirmative action but also built on UM's national leadership role in advancing the benefits of diversity, existing institutional strengths, and a strong commitment to equity.

INNOVATIVE DIVERSITY RESEARCH AND TRAINING (2005)

During the 2002–2014 Coleman era, the Provost Office supported Professor James Jackson's strategic efforts as director of the UM's world-renowned Institute for Social Research (ISR) to institutionalize several innovative diversity research and training initiatives. As the Daniel Katz Distinguished Professor of Psychology, Jackson was internationally renowned for his ISR-based national studies on the social psychology of race and culture. Since the 1970s, Jackson had played an especially pivotal role in diversifying faculty at UM in several leadership roles within ISR and the Department of Psychology, and serving as director of the Center for Afro-American and African Studies.

With support from the Provost Office, Jackson strategically leveraged a unique ISR-based Program for Research on Black Americans (PRBA) to diversify the faculty at UM and other universities across the nation. Innovative ISR-PRBA mentoring and training activities continue to provide rigorous research methods and skill development for talented junior faculty, postdoctoral, and doctoral scholars from diverse backgrounds. Since the 1970s, Jackson and ISR-PRBA colleagues have developed a stellar reputation for diversifying faculty at UM and other universities in the social sciences (sociology, psychology, political science, etc.) and related professional schools (public health, social work, education, public policy, etc.). As a foundation for cutting-edge diversity research methods training, Jackson and ISR-PRBA colleagues developed a series of landmark national studies with international significance (P. J. Bowman, 1982; Jackson, 1991; Jackson et al., 2006). In addition, a growing number of related ISR-PRBA publications provide new insight into pressing policy-relevant issues, including racial/ethnic disparities in mental and physical health and a range of related risk factors (discrimination and other psychosocial stressors) and protective factors (family support, religion, identity, and political engagement).

New National Center for Institutional Diversity (2006)

With support from President Coleman and the Provost Office, Senior Vice Provost Monts launched another major UM diversity initiative in 2002. Based on a strategic meeting with 100 UM diversity leaders, a diversity steering committee with 30 members was established (senior faculty, center directors, four deans, and other key leaders). This steering committee secured Ford Foundation support for a 2005 "Futuring Diversity" planning conference that recommended the establishment of a new UM National Center for Institutional Diversity (NCID). In 2006, NCID was launched to (1) address complex diversity challenges facing higher education and other major social institutions; (2) provide institutions with innovative scholarship, models, support, and resources to promote the benefits of diversity; and (3) develop strategic institutional partnerships to address both campus and national diversity challenges.

Following a national search, Phillip Bowman was selected in 2006 as the founding director of NCID as well as professor of higher education and faculty associate at ISR. As a UM social psychologist with expertise on race and public policy issues, Bowman had collaborated with James Jackson in the 1970s to establish the ISR-based Program for Research on Black Americans. While founding NCID director from 2006 to 2013, Bowman worked closely with the senior vice provost, a steering committee, deans, directors, and other key stakeholders to advance an innovative agenda. To build on UM's strengths, the NCID strategic agenda focused on addressing the challenges and opportunities of diversity in four core priority areas: (a) scholarship, education and innovation; (b) science, health, and pipeline development; (c) organizations and urban and economic development; and (d) public policy, culture, and social change.

Guided by these four priority areas, from 2006 to 2013, NCID annually sponsored national conferences, meetings, presentations, conversations, and dialogues. In addition, NCID strategic partnerships—campus and external—promoted national exemplars by bridging scholarship, engagement, and innovation through seven programmatic activities: (1) an Annual Grants Program to seed, incubate, and advance diversity innovation; (2) Diversity Scholarship and Innovation Awards to promote diversity champions at the UM and beyond; (3) a Postdoctoral Fellows Program for exceptional early career diversity scholars; (4) a National Diversity Scholars Network to promote scholars at various career stages engaged in exemplary work across the nation; (5) a Readings on Equal Education book series focusing on diversity interventions to address K–career educational inequalities; (6) a Diversity Research And Policy Program to conduct sponsored studies on critical higher education and career diversity challenges; and (7) a Diversity Blueprints Strategic Planning process to develop innovative initiatives that advance the benefits of diversity at UM and beyond.

Since 2013, the NCID has continued to refine its mission, expand its strategic agenda, and organize new initiatives to maintain a distinctive national niche under the directorship of Professors John Burkhardt (2013–2016) and Tabbye Chavous (2016–present). Under Burkhardt's and Chavous's leadership, NCID has consolidated several inaugural programmatic activities and added a growing number of new activities, including national forums on immigration issues, an expanding International Diversity Scholars Network, and several fellowships and awards to promote diversity, equity, and inclusion.

Schlissel Era (2014–2022): Institutional Diversity to DEI Strategic Planning Strategy

Mark Schlissel became the 14th president of UM in 2014 after serving as provost at Brown University. President Schlissel advanced UM's strategic agenda with support from three provosts, including Martha Pollack (2013–2017), Martin Philbert (2017–2020), and Susan Collins (2020–2022). In addition, Schlissel and a series of three provosts have provided strong support for Robert Sellers as UM's chief diversity leader since 2014 to spearhead a new DEI strategic planning process. As UM's first chief diversity officer (CDO), Sellers is also the vice provost for equity and inclusion and Charles Moody Collegiate Professor of Psychology and Education.

To further advance the ideals of academic excellence and its interdependence with diversity, Vice Provost Sellers launched the first 5-year DEI strategic planning process in 2016. As a model for future UM-CDOs, Sellers has led a 2016–2021 DEI strategic planning process that systematically mobilized UM's vast energies and intellectual resources. The DEI planning process engaged all UM sectors and constituents within a decentralized planning structure with over 90 leads in every school, college, and unit. A central Office of DEI (ODEI) oversees both major institutional diversity initiatives and the decentralized DEI strategic planning process. To effectively manage campus-wide DEI activities, CDO Sellers is assisted by Katrina Wade-Golden as deputy chief diversity officer to engage 51 UM units in a yearlong process. Wade-Golden coordinates a complex decentralized DEI strategic planning accountability structure in which different UM academic and administrative units have their own diversity officers.

To advance the innovative DEI agenda, UM initially committed $85 million in new investment in addition to over $40 million in annual funding for 20 university programs addressing critical campus diversity issues. This substantial investment supports the implementation and progress of new DEI initiatives to advance UM's mission and operations further. ODEI also advances the unique DEI strategic planning process with an array of innovative awards, summits, symposia, reports, and online resources to further reinforce UM's historical reputation as a national DEI leader. For example, annually, the ODEI sponsors UM's Distinguished Diversity Leaders Awards, the annual DEI Summit, and the extensive Martin Luther King Jr. Celebration activities.

Under CDO Sellers's leadership, ODEI maintains an innovative online resource that provides historical, current, and future-oriented information about

DEI at UM. This website serves as a gateway for DEI news, information, and resources that benefit faculty, staff, students, and the UM community. At this stage in the 21st century, UM's online portal is an increasingly powerful tool to further advance the four foundational pillars and goals that guide ODEI's strategic engagement. This tool allows UM stakeholders to form mission-focused, mutually beneficial partnerships around the four pillars: (1) diversity: working to create a university community that reflects the vast, rich heterogeneity of the state and the broader society; (2) equity: working to create a university environment that fosters equal opportunity for all members and promites a university culture that discourages individual bias and commits to eliminating institutional bias in all of its forms at our university; (3) inclusion: working to create a university where every individual has a sense of belonging and the opportunity to contribute to the whole; and (4) partnerships: working to discover, develop, foster, and celebrate mutually beneficial mission-focused partnerships within and outside the university community.

In January 2022, Mary Sue Coleman returned to serve again as the UM interim president while the board of regents searches for a permanent replacement for former President Mark Schlissel, who was dismissed for an inappropriate relationship with a subordinate. In May 2022, Provost Susan Collins named Tabbye Chavous to succeed Robert Sellers as the new CDO and vice provost for equity and inclusion for a five-year term. Chavous is a professor of psychology and education and brings a wealth of expertise to the CDO position, including DEI-related leadership experience at both UM and national levels. As CDO and vice provost, Chavous reports to the provost as a member of the provost leadership team with a major focus on academic affairs, including faculty recruitment and retention, tenure and promotion, and faculty development. She also meets regularly with the UM president as a principal adviser and campus leader on DEI issues. Chavous becomes the CDO at a pivotal time, when UM is in the midst of an evaluation process at both the unit and university levels of DEI 1.0, its initial DEI five-year plan. This evaluation will be followed by a yearlong campus-wide engagement period to inform and launch UM's next DEI strategic plan—DEI 2.0—in fall 2023.

Conclusions and Implications

This chapter contextualizes and highlights the evolving story of strategic diversity leadership at HWCUs, focusing on the UM. At this stage in the

21st century, a better understanding of this evolving story can help to guide future scholarship and strategic interventions to address ongoing DEI challenges in higher education. The UM continues to be a national exemplar for innovative responses to historical shifts in national racial/ethnic policies and related campus diversity challenges. Therefore, this chapter provides a historical context and multilevel conceptual framework for a deeper understanding of the evolving UM story of strategic diversity leadership. From its founding in 1817, the UM has been a national leader in diversifying higher education despite the persistent Eurocentric legacies that continue to challenge UM and all HWCUs in the United States as they strive to achieve the core values of institutional diversity.

Since the 1950s, there have been seven presidential eras at UM. After the long history of legal segregation in the United States, the Hatcher era required strategic diversity leadership to respond to the new transformative mandates of desegregation and civil rights policies. As national racial/ethnic policies have continued to shift, each subsequent UM president from Fleming to Schlissel has relied on a strategic diversity leadership team, including the provost and a chief diversity leader. The specific priorities of these successive UM diversity leadership teams have also continued to evolve from early desegregation to current DEI strategic planning strategies to address shifting national and campus diversity challenges.

The specific title of UM's chief diversity leaders also continues to evolve from "special assistant to the president" during the early Fleming era to "chief diversity officer" during the current Schlissel era. From the Fleming to the Schlissel eras, UM's chief diversity leaders have promoted innovative responses to the shifting sociopolitical and campus diversity challenges that reinforce UM's legacy as a national model for strategic diversity leadership. Guided by our preliminary analysis, future scholarship should further clarify the historical evolution of strategic diversity leadership at the UM and other HWCUs. In addition, future scholarship should also provide greater insight into the: (1) evolving roles of chief diversity leaders, (2) specific functions of strategic diversity leadership teams, and (3) multilevel factors that impede and promote the efficacy of DEI strategic planning in higher education.

A book by Williams and Wade-Golden (2013) titled *The Chief Diversity Officer* provides several directions for future research on the critical role of chief diversity leaders in organizational strategy, structure, and change management in higher education. Studies have long shown that diversity leaders in HWCUs often face especially stressful challenges (Poussaint, 1974; Rist, 1979) and that higher education diversity initiatives are often impeded by campus resistance, tension, and conflict (Peterson et al., 1978; Record, 1973). A related book by Damon Williams (2013) titled *Strategic Diversity Leadership* also provides several directions for future research on how strategic diversity leadership teams can effectively activate change and transform higher education in the 21st century. In order to improve the benefits of diversity, future studies need to clarify further how strategic diversity leadership teamwork may be stressful and may face resistance from multiple sources—team members, organizations, and external environment (Phillips, Liljenquist, & Neale, 2009; Phillips et al., 2014).

After a decade of solid enforcement in the 1970s, affirmative action to promote diversity in higher education begins to face strong resistance in the 1980s. Next, faced with growing legal opposition, race-based affirmative action has been increasingly replaced by more popular class-based affirmative action and race-neutral strategies to promote diversity (Guiner, 2015; Kahlenberg, 2014; Sedlacek, 2004). From the Hatcher to the Schlissel era, UM leaders have faced external resistance (national and state) and internal campus resistance to their innovative diversity efforts. Future studies should further clarify how such multilevel resistance may impede the efficacy of innovative DEI initiatives (Kalev, Dobbin, & Kelly, 2006; K. L. Williams, 2014). For example, macrosocietal legal opposition to affirmative action at the national and state levels grew especially strong during the Shapiro, Duderstadt, Bollinger, and Coleman eras at UM (*Gratz v. Bollinger*, 2003; *Grutter v. Bollinger*, 2003). In addition to the external backlash, we need to understand better how DEI initiatives are often impeded by internal opposition from meso-organizational resistance (Kelly & Dobbin, 1998) and more subtle micro-psychosocial bias (Steele, 2010).

At the macrosocietal level, the racial/ethnic hierarchy and racist status beliefs produce resistance to campus diversity initiatives and biased group processes and individual behaviors. At the meso-organizational level, resistance to campus diversity initiatives can be exacerbated by biased racial ideology and attitudes that, in turn, reinforce campus inequalities, climate problems, and conflicts (Bell & Kravitz, 2008; Dobbin & Sutton, 1998; Kalev, Dobbin, & Kelly, 2006). Finally, at the micropsychosocial level, racial attitude studies show how resistance to diversity initiatives is also exacerbated by (a) priming negative stereotypes; (b) perceived threats to privileges and scarce resources; and (c) perceived threats to existing norms and color-blind ideology (Bobo & Hutchings 1996; Bonilla-Silva, 2013; Steele, 2010).

Consistent with status characteristics theory, future research should also provide greater insight into whether the popular business case for diversity initiatives may sometimes exacerbate resistance rather than enhance the efficacy of innovative DEI efforts (e.g., P. J. Bowman, 2013; Ridgeway, 2014). For example, in contrast to prior research, a related study by Jamillah Bowman Williams (2017) suggests that diversity leaders may exacerbate resistance to innovative DEI initiatives when they promote the popular business case but reduce resistance by emphasizing legal and moral rationales.

Bridging DEI Strategic Evaluation and Related Scholarship: Reciprocal Translation

The UM and other HWCUs increasingly rely on strategic DEI leadership, planning, and evaluation to better leverage institutional diversity to promote academic excellence in a rapidly diversifying nation. For example, UM's CDO has organized the Office of DEI (ODEI) to launch a series of 5-year DEI strategic plans to advance the ideals of academic excellence and its interdependence with diversity. With a decentralized agenda, the ODEI coordinates both campus-wide and unit-specific DEI strategic plans along with a systematic implementation, evaluation, and assessment system to monitor progress toward specific objectives. Annually, quantitative and qualitative data provide formative assessments to improve DEI strategic plan implementation and evaluation metrics to track progress toward longer-term outcomes.

In addition to ODEI evaluation studies, more multidisciplinary scholarship on innovative DEI strategic planning and initiatives is also needed in the 21st century. A reciprocal translation approach can help chief diversity leaders better bridge insights from DEI evaluation studies with a multidisciplinary scholarship for a deeper understanding of the complex DEI strategic planning process (J. E. Bowman, 2013; Bowman, St. John, Kreger Stillman, 2011). With regard to evaluation, both formative and outcome evaluation studies are essential to guide practical DEI policy and program decision making. Formative evaluation can help refine campus-wide and unit-specific DEI strategic plans, initiatives, and programs. In addition, outcome evaluation can demonstrate the effectiveness of specific DEI programs and track progress toward long-term outcomes for external stakeholders.

In order to complement ODEI evaluation studies, more multidisciplinary scholarship is also needed for a deeper *understanding* of critical DEI issues, including chief diversity leaders' evolving role. Multidisciplinary studies by scholars from the social/behavioral sciences, humanities, and professional fields can deepen understanding of critical DEI trends, issues, and complexities. Jamillah Bowman (2013) highlights a reciprocal translation approach that can help to better bridge innovative "DEI scholarship" with "DEI strategic evaluation." Reciprocal translation promotes both (a) the "traditional translation" of DEI scholarship to guide DEI practice, and (b) the "reverse translation" of DEI evaluation studies to "inspire" new DEI scholarship. This reciprocal translation approach to DEI strategic planning also extends a classic "action research" adage by the eminent social psychologists Kurt Lewin: "There is nothing so practical as a good theory and nothing so theoretical as a good practice" (Bowman, 2019, p. xv). With such action research, strategic diversity leadership in higher education can benefit from the "deeper understanding" provided by reciprocal insights from DEI evaluation studies and related DEI theory-driven scholarship.

References

Allen, W. R. (1982). Black and blue: Black students at the University of Michigan. *LS&A Magazine.* University of Michigan.

Allen, W. R. (1985). Black students, White campus: Structural, interpersonal and psychological correlates of success. *Journal of Negro Education, 54*(2), 134–147.

Allen, W. R., & Solorzano, D. (2001). Affirmative action, educational equity, and campus racial climate: A case study of University of Michigan Law School. *Berkeley La Raza Law Journal, 12*(2), 237–263.

Altbach, P. G., Lomotey, K., & Rivers, S. (2002). Race in higher education: The continuing crisis. In W. A. Smith, G. Altbach, & Lomotey, K. (Eds.), *The racial crisis in higher education* (pp. 23–42). SUNY Press.

Anderson, J. D. (1988). *The education of Blacks in the south, 1860–1935.* University of North Carolina Press.

Anderson, J. D. (1993). Race, meritocracy and the American academy during the immediate post–World War II era. *History of Education Quarterly, 33*(2), 152–175.

Anderson, J. D. (2002). Race in American higher education. In W. A. Smith, G. Altbach, & K. Lomotey (Eds.), *The racial crisis in higher education: Continuing challenges for the 21st century* (pp. 3–23). SUNY Press.

Astin, A., Astin, H. S., Boyle, A. E., & Bisconti, A. S. (1975). *The power of protest: National study of student and faculty disruption with implications for the future.* Jossey-Bass.

Bell, M. P., & Kravitz, D. A. (2008). From the guest co-editors: What do we know and need to learn about diversity education and training? *Academy of Management Learning & Education, 7*(3), 301–308.

Bicentennial StoryCorps. (2018, January 29). Interview No. 4, Taking care of a community. *Arts & Culture.* https://arts.umich.edu/news-features/bicentennial-storycorps-interview-no-4-taking-care-of-a-community/

Blassingame, J. W. (1973). *New perspectives on Black studies.* University of Illinois Press.

Blauner, R. (1972). *Racial oppression in American.* Harper & Row.

Bobo, L., & Hutchings, V. (1996). Perceptions of racial group competition: Extending Blumer's theory of group position to a multiracial social context. *American Sociological Review, 61*(6), 951–972.

Bonilla-Silva, E. (2013). *Racism without racists: Color-blind racism and the persistence of racial inequality* (4th ed.) Rowman and Littlefield.

Bowen, W. G., & Bok, D. (1998). *The shape of the river: Long-term consequences of considering race in college admissions.* Princeton University Press.

Bowman, J. E. (2013). *Status processes and organizational inequality: The social psychology of inclusion.* (Unpublished PhD diss.). Stanford University.

Bowman, P. J. (1982). Significant involvement and functional relevance: Challenges to survey research. *Social Work Research and Abstracts, 19*(4), 21–26.

Bowman, P. J. (2013). A strengths-based social psychological approach to resiliency: Cultural diversity, ecological and life span issues. In S. Prince-Embury & D. H. Saklofske (Eds.), *Resilience in children, adolescents, and adults: Translating Research into Practice* (pp. 299–324). Springer.

Bowman, P. J. (2019). Foreward. In E. P. St. Johm & F. Girmay (Eds.), *Detroit school reform in comparative contexts* (p. xv). Springer.

Bowman, P. J., & Betancur, J. J. (2010). Sustainable diversity and inequality: Race in the USA and beyond. In M. Janssens, M. Bechtold, G. Prarolo, & V. Stenius (Eds.), *Sustainability of cultural diversity: Nations, cities, and organizations* (pp. 55–78). Edward Elger.

Bowman, P. J., & Smith, W. A. (2002). Racial ideology in the campus community. In W. A. Smith et al. *The racial crisis in higher education* (pp. 103–120). SUNY Press.

Bowman, P. J., St. John, E., & Kreger Stillman, P. (2011). *Diversity, merit, and higher education: Toward a comprehensive agenda for the 21st century.* Readings on Equal Education. AMS Press.

Bowman Williams, J. E. (2017). Breaking down bias: Legal mandates vs. corporate interests. *Washington Law Review, 92*(3), 1473–1514.

Boyd, W. M. (1971). *Desegregating America's colleges: A National study of Black students.* Praeger.

Cantor, N., & Engot, P. (2014). Why we cannot leave the nation's diverse talent pool behind and thrive. In R. D. Kahlenberg (Ed.), *The future of affirmative action: New paths to higher education diversity after Fisher v. University of Texas* (pp. 27–35). The Century Foundation Press.

Catlin, J. B., Seeley, J. A., & Talburtt, M. (1974). *Affirmative action: Its legal mandate and organizational implications.* University of Michigan, Center for the Study of Higher and Postsecondary Education.

Centra, J. (1970). Black students at predominantly white colleges: A research description. *Sociology of Higher Education, 43*(3), 325–339.

Dobbin, F., & Sutton, J. R. (1998). The strength of a weak state: The rights revolution and the rise of human resources management divisions. *American journal of sociology, 104*(2), 441–476.

Duderstadt, J. (1990). *The Michigan Mandate: A strategic linking of academic excellence and social diversity*. Millennium Project. https://ece.engin.umich.edu/wp-content/uploads/sites/4/2019/10/um-social-diversity-millennium-project.pdf

Duderstadt, J. (2015). 50-year history of social diversity at University of Michigan. Millennium Project.

Feagin, J. R, & Feagin, C. B. (2011). *Racial and ethnic relations*. Prentice-Hall.

Forgianni, D. A. (1973). Impact of black student activism on institutional responses to blacks in higher education. (Unpublished PhD Diss.). Indiana University.

Gamson, Z. F., & Arce, C. H. (1978). Implications of the social context for higher education. In M. W. Peterson, R. T. Blackburn, Z. F. Gamson, Z. F., C. H. Arce, R. W. Davenport, & J. R. Mingle, J. R. (Eds.), *Black students on White campuses: Impact of increased Black enrollments* (pp. 23–42). University of Michigan: Institute for Social Research.

Gratz v. Bollinger, 539 US 244 (2003).

Grutter v. Bollinger, 539 US 306 (2003).

Guiner, L. (2015). *The tyranny of the meritocracy: Democratizing higher education in America*. Beacon Press.

Gurin, P., Dye, E. L., Hurtado, S., & Gurin, G. (2002). Diversity and higher education: Theory and impact on educational outcomes. *Harvard Education Review, 72*(3), 330–367.

Gurin, P., & Epps, E. (1975). *Black consciousness, identity, and achievement: A study of students in historically black colleges*. John Wiley.

Gurin, P., Lehman, J., & Lewis, E. (2004). *Defending diversity: Affirmative action at the University of Michigan*. University of Michigan Press.

Gurin, P., Nagda, B. A., & Lopez, G. E. (2004). The benefits of diversity in education for democratic citizenship. *Journal of Social Issues, 60*(1), 31–32.

Herring, C. (2009). Does diversity pay: Race, gender and the business case for diversity. *American Sociological Review, 74*(2), 208–224.

Hurtado, S. et al. (1998). Enhancing campus climate for racial/ethnic diversity through educational policy and practice. *Review of Higher Education, 21*(3), 279–302.

Jackson, J. S. (1991). *Life in Black America*. Sage.

Jackson, J. S., Torres, M., Caldwell, C. H., Neighbors, H. W., Nesse, R. M., Taylor, R. J., Trierweiler, S. J., & Williams, D. R. (2006). The national survey of American life: A study of racial, ethnic and cultural influences on mental disorders and mental health. *International Journal of Methods in Psychiatric Research, 13*(4), 196–207.

Janssens, M., Bechtoldt, M., de Ruijter, A., Pinelli, D., Prarolo, G, & Stenius, V. M. K. (2010). *Sustainability of cultural diversity: Nations, organizations, and cities*. Elger.

Jayakumar, U. M., & Garces, L. M. (2015). *Affirmative action and racial equity: Considering the Fisher Case to forge the path ahead*. Routledge.

Kahlenberg, R. (2014). *The future of affirmative action: New paths to higher education and diversity after Fisher v. University of Texas*. The Century Foundation Press.

Kalev, A., F. Dobbin, and E. Kelly. (2006). Best practices or best guesses? Assessing the efficacy of corporate affirmative action and diversity policies. *American Sociological Review, 71*(4), 589–617.

Kelly, E. and F. Dobbin. (1998). How affirmative action became diversity management: Employer responses to antidiscrimination law 1961–1996. *American Behavioral Scientist, 41*(7), 960–984.

Kerner Commission (1968). *Report of the National Advisory Committee on Civil Disorders*. US Government Printing Office.

Lewis, E. (2004). Why history remains a factor in the search for racial equality. In P. Gurin, J. Lehman, & E. Lewis, E. (Eds.). *Defending diversity: Affirmative action at the University of Michigan* (pp. 17–60). University of Michigan Press.

Meier, A., & Rudwick, E. (2007). *Black Detroit and the rise of the UAW*. University of Michigan Press.

Milburn, N., & Bowman, P. J. (1991). Neighborhood life (pp. 31–45). In J. S. Jackson (Ed.), *Life in Black America*. Sage Publications.

Morris, A. (1984). *Origins of the civil rights movement: Black communities organizing for social change*. Free Press.

Natour, R., Locks, A., & Bowman, P. J. (2011). Diversity, merit and college choice: The role of a dynamic socio-political environment. In P. J. Bowman, & E. St. John (Eds.), *Diversity, merit, and higher education: Toward a comprehensive agenda for the 21st century* (Vol. 25, pp. 111–140). Readings on Equal Education. AMS Press.

Page, S. (2007). *The difference: How the power of diversity creates better groups, firms, schools, and societies*. Princeton University Press.

Page, S. (2017). *The diversity (bonus): How great teams pay off in the knowledge economy*. Princeton University Press.

Perry, B. A. (2007). *The Michigan affirmative action cases*. University Press of Kansas.

Peterson, M.W, Blackburn, R. T., Gamson, Z. F., Arce, C. H., Davenport, R. W., & Mingle, J. R. (1978). *Black students on White campuses: Impact of increased Black enrollments*. University of Michigan: Institute for Social Research, Survey Research Center.

Phillips, K. W. (2014). How diversity makes us smarter. *Scientific American, 311*(4), 43–47.

Phillips, K. W., Liljenquist, K., and Neale, M. A. (2009). Is the pain worth the gain? The advantages and liabilities of agreeing with socially distinct newcomers." *Personality and Social Psychology Bulletin, 35*(3), 336–350.

Phillips, K. W., Medin, W. D., Lee, C. D., Bang, Bishop M. S., & Lee, D. N. (2014). How diversity works. *Scientific American, 311*(4), 42–47.

Poussaint, A. (1974). The Black administrator in the White university. *The Black Scholar—Journal of Black Studies and Research, 6*(September), 8–14.

Rai, K. B., & Critzer, J. W. (2000). *Affirmative action and the university: Race, ethnicity, and gender in higher education employment.* University of Nebraska Press.

Record, W. (1973). Some implications of the Black studies movement for higher education. *Journal of Higher Education, 44*(March), 191–216.

Ridgeway. C. L. (2011). *Framed by gender: How gender inequality persists in the modern world.* Oxford University Press.

Ridgeway. C. L. (2014). Why status matters for inequality. *American Sociological Review, 79*(1), 1–16.

Rist, R. C. (1970). Black staff, Black studies at White universities: A study in contradictions. *Journal of Higher Education, 41*(November), 618–629.

Rojas, F. (2007). *From Black Power to Black studies: How a radical social movement became an academic discipline.* John Hopkins University Press.

Schuette v. Coalition to Defend Affirmative Action. (2014). Integration & Immigrant Rights and Fight for Equal By Any Means Necessary (BAMN), US Supreme Court, 134 S. Ct. 1623.

Sedlacek, W. E. (1987). Black students on White campuses: Twenty years of research. *Journal of College Student Personnel, 28*(6), 484–495.

Sedlacek, W. E. (2004). *Beyond the big test.* Jossey-Bass.

Smith, W. A., Altbach, G., & Lomotey, K. (2002). *The racial crisis in higher education: Continuing challenges for the 21st century.* SUNY Press.

Steele, C. M. (2010). *Whistling Vivaldi: How stereotypes affect us and what we can do.* W. W. Norton.

Tatum, B. (2017). *Why are all the Black kids sitting together in the cafeteria? And other conversations about race.* Basic Books.

Teddlie, C., & Freeman, J. A. (2002). Twentieth-century desegregation in US higher education. In W. A. Smith, G. Altbach, & K. Lomotey (Eds.), *The racial crisis in higher education* (pp. 77–99). SUNY Press.

Wilkerson, I. (1990, January 15). U. of Michigan fights the taint of racial trouble. *The New York Times.* https://www.nytimes.com/1990/01/15/us/u-of-michigan-fights-the-taint-of-racial-trouble.html

Williams, D. A. (2013). *Strategic diversity leadership: Activating change and transformation in higher education.* Stylus.

Williams, D. A., & Wade-Golden, K. C. (2013). *The chief diversity officer: Strategy, structure, and change management.* Stylus.

Williams, K. L. (2014). Strains, strengths, and intervention outcomes: A critical examination of intervention efficacy for underrepresented groups. *New Directions for Institutional Research, 2013*(158), 9–22.

Winkle-Wagner, R., & Locks, A. (2014). *Diversity and inclusion on campus: Supporting racially and ethnically underrepresented students.* Routledge.

Afterword

Equity, Justice, and *The Racial Crisis*

VALERIE KINLOCH

In the introduction to the second edition of *The Racial Crisis in American Higher Education,* William A. Smith, Philip G. Altbach, and Kofi Lomotey open with the following: "In 1991 two of us (Altbach and Lomotey) published the first edition of *The Racial Crisis in American Higher Education.* When we started working on the book in 1989, race-based campus conflict was much in the news. The scenarios were similar. A hate speech, a racist poster, or some other race-related campus incident stimulated protests and debate." They continue, "Meetings were organized, protest marches took place, and controversy ensued. In more than a few cases, antiracist demonstrations organized by student groups, often with broad campus support, led to conflicts with university administrators and occasionally arrests" (Smith et al., 2002, p. xv).

As I write this afterword for the third edition of *The Racial Crisis in American Higher Education,* co-edited by Kofi Lomotey and William A. Smith, the year is 2023, and not much has changed. Universities are still grappling with institutional racism and, in many cases, functioning as if present-day "race-based campus conflict" does not exist. Student groups and organizations are still demanding that college and university leaders enact system-wide policy changes to ensure safe working conditions and antiracist learning environments. Educational researchers are engaging in #ScholarStrike and collectively speaking against federal efforts that seek to undermine the significance of critical race theory. Many educational practitioners are insisting on professional development that focuses on race-centered, equity-driven approaches to teaching, learning, and engagement. Community members and activists are still protesting against persistent racial, economic, and social inequalities. In cities across the United States, communities of people are still mobilizing against racist, classist, sexist, transphobic, and xenophobic discourses, behaviors, and ways of thinking. People across this country and around the world are marching, advocating, and fighting for human rights, for fairness and freedom, for justice and equality, and for Black lives mattering.

Let's remember George Floyd.

This third edition of *The Racial Crisis* also comes after the police killing of 46-year-old George Floyd in Minneapolis, Minnesota. In addition, it comes after Ahmaud Arbery was murdered as he was jogging in Glynn County, Georgia. In fact, this edition of *The Racial Crisis* comes in light of ongoing, increased, and hypervisible racial violence directed toward Black, Indigenous, Latinx, and other Peoples of Color and Communities of Color during a time in America that some have referred to, rather falsely, as post-racial.

Let's remember Breonna Taylor.

This third edition of *The Racial Crisis* also comes after 26-year-old Breonna Taylor was killed in her apartment by police officers in Louisville, Kentucky. It also comes as we still mourn the lost lives of many other Black people, including Eric Garner, who, gasping for breath, was killed after police officers placed him in a chokehold in New York, New York. We also mourn for Tanisha Anderson, Sandra Bland, Rekia Boyd, Philando Castile, Terence Crutcher, Oscar Grant, Freddie Gray, Botham Jean, Corey Jones, Walter Scott, and, among so many others, Trayvon Benjamin Martin.

Let's remember their names and their lives.

The Racial Crisis also comes during the time of a global health pandemic, COVID-19. According to a story written by Ana Sandoiu for *Medical News Today*, "The evidence reveals enormous disparities and a bitter reality: COVID-19 is disproportionately affecting black people in the United States, and black people are dying as a result of COVID-19 at an alarming rate." Sandoiu continues, "Experts have been saying for years that we need to tackle systemic racism and the toll that it takes on the health of communities of color" (Sandoiu, 2020).[1] Although COVID-19 has had a tremendous impact on Black people, in particular, the United States, to date, has not provided an adequate response or intervention to what inequities the pandemic has brought increased attention. The safety, health, and well-being of Black people and many other People of Color in this country continue to be minimized and disregarded by systems and people who are supposed to protect us.

Both the COVID-19 pandemic and racism have an impact on every aspect of our lives, including education. The third edition of *The Racial Crisis* reveals an urgent need to reimagine postsecondary education by thinking deeply about, as William A. Smith and Kofi Lomotey write in the introduction to this volume, "becoming a racially inclusive environment that does not uphold institutionalized white supremacy." They engage in this reimagining by elevating important research on a variety of interconnected topics, some of which include a focus on diversity and equity in university leadership, historical perspectives on campus racism, activism at historically Black colleges and universities, the impact of racism and anti-Blackness in US higher education, Black women professors creating online spaces for students, Latinx faculty and "servingness" at Hispanic-serving institutions, and, among others, Pacific Islanders and Native erasure. Collectively, the contributors engage in powerful descriptions and analyses of race and racism within US higher educational contexts, and they do so by relying on historical, contemporary, ethnographic, or autoethnographic perspectives. I am left inspired, hopeful, and committed to be in conversation with these scholars and many others who continue to reimagine and reposition education, generally, and postsecondary education, specifically, within equitable, socially just, and humanizing perspectives.

I entered into reading the third edition of *The Racial Crisis* excited to continue learning from colleagues about how "social justice is a collective and collaborative responsibility," as Lomotey and Smith write at the end of the introduction. I leave with even more concrete ideas for creating anti-racist spaces for deep inquiry and activism within higher education, for committing to educational equity even in the face of systemic racism, for justice leading within institutions, and for examining how we bring ourselves into teaching and learning.

It is my hope that, whenever the fourth edition of *The Racial Crisis* is written, our organized meetings; protest marches; anti-racist demonstrations; letter-writing campaigns; arguments against racial, economic, and social inequalities; commitments to combat racist and xenophobic discourses; efforts to prevent further deaths by COVID-19 and by systemic racism; and our calls for Black lives mattering will no longer be questioned or in question. It is my hope that equity and justice will be the overarching framing for how we work together, think together, and resist together the unjust practices, policies, and procedures within higher education institutions, within our communities, and throughout the world.

Note

1. See https://www.medicalnewstoday.com/articles/racial-inequalities-in-covid-19-the-impact-on-black-communities#What-explains-the-disparities?-And-how-does-racism-play-into-it?-.

References

Sandoiu, A. (2020, June 5). Racial inequities in COVID-19: The impact on black communities. *Medical News Today.* Retrieved from https://www.medicalnewstoday.com/articles/racial-inequalities-in-covid-19-the-impact-on-black-communities

Smith, W. A., Altbach, P. G., & Lomotey, K. (2002). The racial crisis in American higher education: Continuing challenges for the twenty-first century (Rev. ed.). State University of New York Press.

Contributors

Editors

Kofi Lomotey is the Bardo Distinguished Professor of Educational Leadership at Western Carolina University. His research and publications focus on Black principals, urban schools, independent African-Centered schools, and Blacks in higher education. He has published more than fifty books, book chapters, and refereed journal articles. He has degrees from Oberlin College (BA), Cleveland State University (MEd), and Stanford University (MA and PhD).

William A. Smith currently serves as the chief executive administrator at the Huntsman Mental Health Institute and he holds full professorships in the Department of Education, Culture, & Society and the Ethnic Studies Program (African American Studies division) at the University of Utah. Dr. Smith is credited with coining racial battle fatigue, where his research focuses on the impact of micro-level and macro-level racial aggressions on racially marginalized communities. He is widely recognized for his contributions to the field of mental health and social justice.

Contributors

Walter R. Allen is Allan Murray Cartter Professor of Higher Education and distinguished professor of education, sociology, and African American studies at the University of California, Los Angeles

Maria Ashkin is a MEd candidate in the Education, Culture, and Society Department at the University of Utah. Her career and research interests include the incorporation of radical, liberational, and transformative pedagogies into the classroom—encouraging healthy and adaptive coping strategies for adolescents in the US education system.

Phillip J. Bowman is a University of Michigan professor of higher education, director of the Diversity Research and Policy Program, and Institute for Social Research faculty ssociate. A social psychologist, Bowman was founding director of UM's National Center for Institutional Diversity and University of Illinois Chicago's Institute for Research on Race and Public Policy.

Cherese Childers-McKee, PhD is an assistant teaching professor at Northeastern University, College of Professional Studies. Her research interests include language and identity, community-engaged research, urban schools, critical literacy, teacher leadership, social justice education, and intercultural relations. She is coeditor of *Postcards from the Schoolhouse* (2013).

Cheryl Ching is an assistant professor of higher education at the University of Massachusetts Boston. Her work examines how practitioners and policy makers make sense of and enact educational equity, particularly for racially minoritized students. She previously served as a program officer at the Teagle Foundation in New York City.

Eddie R. Cole is an associate professor of higher education and affiliated faculty of history at William & Mary, and has been a fellow of the National Academy of Education, Spencer Foundation, and Woodrow Wilson Foundation. His forthcoming book about college presidents and the Black freedom movement will be published by Princeton University Press.

Angela Ebreo is associate research scientist with the Center for the Study of Higher and Postsecondary Education at the University of Michigan. Ebreo's primary research interests include the social psychology of social support, stress, coping, and cross-cultural behaviors, as well as racial, ethnic, and gender disparities in health within community contexts.

Rose Ann Rico Eborda **Gutierrez** is a doctoral student in the Graduate School of Education and Information Studies and a research associate with the Institute for Immigration, Globalization, and Education at the University of California, Los Angeles.

Evelyn Ezikwelu is a doctoral student in the Department of Education, Culture, and Society at the University of Utah. She is investigating how identities such as race and class relate to racial battle fatigue and socioeconomic status discrimination, and their implications on the cognitive thought processes of Black elementary school students.

Nia D. Holland is a University of Michigan graduate student in the School of Public Health's Department of Health Behavior and Health Education. A Spelman College graduate, her scholarly interests include the social psychology of racial/ethnic discrimination and health disparities, and the role of racial socialization, higher education, and strengths-based interventions in promoting health equity.

Jerlando F. L. Jackson is the dean of the Michigan State University College of Education and the MSU Foundation Professor of Education. His research examines hiring practices, career mobility, workforce diversity, workforce discrimination, and organizational disparities.

Uma Mazyck Jayakumar is an associate professor in the Graduate School of Education at the University of California, Riverside. Her scholarship addressing issues of racial justice and higher education policy is featured in *Educational Researcher, Journal of Higher Education, Harvard Educational Review,* and in numerous Supreme Court amicus briefs in the *Fisher v. University of Texas* cases.

Chantal Jones is a doctoral candidate in higher education at the University of California, Los Angeles.

Jimmy Kendall is a doctoral student in the Department of Education, Culture, and Society at the University of Utah. At present, he is studying neoliberal restructuring within both secondary and higher education systems and examining the implications for mental health and wellness across student and staff populations.

Valerie Kinloch is the Renée and Richard Goldman Endowed Dean of the School of Education and professor at the University of Pittsburgh. She is also president-elect of the National Council of Teachers of English (NCTE) and co-chair of Remake Learning. Her scholarship examines the literacies and engagements of youth and adults in school and community spaces. The author of publications on race, place, literacy, and equity, she has written books on the poet June Jordan, on critical perspectives on language and learning, and on community engagement. Her book *Harlem on Our Minds: Place, Race, and the Literacies of Urban Youth* received the 2010 Outstanding Book of the Year Award from the American Educational Research Association (AERA). Her most recent coedited book is *Race, Justice, and Activism in Literacy Instruction,* published in 2020 with Teachers College Press.

Annie Le is a doctoral student in the Graduate School of Education and Information Studies and a research associate with the Institute for Immigration, Globalization, and Education at the University of California, Los Angeles.

María C. Ledesma is an associate professor in the Department of Educational Leadership and Policy at the University of Utah. Her research interests include the sociology of race-conscious policy in higher education as well as the experiences of historically underrepresented faculty of color who identify as first-generation.

Na Lor is an assistant professor of sociology and education in the Department of Education Policy and Social Analysis at Teachers College, Columbia University, where she teaches mixed methods, activity theory, and sociology of higher education. Her research focuses on culture in higher education.

Bianca M. Mack is a native of Atlanta, Georgia. She earned her BS in psychology and shortly after began her career in health care. She served as a behavioral therapist before earning her MEd in counseling from Loyola University Chicago. She is currently a counseling psychology PhD student at Howard University.

Channel C. McLewis is an assistant project scientist at the University of California–Los Angeles.

Mounira Morris is an associate teaching professor in the Graduate School of Education at Northeastern University. Dr. Morris has held administrative and faculty roles in higher education contributing to a depth of professional experience in diversity, social justice, and student affairs that informs her teaching, writing, research, and professional practice.

Donald B. Pope-Davis is a professor and dean of the College of Education and Human Ecology at The Ohio State University. He is an elected fellow of the American Psychological Association's (APA) Society for Psychological Study of Ethnic Minority Issues and a fellow of the Society of Counseling Psychology. He is the current chair of the APA Committee on Ethnic Minority Affairs. He is a member of the steering committee of Deans for Social Justice and Equity in Education, the AERA-Consortium of University and Research Institutions, and the Council of Academic Deans from Research Education Institutions. He received his doctorate from Stanford University.

Temple R. Price earned her master of arts degree in clinical mental health counseling at Xavier University of Louisiana. Temple has worked in children's mental health, as well as nonprofits addressing substance abuse and HIV. She has done research on Black students in STEM and women of color on social media.

Gadise Regassa is a doctoral candidate in higher education at the University of California, Los Angeles.

Shiver is a doctoral student in the Education, Culture, and Society Department and an education professional at the University of Utah. With an academic background in philosophy and social theory, they hope to continue their work to address systemic injustice in US higher education.

Robert T. Teranishi is professor of social science and comparative education, the Morgan and Helen Chu Endowed Chair in Asian American Studies, and the director for the Institute for Immigration, Globalization, and Education at the University of California, Los Angeles.

Ivory A. Toldson is the president and CEO of the QEM Network, professor of counseling psychology at Howard University, and editor-in-chief of the *Journal of Negro Education*. Additionally, Dr. Toldson currently serves as the national director of Education Innovation and Research for the NAACP. Previously, Dr. Toldson was appointed by President Barack Obama to devise national strategies to sustain and expand federal support to HBCUs as the executive director of the White House Initiative on Historically Black Colleges and Universities. He also served as senior research analyst for the Congressional Black Caucus Foundation and contributing education editor for the *Root*.

Kēhaulani Vaughn (Kanaka Maoli) is an assistant professor in the Department of Education, Culture, and Society and the Pacific Islands Studies Initiative at the University of Utah. Formerly a higher education practitioner, her research intersects Pacific Island and Indigenous studies, higher education, and decolonial methods and pedagogies.

M. Billye Sankofa Waters is an assistant professor of educational leadership at the University of Washington Tacoma. She identifies as a hip-hop generation Blackgirl from Chicago and grounds her work in Black feminism, critical race theory, abolitionist teaching, Black women writers, and qualitative inquiry. Sankofa Waters created the Radical Identity Praxis (RIP) curriculum; is the founding executive director of the nonprofit charity Blackgirl Gold Unapologetic, Inc.; and is the author of *We Can Speak for Ourselves* (2016) and coeditor of *The Lauryn Hill Reader* (2019) and *How We Got Here* (2020).

Kenyon L. Whitman is a PhD candidate and director of the Office of Foster Youth Support Services at the University of California, Riverside. His research focuses on underrepresented students in higher education, specifically the college-going experiences of foster youth. Kenyon has a passion for this population, as he emancipated from the foster care system.

Jamillah Bowman Williams is professor and faculty director of the Workers Rights Institute at Georgetown University Law Center. Williams's scholarly interests include the social psychology of contemporary bias and the law, civil rights, employment law, the effectiveness of antidiscrimination law, and the capacity of the law to promote compliance and social change.

Index

1619 Project, 175, 321
1958 National Defense Education Act, 323
#abolishICE, 297
#BlackandHooded, 198
#blackgirlmagic, 303
#BlackLivesMatter, 106, 113, 148, 272, 297
#BlackMalePhD, 198
#BlackWomenPhD, 198
#CiteASista, 198
#metoo, 297
#NoDAPL, 297
#ScholarStrike, 347

Aboh, Sessi, 17
abolitionist teaching, 305
academic freedom, 90
adaptive racial socialization, 152
affirmative action, race-conscious, 97–100, 242, 245, 323–24
    anti-affirmative action efforts, 180, 325, 329, 331, 332, 339
    Black student activism and, 324–25
    institutional accountability and advocacy, 114
    opponents of, 97, 98–100
    University of Michigan and, 320
    White backlash to, 103–5, 113

See also race-conscious admissions practices
African and African American Studies, 18
Africans, discovery of the Americas, 12
Africana Studies, 272
Afrisandric-centered analysis, 134–35
Afrocentric movement, 270–72
Afrocentricity
    definition of, 270–71
    origin of term, 270
Afropenia, 140
Alito, Samuel, 113
Allen, Evette, 197
Allen, Julie Ober, 60
Allen, Walter R., 139, 193
Amateur Athletic Union, 81
American Trends Panel (ATP), 125
American Veterans Committee, 83
Anderson, James, 10, 323
Anderson, Riana, 152
Angell, Donald, 87
Annamma, Subini Ancy, 137
anti-affirmative action challenges, 180, 325, 329, 331, 332, 339
anti-Black ableism, 137
anti-Black racism, 127, 128, 129
anti-Blackness, 169, 192, 193, 194

Anti-Defamation League (ADL), 127
Arbery, Ahmaud, 13, 154, 348
arbitrary-set system, 134
Arce, Charles, 323
Archibald, Ashley, 47
Arnold, Noelle Witherspoon, 148
Asian American and Pacific Islander (AAPI), 25
Asian American faculty, discrimination against, 239–40, 249–51
  additional workload expectations, 243–44
  affirmative action and, 245
  Asian American women faulty, 248–49
  Asian Americans, Asians and, 244–45
  conflation of data regarding, 244–45
  as endowed professors of education, 245
  implication for inclusion of, 244–49
  low levels of employment satisfaction among, 246
  as "model minority," 245
  Moreno Report and, 239, 240, 246
  racial battle fatigue and, 246–47
  tenure process and, 246
Asian American studies, 18
Asian or Pacific Islander (API), 25
Asian Americans Advancing Justice, 34
Asian Americans, Native Hawaiians, and Pacific Islanders (AANHPI), 29, 30, 31, 32, 33
Association for the Study of Negro Life and History, 264
Atlanta, Georgia, 38
  arrest rates in, 46
  high school graduation rates for Black males, 49–50
  infant mortality rates and, 43
  out-of-school suspensions of Black males, 45
  police killings and, 49
  See also University System of Georgia

B&B Club, 82
Bad Boys, 54
bait and switch, 210, 216
Baker, Rachel, 111
Ball, Daisy, 149
Balsam, Kimberly, 136
Baltimore Afro-American, 80
Baptist Ministers Conference, 82
Barden, Jamie, 274
Barnes, Natasha B., 175
Barnett, Ross, 87
Barrett, Amy Coney, 108
Beadle, George W., 85
Beckery, 308
Becton, Dajerria, 306
Bell, Chris, 138
Bell, Derrick, 99, 154, 174, 299
Bennett College, 268
Bennett, Jessica, 174, 176
Bensimon, Estela, 280, 281, 292
Bettez, Silvia, 312
Biden, Joseph, 104
biopsychosocial equilibrium, 128
Black art, 263
Black critical theory, 169
Black feminist tenets, 303
Black life making, 197–98
Black Lives Matter, 48, 105, 107
  civil rights movement and, 274
  HBCUs and, 272–74
Black male genocide, 37–42
  arrests and, 46
  arrests and deaths among college-aged males, 54–55
  enrollment in higher education, 51–52
  four factors identifying in case study, 41

health, life expectancy and, 59–62
higher education and, 50–57
incarceration rates and, 46–47
infant mortality rates and, 42–43
issues from infancy, 42–44
negative health outcomes and, 59–60
postgraduation employment and income, 56–57
professional occupations and, 58–59
pull-out rates and, 47–48
push-out rates among, 45–46
racial battle fatigue and, 43–44
racialized stress and, 60–62
school-to-prison pipeline (STPP), 41–42, 44–50
violent deaths, murders and, 48–50
zero tolerance, suspensions and, 44–46
Black Panther Party, 88, 267
Black power movement, 267–70
  Black women activists and, 268
Black-serving institutions, 171, 180
Black Student Union, 105
Black studies, 18
Black studies movement, 268–69
Black Studies in the University, 269
Black tax, 176, 308
Black women
  Black power movement and, 268
  co-mentorship and, 195
  faculty at HBCUs, 176
  institutional racism and, 134
  subjective cognitive functioning and, 133
  See also Black women faculty
Black women faculty, 297–99
  Black faculty and, 175, 177–78, 224–25
  encounters with students, 303–4
  exhaustion from teaching, 308–11
  as othermothers, 299

reason for teaching, 299–303
tenure track and, 191
See also Black women
Blacks
  adultification of Black youth, 50–51
  arrest rates, 46
  attrition rates in higher education, 52–54
  COVID-19 and, 348–49
  degree attainment in higher education and, 52–54
  economic exclusion of, 57–59
  health, life expectancy and, 59–62
  higher education and, 50–57
  issues from infancy, 42–44
  LGBT, 135
  racial battle fatigue and, 43–44
  school-to-prison pipeline and, 44–50
  states with largest populations, 178–79
Blake, Jr., Jacob, 154
Blum, Edward, 107–8
Boddie, Elise, 106
Bogart, Kathleen R., 137
Bok, D., 109
Bollinger, Lee, 320, 326, 331–32
Boone, Sylvia, 178
Bowen, W. G., 109
Bowman, Jamilla, 340
Bowman, Phillip J., 150, 335
Bowman role strain and adaptation model, 150
Brame, Robert, 54
Brondolo, Elizabeth, 131
Brown, Leonard, 269
Brown, Michael, 106, 273, 306
Brown University, 336
Brown v. Board of Education, 266, 267, 323, 326, 327
Brownies Book, The, 263
Bureau of Labor Statistics, 56
Burkhardt, John, 335

Burroughs, Allison, 103

California Civil Rights Initiative, 102
Calloway, Nathaniel Oglesby, 85
Campaign for College Opportunity, 23, 31, 33
campus racism, presidential responses to, 87–88
   Hampton Institute, 82–83
   hesitancy to directly condemn racism, 90
   Johns Hopkins University and, 80–82
   Northwestern University, 84
   Syracuse University, 86
   University of California, Los Angeles, 88–89
   University of Chicago and, 83–86
Canaday, John E., 89
Cantor, Nancy, 331, 332
Carmichael, Stokely, 142
Carpenter, Joseph, 174
Carpenter v. Board of Regents of University of Wisconsin System, 174, 175
Carr, Gregory, 272
Carroll, Grace, 139
Carruthers, J., 17
Caruthers, Loyce, 311
Case for Reparations, The, 314
Cash, William, 328
Cato Institute, 107
Caton, Marcia, 44–45
Ceja, Miguel, 139
Center for Individual Rights, 107
Center on Extremism, 127
Chan, Kenyon, 246
Chan, Sucheng, 245
Charleston 9, 306
chattel slavery, 321, 323
Chavous, Tabbye, 335, 337
Cheyney University, 259–60, 261

Chicago, Illinois
   racist housing practices and, 83–84
   urban renewal projects and, 85
Chicago State University, 181, 184, 190, 191
Chicago Urban League, 85
Chico State, 52
Chief Diversity Officer, The, 338
Chin, Vincent, 13
Cho, Sumi, 246
chronic stress, 60
City-Wide Young People's Forum, 264
Civil Rights Congress, 130
civil rights movement, 265–67, 274
Clark Atlanta University, 273
Clayton, Dewey, 274
Clinton, Hilary Rodham, 125, 273–74
Coates, Ta-Nehisi, 175
Coleman, Mary Sue, 332–33, 334, 337
Collier, Joan Nicole, 198
Collins, Susan, 336, 337
colonialism, 126, 321
color-blind ideologies, 298
Columbia University, 329
Columbus, Christopher, 12
Committee on Racial Equity, 83
Community of Contrasts Report, 26, 34
community walks, 299
community wealth and protest, 305
Congress of Racial Equity, 83, 85–86
Contreras, Frances, 280
Coogan, Patricia, 133
Cooper, Brittney, 299
Corbin, Nicola A., 148
counterspace, 310
Courant, Paul N., 332
Crawford, Emily R., 148
Crenshaw, Kimberlé, 97
Crisis, The, 263
critical community building, 312
critical pedagogy online, 311

critical race theory (CRT), 114, 139, 175, 193, 348
   disability studies and, 137–38
   Donald Trump and, 154
   higher education and, 168–69
   Ten Pillars of, 146–47
critical social justice curriculum. *See* social justice curriculum
Crouch, Stanley, 271
Cuevas, Adolfo, 131
Cullors, Patrisse, 273
cultural taxation, 229
culturally relevant curriculum, 17
culturally relevant teaching, 17
CUNY, City College, 190
CUNY, Medgar Evers College, 181, 184
curriculum reform, 16, 17–19
   four suggestions for, 18–19
Curry, Tommy J., 128, 132

Daily Bruin, 248
Daily Northwestern, 84
Daily Orange, 86
Dancy II, T. Elon, 176
data aggregation. *See* Pacific Islanders
Davis, Angela, 88–89
Davis, James Earl, 176
Davis, Lori Patton, 192
Day O'Connor, Sandra, 242
decolonization, 305
deficit frameworks, 37, 292
Denson, Nida, 249
desegregation, 323–24
Desnoyers-Colas, Elizabeth F., 148
Dillard, Cynthia, 304, 313–14
dis/ability critical race studies, 138
disability studies, 137–38
Discrimination Beta, 45
DisCrit, 137–38
disequilibrium, 128
distributive justice, 113

Diverse Issues in Higher Education, 250
diversity, 23, 169
diversity, equity and inclusion, 297, 319–21, 337–41
   future scholarship about, 338
   historical shifts in societal diversity policies, 321–23
   three major goals of, 330–31
diversity leadership. *See* diversity, equity and inclusion; University of Michigan
diversity mules, 195
diversity within diversity, 110
Dowd, A. C. 281–82
Dred Scott Supreme Court decision, 321, 326
Du Bois, W. E. B., 81, 130, 145, 263, 299, 314
   "The Talented Tenth" and, 263
Duderstadt, James, 328, 329–31
Dumas, Michael, 169
Dumas, Rhetaugh, 330
Dunn, Dana S., 137
Durham, North Carolina, 38
   high school graduation rates for Black males, 49
   infant mortality rates and, 43
Durkee, James Stanley, 265

education
   versus schooling, 15–17
   zero tolerance and suspensions for Black males, 44–46
Edwards, Breanna, 274
Edwards, Kirsten T., 176
Ellis, Katrina, 60
Emdin, Chris, 299
Emory University, 55
Empowering Pacific Islander Communities, 34
endogenous biopsychosocial effects, 143

endogenous microaggressions, 145
Equal Protection Clause, 101, 102
ethic of care, 304
ethnic studies, 18
European cultural studies, 18
Evers, Medgar, 270
Everytown for Gun Safety, 153
Excelencia in Education, 279
Executive Order 10925, 324, 327
Executive Order 11246, 98, 210
Executive Order 13950, 114
exogenous raciam, 146
extrajudicial killings, 49

Fanon, Frantz, 132, 145
Fasching-Varner, Kenneth, 148
Feagin, Joe R., 128, 142
Federal Student Aid, 211
Ferguson, A., 54
Ferguson, R., 106
first-few-only, 299
Fisher, Abigail, 101
Fisher v. University of Texas, 100, 101–2, 103, 106, 107, 110, 113
Fisk Strike, 263
Fisk University, 263
Fleming, Robben, 327–28, 338
Florida A&M University, 189, 190, 191, 268, 272
Floyd, George, 13, 48, 105, 154, 297, 348
Follins, Lourdes D., 135, 136
Francis Marion University, 181, 184
Franklin, Jeremy D., 148
free speech policies, 90
Freedmen's Bureau, 104
freedom dreaming, 305
Freire, Paulo, 312
Friend, Jennifer, 311
Frye, Billy, 328

Gamson, Zelda, 323

Garcia, G. A., 280, 282
Garcia, J. Roberto, 148
Garner, Eric, 348
Garza, Alicia, 273
gender, history of the concept of, 132
gendered racism, 37
Gender(s), 132
General Assembly of the United Nations, 130
genocide, 129–38
    bodily or mental harm and, 130
    disaggregating ethnic gender groups, 132
    LGBTQ+ community and, 130
    See also Black male genocide
George Floyd Scholarship, 15
Georgia College and State University, 55
Georgia State University, 55, 181, 184, 191
Georgia Technical Institute, 55
GI Bill, 323
Gibbs, Phillip, 269
Ginsberg, Ruth Bader, 103
Goheen, Robert F., 87
Goodnow, Frank J., 81–82
Goodyear-Ka'ōua, Noelani, 26–27
Gordon, B., 60
Gorski, Paul C., 148
Gorsuch, Neil, 108
Gratz v. Bollinger, 100, 103, 172, 320, 325, 326, 331, 333, 339
Gray, Freddie, 306
Green, James Earl, 269
Gregg, James E., 82
Griffin, Kimberly, 240
Griffith, Derek, 60
Griffin, Kimberly, 174, 176
Grutter v. Bollinger, 100, 103, 172, 193, 320, 325, 326, 331, 333, 339
Guardado, Andrés, 13

Guinier, Lani, 110
Gurin, Patricia, 332

Hafoku, 'I., 34
Hamilton, Charles, 142
Hampton Institute, 82–83
Hanlon, Philip, 332
Hannah-Jones, Nikole, 175
Harlem Renaissance, 263, 264
Harnwell, Gaylord P., 87
Harper, Shaun, 168
Harriet Tubman Collective, 137
Harris III, Frank, 140
Harris, Jessica, 174, 176
Harris, Paul C., 175
Hartlep, Nicholas D., 148, 245
Harvard University, 79, 87, 103, 108, 111, 154
Hatcher, Harlan, 327, 338, 339
Hernández, Rafael J., 148
hashtag activism, 198
Herring, Cedric, 130
Heyns, Roger, 327
higher education, (U.S.), 14–15
  anti-Blackness and, 194
  Black male professional occupations and, 58–59
  Black males and, 38, 50–57
  Black student statistics, 167–68, 223
  curriculum reform, 16, 17–19
  enrollment of students of color in, 209
  geography of African Americans in, 213–19
  importance of faculty of color in, 241–42
  racial crisis in, 41, 80, 148
  schooling versus education, 15–17
  underrepresentation of Black students and faculty, 88
  See also affirmative action, Black faculty and administrators; race-conscious admissions practices, higher education
Higher Education Act of 1965, 259
higher education, Black faculty and administrators, 167–68, 209–11, 229–30
  academic freedom and, 174–75
  administrators at research institutes and two-year institutions, 222–23
  African American female faculty and, 224–25
  African American male faculty and, 224
  anti-Blackness and, 169
  Black critical theory and, 169
  campus racial climate and cultures and, 172–73
  changing representation in, 223–28
  critical race theory and, 168–69
  data regarding, 211–12
  diversity and opportunity hiring programs, 172
  diversity at the expense of, 193–94
  doctorate-granting institutions and, 220–21, 222–23
  faculty at private sector and two-year institutions, 220–21
  faculty not on tenure track, 190–91
  findings of study of, 181–91
  gender and tenure status of, 180
  geographic mobility among administrators, 216–18, 218–19
  geographic mobility among faculty, 214, 214–16
  HCBUs and, 190
  importance of campus climate for, 242–43
  inclusion and, 194–96
  locating Black faculty in the academy, 181–84
  national data on, 210–11
  obstacles encountered by, 171–75

higher education, Black faculty and administrators *(continued)*
　patterns of employment among, 220–23
　private sector and two-year institutions, 220–21
　promotion, tenure and, 173–75
　race, gender and, 176–78, 191
　racial bias, systemic barriers and, 210
　ration of Black students to Black faculty, 168
　recommendations for improvement for, 196–97, 230–32
　recruitment, retention and, 228–29
　representation among African American administrators, 226–28
　retention and, 172–73
　search committees and, 172
　statistics on Faculty of Color, 169–71
　study examining, 178–80, 192–99
　teaching, mentoring, service and, 176
　tenure and, 184–89
　tenure track and, 189
　theoretical framework of study of, 212–13
　turnover among faculty of color in, 243
　types if institutions studied, 180
　underrepresentation in, 209–10
　vice presidents for student affairs (VPSAs) and, 211–12
　See also Black women, higher education
Hines, Dorothy E., 177–78
hip-hop culture, 272
hip-hop music, 272
Hiroshige, Ernest, 248
Hispanic-serving institutions (HSIs), 279, 280, 291
　faculty with tenure at, 281
　originating as PWIs, 280

Hispanic-serving Institutions Division (USDoE), 280
historically Black colleges and universities (HCBUs), 52, 91, 170, 175, 180, 184, 192, 213, 230, 275, 280, 323
　activism at, 259–60
　Black Lives Matter movement and, 272–74
　Black women faculty at, 176
　definition of, 259
　during the Afrocentric movement, 270–72
　during the Black power movement, 267–70
　during the civil rights movement, 265–67
　during the New Negro movement, 262–65
　during reconstruction and post-reconstruction, 260–62
　enrollment surges at, 223
　presidents at, 197
　three-dimensional function of, 259
　underfunding of, 194
historically White institutions (HWIs), 59, 60, 64, 171, 172, 189, 243, 247
　Black women and, 195
　HBCUs and, 192–93
　University of Michigan and, 320
homophobia, 126
Hopkins, Johns, 81
Hopwood v. Texas, 332
Housing Act of 1949, 85
Howard University, 175, 192, 263, 264–65, 272
Howe, Arthur, 82
Hsu, Madeline, 250
Huang, Belinda, 246, 248–49
Hughey, Matthew, 103
Hune, Shirley, 246

Husband, Miracle, 148
Hutchins, Mary F., 84
Hutchins, Robert M., 83–84
hyperinvisible, 303

Iddind, Henry, 81
incarceration, 46–47
inclusion, 23
   aggregation of data and, 30
Indiana State University, 181, 190
Indiana University Bloomington, 190
Indiana University Purdue University Indianapolis, 181, 190
Indigenous peoples, land loss and, 10
Indigenous studies, 18
Ingram-Lopez, Carlos, 13
Inside Higher Ed, 243
Institute for Social Research (ISR), 333
institutional White racism, 9–10, 19, 126, 347
   contemporary responses to, 13–14
   overview of, 9–10
   power and, 10–12
   US higher education and, 14–15
   White privilege and, 12–13
institutionalized discrimination, 37
Integrated Postsecondary Education Database System (IPEDS), 178, 211, 212
interest convergence dilemma, 99
invisible, 303
Iowa State University, 85

Jackson, James, 333, 334, 335
Jackson State University, 189, 190, 267, 269–70
Japanese Americans, internment of, 12–13
Jean, Brandt, 314
Jet, 269
Jewish problem, 111
Jim Crow laws, 80, 83, 261, 265, 268, 324

Joe, Sean, 61
John and Jane Henryism, 143
Johns Hopkins Hospital, 80–81
   Provident Hospital and, 80–81
Johns Hopkins University, 80–82
   racism at, 80–82
Johnson, Harold, 329
Johnson, Henry, 328
Johnson, Lyndon B., 98, 327
Joseph, Nicole, 197
justice, equity, diversity, and inclusion (JEDI), 154

Kambon, Kobi, 272
Kauanui, J. Kēhaulani, 27
Kavanaugh, Brett, 108
Kean University, 189
Keith, Verna, 130
Kendi, Ibram X., 88–89
Kennedy, Anthony, 103, 107
Kennedy, John F., 327
Kent State, 269
Kerr, Clark, 88
Khalifa, Muhammad, 148
Kimpton, Lawrence A., 84, 85
King, Jr., Martin Luther, 266, 270
Klasik, Daniel, 111
Kwoh, Stewart, 248

Ladson-Billings, Gloria, 17
Latinx faculty, servingness at HSIs, 279–82, 291–93
   coaching Latinx students, 285–86
   contexts and structures of, 282–83
   definition of, 280
   faculty acts of, 283–84
   STEM and, 287–90
Latinx-servingness. *See* Latinx faculty
Latinx students
   career options and, 289
   coaching of by faculty, 285–86
   cultural wealth and, 299

Latinx students *(continued)*
 deficit framing and, 292
 enrolled in STEM programs, 281–82, 283, 287–90
 navigating college, 285–87
 statistics about, 279
Latinx studies, 18
Lawrence, Charles R., 193
Lee, Jennifer, 55
Lee, Sharon, 241
Left Out, 23–24, 34–35
 California institutions of higher education, 25, 28–30
 faculty representation in, 31–32
 need for disaggregating data, 32–34
 need for race in, 28–30
 race statistics reported in, 31–32
Lemon, Don, 273–74
Lempert, Richard, 106–7
Lewin, Kurt, 341
Lewis, John, 273–74
Lewis, Michelel K., 135, 136
LGBT People of Color Microaggression Scale, 136
LGBT Relationship Racism subscale, 136
LGBTQ+
 Black, 135
 People of Color and, 135–36
 racially minoritized, 135
 White, 136
Lincoln University, 181, 189, 260, 329
Loftin, R. Bowen, 79
Lomotey, Kofi, 17
Los Angeles Times, 89, 248
Los Angeles Unified School District, 248
Louisiana State University, 184, 189
love language, 308
Lyiscott, Jamila, 299
Lynch, Loretta, 306

Machen, J. Bernard, 330
Magazine of Higher Education, 245
Malcom, Lindsey, 280
Man-Not, The, 132
mansplaining, 308
March on Washington for Jobs and Freedom, 86
Martin, Jennifer L., 148
Martin, Trayvon, 272, 273, 348
Matlock, Lester, 330
Matsuda, Gann, 247
Mayer, Milton, 83
McCarn, Ruth, 84
McKenzie, Fayette Avery, 263
Medical News Today, 348
Mercator projection map, 11–12
meritocracy, 110–11, 193
meritocracy ideologies, 298
Meritorious Manumission Act of 1710, 145
Michigan Civil Rights Initiative, 325
Michigan Mandate, 330
Michigan State University, 181
microaggressions, 61, 127, 131, 137, 138–45, 148, 301, 308
Minami, Dale, 247
mismatch hypothesis, 110
Monts, Lester, 330, 331, 333, 334
Moody, Charles, 330
Morehouse College, 261
Moreno, Carlos, 239
Moreno Report, 239, 240, 246
Morgan State University, 263
Morrill Land Grant Act, 260–61
multiculturalism, 169, 330
Murphy, Franklin D., 88
Museus, S. D., 246
Mustaffa, Jalil Bishop, 197
Myers, Samuel, 171
myth of meritocracy, 110–11

Nakanishi, Don, 247–48

NASPA Research and Policy Institute, 211
NASPA Salary Tool, 212
National Association for the Advancement of Colored People (NAACP), 263, 264
National Association of Colored Women, 264
National Association of Student Personnel Administrators (NASPA), 211
National Center for Educational Statistics (NCES), 51, 52, 241
National Center for Institutional Diversity, 333, 334–35
National Study of Postsecondary Faculty (NSPOF), 211
National Survey of Black Americans, 130
National Urban League, 264
National Youth Conference (NAACP), 264
native erasure. *See* Pacific Islanders
Native Hawaiian and Pacific Islander (NHPI), 24, 31, 32, 33
neoliberal-multicultural imagination, 169
Netterville, George Leon, 269
New Commonwealth, 305, 308, 310
New Negro movement, 262, 264–65
New York Times, The, 81, 321
Niagara movement, 263, 264
Niehuss, Marvin, 327
Nobles, Wade, 10
nonbeing, 133
North Central University, 15
North Carolina A&T University, 189, 190, 268
Northwestern State University of Louisiana, 181, 184, 190
Northwestern University, 83, 84, 269
Núñez, A. M., 280, 282

Oakland, California, 38
  high school graduation rates for Black males, 49
  infant mortality rates and, 43
Obadele, Imari, 272
Obama, Barack, 104, 125
Office of Civil Rights (USDoE), 324
Office of the Special Advisor on the Prevention of Genocide (OSAPG), 39, 50, 54, 57
  eight factors defining genocide, 40–41, 62–63
Ohio State University, The, 190
Okello, Wilson K., 149
Old Dominion, 191
Oliver Brown et al. v. Board of Education of Topeka, 303
othermothers, 299
other/othering, 298, 299

Pacific Islanders, 23–24
  aggregated with Asian Americans, 23–24, 27
  California higher education and, 25, 28–30, 29
  culturally relevant education system for, 25, 27
  defining, 24–25
  history of the category, 25–26
  as Indigenous People, 26–28
  need for disaggregating data about, 32–34
  place in the academy, 24, 28
  within California's higher education leadership, 29–30
Parents Involved in Community Schools v. Seattle School District No. 1, 100
Patterson, Wilhelmina B., 82
Patterson, William L., 134
Pendleton, Hadiya, 305

368 | Index

Pennsylvania State College, University Park, 190
Perrin, Paul B., 135
Peterson, Richard, 105
Pew Research Center (PRC), 125, 241
Phenix, George P., 82
Philbert, Martin, 337
Phillip Merrill College of Journalism, 272
Pierce, Chester M., 138, 142
Pittman, Chavella T., 177
Plessy v. Ferguson, 261, 262, 264, 323, 326, 327
pluralistic ignorance, 145
police brutality, 48
Pollack, Martha, 337
Poon, OiYan A., 26
post-racial myths, 111–12
Post-Standard, The, 86
Powell, Lewis, 98–99, 108
power, 9, 10–12
Prairie View A&M University, 272
Pratto, Felicia, 134
predominately White institutions (PWIs), 52, 87–88, 210, 215–16, 218
   evolving into HSIs, 280
Price, Gregory, 195
Priest, Myisha, 178
Princeton University, 15, 90, 111, 328
   Ross Barnett and, 87
Prison Policy Initiative, 50
proactive racial socialization beliefs, 152
Program for Research on Black Americans (PRBA), 334, 335
Project on Fair Representation, 107
Proposition 16, 102
Proposition 209, 102
protective racial socialization, 150–52
Provident Hospital, 80–81
pull-out rates, 46, 58

push-out rates, 45–46, 58

Quaye, Stephen, 149

race as a social construct, 30
race-based campus conflict, 341
race-conscious admissions practices, 98, 112–15
   banned in seven states, 102
   current court cases, judicial updates and, 107–8
   five defenses of, 99
   framework challenges and myths, 108–12
   mismatch hypothesis, 110
   myth of meritocracy and, 110–11
   the new millennium and, 100–3
   post-racial myths and, 111–12
   race-neutral alternatives to, 109–10
   student activism and, 105–7
   See also affirmative action
racelighting, 140
race-neutral language, 30
racial battle fatigue (RBF), 39–40, 43–44, 58, 60, 61, 64, 125–27, 153–55
   applying trauma-informed care to, 149–53
   Asian American faculty and, 246–47
   biopsychosocial responses to, 143–45
   Black women faculty and, 308
   definition of, 143
   operationalizing as a theoretical framework, 142–49
   psychosocial antecedents of, 126
   signs and symptoms of, 150
   in society and schools, 138–42
   symptoms of, 40
racial disequilibrium, 129
racial diversity, 101
racial gesture politics, 194
racial identity, 271

racial misandry, 129
racial misogyny, 129
racial realism, 150, 155
racial subcategories, 133
racial uplift, 261
racialized ableism, 137
racialized microaggressions, 61, 138, 139
  three types of, 140
racialized stress, 64
racism
  definition of, 127–29
  levels of, 128, 131
  on campus, 79–91
  higher education and, 169
  as a public and mental health illness, 138
  subordinate-racialized groups and, 127–29
racially minoritized queer people, 129
Reagan, Ronald, 89, 325
Reardon, Sean, 111
RECASTing theory, 152
redlining, 12, 47, 56, 58
reflexivity journals, 299
Regents of the University of California v. Bakke, 98–99, 103, 108, 113, 332
Rendón, Laura, 291
representation, 25
resistance, 152–53
Rhodes, Frank, 328
Ricci, Frank, 101
Ricci v. DeStefano, 100, 101
Rice, Tamir, 306
Roberts, John, 101, 113
Robeson, Paul, 130
Robinson, Kimberly, 103
Rollock, Nicola, 194
ross, kihana, 169
Royster-Harper, E., 331
Rutgers University, New Brunswick, 190, 191

Samson, Frank, 111
San Francisco State College, 105
San Francisco State University, 105
Sandler, Richard, 110
Sandoui, Ana, 348
Sansone, V. A., 280, 282
Savannah State University, 190, 191
Scanlan, Martin, 15
Schlissel, Mark, 336–37, 338, 339
school-to-prison pipeline (STPP), 41–42, 44–50, 58, 60, 63
schooling, education versus, 15–17
Schuette v. Coalition to Defend Affirmative Action, 100, 101, 102, 103, 107, 108, 325
Schuette, William, 102
science, technology, engineering and math (STEM), 281, 281, 283, 287–90, 291
Scott, Lawrence, 53
Scott, Nolvert, 173
Scott v. University of Delaware, 172, 174
segregation, legal, 323
Sellers, Robert, 336, 337
Sentencing Project, 46–47
seven continents, 11
sexism, 126
Shapiro, Harold, 328–29
Sharp, Laurie, 53
Sharpe, Rhonda, 195
Shelby County v. Holder, 107
Shelley v. Kraemer, 84
Shujaa, Mwalimu J., 16
Sidanius, Jim, 134, 135
Simmons, Isaiah, 168
Sinclair-Chapman, Valeria, 175
Sistah Network, 197
Sitting Bull, 13
Sloan, Lloyd, 274
Smith, Allen, 327, 328
Smith, Denver, 269

Smith, Linda, 25
Smith, W. A., 40
Smith, William A., 139, 148
Snyder, Franklin B., 84
social closure theory, 212, 216, 229
social dominance theory (SDT), 39, 62, 135, 137
 three identity features of, 39
Social Dominance Theory of Social Hierarchy and Oppression, 134
social justice curriculum, 299–303, 303–14
 effective design of, 312–13
 ethic of care and, 303
 five core questions about, 303
 resistance to, 308–9
 re/imaging space, 313–14
 setting boundaries, 313
 teaching online, 307
 two challenges for creating, 298
 See also Black women faculty
social justice leadership, 15–16
socioeconomic status (SES), 60
Solórzano, Daniel G., 139
Sotomayor, Sonia, 108–9
Souls of Black Folk, The, 314
South Atlantic Championships, 81
South Atlantic Committee, 81
South East Chicago Commission, 85
Southeastern Conference, 15
Southern University, 267, 269
Southern University and A&M College, 189, 190
Special Report on Student Unrest at Black Colleges, 269
Spencer, Ted, 333
spiral of ignorance, 145
spirit-murdering, 177
standardized achievement examinations, 15
standardized testing, 99, 111
Stanford University, 18

State of Higher Education in California, The, 31, 32, 33
state-sponsored surveillance, 54
status characteristics theory, 339
Stevenson, Howard, 150, 152
Stevenson, Tamara N., 148
Stewart, D.-L., 136
Stockholm syndrome, 145
Stockton, Kathryn, 132, 133
Strategic Diversity Leadership, 339
structural racism, 41, 113
structures of serving, 282–83
Students for Fair Admissions, 107
Students for Fair Admissions v. Harvard, 103, 107
Students for Fair Admissions v. University of North Carolina at Chapel Hill, 103, 107
subjective cognitive functioning (SCF), 133
subordinate-male target hypothesis (SMTH), 39, 42, 44, 49, 62, 134, 135, 137
Sudarkasa, Niara, 329
Sue, Derald Wing, 139–40, 142
Suggs, Ernie, 52
Sullivan, Teresa, 79, 332
SUNY, Albany, 184, 189, 190
supply-side theory, 196
Sutter, Megan, 135
Syracuse, New York, 86
 urban renewal projects and, 86
Syracuse university, 86
systemic land loss, 10
systemic racism, 37, 38, 44, 53, 54, 57, 58, 106, 128, 196
Szelényi, Katalyn, 249

Talented Tenth, The, 263
targets of White supremacy (ToWS), 127, 128–29, 130, 137, 140, 143, 147, 150

Taylor, Breonna, 13, 105, 348
Taylor, Hobart, 327
Taylor, Stuart, 110
Temple University, 191
Temple University School of Scholars, 270
Ten Pillars, 146–47
Tennessee State University, 190
"tequila Sunrise" party, 91
Texas Southern University, 189, 190
Theoharis, George, 15
theory of gender prejudice (TGP), 135, 137
thirdspace, 311
Third World Liberation Front, 105
Thomas, Clarence, 113
Thomas, Laurita, 333
Tichavakunda, Antar, 153
Till, Emmett, 13
tokenism, 195
Tolley, William Pearson, 86–87
Tometi, Opal, 273
Top Ten Percent Plan (TTPP), 101, 102, 109, 113
Torres, Gerald, 110
Transnational Racial Justice Initiative, 12–13
transphobia, 126
tribal colleges and universities (TCUs), 280
Trump, Donald, 91, 104, 105, 108, 113, 114, 125, 274, 306
  denial of systemic racism, 153–54
  voter statistics, 126–26
Ture, Kwame, 142
Turner, Caroline, 171, 246
Tuskegee Institute, 327

UCLA Asian American Studies Center, 248
Union of White Connell Students, 114
Unite the Right, 79
United States, "discovery" of, 12
University of Alabama, 104, 191
University of California, 51, 109, 332
University of California, Berkeley, 109, 189, 190, 191
University of California, Los Angeles, 88–89, 109, 181, 189, 190, 191
  Angela Davis and, 88–89
  Don Nakanishi and, 247–48
  study of racial bias and discrimination at, 239
University of California, San Diego, 178
University of Chicago, 83–86
  urban renewal programs at, 84–85
University of Delaware, 173
University of Georgia, 55, 190
University of Illinois, 85
University of Illinois, Urbana-Champaign, 190
University of Maryland, 272
University of Michigan, 100
  affirmative action and, 320
  anti-affirmative action efforts at, 325, 331
  benefits of diversity plan at, 320, 325, 331
  Black student activism at, 328
  diversity, equity and inclusion efforts at, 319–21
  early race history at, 320–21
  evolution of diversity leadership at, 325–27
  four pillars of DEI at, 337
  Harlan Hatcher presidency and, 327
  Harold Shapiro presidency and, 328–29
  innovative diversity research and training at, 333–34
  Institute for Social Research and, 333
  James Duderstadt presidency and, 329–31

University of Michigan *(continued)*
  Lee Bollinger presidency and, 331–32
  Mark Schlissel presidency and, 336–37
  Mary Sue Coleman presidency and, 332–33
  Michigan Mandate, 330
  National Center for Institutional Diversity, 333, 334–35
  Office of DEI (ODEI), 340
  Robben Fleming presidency and, 327–28
  seven presidential eras at, 326, 338
  three major diversity goals at, 330–31
University of Michigan, Ann Arbor, 191
University of Mississippi, 181, 190, 191
University of Missouri, 79, 106
University of Missouri, Columbia, 184, 190
University of Missouri, St. Louis, 190
University of North Carolina, 51
University of North Carolina, Chapel Hill, 108, 175
University of Pennsylvania, 87
University of Southern Mississippi, 181, 184
University of Tennessee, Knoxville, 184, 190
University of Texas, 101, 102, 109, 113, 190, 325, 332
University of Texas at Austin, 250
University of Virginia, 79, 126, 190
University of Wisconsin, 174
University System of Georgia, 51–52
  Black male graduation rates and, 55
urban renewal programs, 84–85, 86, 90
US Department of Education, 55, 280, 324

US Equal Employment Opportunity Commission, 244
US Supreme Court, 14, 100, 320, 326, 333

Van Camp, Debbie, 274
Vest, Charles, 330
Villodas, Miguel T., 148

Wade-Golden, Katrina, 336, 338
Walker, J. J., 135, 136
Wallace, George C., 87, 104
Warren, Christiane, 19
Washington, Booker T., 263
Washington, Michael, 52
Washington Post, The, 274
Watkins, William, 10
Waugh, Scott, 23
Wayne State university, 191
We Charge Genocide, 37, 130
West, Cornell, 175
Wheller, Albert, 327
Whitaker, Gilbert, 330
White backlash, 103–5, 113
White disability studies, 138
White fragility, 114
White innocence, 104, 108
White nationalism, 113, 114
White privilege, 9, 12–13, 19
White Privilege: Unpacking the Invisible Knapsack, 308
White racism, institutional. *See* institutional White racism
white rage, 81
White supremacy, 9, 19, 38, 106, 126, 137, 168, 169
  statistics on, 127
White victimhood, 104–5
whitesplaining, 308
Why Are All the Black Kids Sitting Together in the Cafeteria?, 308
Wilberforce University, 260

Williams, Brittany Marie, 198
Williams, D. A., 338
Williams, Damon, 339
Williams, David R., 60
Williams, Jamilla Bowman, 340
Williams, Sherley Anne, 178
Wilson, Darren, 273
Winchester, Paul, 81
Wingfield, Adia Harvey, 58
Winona School, 82
Wolfe, Tim, 79

Woode, J. Luke, 140

X, Malcolm, 270

Yale University, 87, 111, 178, 269
Yan, W., 246
Yosso, Tara J., 139
Young, Charles E., 88, 89, 248
Young, Jemimah L., 177–78

Zimmerman, George, 272